Android™
Tips and Tricks

Second Edition

lollipop

Guy Hart-Davis

que®

800 East 96th Street
Indianapolis, Indiana 46240 USA

ANDROID TIPS AND TRICKS
SECOND EDITION
GUY HART-DAVIS

COPYRIGHT © 2016 BY PEARSON EDUCATION, INC.

ISBN-13: 978-0-7897-5583-4

ISBN-10: 0-7897-5583-1

Library of Congress Control Number: 2016937243

1 16

TRADEMARKS

WARNING AND DISCLAIMER

SPECIAL SALES

For information about buying this title in bulk quantities, or for special sales opportunities (which may include electronic versions; custom cover designs; and content particular to your business, training goals, marketing focus, or branding interests), please contact our corporate sales department at corpsales@pearsoned.com or (800) 382-3419.

For government sales inquiries, please contact governmentsales@pearsoned.com.

For questions about sales outside the U.S., please contact intlcs@pearson.com.

EDITOR-IN-CHIEF
Greg Wiegand

ACQUISITIONS EDITOR
Michelle Newcomb

DEVELOPMENT EDITOR
Bill Abner

MANAGING EDITOR
Sandra Schroeder

PROJECT EDITORS
Seth Kerney
Tonya Simpson

COPY EDITOR
Karen Davis

INDEXER
Lisa Stumpf

PROOFREADER
Leslie Joseph

TECHNICAL EDITORS
Vince Averello
Christian Kenyeres

EDITORIAL ASSISTANT
Cindy Teeters

COVER DESIGNER
Mark Shirar

COMPOSITOR
Bumpy Design

CONTENTS AT A GLANCE

TABLE OF CONTENTS

ABOUT THE AUTHOR

Guy Hart-Davis is the author of *Windows 10 Tips and Tricks* and the coauthor of *My Samsung Galaxy Note 5*, both from Que.

DEDICATION

I dedicate this book to my son, Edward, who doggedly tests Android[†] hardware and software to destruction so that I don't have to.

[†] and other!

ACKNOWLEDGMENTS

My thanks go to the people whose hard work helped create this book you're reading. In particular, I'd like to thank the following people:

- Michelle Newcomb, for asking me to write the book.
- William Abner, for developing the outline and content.
- Vince Averello and Christian Kenyeres, for reviewing the manuscript for technical accuracy and contributing suggestions for improving the book.
- Seth Kerney and Tonya Simpson, for coordinating the book project.
- Karen Davis, for editing the manuscript with a light touch.
- Leslie Joseph, for proofreading the book.
- Lisa Stumpf, for creating the index.

WE WANT TO HEAR FROM YOU!

As the reader of this book, *you* are our most important critic and commentator. We value your opinion and want to know what we're doing right, what we could do better, what areas you'd like to see us publish in, and any other words of wisdom you're willing to pass our way.

We welcome your comments. You can email or write to let us know what you did or didn't like about this book—as well as what we can do to make our books better.

Please note that we cannot help you with technical problems related to the topic of this book.

When you write, please be sure to include this book's title and author as well as your name and email address. We will carefully review your comments and share them with the author and editors who worked on the book.

Email: feedback@quepublishing.com

Mail: Que Publishing
ATTN: Reader Feedback
800 East 96th Street
Indianapolis, IN 46240 USA

READER SERVICES

Register your copy of *Android Tips and Tricks* at quepublishing.com for convenient access to downloads, updates, and corrections as they become available. To start the registration process, go to quepublishing.com/register and log in or create an account.* Enter the product ISBN, 9780789755834, and click Submit. When the process is complete, you will find any available bonus content under Registered Products.

*Be sure to check the box that you would like to hear from us to receive exclusive discounts on future editions of this product.

Introduction

This short introduction is intended to make sure you know the essentials for navigating your Android device.

If you're already familiar with Android, feel free to skip the Introduction and dive straight into Chapter 1, "Getting Up to Speed with Android"—or into whichever chapter will be most helpful to you.

GRASPING THE ESSENTIALS OF ANDROID NAVIGATION

Google has made Android as easy to navigate as possible using straightforward taps and gestures on the touch screen.

This section covers navigating the lock screen, the Home screen, and the Apps screen; opening the Notifications panel and the Quick Settings panel; and opening the Settings app.

> **NOTE** This book focuses on Android version 5, which is known as Lollipop, and Android version 6, which is known as Marshmallow. Earlier versions of Android, such as KitKat (version 4.4) and Jelly Bean (versions 4.1–4.3), have different features and respond in different ways.

NAVIGATING THE LOCK, HOME, AND APPS SCREENS

As you work with your device, you will likely use three screens the most. These are the lock screen, which protects your security; the Home screen, which is your home base in Android; and the Apps screen, from which you launch the apps you want to use.

UNLOCKING THE LOCK SCREEN

When you start your Android device, it normally displays the lock screen. This security screen has two purposes: to prevent Android from responding to accidental touches on the screen and (optionally) to make the user authenticate himself by using the unlock method that the owner has set.

You can apply different unlock methods to the lock screen. The default unlock move is a simple swipe that provides no security at all, but you can apply strong security by requiring a PIN or passcode. The left screen in Figure I.1 shows the lock screen with security in place. The right screen in Figure I.1 shows the screen for entering a password to unlock the device.

> **CAUTION** You can turn off the lock screen by tapping the None button on the Choose Screen Lock screen in the Settings app. This move is seldom wise except for devices you are using for demonstration purposes.

GETTING AROUND THE HOME SCREEN AND USING THE BUTTONS

After you've unlocked your device, the Home screen appears. The Home screen is your base for taking actions in Android and typically contains several types of items. Figure I.2 shows a Home screen with its essential parts labeled:

- **Status bar.** The status bar appears at the top of the Home screen and most other screens.
- **Google Search box.** This box enables you to search quickly straight from the Home screen. You can tap the microphone icon and speak your search terms.

FIGURE I.1

Swipe the lock icon at the bottom of the lock screen (left) to start unlocking your device. On the screen that appears, perform your unlocking move, such as entering your password on the password screen (right).

- **Clock widget.** A *widget* is a small, single-purpose app, such as the Clock widget shown here. You can put any of various widgets on the Home screen to display the information you find useful or entertaining.

- **App icon.** You can place icons for apps on the Home screen so that you can access them quickly.

- **Folder icon.** You can put your Home screen icons into folders to keep them organized.

- **Home screen panel indicator.** The Home screen consists of a series of panels that you can scroll among by swiping or dragging left or right. The larger dot shows the current panel in the series of panels.

- **Apps button.** Tap this button to display the Apps screen (discussed in the next section).

- **Favorites tray.** This tray contains a handful of icons for apps that you want to have available on every Home screen panel.

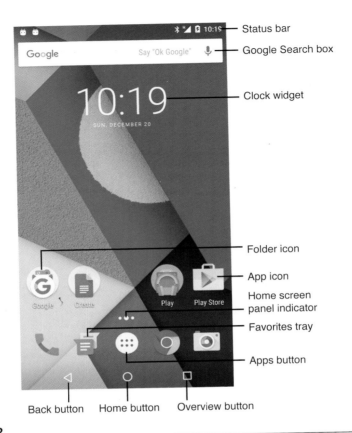

FIGURE I.2

The Home screen consists of a series of horizontal panels that give you access to many different Android features.

- **Back button.** Tap this button to return to the previous screen or to cancel out of a dialog box.

- **Home button.** Tap this button to display the Home screen. Android displays whichever Home screen panel you used last. Tap the Home button again to display your main Home screen panel.

> ✅ **TIP** Swipe up across the Home button to access the Google Now information feature. In Marshmallow, you can tap and hold the Home button to bring up the Now on Tap feature.

- **Overview button.** Tap this button to display the Overview screen. You can then tap the app or window you want to display.

USING THE APPS SCREEN

From the Home screen, tap the Apps button to display the Apps screen. This screen contains a list of apps. (See the left screen in Figure I.3.) If all the apps don't fit on the screen at once, swipe up to display further apps.

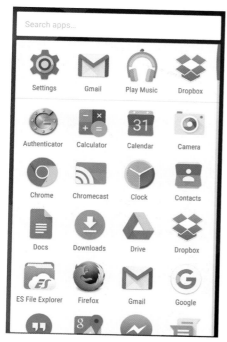
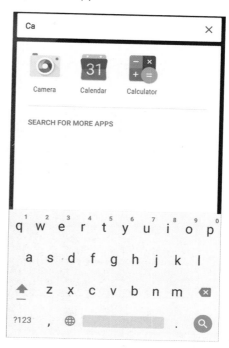

FIGURE I.3

On the Apps screen (left), drag or swipe up to find the app you want, and then tap its icon. You can locate an app by tapping the Search Apps box and typing the beginning of the app's name (right).

The Apps screen is easy to use:

- The top row shows apps you have recently used.
- The following rows show the full list of apps in alphabetical order.
- You can tap the Search Apps box at the top and start typing the name of the app you want. (See the right screen in Figure I.3.)

When you find the app you want to use, tap its icon. That app's screen then appears.

OPENING THE NOTIFICATIONS PANEL

The Notifications panel contains notifications raised by apps to alert you to events. For example, when you receive a message in Gmail, the Gmail app raises a notification in the Notifications panel. Similarly, when Android detects that a software update has become available, it displays a notification to let you know about the update.

To open the Notifications panel (shown in Figure I.4), drag or swipe down from the top of the screen with one finger. You can then view your notifications, deal with any that need your attention, and close the Notifications panel again by dragging or swiping upward.

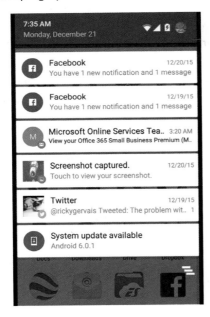

FIGURE I.4

Drag or swipe down from the top of the screen to open the Notifications panel (left). The Quick Settings panel (right) gives you instant access to essential settings.

OPENING THE QUICK SETTINGS PANEL

The Quick Settings panel is a screen that gives you swift access to frequently used settings. You can open the Quick Settings panel in one of two ways:

- Pull down from the top of the screen with two fingers.
- Open the Notifications panel and then tap the bar at the top.

The right screen in Figure I.4 shows the Quick Settings panel on a phone. To close the Quick Settings panel, drag or swipe up.

> **☑ TIP** Tap at the top of the Quick Settings panel to switch to the Notifications panel.

OPENING THE SETTINGS APP

Android has a vast number of settings that you can customize to configure your device the way you want it. You configure most of the settings through the Settings app. You can open the Settings app in three easy ways, as explained next. From here on, this book tells you to "Open the Settings app" rather that telling you which way to open it.

The quickest way to open the Settings app is to use the Quick Settings panel:

1. Open the Quick Settings panel by pulling down from the top of the screen with two fingers.
2. Tap the Settings icon (the gear icon) to open the Settings app.

Alternatively, you can open the Settings app from the Notifications panel:

1. Pull down from the top of the screen with one finger to open the Notifications panel.
2. Tap the bar at the top to display the Quick Settings panel.
3. Tap the Settings icon (the gear icon) to open the Settings app.

Or you can simply open the Settings app from the Apps screen like any other app:

1. Tap the Home button to display the Home screen.
2. Tap the Apps icon to display the Apps screen.
3. Tap the Settings icon to open the Settings app.

> **☑ NOTE** Some Android skins make major changes to the Settings app, so if your device uses a skin, you may need to find your own way to the settings. See Chapter 14, "Using Samsung TouchWiz," for coverage of the changes in the Samsung TouchWiz skin.

USING THE NAVIGATION PANEL, MENUS, CONTROLS, AND DIALOG BOXES

To enable you to give commands easily and clearly, Android uses a large menu called the navigation panel; smaller menus; controls such as switches, check boxes, and radio buttons; and dialog boxes.

USING THE NAVIGATION PANEL

In Lollipop and Marshmallow, many apps use the navigation panel, a wide menu-like panel on the left side of the screen, to enable you to navigate the app and give commands.

To display the navigation panel, you either tap the Navigation Panel button (see the left screen in Figure I.5, which shows the Play Store app) or swipe right from the left edge of the screen. Tapping the Navigation Panel button is usually easier because some apps have laterally scrolling sections that accept the swipe gesture, which means you need to avoid such sections when you're swiping to open the navigation panel.

Navigation
Panel button

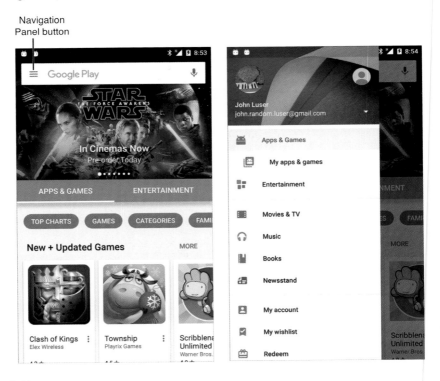

FIGURE I.5

Tap the Navigation Panel button (left) to display the navigation panel (right).

After the navigation panel is open, you can tap one of the buttons or other controls on it to take an action. (See the right screen in Figure I.5.) For example, you can tap the My Account button on the navigation panel in the Play Store app to display the My Account screen, on which you can configure settings.

If you decide not to take an action on the navigation panel, you can close it either by swiping the navigation panel to the left or by tapping in the app to the right of the navigation panel.

USING THE MENUS

Many apps include a Menu button that you can tap to display a menu of commands. For example, in Google's browser app, Chrome, you tap the Menu button (an icon with a vertical line of three dots) to display the menu (see Figure I.6), and then tap the command you want to use.

FIGURE I.6

Tap the Menu button (the three-dot icon, left) to open the menu (right), and then tap the command you need.

WORKING WITH SWITCHES, CHECK BOXES, AND RADIO BUTTONS

Android uses switches and check boxes to enable you to turn individual options on and off.

For example, in the left screen in Figure I.7, the Adaptive Brightness switch is set to Off and the Press Power Button Twice for Camera switch is set to On. In the right screen in Figure I.7, the Show Addresses and Credit Cards from Google Payments box is checked, indicating that this feature is enabled.

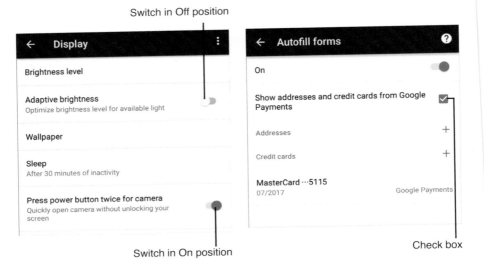

FIGURE I.7

Set a switch to On to enable a feature or to Off to disable it (left). Check a check box (right) to enable a feature.

> **NOTE** This book uses the term *check* to mean tapping a box to put a check mark in it and the term *uncheck* to mean tapping a box to remove the check mark from it. If the box is already checked or unchecked (as appropriate), you don't need to change the setting.

Android uses groups of radio buttons, also called *option buttons*, to enable you to make a choice among two or more mutually exclusive options. For example, in the Prefetch Page Resources dialog box shown on the left in Figure I.8, the Only on Wi-Fi radio button is selected, showing the blue circle. Tapping the Always radio button or the Never radio button selects the radio button you tap and deselects the Only on Wi-Fi radio button; only one radio button in the group can be selected at any time.

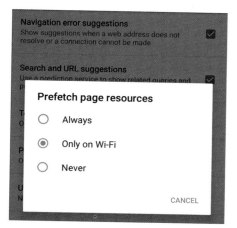

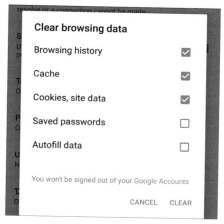

FIGURE I.8

Tap a radio button to select that option, deselecting whichever other option in the group is currently selected (left). Many dialog boxes contain command buttons, such as the Clear button and Cancel button shown in the Clear Browsing Data dialog box (right).

MAKING CHOICES IN DIALOG BOXES

When you need to make a decision, Android displays a dialog box to present the choices clearly. You can't take other actions until you have dismissed the dialog box.

If a dialog box contains only radio buttons, tapping a radio button closes the dialog box.

Otherwise, you normally tap a command button, such as the OK button or the Cancel button, to dismiss the dialog box. For example, in the Clear Browsing Data dialog box (see the right screen in Figure I.8), you tap the five check boxes to specify which of your browsing data you want to clear. The dialog box remains open until you tap the Clear button (to clear the selected items) or tap the Cancel button to close the dialog box without taking action.

Some dialog boxes appear only to confirm an action you have taken and so contain only an OK button.

USING THE TOUCHSCREEN

Android uses seven main gestures on the touchscreen:

- **Tap.** Tap the screen and then lift your finger.
- **Tap and hold.** Tap the screen and keep your finger on it, usually until a menu appears or another change occurs. This action is also called *long-press*.
- **Double-tap.** Tap the screen twice in rapid succession.
- **Drag.** Tap an item on the screen, keep your finger on the screen, and then drag the item to its destination. In many cases, you need to tap and hold for a moment before the item becomes free for dragging.
- **Swipe.** Move your finger left, right, up, or down across the screen.
- **Pinch in.** Place your finger and thumb (or two fingers, if you prefer) apart on the screen and then pinch them together. This action is often used for zooming out (for example, on a map or a photo).
- **Pinch out.** Place your finger and thumb (or two fingers) together on the screen and then spread them apart. This action is often used for zooming in.

PREVENTING THE SCREEN FROM ROTATING

Most Android devices include sensors (such as accelerometers) that detect the device's orientation. Android can automatically rotate the display to match the way the screen is pointing.

This automatic rotation is often handy, but you may want to turn it off at times, such as when you are holding your device nearly flat rather than upright. To turn off automatic rotation, open the Quick Settings panel by pulling down with two fingers from the top of the screen, and then tap the Auto-Rotate icon. When you tap it, the Auto-Rotate icon changes to the Portrait icon or the Landscape icon, depending on the device and its current orientation.

IN THIS CHAPTER

- Identifying skins, managing notifications, and entering text
- Setting up a phone or tablet for multiple users
- Optimizing battery performance and managing storage

1

GETTING UP TO SPEED WITH ANDROID

This chapter will familiarize you with your Android device so that you can get the most benefit out of the rest of this book. You'll start by establishing which version of Android your device is running and whether it uses stock Android or a skin. You'll then move into setting volume levels for your various audio sources; managing your notifications; and entering text using the onscreen keyboard, hardware keyboards, and dictation. After that, it's time to examine how you set up a tablet for multiple users, get the best battery performance from your device, and manage files and storage on it.

IDENTIFYING YOUR DEVICE'S ANDROID VERSION AND ITS SKIN

As of this writing, you can choose from a vast range of devices that run the Android operating system (OS). These devices not only have widely varying capabilities but also run many different versions of Android. To make matters even more confusing, many devices use what's called a *skin*, a layer of software that runs on top of the Android OS to make it look different and give it additional capabilities.

All this means that, to get the most out of this book, you need to know not only exactly what device you have but what version of Android it's running—and what skin, if any. Armed with this knowledge, you can identify which tips and tricks apply to your device, its version of Android, and its skin.

UNDERSTANDING ANDROID VERSION NUMBERS AND NAMES

Table 1.1 shows Android's versions as of April 2016, starting with the latest version. Each version has a number and a name. For example, the latest version is Android 6, which is called Marshmallow.

Table 1.1 Android Version Numbers and Names

Version Numbers	Version Name
6.0	Marshmallow
5.0–5.1	Lollipop
4.4–4.4.4	KitKat
4.1–4.3	Jelly Bean
4.0–4.0.4	Ice Cream Sandwich
3.0–3.2.6	Honeycomb
2.3–2.3.7	Gingerbread
2.2	Froyo
2.0–2.1	Éclair
1.6	Donut
1.5	Cupcake

As of this writing, the current version of Android is Marshmallow (6.0), but relatively few devices are running it. Many devices have only just updated to Lollipop (version 5.0–5.1), and a large number of devices are still using KitKat (4.4) and

Jelly Bean (4.1–4.3). The next version of Android is known only as "Android N" but is expected in mid-2016.

FINDING OUT WHICH ANDROID VERSION YOUR DEVICE IS RUNNING

To find out which version of Android your device is running, follow these steps:

1. Open the Settings app.
2. Scroll down to the bottom of the list.
3. Tap the About Phone button or the About Tablet button to display the About Phone screen or the About Tablet screen. (On some devices, the button and screen may be called About Device.)
4. Look at the Android Version readout. You'll see a number such as 6.0.1 (which means your device is running Marshmallow) or 5.1.1 (which indicates Lollipop).

ESTABLISHING WHETHER YOUR DEVICE IS USING A SKIN

Skins typically provide extra functionality that is not available in stock Android, so by adding a skin, a manufacturer can provide additional features to a device, make it more attractive, or make it easier to use.

These are all points in favor of skins. But because implementing a skin involves running extra software, a skin tends to make your Android device respond more slowly. If the device has a powerful processor and plenty of RAM, it may have enough punch to run Android and the skin without slowing down. But if the device is underpowered, a skin may make it slow and cumbersome to use.

Google periodically issues new versions of Android with new features, new looks, or other improvements. If you have one of Google's branded devices, such as the Nexus 6 phone or the Nexus 9 tablet, you can update to the newest version imme-diately. By contrast, manufacturers that provide custom versions of Android need to create new custom versions for their devices, which takes time and money. So if your device has a skin, you will likely have to wait months before a new version becomes available—and that's for one of the manufacturer's latest or biggest-selling devices. For older or lesser devices, manufacturers may not provide updated versions of Android.

The easiest way to tell whether your device has a skin is to see whether it's dif-ferent from the stock Android screens shown in most of this book. For example, Figure 1.1 shows the Settings screen in stock Android on the left and the Settings screen in Samsung's TouchWiz skin on the right. You can clearly see the huge differences between the two.

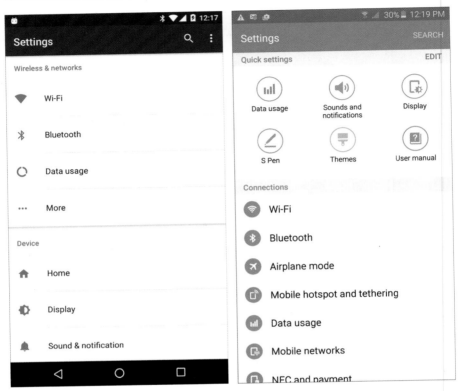

FIGURE 1.1

Samsung's TouchWiz skin (right) makes huge visual changes from stock Android (left).

TIPS FOR CHOOSING AN ANDROID DEVICE

If you're looking for an Android device, take your time because there's an array of options. Here are four suggestions to help:

- **Android version.** If possible, get a device that has the latest version of Android. At this writing, that means Marshmallow (Android 6). You can get bargains on older devices, but be clear that you may not be able to update them to newer versions of Android.

- **Battery.** If you plan to use your device extensively, look for a model that enables you to easily change the battery.
- **Budget device.** When buying a budget Android device, choose a vanilla device—one without a skin—for better performance. A vanilla device is also more likely to receive Android OS updates more quickly than a device with a skin.
- **SD card.** Look for one that accepts an SD card so that you can easily increase the memory, load your media files, and switch quickly between libraries of content.

SETTING DIFFERENT VOLUME LEVELS FOR DIFFERENT AUDIO SOURCES

Android enables you to set different volume levels for media playback, ringtones and notifications, and alarms. You can adjust the levels to make sure that notifications don't swamp the music you're enjoying and that alarms are loud enough to wake you or get your attention.

Here's how to set different audio levels for different audio sources:

1. Open the Settings app.
2. Tap the Sound & Notification button in the Device section to display the Sound & Notification screen.
3. Drag the Media Volume slider to set the playback volume for music, movies, games, and so on.
4. Drag the Alarm Volume slider to set the alarm volume.
5. Drag the Ring Volume slider to set the volume for ringtones.

> **NOTE** The Sound & Notification screen on your device may have different volume sliders than the standard ones explained here. For example, it may have a Ringtone slider and a Notifications slider instead of a Ring Volume slider.

USING MANUAL BRIGHTNESS AND ADAPTIVE BRIGHTNESS

Most Android devices enable you to manually set the screen brightness to exactly the level you want. Many devices also offer an Adaptive Brightness feature that automatically changes the screen brightness to suit the level of light that sensors in or around the screen detect.

> ☑ **TIP**   The quickest way to set the screen brightness manually is to open the Quick Settings panel and drag the Brightness slider at the top. As you drag the slider, Android hides the rest of the Quick Settings panel so that you can see the rest of the screen and judge the brightness level.

Follow these steps to set the brightness level in the Settings app and enable or disable Adaptive Brightness:

1. Open the Settings app.
2. Tap the Display button in the Device section to show the Display screen.
3. Tap the Brightness Level button to display the Brightness slider, and then drag it left or right as needed.
4. Set the Adaptive Brightness switch to On or Off, as needed.

SET AMBIENT DISPLAY AND TAP TO WAKE IF YOUR DEVICE HAS THEM

While you're on the Display screen, look to see if your device has a couple of other settings. First, if the Ambient Display switch appears, set it to On if you want your device's screen to automatically wake when you pick up the device or when you receive notifications. This feature can be helpful for keeping an eye on what's happening without having to wake your device fully.

Second, if the Tap to Wake switch appears, set it to On if you want to be able to wake your device by double-tapping anywhere on the screen. This feature can be a time-saver, but only some devices have it.

MANAGING YOUR NOTIFICATIONS

Android displays notifications to help you keep up with your messages, appointments, and other events. You can choose which apps can give you notifications.

If your device has a notification light, you can control whether Android pulses the light to make you aware of notifications you have not yet viewed.

RESPONDING TO A NOTIFICATION

When an app raises a notification, the notification appears briefly at the top of the screen and then disappears. The left screen in Figure 1.2 shows the notification for an incoming phone call. Drag down from the top of the screen to display the Notifications panel. (See the right screen in Figure 1.2.) You can then take the following actions:

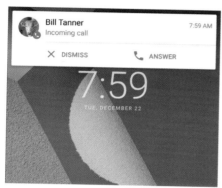
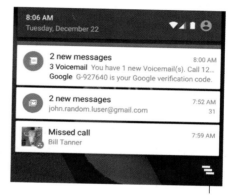

Clear All button

FIGURE 1.2

A notification appears briefly at the top of the screen (left), including any action buttons needed, such as Answer for a phone call. Drag down from the top of the screen to display the Notifications panel (right).

- Tap a button on the notification to take an action. For example, on a Missed Call notification, you can tap the Call Back button to return the call or tap the Message button to send a message to the caller.
- Swipe a notification left or right to dismiss it.
- Tap the Clear All button (the button that shows three horizontal bars staggered like a staircase) to clear all the notifications you can dismiss.

NOTE   There are some important notifications that Android prevents you from dismissing by swiping or by tapping the Clear All button. To get rid of these notifications, you must deal with the issues that raised them.

■ If the notification is collapsed, tap it and drag down to expand it. For example, dragging down on the 2 New Messages notification shown in the right screen in Figure 1.2 displays brief details of the messages and the email account involved. (See the left screen in Figure 1.3.) Similarly, dragging down on the Missed Call notification reveals the Call Back button for returning the call and the Message button for sending a text message to the caller. (See the right screen in Figure 1.3.)

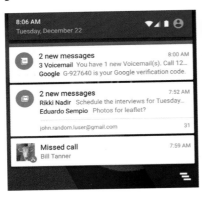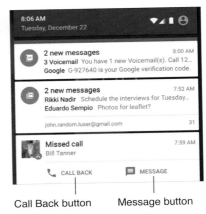

Call Back button   Message button

FIGURE 1.3

Drag down on a collapsed notification to display its details, such as the senders and subjects of email messages (left) or the Call Back button and Message button for a missed phone call (right).

■ Tap and hold the notification until the App Info pop-up button appears, and then tap the button to display the App Notifications screen for the app.

■ Tap a notification to go to the app that raised it.

CATCHING UP WITH NOTIFICATIONS YOU MISSED

If you clear all notifications by mistake, or you clear them deliberately and realize that you didn't read something vital, don't worry—you can easily catch up with them by using a Settings Shortcut widget to display the Notifications screen.

Tap and hold empty space on the Home screen until the customization controls appear; then tap the Widgets icon to display the widgets list. Tap and hold the Settings Shortcut widget until it appears on the Home screen. When you lift your finger, the Settings Shortcut screen appears. Tap the Notification Log button to make the Settings Shortcut widget take you to the Notification Log screen.

You can now tap your Notification Log widget to display the Notification Log screen. This screen shows all your recent notifications, so you can easily catch up on what you missed. You can tap a notification to display the App Info screen for the app that raised the notification, not to go to the app itself.

Android clears the Notification Log screen when you restart your device.

TURNING THE NOTIFICATION LIGHT ON OR OFF

If your device has a notification light, you can make the light blink to alert you to notifications you haven't yet seen. Here's how to control whether the light blinks:

1. Open the Settings app.

2. Tap the Sound & Notification button to display the Sound & Notification screen.

3. Set the Pulse Notification Light switch to On or Off, as needed.

   Some skins do not include the Pulse Notification Light setting.

CONFIGURING NOTIFICATIONS FOR AN APP

Both Marshmallow and Lollipop enable you to configure notifications for an app. In Lollipop, the decision is simple: You can either turn on notifications or turn them off. In Marshmallow, you can turn notifications on or off; but if you turn them on, you can choose whether to treat them as priority notifications and whether to allow peeking at them.

CONFIGURING NOTIFICATIONS FOR AN APP IN MARSHMALLOW

Here's how to configure notifications for an app in Marshmallow:

1. Open the Settings app.

2. Tap the Apps button in the Device section to display the Apps screen.

3. Tap the Notifications button to display the App Notifications screen. (See the right screen in Figure 1.4.)

4. Tap the button for the app you want to affect. The App Info screen appears. (See the left screen in Figure 1.4.)

> **✓ TIP**   You can display the App Notifications screen quickly from the Notification panel. Tap and hold the notification until its background changes from light to dark, and then tap the App Info button on the right of the notification.

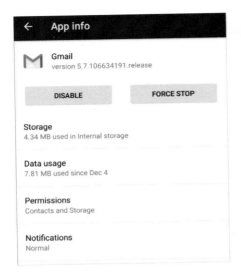
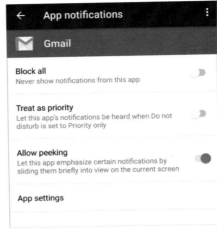

FIGURE 1.4

On the App Info screen for an app in Marshmallow (left), tap the Notifications button to display the App Notifications screen (right), where you can enable or block notifications, treat them as priority, and allow peeking.

5. Set the Block All switch to On if you want to prevent this app from giving you notifications. When you set this switch to On, the other controls on this screen disappear because they're relevant only when you're allowing notifications.

6. Set the Treat as Priority switch to On if you want this app to be able to raise notifications when you have set the Do Not Disturb mode to Priority Only.

7. Set the Allow Peeking switch to On if you want this app to be able to display notifications briefly in front of whichever screen you're using.

> **TIP** Notification peeking—arguably, it should be called "notification flashing," because the app is exposing the notifications briefly to you—is useful for any app you need to monitor in real time. For example, you may find peeking useful for apps such as Gmail, Hangouts, Calendar, and perhaps social-media apps. For anything that's not time critical, you'll likely want to turn peeking Off to spare yourself unhelpful interruptions.

> **NOTE** The App Notifications screen for some apps includes the App Settings button, which you can tap to go to the Settings screen (or one of the Settings screens) in that app. For example, tapping the App Settings button on the App Notifications screen for the Chrome app takes you to the Notifications screen in Chrome, which contains a Notifications switch that you can set to On to make Chrome prompt you before sending notifications.

TURNING OFF NOTIFICATIONS FOR AN APP IN LOLLIPOP

Here's how to turn off notifications for an app in Lollipop:

1. Open the Settings app.
2. Tap the Apps button in the Device section to display the Apps screen. The Apps screen displays the Downloaded tab at first.
3. If the app for which you want to turn off notifications does not appear on the Downloaded tab, swipe left twice to display the All tab.
4. Tap the app's button to display its App Info screen.
5. Tap to clear the Show Notifications check box.

CLEARING REPEAT NOTIFICATIONS

Sometimes Android displays the same notifications repeatedly. Usually this happens with download notifications, but other apps can also raise notifications more than once.

If you find this happening, first restart your device. Restarting can solve any number of problems, and it takes only a minute or two.

If restarting doesn't suppress old download notifications, you may need to clear the cache and data for the Download Manager app.

CLEARING THE CACHE AND DATA FOR DOWNLOAD MANAGER IN MARSHMALLOW

Here's how to clear the cache and data for the Download Manager app in Marshmallow:

1. Open the Settings app.
2. Tap the Apps button in the Device section to display the Apps screen.
3. Tap the Downloads button to display the App Info screen for Downloads.

4. Tap the Storage button to display the Storage screen for Downloads.

5. Tap the Clear Data button.

6. Tap the Clear Cache button.

7. Restart your device.

CLEARING THE CACHE AND DATA FOR DOWNLOAD MANAGER IN LOLLIPOP

Here's how to clear the cache and data for the Download Manager app in Lollipop:

1. Open the Settings app.

2. Tap the Apps button in the Device section to display the Apps screen.

3. Swipe left twice to display the All list.

4. Tap the Download Manager button to display the App Info screen for the Download Manager app.

5. Tap the Clear Cache button to clear the cached data.

6. Tap the Clear Data button. The Delete App Data dialog box opens.

7. Tap the OK button.

8. Tap the Force Stop button. The Force Stop dialog box opens.

9. Tap the OK button.

10. Restart your device.

> **✓ TIP** Another way to clear old notifications is to install a notification-management app. You can find various notification-management apps on the Play Store, but watch out for two things. First, make sure the app doesn't require Internet access. Second, make sure that the app doesn't require your phone to be rooted. Rooting gives you access to the root account, which enables you to take full control of your device's software and hardware and install unapproved software on it.

CONFIGURING AND USING DO NOT DISTURB AND INTERRUPTIONS

Both Marshmallow and Lollipop include settings that enable you to avoid receiving notifications when you don't want them.

In Marshmallow, this feature is called Do Not Disturb. In Lollipop, the feature is called Interruptions.

CONFIGURING AND USING DO NOT DISTURB IN MARSHMALLOW

To start configuring the Do Not Disturb feature, open the Settings app and display the Do Not Disturb screen:

1. Open the Settings app.

2. Tap the Sound & Notification button in the Device section to display the Sound & Notification screen.

3. Tap the Do Not Disturb button to display the Do Not Disturb screen. (See the left screen in Figure 1.5.)

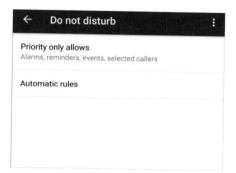 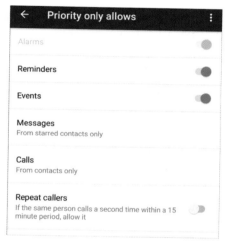

FIGURE 1.5

In Marshmallow, tap the Priority Only Allows button on the Do Not Disturb screen (left) to display the Priority Only Allows screen (right), and then choose which apps and callers can disturb you in Priority Only mode.

SETTING YOUR PRIORITY ONLY ALLOWS NOTIFICATIONS

Next, follow these steps from the Do Not Disturb screen to set up your Priority Only Allows notifications:

1. Tap the Priority Only Allows button to display the Priority Only Allows screen. (See the right screen in Figure 1.5.) This is where you specify which notifications you want to receive when your device is set to the Priority Only mode.

2. Set the Reminders switch to On if you want to receive reminders in Priority Only mode.

3. Set the Events switch to On if you want to receive events notifications (such as upcoming appointments) in Priority Only mode.

4. Tap the Messages button to display the pop-up menu, and then tap the appropriate button on it: From Anyone, From Contacts Only, From Starred Contacts Only, or None.

5. Tap the Calls button to display the pop-up menu, and then tap the appropriate button on it: From Anyone, From Contacts Only, From Starred Contacts Only, or None.

6. Set the Repeat Callers switch to On if you want Android to override your Calls setting if the same person calls twice within 15 minutes.

> **!CAUTION** The Repeat Callers switch gives you a hard choice. On the one hand, you likely want to be able to receive urgent calls in case of an emergency. On the other hand, setting the switch to On may expose you to determined cold callers.

7. Tap the arrow button or the Back button below the screen to return to the Do Not Disturb screen.

CONFIGURING THE DEFAULT AUTOMATIC RULES

Here's how to configure the default automatic rules for Do Not Disturb, starting from the Do Not Disturb screen:

1. Tap the Automatic Rules button to display the Automatic Rules screen. (See the left screen in Figure 1.6.) This screen starts you off with three default rules—Weekend, Weeknight, and Event—that you can configure as needed. You can also create new rules of your own.

2. Tap the Weekend button to display the Weekend screen. (See the right screen in Figure 1.6.)

3. Set the switch at the top to On if you want to enable the rule.

4. If you need to change the rule's name, tap the Rule Name button to display the Rule Name dialog box, type the new name, and then tap the OK button.

5. Tap the Days button to display the Days dialog box, check the box for each day you want the rule to apply to, and then tap the Done button.

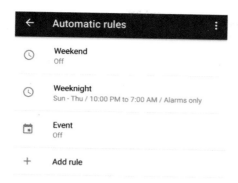

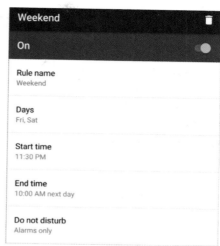

FIGURE 1.6

On the Automatic Rules screen (left), tap each automatic rule and use the resulting screen, such as the Weekend screen (right), to configure it. You can also tap the Add Rule button to add new rules as needed.

6. Tap the Start Time button to display the time controls, set the start time, and then tap the OK button.

7. Tap the End Time button to display the time controls, set the end time, and then tap the OK button.

8. Tap the Do Not Disturb button to display the pop-up menu, and then tap the Priority Only button, the Alarms Only button, or the Total Silence button on it, as needed.

9. Tap the Back button below the screen to display the Automatic Rules screen again.

10. Repeat steps 2–9 as needed to configure the Weeknight rule.

11. Tap the Event button to display the Event screen. (See the left screen in Figure 1.7.)

12. Set the switch at the top to On if you want to enable the rule.

13. Tap the During Events For button to display the pop-up menu, and then specify which calendars to affect by tapping either the Any Calendar button or the button for a specific calendaring account.

14. Tap the Where Reply Is button to display the pop-up menu, and then tap the Yes, Maybe, or Not Replied button; the Yes or Maybe button; or the Yes button, as needed.

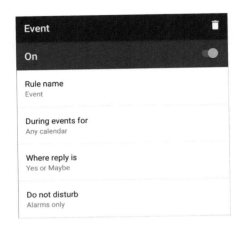 

FIGURE 1.7

On the Event screen (left), choose which calendars and reply types the Event rule affects and whether Do Not Disturb allows alarms. In the Add Rule dialog box (right), name your new rule and select the Time Rule radio button or the Event radio button.

15. Tap the Do Not Disturb button to display the pop-up menu, and then tap the Priority Only button, the Alarms Only button, or the Total Silence button.

16. Tap the Back button below the screen to display the Automatic Rules screen again.

CREATING CUSTOM AUTOMATIC RULES

If configuring the Weekend, Weeknight, and Event automatic rules doesn't cover all your needs for Do Not Disturb, you can create custom automatic rules. You can create either a time rule or an event rule.

To create a new rule, tap the Add Rule button on the Automatic Rules screen. In the Add Rule dialog box that opens, type the name for the rule; tap the Time Rule radio button or the Event Rule radio button, as needed; and then tap the OK button. (See the right screen in Figure 1.7.)

The screen for configuring the rule then appears. You can configure it using the techniques explained in the previous section. For example, for a time rule, you can specify which days to affect by tapping the Days button; set the start time and end time by tapping the Start Time button and the End Time button; and choose between priority only, alarms only, and total silence by tapping the Do Not Disturb button.

TURNING DO NOT DISTURB ON AND OFF

After you've set your preferences for Do Not Disturb, the feature runs automatically at the times specified.

You can override the Do Not Disturb setting at any time. Follow these steps:

1. Pull down from the top of the screen with two fingers to open the Quick Settings panel. (See the left screen in Figure 1.8.)

Do Not Disturb button

FIGURE 1.8

Tap the Do Not Disturb button on the Quick Settings panel (left) to display the Quick Settings panel for Do Not Disturb (right). You can then tap Total Silence, Alarms Only, or Priority Only, and then specify the length of time for Do Not Disturb.

2. Tap the Do Not Disturb button to display the Quick Settings panel for Do Not Disturb. (See the right screen in Figure 1.8.)
3. Make sure the Do Not Disturb switch at the top is set to On.
4. Tap the Total Silence button, the Alarms Only button, or the Priority Only button, as needed.
5. Tap the Until You Turn This Off radio button or the For One Hour radio button. If you tap the For One Hour radio button, tap the + button or the – button to set the length of time.
6. Tap the Done button. The Quick Settings panel appears again, showing the setting you chose—for example, Priority Only.

> 🖊 **NOTE**   You can tap the More Settings button on the Quick Settings panel for Do Not Disturb to jump to the Do Not Disturb screen in the Settings app.

When you're ready to turn Do Not Disturb off again, open the Quick Settings panel and tap the Priority Only icon, the Alarms Only icon, or the Total Silence icon. The Do Not Disturb icon then appears again.

CONFIGURING AND USING INTERRUPTIONS IN LOLLIPOP

In Lollipop, you configure the Interruptions feature to avoid receiving notifications when you don't want them. You can then turn on Interruptions as needed.

CONFIGURING INTERRUPTIONS

Here's how to configure Interruptions in Lollipop:

1. Open the Settings app.
2. Tap the Sound & Notification button to display the Sound & Notification screen.
3. Tap the Interruptions button to display the Interruptions screen. (See the left and right screens in Figure 1.9.)
4. Tap the When Calls and Notifications Arrive button to display the pop-up menu, and then tap the appropriate button: Always Interrupt, Allow Only Priority Interruptions, or Don't Interrupt. If you tap Allow Only Priority Interruptions, the Allow Only Priority Interruptions dialog box opens; if you tap Don't Interrupt, the Don't Interrupt dialog box opens. In either case, tap the radio button for the appropriate length of time—such as Indefinitely, For 4 Hours, or For 30 Minutes—and then tap the OK button.
5. In the Priority Interruptions area, set the Events and Reminders switch, the Calls switch, and the Messages switch to On or Off, as needed, to specify which types of interruptions you want to treat as priority interruptions.
6. If you set the Calls switch, the Messages switch, or both to On, tap the Calls/Messages From button to display the pop-up menu, and then tap the Anyone button, the Starred Contacts Only button, or the Contacts Only button, as needed.
7. In the Downtime area, tap the Days button to display the Days dialog box. Check the box for each day to which you want the downtime to apply, and then tap the Done button.

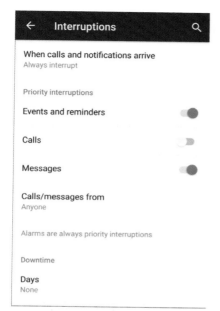
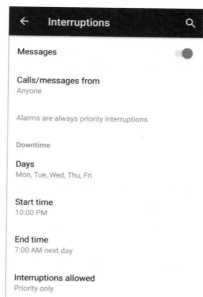

FIGURE 1.9

In Lollipop, use the controls on the Interruptions screen to specify which interruptions you will allow when.

8. Tap the Start Time button to display the time controls, set the start time, and then tap the OK button.

9. Tap the End Time button to display the time controls, set the end time, and then tap the OK button.

10. Tap the Interruptions Allowed button to display the pop-up menu, and then tap the Priority Only button or the None button, as needed.

TURNING INTERRUPTIONS ON AND OFF

When you're ready to turn on Interruptions, follow these steps:

1. Press the Volume Up button, the Volume Down button, or both buttons. The Volume panel appears. (See the left screen in Figure 1.10.) At first, the All button is selected, meaning that you're getting all your notifications.

2. Tap the None button or the Priority button, depending on how few interruptions you want. This example uses Priority, but the None controls work in a similar way. The None controls or the Priority controls appear. (See the right screen in Figure 1.10, which shows the Priority controls.)

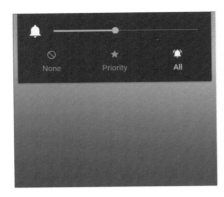

FIGURE 1.10

In Lollipop, open the Volume panel (left) and tap the None button or the Priority button when you need to cut out or reduce interruptions. On the expanded panel, choose the time period.

3. Tap the Indefinitely radio button or the For One Hour radio button, as needed. If you tap the For One Hour radio button, tap the + button or the – button to set the length of time.

4. Tap outside the Volume panel to close the panel.

When you're ready to allow interruptions (or more interruptions) again, open the Volume panel and tap the All button.

ENTERING TEXT

To enter text on your Android device, you can use the onscreen keyboard, a hardware keyboard, or dictation. You can also enter emoticons to liven up your messages or documents.

USING THE KEYBOARD AND SPELLING CORRECTION

The most straightforward means of entering text in a document is the onscreen keyboard. Android automatically displays the onscreen keyboard when you touch a text field in a document or the user interface. The keyboard has a letters layout, a symbols and numbers layout, and an extended symbols layout.

Here's what you need to know about the keyboard:

- **Switch among layouts.** Tap the ?123 button to display the symbols and numbers layout. From there, tap the ABC button to return to the letters layout or tap the =\< button to display the extended symbols layout. From the extended symbols layout, tap the ABC button to display the letters layout or tap the ?123 button to return to the symbols and numbers layout.

> **NOTE** You can hide the keyboard by tapping the Back button. (This button appears as a downward-triangle icon when the keyboard is displayed.) You may want to hide the keyboard so that you can read larger amounts of text or navigate to other text fields. To display the keyboard once more, tap in the text field again.

▪ **Type numbers from the letters keyboard.** The top row of letters on the letters layout has a number in the upper-right corner, from 1 on the Q key to 0 (zero) on the P key. To type the number, tap and hold the appropriate key until the pop-up panel appears, and then lift your finger. Some of the pop-up panels also contain alternate characters (discussed next), but the numbers are the default characters.

▪ **Type alternate characters.** The vowel keys, some letter keys (such as N, S, and C), and many of the symbol keys give access to pop-up panels containing alternate characters. For example, tapping and holding the A key opens a pop-up panel with alternate characters such as ã and æ. (See the left screen in Figure 1.11.) Furthermore, tapping and holding the asterisk key gives you access to star, dagger, and double-dagger symbols. So when you need to type a character that does not appear on any of the keyboard layouts, tap and hold the key for the base character, and then tap the character on the pop-up panel.

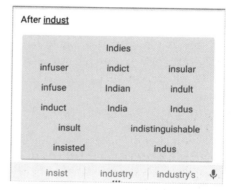

FIGURE 1.11

Tap and hold a character to display a pop-up panel of alternate characters (left), and then tap the character that you want to enter. Tap and hold a suggestion (right) to display the full list of suggestions, and then tap the appropriate suggestion.

- **Type real fractions.** To type a real fraction, display the symbols and numbers layout, tap and hold the number key for the first part of the fraction, and then tap the fraction on the pop-up menu that appears. For example, tap and hold the 1 key to type 1/3, or tap and hold the 5 key to type 5/8.

- **Type quickly with Gesture Typing.** The Gesture Typing feature enables you to type words by sliding your finger from one letter to another over the keyboard without removing it. At the end of a word, you can either swipe over the spacebar to type a space and continue swiping the next word, or you can lift your finger off the screen and then put it back down to start the next word.

- **Using suggestions.** By default, the Google Keyboard displays suggestions as you type in the suggestion strip above the top row of the keyboard. The suggestion with three dots below it is the default one; you can enter this word by tapping the spacebar or a punctuation key (such as the period key). You can enter another suggestion by tapping it. To see the full list of suggestions, tap and hold any of the suggestions until the pop-up panel appears. (See the right screen in Figure 1.11.)

TURNING ON AND CONFIGURING GESTURE TYPING

If Gesture Typing doesn't work on your device, you may need to turn it on. You may also need to configure it to work the way you prefer. Follow these steps:

1. Open the Settings app.
2. Tap the Language & Input button in the Personal section to display the Language & Input screen.
3. Tap the Google Keyboard button to display the Google Keyboard Settings screen.
4. Tap the Gesture Typing button to display the Gesture Typing screen.
5. Set the Enable Gesture Typing switch to On to enable Gesture Typing.
6. Set the Dynamic Floating Preview switch to On if you want to see a preview of the word as you slide.
7. Set the Show Gesture Trail switch to On if you want to see a trail following your finger across the keyboard.

In Lollipop, you can use a shortcut to get to the Google Keyboard Settings screen. Follow these steps:

1. Tap and hold the key to the left of the spacebar on the keyboard. Depending on your device and the keyboard, this may be the comma key, the Voice Input key (the microphone icon), or another key.

2. When the Settings icon appears, release the button to display the Input Options pop-up menu.

3. Tap the Google Keyboard Settings button to display the Google Keyboard Settings screen.

CONFIGURING TEXT CORRECTION

Android's Text Correction feature automatically corrects words and phrases you type that appear to be wrong. You can control how aggressively Text Correction corrects text, so if you find Android changing too many words and phrases that you actually want to use, try turning down the degree of correction.

Here's how to configure Text Correction:

1. Open the Settings app.

2. Tap the Language & Input button in the Personal section to display the Language & Input screen.

3. Tap the Google Keyboard button to display the Google Keyboard Settings screen. (See the left screen in Figure 1.12.)

4. Tap the Text Correction button to display the Text Correction screen. (See the right screen in Figure 1.12.)

> **TIP** If you want to load or remove add-on dictionaries, tap the Add-On Dictionaries button on the Google Keyboard Settings screen. On the Add-On Dictionaries screen that appears, tap the Refresh button to get the latest list of add-on dictionaries. You can then install an add-on dictionary by tapping its button and then tapping the Install button that appears, or you can delete a dictionary by tapping its button and then tapping the Delete button that appears.

5. Set the Block Offensive Words switch to On if you want Android to suppress words that some people may find offensive.

6. Set the Auto-Correction switch to On if you want Android to automatically correct mistyped words when you tap the spacebar or type punctuation.

7. Set the Show Correction Suggestions switch to On if you want Android to display suggested words as you type.

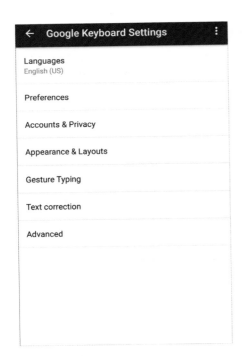
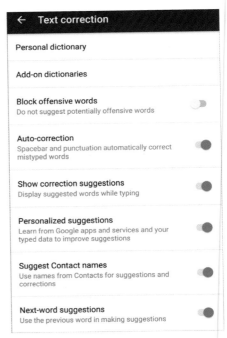

FIGURE 1.12
Tap the Text Correction button on the Google Keyboard Settings screen (left) to display the Text Correction screen (right). You can then configure automatic corrections, correction suggestions, and add-on dictionaries.

8. Set the Personalized Suggestions switch to On if you want Google Keyboard to learn words and phrases from what you type. Personalized suggestions are usually helpful.

9. Set the Suggest Contact Names switch to On if you want Android to use contact names for suggestions and for corrections. This, too, is usually helpful.

10. Set the Next-Word Suggestions switch to On if you want Android to evaluate the previous word when making suggestions for the current word. This feature can make suggestions more accurate, but it takes more processing power, so you might want to set the switch to Off if your device lags when you're typing.

ADDING WORDS TO YOUR PERSONAL DICTIONARY

Android enables you to maintain a personal dictionary containing words that are correctly spelled but do not appear in Android's dictionary. By adding words to your personal dictionary, you can prevent Android from querying them. You can also create a shortcut for any word or phrase so that you can enter it by typing the shortcut.

1. Open the Settings app.
2. Tap the Language & Input button in the Personal section to display the Language & Input screen.
3. Tap the Google Keyboard button to display the Google Keyboard Settings screen.
4. Tap the Text Correction button to display the Text Correction screen.
5. Tap the Personal Dictionary button to display the Personal Dictionary screen.
6. Tap the button for the personal dictionary you want to affect, such as the English (United States) button.

> **NOTE** You may find only one personal dictionary button on the Personal Dictionary screen. But if multiple buttons appear, you also have the option of tapping the For All Languages button to affect all the personal dictionaries.

7. Tap the + button to display an input screen.
8. Type the word or phrase on the upper line, which has no label but shows the prompt "Type a word".
9. Tap the Shortcut field and type any shortcut you want to use for the word or phrase.
10. Tap the arrow button or the Back button below the screen to finish adding the word.

> **NOTE** To edit or delete a word or shortcut, tap it on the Personal Dictionary screen. Android opens the word for editing. You can then change the word or shortcut or tap the Delete icon (the trash can) to delete it.

ENTERING TEXT USING A HARDWARE KEYBOARD

The stock Android onscreen keyboard is easy enough to use, but few people are able to touch-type on it, especially on a phone rather than a tablet. So if you need to type large amounts of text on your Android device, you should think seriously about connecting a hardware keyboard to it.

You can connect a variety of keyboards via either Bluetooth or a cable. Bluetooth is handy, especially if you get a Bluetooth keyboard built into a case that fits your device. See Chapter 4, "Connecting to Networks and Devices," for instructions on connecting Bluetooth devices.

But if you simply need to enter a lot of text quickly, any regular USB keyboard can do the trick as long as your device supports the USB On-The-Go standard. Get a USB A female to micro USB B male adapter cable that also supports USB OTG, plug the keyboard into the USB female port, and plug the micro USB jack into your device.

> **NOTE** USB OTG is short for USB On-The-Go. USB OTG enables a device (such as an Android phone or tablet) to act as a USB host, so you can plug in USB hardware and use it.

After connecting a hardware keyboard, you can use the keyboard shortcuts explained in Table 1.2 to navigate through text.

Table 1.2 Keyboard Shortcuts for Hardware Keyboards

Keyboard Shortcut	What It Does
Left arrow	Moves the insertion point one character to the left.
Right arrow	Moves the insertion point one character to the right.
Up arrow	Moves the insertion point up one line.
Down arrow	Moves the insertion point down one line.
Ctrl+Left arrow	Moves the insertion point to the beginning of the current word (if the insertion point is within a word) or to the beginning of the previous word (if it is not).
Ctrl+Right arrow	Moves the insertion point to the beginning of the next word.
Alt+Left arrow	Moves the insertion point to the beginning of the line.
Alt+Right arrow	Moves the insertion point to the end of the line.

Keyboard Shortcut	What It Does
Alt+Up arrow	Moves the insertion point to the beginning of the document or text field.
Alt+Down arrow	Moves the insertion point to the end of the document or text field.
Alt+Delete	Deletes the current line.
Ctrl+A	Selects all the content of the document or the active field.
Ctrl+C	Copies the selection (if there is one) or the entire document (if not).
Ctrl+X	Cuts the selection (if there is one) or the entire document (if not).
Ctrl+V	Pastes the most recent Clipboard item.

TIP You can select text using the keyboard by holding down Shift while you press the navigation keys or keyboard shortcuts. For example, press Shift+Right arrow to select the character to the right of the insertion point (or to extend the existing selection by one character to the right) or press Shift+Alt+Right arrow to select from the insertion point's current position to the end of the line.

CHANGING THE LOGICAL LAYOUT OF A HARDWARE KEYBOARD

After connecting a hardware keyboard, you can change the logical layout if necessary. For example, you may prefer the Dvorak layout to QWERTY, or you may want the layout for a different language or region.

Open the Settings app, tap the Language & Input button, and then go to the Physical Keyboard section of the Language & Input screen. The Physical Keyboard section appears above the Speech section, but it's only there when the physical keyboard is connected.

Tap the keyboard's button (this shows the keyboard's description, such as Logitech USB Keyboard) to display the Choose Keyboard Layout dialog box. If the layout you want appears, tap it to apply it. If not, tap the Set Up Keyboard Layouts button to display the Keyboard Layouts screen, and then tap the check box for each keyboard layout you want to make available. The Keyboard Layouts screen shows an alphabetical list of widely used keyboards at the top, followed by the full list of keyboards (again in alphabetical order). You may need to scroll beyond the first list to find the keyboard you're looking for.

Tap the Back button below the screen, tap the appropriate keyboard in the Choose Keyboard Layout dialog box, and then start typing using that layout.

ENTERING TEXT USING DICTATION

Typing is the standard way of entering text, but you may be able to enter text more quickly—and accurately—by using the Google Voice Typing feature.

Google Voice Typing may already be set up on your phone or tablet. If so, you're good to go, but you may want to set up your input languages or install offline speech recognition.

Follow these steps to set up and configure Google Voice Typing:

1. Open the Settings app.

2. Tap the Language & Input button in the Personal section to display the Language & Input screen.

3. Tap the Google Voice Typing button to display the Settings screen for Google Voice Typing. (See the left screen in Figure 1.13.)

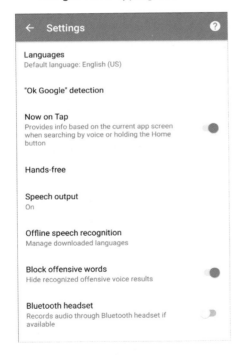
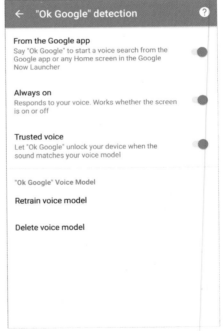

FIGURE 1.13

On the Settings screen for Google Voice Typing (left), choose which Google Voice Typing features you want to use. On the "OK Google" Detection screen (right), enable or disable "OK Google" features as needed.

4. If you want to select input languages, tap the Languages button to open the Languages dialog box. Check the box for each language you want to use; tap and hold the language you want to make the default; and then tap the Save button.

5. Tap the "OK Google" Detection button to display the "OK Google" Detection screen. (See the right screen in Figure 1.13.) Set the From the Google App switch and the Always On switch to On or Off, as needed. Tap the arrow button or the Back button below the screen to return to the Google Voice Typing screen.

> **NOTE** Depending on your device, you may see a Personal Results switch instead of the Trusted Voice switch on the "OK Google" Detection screen. Set this switch to On if you want to get personal results for your voice searches. Be aware that this feature works even when your device is locked.

6. Tap the Hands-Free button to display the Hands-Free screen. In the Allow Requests with Device Locked section, set the For Bluetooth Devices switch and the For Wired Headsets switch to On or Off, as needed. Tap the arrow button or the Back button below the screen to return to the Google Voice Typing screen.

7. Tap the Speech Output button to open the Speech Output dialog box, and then tap the On radio button or the Hands-Free Only radio button, as needed.

8. Tap the Offline Speech Recognition button to display the Download Languages screen. This screen has three tabs: Installed, All, and Auto-Update. The Installed tab appears first.

9. Review your current languages on the Installed tab.

10. If you need to install another language for offline speech recognition, tap the All tab, and then tap the language you want to download and install.

11. Tap the Auto-Update tab to reveal its controls, and then tap the radio button for the way you want to update. Your choices are the Do Not Auto-Update Languages radio button; the "Auto-Update Languages At Any Time. Data Charges May Apply" radio button; and the Auto-Update Languages over Wi-Fi Only radio button.

> **TIP** The Auto-Update Languages over Wi-Fi Only setting is the best choice for keeping your Google Voice Typing languages up to date without incurring data charges from downloading over the cellular network.

12. Tap the arrow button or the Back button below the screen to return to the Settings screen for Google Voice Typing.

13. Set the Block Offensive Words switch to On if you want Google Voice Typing to censor your input.

14. Set the Bluetooth Headset switch to On if you want to be able to record audio for Google Voice Typing through a Bluetooth headset when one is connected.

After you've turned on Google Voice Typing, tap the microphone button at the right end of the suggestions strip to start dictation.

> **TIP** If you plan to dictate a lot, use a high-quality headset microphone. Google Voice Typing delivers impressive results with just the open microphone built into your device, but you can get much clearer input by using a headset microphone.

ENTERING EMOJI

The Google Keyboard provides a large selection of emoticons, or *emoji*, that you can enter in your messages and documents. To access the emoticons, tap and hold the Enter key at the lower-right corner of the onscreen keyboard, and then slide your finger to the smiley-face icon on the pop-up panel.

> **NOTE** Depending on your device and keyboard configuration, you may be able to access emoticons by tapping an emoticon key that appears on the keyboard or by tapping and holding the key to the left of the keyboard and then tapping the Emoticons button on the pop-up panel.

With the emoticons displayed, tap the tab button for the category you want to view, swipe left to see further characters, and then tap the character you want to insert. (See Figure 1.14.) Tap the Recents tab button (the leftmost button, with the clock icon) to see the characters you've used recently. Tap the ABC button to return to the letters keyboard.

Recents tab button

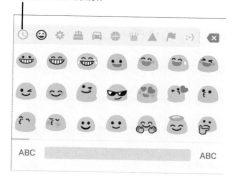 

FIGURE 1.14

*You can easily enter emoticons in your messages and documents by using the Google Keyboard.
Tap the tab button at the top to select the emoticon category, and then swipe left as needed to
find the right emoji.*

USING ALTERNATIVE KEYBOARDS

If you find the Google Keyboard difficult to use, you can install another keyboard
that suits you better. You'll find various alternative keyboards in the Play Store.
Here are three alternative keyboards to consider:

- Hacker's Keyboard (free) is a highly customizable keyboard that includes keys
  you normally find on hardware keyboards, such as Ctrl and Tab, but not on
  Android keyboards. This keyboard is great for remote access to computers.

- SwiftKey Keyboard (free, but with in-app purchases) is a trace keyboard (like
  the Gesture Typing feature on the Google Keyboard) with strong predictive
  text features.

- Smart Keyboard Pro ($2.50) is a customizable keyboard that includes skins
  for different looks and optional transparency. You can customize the key
  height separately for portrait and landscape orientations; hide the period
  and comma keys; and switch among Normal mode, T9 mode, and Compact
  mode. Smart Keyboard Pro includes a calibration tool that you can run to
  improve accuracy if you tend to tap the wrong keys. Download the free
  Smart Keyboard Trial to test; you can then pay for the upgrade to Pro if you
  like it.

SETTING UP A PHONE OR TABLET FOR MULTIPLE USERS

Android includes multiuser features, so you can set up your device with a separate account for each user. By creating user accounts, you give each user his own Home screen, settings, and storage for documents. Each user can send and receive email and browse the Web without sharing his messages and history with other users. Each user can choose a different unlock method to keep his data safe.

On tablets, you have another option: Instead of creating a user account for another person, you can create a *restricted profile*, a kind of limited account that enables the user to access only some apps and content on your account. Like a user account, a restricted profile has a separate space and data on the tablet. You might want to create a restricted profile for a child that you allow to occasionally use your tablet.

CREATING A USER ACCOUNT

When you create a new user account, it is best to have the person who will use the account with you so that she can set up the account immediately. In this way, you can ensure that the right person sets up the user account; you can also insist that the person sets an unlock method on the account to help protect the device.

If you must set up the new user account when the person is not available, the account appears on the lock screen without a security method. Anyone with access to the device can set up the user account, and there is no obligation to set an unlock method.

Here's how to create a user account:

1. Open the Settings app.
2. Tap the Users button in the Device section to display the Users screen.
3. On a phone, tap the Add User button to display the Add New User dialog box. (See the left screen in Figure 1.15.) On a tablet, tap the Add User or Profile button to open the Add dialog box, which lets you choose between adding a user and adding a restricted profile; and then tap the User button to open the Add New User dialog box.
4. Tap the OK button. Android displays the Set Up User Now dialog box. (See the right screen in Figure 1.15.)
5. If the user is with you and can set up the account now, tap the Set Up Now button and hand over the device to the user. Otherwise, tap the Not Now button.

FIGURE 1.15

In the Add New User dialog box (left), tap the OK button. In the Set Up User Now dialog box (right), tap the Set Up Now button if the new user is available to set up her user account; otherwise, tap the Not Now button.

6. Assuming you tap the Set Up Now button, the lock screen for the new account appears. The user can swipe to unlock the screen, tap to select the Continue radio button on the Set Up New User screen that appears, and tap the Next button to begin the rest of the process for setting up the new account.

If you tap the Not Now button in the Set Up User Now dialog box, the user account appears in the Users & Profiles list on the Users screen as New User, Not Set Up. When the user is present and can set up the account, open the Quick Settings panel and tap the User icon in the upper-right corner. On the User section of the Quick Settings panel, tap the New User button to switch to the new account. The user can then swipe to unlock the screen and start setting up the account.

UNDERSTANDING OWNER AND NONOWNER ACCOUNTS

To create a new user account on your device, you must log in using the owner account. This is the account you used when you first set up the device. As long as that account is the only account that your device contains, there's no confusion; but if your device already contains multiple user accounts, and you find that the Add User button (on a phone) or the Add User or Profile button (on a tablet) does not appear on the Users screen, the reason is most likely that you are using a nonowner account.

CREATING A RESTRICTED PROFILE

On a tablet, you can create a restricted profile for a user. Here's how to do so:

1. Open the Settings app.
2. Tap the Users button in the Device section to display the Users screen.
3. Tap the Add User or Profile button to display the Add dialog box.
4. Tap the Restricted Profile button to display the App & Content Access screen. (See the left screen in Figure 1.16.)

FIGURE 1.16

On the App & Content Access screen (left), choose which apps and content items to make available in the restricted profile. Use the Profile Info dialog box (right) to name the profile and add a picture to it.

SETTING A SCREEN LOCK TO PROTECT YOUR APPS AND DATA

For the restricted profile feature to work, you must use a screen lock to protect your apps and data. So if you haven't yet set a screen lock, Android prompts you to set a lock when you tap the Restricted Profile button in the Add dialog box. Tap the Set Lock button to display the Unlock Selection screen, type the lock type you want (Pattern, PIN, or Password), and then follow through the steps for setting the lock. Android then displays the App & Content Access screen, and you can continue with step 5 in the main text.

5. Tap the New Profile button at the top to display the Profile Info dialog box. (See the right screen in Figure 1.16.)

6. To add a custom icon to the profile, tap the default icon on the left side of the dialog box, tap the Take Photo button or the Choose Photo from Gallery button on the pop-up menu, and then take the photo or select the existing photo to use. You can then crop the photo as needed.

7. Type the name for the profile, replacing the default name, New Profile.

8. Tap the OK button to close the Profile Info dialog box and apply the name.

9. Specify which apps and content items you want the user to be able to use by setting each item's switch to the On position. Make sure the switch for each app or content item you don't want the user to use is set to the Off position.

10. Tap the arrow button or the Back button below the screen to return to the Users screen.

SWITCHING USER ACCOUNTS AND PROFILES

After you set up an account for each full user and (on a tablet) a restricted profile for each person who needs less freedom, you can easily switch among the accounts and profiles.

You can switch accounts either while you're logged into your account or while your device is locked. Follow these steps to switch accounts:

1. Open the Quick Settings panel.

2. Tap the account icon in the upper-right corner to display the User section of the Quick Settings panel.

3. Tap the user account or restricted profile to which you want to switch. For example, type the password and press the Enter key.

The lock screen for that user account or profile appears. You can unlock it using the unlock method set for that account or profile.

> **TIP**   You can also lock your device by briefly pressing the Power button. The device turns off, and the screen goes dark. Press the Power button again to wake the device. The lock screen appears, and you can choose which account or profile to use.

DELETING A USER ACCOUNT OR RESTRICTED PROFILE

If you no longer need a particular user account or restricted profile, you can delete it from your device. Follow these steps:

1. Open the Settings app.
2. Tap the Users button in the Device section to display the Users screen.
3. Tap the Settings button (the gear icon) on the button for the account. A screen showing the name of the user account appears.
4. Tap the Remove User button. The Remove This User dialog box opens.
5. Tap the Delete button. Android removes the account.

On a tablet, you use a similar technique to remove a restricted profile. Open the Settings app, tap the Users button to display the Users screen, and then tap the Settings button (the gear icon) on the button for the profile. The App & Content Access screen appears. Tap the Delete button (the trash-can icon) on the right of the button showing the profile's name, and then tap the Delete button in the Remove This Profile dialog box that opens.

UNDERSTANDING AND AVOIDING PROBLEMS WHEN SHARING YOUR DEVICE

Sharing a device with others can be a great way to get more computing out of your hardware budget, but it may bring some problems with security, storage space, and performance.

Apart from actually having to share the physical device, you need to ensure security for your data and that of each other user. Make sure you lock the device consistently so that nobody can access it without entering a PIN or passcode.

Be aware that each user can accept updated app permissions for the device as a whole. This means you should create full user accounts only for people you can trust to deal sensibly with app updates. On a tablet, you can create a restricted profile for users who don't inspire this level of trust. On a phone, you don't have this choice, so you're realistically looking at getting such a user his own device or leaving him incommunicado.

With several users storing data and files (especially media files) on the device, space may run low. You need to manage the device's storage using the techniques discussed later in this chapter.

If several users have sessions open at the same time, the device may start running more slowly because it is low on memory. You can try closing apps or getting other users to close their apps so yours will run better, but restarting the device is usually a better choice.

GETTING THE BEST BATTERY PERFORMANCE

To get the most use out of your Android phone or tablet, you need to manage its battery life. You can do this using either the tools that come with the device or extra tools that you add. You can identify features and apps that consume large amounts of power so that you can either disable them or simply not use them. You can reduce the amount of power your device needs by choosing settings to spare power. And you can give yourself the means to recharge your device at every opportunity.

IDENTIFYING POWER HOGS

To identify power-hogging features and apps, follow these steps:

1. Open the Quick Settings panel. For example, pull down from the top of the screen with two fingers.

2. Tap the Power icon to display the Battery screen (see the left screen in Figure 1.17). This screen shows currently running features and apps listed in descending order by power consumption—in other words, greediest first.

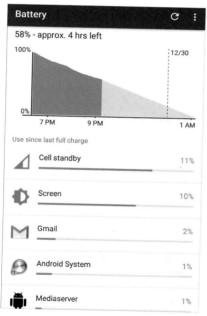
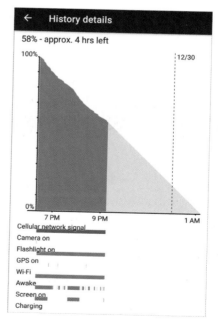

FIGURE 1.17

Look at the Battery screen (left) to see which features and apps have been consuming the most battery power. Tap the Battery graph to display the History Details screen (right), which shows you exactly when each feature was consuming power.

3. Tap the Battery graph at the top to display the History Details screen. (See the right screen in Figure 1.17.) This screen shows a larger battery chart, enabling you to see the relative rates of power consumption more clearly, and bar charts showing when each feature was consuming power.

4. Tap the arrow button or the Back button below the screen to return to the Battery screen.

5. Tap the button for a feature or app whose usage details you want to view. The Use Details screen appears, showing details of any measures you can take to adjust the app's power usage, plus details of the resources the app has consumed, such as the amount of CPU (processor) time, the number of Wi-Fi data packets sent and received, and the app's computed power use.

EKING OUT BATTERY LIFE

To get the most runtime out of your device, you need to reduce power consumption to an acceptable minimum. What that means depends on what the device is and what you're doing with it.

Here are 10 ways you can easily reduce the amount of power your device consumes:

- **Turn down the display brightness.** Open the Quick Settings panel, tap the Brightness icon, and then drag the slider as far to the left as you can bear. The display gets through a huge amount of power, especially on a tablet with a large screen.

- **Set a short sleep interval.** Open the Settings app, tap the Display button, and then tap the Sleep button to display the Sleep dialog box. Tap a short time, such as 15 Seconds or 1 Minute, to save power by turning off the screen quickly when you're not using it.

- **Use Airplane mode when you can go offline.** Open the Quick Settings panel and tap the Airplane Mode icon to quickly shut down all communications services. Repeat the move when you need to go back online.

> ☑ TIP   Turn on Airplane mode when you don't absolutely need connectivity and you're in a place with no signal or poor signal, such as rural wastelands or convention centers. Otherwise, your device happily squanders valuable battery power on chasing will-o'-the-wisp signals.

Turn off communications services you don't need. Open the Quick Settings panel and tap the icon for any communications service that is currently turned on but which you can afford to turn off: Cellular (on a phone or cellular-capable tablet), Wi-Fi, or Bluetooth. If your device has Near Field Communication (NFC), turn that off as well in the Settings app: Tap the More button in the Wireless & Networks section, and then set the NFC switch to Off.

Set the Location mode to Battery Saving. Open the Settings app and tap the Location button in the Personal section to display the Location screen. Tap the Mode button at the top to display the Location Mode screen, and then tap the Battery Saving button. Alternatively, set the Location switch on the Location screen to the Off position to turn off location tracking entirely.

Check for email less frequently. Unless it's vital that you receive all your messages as soon as possible, reduce the frequency of checking for new messages to a minimum. See Chapter 6, "Taking Gmail to the Pro Level," for instructions on configuring the Gmail app.

Store copies of cloud files on your device. Services such as Dropbox are great because they enable you to access your documents from anywhere you have an Internet connection. But to save power, you can store copies of files on your phone or tablet so that you don't need to download them. For example, in Dropbox, you can mark a file as a favorite to make Android store a copy of it locally.

Avoid playing videos and music. Playing videos eats through battery power quickly because it uses the screen, but even playing music takes a fair amount of power. If you find your Android device runs out of power regularly, consider getting a small music player (such as an iPod shuffle or one of its competitors) so that you can listen to your essential music without running down the battery on your phone or tablet.

Turn off live wallpapers. Live wallpapers look pretty, but they make your device's processor work harder and consume power. To turn off live wallpapers, open the Settings app, tap the Display button to go to the Display screen, and then tap the Wallpaper button to display the Choose Wallpaper From screen. You can then tap the Wallpapers button to set a static wallpaper or tap the Photos button to use a photo from the Photos app.

Streamline your Home screens. Widgets that require updating, such as those for email or social networking, consume power both through updating and network connections, so run as few widgets as possible if you're trying to squeeze more time out of your battery.

> **✅ TIP** Some skins and devices offer extra power-management features. For example, the Ultra Power Saving mode on some Samsung Galaxy models enables you to shut off all nonessential features and even uses black-and-white output to reduce the power draw. Look into any extra features that your device provides for getting you through power shortages.

RECHARGING SECRETS

As you saw in the previous sections, you can take various actions to reduce your device's power consumption. But given that most of these actions make your device not only less useful but also harder to use, you may prefer to take a damn-the-torpedoes approach and confront the power problem head on by running your device at full bore but also recharging it whenever you get the chance.

Here are suggestions for recharging your Android device:

- **Carry a spare battery.** If your phone or tablet enables you to easily change batteries, carry one or two spare—and fully charged—batteries with you wherever you go and swap them out as needed.

> **✏️ NOTE** Samsung used to make many phones with easily swappable batteries, up to its 2014 flagship models, the Galaxy Note 4 and the Galaxy S 5; but since then, Samsung has moved to sealed designs with nonswappable batteries. Other vendors still make models with swappable batteries, such as LG with its LG G4 and LG V10 models.
>
> If you can't get a phone with a swappable battery, you may be able to get one with a higher-capacity battery. For example, Motorola's Droid Turbo 2, which is known as the Motorola X-Force in some markets, has a 3750mAh (milliamp-hour) battery that should give two days of use. As of this writing, the holder of the big-battery award is the Oukitel K10000, which has a 10,000mAh battery that claims 10 days of normal use.

- **Get a battery case.** If your phone or tablet is a high-profile device, you may be able to find a case with a built-in battery. If you consistently need more battery power than the built-in battery delivers, a battery case can be a great solution.

- **Get an external battery or portable charger.** No matter which device you have, you can choose from a range of external batteries, also called *portable chargers*, to which you connect your device via USB to recharge it. If you live in a sunny climate, consider getting one with solar charging.

- **Upgrade the battery.** If your device's battery is user-replaceable, you may be able to replace it with a higher-capacity version. First, if your device is still under warranty, check whether replacing the battery invalidates the warranty; if so, decide whether this is a sacrifice you're prepared to make in your pursuit of power or whether to wait until the warranty expires. Next, look up the specs for your device's battery, and then search on the Internet for a higher-capacity version.

> **!CAUTION** When buying a third-party charger or battery for your Android device, read professional and user reviews to make sure you choose a quality unit. A poorly made charger can not only overload your device, damaging the battery, but also be a fire hazard to the place where you use it. A poorly made battery can damage your Android device directly. Also check the battery's date of manufacture before buying. A lithium-ion battery gradually loses capacity over two to three years because of oxidization, so make sure the battery you buy is fresh.

- **Get a car charger.** If you drive a car, get a car charger so that you can plug your device in to charge for the duration of each journey. That should more than offset the power taken by using your device for navigation in the car.

- **Get a spare charger.** Carrying a charger to and from work is a headache, especially when you leave the charger at your workplace for the weekend. Get a spare charger to keep at work.

- **Carry a USB cable.** When no external battery or dedicated charger is available, plug your device into the USB port on whichever computer is handy. The battery may charge more slowly, but you'll pick up at least some power.

UNDERSTANDING HOW DEVICE BATTERIES CHARGE

These days, most devices use lithium-ion batteries, which deliver a good amount of power relative to their size, are usually stable, and prefer frequent charging to full discharging and recharging.

To get the most out of your device's battery, you need to understand the essentials of how it works so that you can charge it in the ways that work best for the battery and for yourself.

Some manufacturers recommend charging the battery fully at the first charge. Most experts agree that this isn't necessary, suggesting that the manufacturers have carried the recommendation over from the days of nickel batteries, which *did* require a full charge at first. But if you want to go ahead and give your device's battery a full charge at first, it does no harm.

A battery's life is measured in charge cycles; a typical lithium-ion battery gives around 500 charge cycles. A *charge cycle* involves charging and discharging the battery fully. Normally, you'll use partial charge cycles rather than full charge cycles for your device's battery, using the device for a while and then plugging it into a power source to recharge. Partial charge cycles add up to full charge cycles as you'd expect, so if you discharge your battery 50% on Monday, 25% on Tuesday, and 25% on Wednesday, charging it up again each evening, you've consumed a full charge cycle.

Using partial charge cycles like this is in general the best way to treat a lithium-ion battery. This is in contrast to some older battery technologies, in which partially discharging and recharging the battery could cause a "memory effect" that reduced the battery's charge capability to the amount you had used.

If you want to keep your device's battery working well, it's a good idea to give it a full discharge and recharge every 30 or so charge cycles—say, once a month if you use your device heavily, or once every couple of months for moderate use. This full discharge and recharge helps to sync the battery's fuel gauge with the actual state of the battery's charge. Without this discharge and recharge, the fuel gauge gradually becomes less accurate, so the power status Android reports to you may not be correct.

Most recent lithium-ion batteries charge relatively quickly up to the 80% level and then charge more slowly for the last 20%. So charging your device for 20 minutes can bump up the level substantially if the battery is depleted, but if the battery is above the 80% level, it may add only a few percent.

Keeping mobile devices charged is a perennial point of pain that device manufacturers are trying to alleviate. Some manufacturers are introducing batteries that charge more quickly, usually when connected to a custom charger. Such batteries appear to be safe but do not always live up to their makers' claims.

Some third-party chargers claim to be able to charge a lithium-ion battery fully in just a few minutes. Experts agree that such instant charging is not possible and that attempting to charge in this way is likely to damage the battery.

Never charge a lithium-ion battery in freezing conditions because doing so can damage the battery. If the battery gets really cold (for example, because you leave your device in the car in winter), allow it to warm up before you try to charge it.

MANAGING FILES AND STORAGE

You might be familiar with Parkinson's Law, which states that "work expands so as to fill the time available for its completion"—but do you know the Law's corollary that states "Storage requirements will increase to meet storage capacity"?

Sadly, this corollary seems to be all too true: Regardless of how much storage space you have, on your Android device in this case, you'll find you want to carry around that quantity of files—or usually more. Between the songs and movies you bring for entertainment, the books and documents you need for work or study, and the files you create directly on your device, the built-in storage can quickly become full. This is especially true if you record video, which can chew through several gigabytes of storage space in next to no time.

Most devices come with only a modest amount of storage space. At this writing, manufacturers pretend that 16GB is a generous size and charge a savage premium for higher-capacity devices. So chances are that you'll need to manage the files and storage on your device.

> **NOTE** Whether you can use SD cards with your device or not, back it up frequently in case it suffers an accident or you delete a priceless file by accident.

ADDING A MICRO SD CARD

If your device accepts a micro SD card, add the highest-capacity SD card that works. If your device's SD card is awkward to insert and remove, you will probably want to leave a single card in place, but if you can swap SD cards easily, you can use several of them. This gives you an easy way to quickly load files onto your device from your computer: Copy them to the SD card, and then insert the card into your Android device.

> **TIP** Before adding an SD card, read your device's documentation to find out the largest size of SD card it supports. Then search online to see if other people who have the device have gotten a larger SD card to work—and if so, which make and model of card. The manufacturers' recommendations are often conservative or out of date, so be prepared to research your device and SD cards if you need the maximum storage possible.

UNDERSTANDING THE SDHC AND SDXC CARD TYPES

Micro SD cards come in various types, but the types you're most likely to need are SDHC and SDXC.

SDHC is the abbreviation for *Secure Digital High Capacity*. SDHC cards come in capacities from 4GB to 32GB, use the FAT32 file system by default (with its limit of 4GB per file), and have a 45Mbps maximum speed for reading and writing data. SDHC is a relatively old standard for memory cards, and users needing high-capacity storage have been bumping up against its 32GB upper limit for several years now.

SDXC is the abbreviation for Secure Digital eXtended Capacity, a newer standard designed for greater capacity. The SDXC standard allows for cards up to 2048GB (in other words, two terabytes, or 2TB) in capacity, but at this writing, 512GB is the largest size widely available. SDXC cards use the exFAT file system by default, which allows for files larger than 4GB.

When choosing a memory card for your device, look at its specifications to see whether it supports SDXC as well as SDHC. If you see "up to 32GB," that usually means SDHC only; but if you see a more generous amount, such as "up to 200GB," you'll know the device supports SDXC as well.

Android expects SDHC cards to use the FAT file system and SDXC cards to use either the FAT file system or the exFAT file system. Most SD cards come formatted with FAT, so if you have a new card, you should be good to go. If the SD card is formatted with a file system other than FAT or exFAT, or if the card is formatted with exFAT and your device accepts only plain FAT, you need to erase or reformat the card before your device can use it.

You can reformat the SD card on your device itself or by using a computer. The following sections explain how to set up an SD card in Marshmallow, how to erase an SD card in Lollipop, how to reformat an SD card in Windows, and how to reformat an SD card on OS X.

> **! CAUTION**   Reformatting an SD card removes any files and folders it currently contains, so if the card contains any files you value, you need to back them up first.

SETTING UP AN SD CARD ON MARSHMALLOW

When you set up an SD card on Marshmallow, you can choose between using the SD card as portable storage and turning it into internal storage:

■ **Portable storage.** Use the SD card as portable storage if you want to be able to use the SD card to transfer items between your device and your computer or if you want to be able to use different SD cards at different times. For example, you might use different SD cards to switch among multiple music libraries or to make movies available for watching.

■ **Internal storage.** Use the SD card as internal storage ("adopting" the card) if your device is short of storage.

> **☑ TIP** For internal storage, you typically want to get a high-capacity SD card with fast performance.

> **❗CAUTION** Adopting the SD card involves reformatting it, which deletes all the card's existing content. So if the card contains any data you care about, back up that data before putting the card in your device.

Here's how to set up an SD card on Marshmallow:

1. Insert the SD card into the slot. Android displays a notification saying that it has detected a new SD card.

2. Tap the notification twice to display the Set Up Your SD Card screen. (This screen shows the manufacturer or brand name of the SD card, such as "Set Up Your Samsung SD Card" or "Set Up Your SanDisk SD Card.")

3. Tap the Use as Internal Storage radio button if you want to adopt the SD card as internal storage; the Format as Internal Storage screen then appears. Otherwise, tap the Use as Portable Storage radio button to use the SD card in the conventional manner, tap the Next button, and then tap the Done button.

4. On the Format as Internal Storage screen, read the warnings about the process requiring the SD card to be formatted and then left in the device. Then tap the Erase & Format button. You see the Formatting SD Card screen (again, with the name of the manufacturer or brand) while Android erases and formats the card. Once the card is formatted, the Move Data to New Storage screen appears, offering to move your photos, files, and some apps to the new card.

NOTE   If Android detects that the SD card you're adopting is slow enough to degrade performance, it displays a dialog box suggesting that you may want to get a faster card.

5. Tap the Move Now radio button if you want to move these items now; you want to do this if you're running out of space in the internal memory already. Otherwise, you can tap the Move Later radio button to postpone the move until a time of your choosing.

6. Tap the Next button. If you selected the Move Now radio button, Android moves the photos, files, and selected apps to the SD card section of the combined internal storage and then displays the SD Card Is Ready screen. If you select the Move Later radio button, the SD Card Is Ready screen appears immediately.

7. Tap the Done button to finish setting up the SD card.

TIP   After you finish adopting an SD card, restart your device. Android may prompt you or force you to restart it; but even if Android doesn't, it's best to restart it.

NOTE   To convert an adopted SD card back to portable storage, first back up your device. Then open the Settings app and tap the Storage & USB button. On the Storage & USB screen, tap the button for the SD card to display the screen for the SD card. Tap the Menu button (the three dots) to display the menu, and then tap the Format as Portable button. Read the warnings on the Format screen that appears, and then tap the Format button if you're sure you want to proceed.

UNDERSTANDING PORTABLE AND INTERNAL MODES IN MARSHMALLOW

Android devices have endured a long and tortuous relationship with SD cards. On the one hand, few manufacturers sell high-capacity devices, so you may well want (or need) to add an SD card to give your device plenty of storage. On the other hand, Google's own devices—and many devices from other manufacturers—don't have SD card slots, so you're stuck with the internal storage. Worse, Google keeps making changes to the ways in which Android apps can use SD cards.

In KitKat, Google largely prevented third-party apps from writing data to the SD card: Even with permission to access the SD card, a third-party app could write only to folders it created or folders of which it took ownership. Uninstalling that third-party app automatically deleted the folders the app had created, along with their contents.

KitKat's restrictions caused howls of protest from developers and users alike. To stifle the screams, Google introduced (in Lollipop) a new way for apps to store data on SD cards. The app prompts the user to grant access to a folder on the SD card; the user selects the folder to use and then grants the permission. Generally speaking, most users find that this arrangement works reasonably well.

Marshmallow enables apps to store data on SD cards. But Marshmallow also goes a step further, allowing you to tell the device to use an SD card as internal storage. Using an SD card as internal storage is called *adopting* the SD card. This is a somewhat unusual move that you should know about but that you will probably not want to perform, even if your device is capable of running Marshmallow and accepting one or more SD cards.

Adopting an SD card is primarily useful for devices that have small amounts of storage, such as the Android One phone models that sell for low prices in India, southeast Asia, and Africa. Some of these devices have only 4GB of storage to help keep down the price—but most of them have an SD card slot, so users can increase the storage as needed.

Adopting an SD card raises several issues that you should understand before you try it.

First, many SD cards are much slower than the internal memory, so adopting an SD card is likely to reduce performance. To minimize the performance hit, make sure the SD card you get has a fast write speed.

Second, once you've adopted a card, you must leave it in place because Android needs the card there to run. So unless your device is one of the few with multiple SD card slots, you're sacrificing your expansion capability. That probably means you'll want to make sure the SD card has as high a capacity as possible as well as a fast write speed.

Third, removing the adopted card tends to be a messy process because if you have used more space in the combined internal memory (the actual internal memory and the adopted SD card) than there is in the actual internal memory, you need to get rid of some apps or data to shrink the system down to fit on the internal memory. Often, the best solution is to back up your device, perform a factory reset to wipe the device clean, and then restore only the apps and data that will fit on the internal memory.

ERASING AN SD CARD ON LOLLIPOP

Here's how to erase an SD card on Lollipop:

1. Insert the SD card into the slot.

> **TIP** If Android displays a Blank SD Card notification (with the detail "SD card is blank or has unsupported filesystem"), you can tap that notification to go straight to the Format SD Card dialog box on the Storage screen. Tap the Format button to format the SD card.

2. Open the Settings app.
3. Tap the Storage button in the Device section to display the Storage screen. (See the left screen in Figure 1.18.)
4. Tap the Erase SD Card button to display the first Erase SD Card screen. (See the right screen in Figure 1.18.)

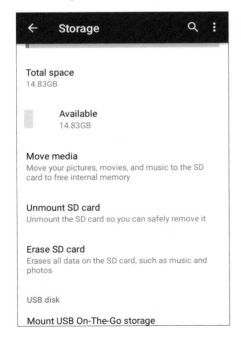
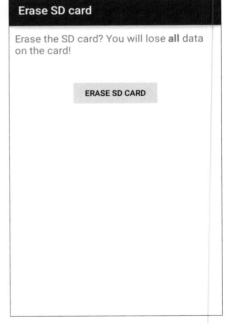

FIGURE 1.18

On the Storage screen (left), tap the Erase SD Card button to display the first Erase SD Card screen (right), and then tap the Erase SD Card button on that screen.

5. Tap the Erase SD Card button.

6. Perform your unlock method to confirm your identity. For example, type your PIN on the Confirm Your PIN screen, and then tap the Next button. The second Erase SD Card screen appears.

7. Tap the Erase Everything button. Android unmounts the SD card, erases it, and then mounts it again. The Storage screen appears, with the SD card mounted.

FORMATTING AN SD CARD IN WINDOWS

Here's how to format an SD card in Windows:

1. Insert the SD card into a card reader built into or connected to your computer.

2. Open a File Explorer window showing This PC (in Windows 8 or Windows 10) or a Windows Explorer window showing Computer or My Computer (on earlier versions).

3. Right-click the SD card and then click Format on the shortcut menu to open the Format dialog box.

4. Click the File System drop-down list and then click FAT32.

5. Clear the Quick Format check box to make Windows check the SD card for errors while formatting it.

6. Click the Start button.

7. Click the OK button in the confirmation dialog box that opens.

8. When the Format Complete dialog box opens, click the OK button.

9. Right-click the SD card and then click Eject to eject the card.

10. Remove the card from the card reader.

FORMATTING AN SD CARD ON OS X

Here's how to format an SD card on OS X:

1. Insert the SD card into a card reader built into or connected to your Mac.

2. Click the Launchpad icon on the Dock, type **dis**, and then click the Disk Utility icon to launch Disk Utility.

3. In the left pane, click the SD card. The right pane displays controls for managing the card.

4. Click the Erase tab to display its controls.

5. Click the Format pop-up menu and then click ExFat.

6. Click the Name field and type the name you want to give the card.

7. Click the Erase button.

8. Click the Erase button in the confirmation dialog that opens.

9. After the format operation finishes, click the Eject button on the toolbar.

10. Remove the card from the card reader.

CONNECTING USB OTG STORAGE

Another means of adding storage to your device is by connecting a USB drive via USB OTG. You can either use a USB drive with a built-in USB OTG connector or simply use a USB OTG cable to connect a regular USB drive to your device's micro-USB port.

> **TIP** Your device's micro-USB port should be able to provide enough power to run a flash drive or a solid-state device (SSD). But if you need to connect a drive with rotating platters, connect a powered USB hub to your device's micro-USB port via a USB OTG cable, and then connect the drive to the USB hub. Using a hub also enables you to connect multiple drives at the same time.

PROS AND CONS OF USB OTG STORAGE FOR ANDROID

Using USB OTG to connect extra storage to an Android device has several clear advantages: It's quick, it's easy, it's inexpensive, and it works with any device.

The disadvantage is equally easy to grasp: The drive is hanging off your device, making it hard to use as normal. If you've connected a hub, a power supply, and a drive or two, your device is about as portable and handheld as a desktop computer, at least temporarily. So you'll likely want to use USB OTG storage only when you need to transfer files quickly, not for long-term use.

USING USB OTG STORAGE IN MARSHMALLOW

In Marshmallow, once you've connected your USB OTG storage to your device, you can access the storage by opening the Settings app and tapping the Storage & USB button. The Storage & USB screen appears, with the Device Storage list showing the internal storage and the Portable Storage list showing the USB OTG storage. Figure 1.19 shows an example of the Storage & USB screen for a tablet that has three flash drives connected via a USB hub.

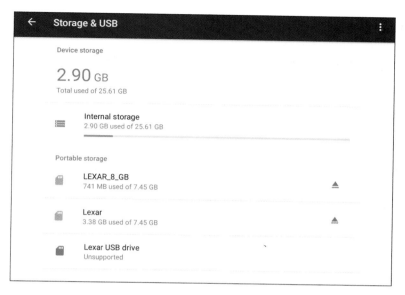

FIGURE 1.19

USB OTG enables you to connect multiple USB drives to your device at once. The drives appear in the Portable Storage list on the Storage & USB screen in Marshmallow.

You can tap a drive in the Portable Storage list to display its contents and then take actions with them as needed. When you finish using a drive, tap the Eject icon on the right side of its button to eject it from the Android file system before you physically disconnect the drive from your device.

If the drive is marked as Unsupported, you need to format it before Android can use it. If you're sure that the drive contains no files you value, tap its button in the Portable Storage list and then follow the prompts to format it. But if you're not sure whether the drive contains anything you want to keep, disconnect it from your Android device, hook it up to a computer, and find out.

USING USB OTG IN LOLLIPOP

In Lollipop, USB OTG works a little differently than in Marshmallow.

Once you've connected your USB OTG storage to your device, you can access the storage by opening the Settings app and tapping the Storage button. At the bottom of the Storage screen that appears, you'll see the USB Disk section. (See the left screen in Figure 1.20.)

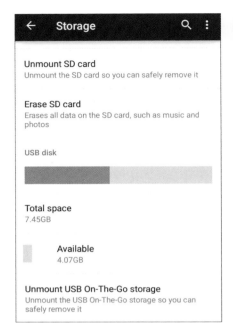
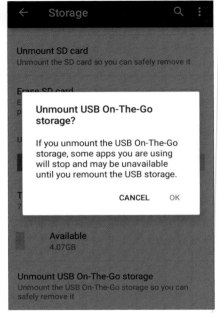

FIGURE 1.20

In Lollipop, a USB OTG drive appears in the USB Disk section at the bottom of the Storage screen (left). Before disconnecting the drive, tap the Unmount USB On-The-Go Storage button and then tap the OK button in the Unmount USB On-The-Go Storage dialog box (right).

If you see the chart of used and unused space, the Total Space readout, and the Available readout, you know that the USB drive is mounted in Android's file system, so you can access the contents by using a file-management app.

If all you see in the USB Disk section of the Storage screen is the Mount USB On-The-Go Storage button, you know that Android hasn't mounted the USB drive. Normally, Android mounts a USB drive automatically—if it can. Anyway, try tapping the Mount USB On-The-Go Storage button to see if Android can mount the drive.

If the drive appears, you're in business; but if the Mount USB On-The-Go Storage button remains visible, it means Android can't mount the drive. In this case, you need to remove the drive and format it differently on another computer or device, such as a PC or Mac, before you can use it.

When you're ready to stop using the USB OTG drive, tap the Unmount USB On-The-Go Storage button at the bottom of the Storage screen, and then tap the OK button in the Unmount USB On-The-Go Storage dialog box that opens. (See the right screen in Figure 1.20.)

CHOOSING AND USING A FILE EXPLORER

You can manage files and folders on your device by running a file explorer on the device itself. Some devices include file explorers, whereas others don't, but you can easily install a file explorer on any device.

EXPLORING YOUR STORAGE ON MARSHMALLOW

Stock versions of Marshmallow include a file explorer that you can access by tapping the Explore button at the bottom of the Storage & USB screen. By using this file explorer, you can browse and search for files, share them with other apps and people, and delete them. (See the left screen in Figure 1.21.)

Sort button

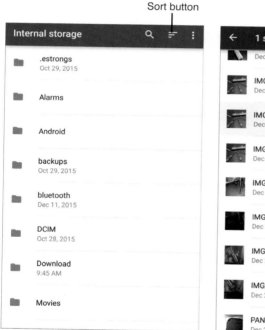

FIGURE 1.21

Marshmallow's file explorer enables you to navigate your device's storage (left). Tap and hold a file to select it (right) so you can take actions with it.

Here's how to use the file explorer:

- **Navigate through folders.** Tap the folder you want to open. Tap the Back button below the screen to move backward along the folder path you've followed.

> 📝 **TIP** You can also navigate quickly back up the folder path by tapping the name of the current location or folder to display a pop-up menu showing the path and then tapping the folder you want to display.

- **Change the sort method.** Tap the Sort button (which shows three horizontal bars of decreasing lengths) to display the pop-up menu, and then tap By Name, By Date Modified, or By Size.
- **Change the view.** On a phone, tap the Menu button (the three dots) and then tap Grid View or List View to switch to that view. (The menu shows only one of those items, for the view you're not currently using.) On a tablet, tap the List icon or the Grid icon in the upper-right corner of the file explorer.
- **Search for a file or folder.** Tap the Search icon (the magnifying glass) and then type your search terms.
- **Select files.** Tap and hold the first file you want to select. After a moment, the file's button becomes highlighted, and the message 1 Selected appears at the top of the screen. (See the right screen in Figure 1.21.) Now that Selection mode is on, you can select other files by tapping them.
- **Share the selected file or files.** Tap the Share button at the top of the screen to display the Share Via panel, and then tap the means of sharing. For example, you can tap Gmail to share the file or files by sending them attached to a message in Gmail, or you can tap Android Beam to share the files by beaming them via NFC.
- **Delete the selected file or files.** Tap the Delete button at the top of the screen. Android doesn't prompt you to confirm the deletion.
- **Copy the selected file or files.** Tap the Menu button to display the menu, and then tap Copy To. The Save To panel opens, and you can tap the location or folder. With that location or folder open, tap the Copy button at the bottom of the screen to copy the file or files.

IDENTIFYING OTHER BUILT-IN FILE EXPLORERS

Stock versions of Lollipop don't include a file explorer, but some manufacturers add custom file explorers—so take a moment to look through the apps on your device and see if you find one. Here are two examples:

- **Samsung: My Files.** Samsung's My Files app suffers from a garish interface but provides strong functionality. (See the left screen in Figure 1.22.) Tap the More button to display the menu of extra commands including Create

Folder, View As (which enables you to choose among List view, Detailed List view, and Grid view), and Show Hidden Files (which does what its name says). (See the right screen in Figure 1.22.)

- **HTC: File Manager.** HTC's File Manager app provides straightforward capabilities for browsing your device's file system and manipulating files.

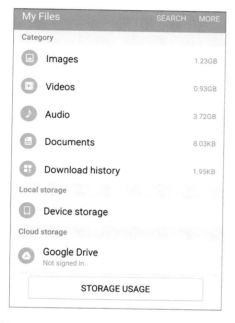

FIGURE 1.22

In Samsung's My Files app, tap the Device Storage button on the My Files screen (left) to display your device's storage. You can then navigate through folders to the file you want, tap the More button, and give a command from the menu (right).

INSTALLING A THIRD-PARTY FILE EXPLORER

If your device doesn't have a file explorer, download and install one from the Play Store.

Both ES File Explorer and ASTRO File Manager are powerful file explorers that are easy to use. (Figure 1.23 shows ES File Explorer running on a phone.) Both are free from the Play Store; ASTRO File Manager also offers a paid version, ASTRO File Manager Pro, which removes the ads.

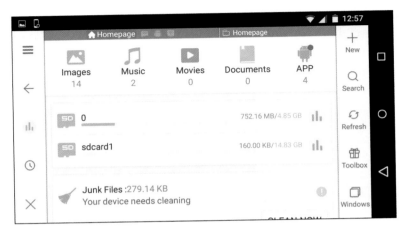

FIGURE 1.23

If your device doesn't come with a file explorer, you can install one such as ES File Explorer from the Play Store.

CHECKING SPACE USAGE AND RECLAIMING SPACE

To see how much space you have left on your device, open the Settings app and then proceed as explained in the next subsection (for Marshmallow) or the subsection after that (for Lollipop).

CHECKING SPACE USAGE AND RECLAIMING SPACE IN MARSHMALLOW

With the Settings app open in Marshmallow, tap the Storage & USB button.

On a device that doesn't have portable storage, Marshmallow takes you straight to the Internal Storage screen. (See the left screen in Figure 1.24.) On a device that does have portable storage, Marshmallow displays the Storage & USB screen, which shows the Internal Storage category and the Portable Storage category. You can tap the one you want to view.

Here's what you can see on the Internal Storage screen:

- **Space Used readout.** The readout at the top shows how much space has been used and the amount of space available—for example, 3.63GB Used of 10.67GB.

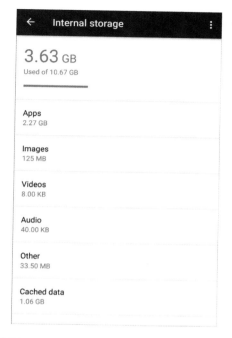

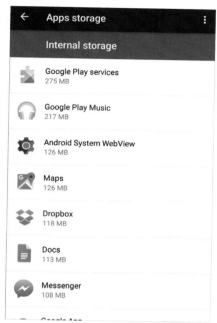

FIGURE 1.24

View the Internal Storage screen in Marshmallow to see how much space is free and how much space the different categories of items are using (left). Tap a category, such as Apps, to display more detail about it, such as the Apps Storage screen (right).

> **NOTE** The Total Space readout on the Storage screen shows a capacity lower than your device's nominal capacity for two reasons. First, manufacturers give the nominal capacity in gigabytes calculated using billions of bytes (1000^3 bytes) rather than the gigabytes that computers actually use (1024^3 bytes), which are 7.4% bigger; so a device with 16GB nominal capacity has a true capacity of 14.9GB. Second, the operating system takes up several gigabytes of space.

■ **Apps.** This button shows how much space the apps are taking up. You can tap the Apps button to display the Apps Storage screen, which shows the apps and their space requirements in descending order. (See the right screen in Figure 1.24.) From here, you can tap an app's button to display the Storage screen for the app, which includes buttons for clearing the app's data and its cache. The Storage screen for an app you've installed includes an Info (i) button. You can tap that button to display the App Info screen for the app, from which you can uninstall the app.

- **Images.** This button shows how much space the various types of image files are occupying. You can tap this button to display the Images screen, which shows the categories of images, such as Camera (photos taken with the Camera app), Screenshots (screens captured on the device), and Bluetooth (pictures received via Bluetooth).

- **Videos.** This button shows how much space the video files are consuming. You can tap the Videos button to display the Videos screen, which shows the folders that contain the video files, such as the Movies folder and the Camera folder (which contains videos you've shot on your device).

- **Audio.** This button shows how much space your audio files—such as songs, ringtones, and podcasts—are occupying. You can tap the Audio button to display the Audio screen, which shows the folders that contain the audio files.

- **Other.** This button shows how much space other files are taking up. When you tap the Other button, Marshmallow displays a dialog box explaining that the category includes files such as those saved by apps and files you've downloaded. You can tap the Explore button to display an Internal Storage screen showing a list of the folders, and then tap a folder to view its contents.

- **Cached Data.** This readout shows how much space is devoted to cached data. You can tap this button to open the Clear Cached Data dialog box and then tap the OK button in it to clear the cached data for all apps.

> **NOTE** *Cached data* is data saved by apps to enable them to display it more quickly; for example, web browsers cache recent web pages in case you visit them again.

CHECKING SPACE USAGE AND RECLAIMING SPACE IN LOLLIPOP

When you tap the Storage button, Lollipop displays the Storage screen whether or not the device has portable storage. (See the left screen in Figure 1.25.) The Internal Storage section appears at the top, the SD Card (if your device has one) appears further down the screen, and the USB Disk section appears at the bottom.

The Storage screen is easy to read:

- **Internal Storage.** The bar chart at the top of the Internal Storage section shows what proportion of your device's storage is in use and how much is free. The color bars show you the file types.

- **Total Space.** This readout gives your device's total capacity.

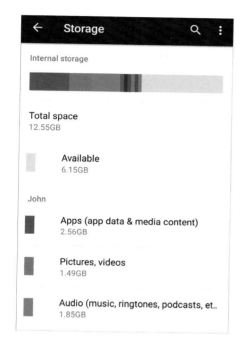
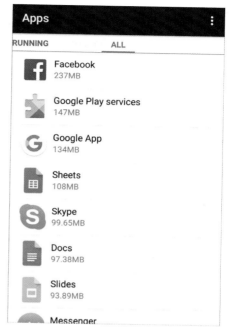

FIGURE 1.25

In Lollipop, use the Storage screen to identify which types of files are taking up your device's storage space (left). Use the Apps screen to see which apps are taking up the most room (right).

> **NOTE** If you have set up multiple accounts on your device, the Storage screen shows a heading for each user. Your account (the account with which you're currently logged in) shows the buttons explained next (such as Apps and Pictures, Video). Each other account shows only a single button that displays the total amount of space the account is occupying.

- **Available.** This readout shows how much space is available.
- **Apps.** This button shows how much space the apps are taking up. You can tap the Apps button to display the Apps screen. (See the right screen in Figure 1.25.) From here, you can tap an app's button to display the App Info screen for the app, and then tap the Uninstall button if you want to remove an app.
- **Pictures, Video.** This button shows how much space your pictures and videos are occupying. You can tap this button to view your photos in the Photos app. You can delete photos using the Photos app if necessary.

- **Audio.** This button shows how much space your audio files—such as songs, ringtones, and podcasts—are taking. You can tap this button to display the Open From panel, which gives you several ways to browse the files. But usually it is easier to manage your music from your computer if you sync your device with it.

- **Downloads.** This button shows the amount of space occupied by files you have downloaded. You can tap the Downloads button to display the Downloads screen, from which you can delete files to free up space.

- **Cached Data.** This button shows how much space is devoted to data that Android and apps have cached so that they can display it again more quickly. You can tap the Cached Data button to open the Clear Cached Data dialog box and then tap the OK button in it to clear the cached data for all apps.

- **Misc.** This button readout shows how much space miscellaneous files are occupying. You can tap the Misc. button to display the Misc Files screen, which allows you to browse the files and delete those you no longer need.

2

LOADING AND SYNCING YOUR DEVICE

To get the most use and enjoyment out of your Android device, you'll probably need to put some of your existing files on it: songs, photos, videos, documents, and so on. Likewise, you'll probably want to copy or move files from your device to your computer or other storage. For example, if you take photos and videos on your device, you will likely want to copy or move them to a computer so that you can enjoy them on a bigger screen—and so that the videos you shoot don't take up all the space on your device.

In this chapter, you'll look at your options for copying and moving files back and forth between your device and your computer. You can either control the copying and moving manually or sync the files between the device and your computer.

> **NOTE** There's no need to sync your Android device with a computer. You can use your phone or tablet as a standalone device if you prefer, loading it with files using whatever means you find convenient and backing it up online.

Later in this chapter, you'll dig into how to keep your device updated, how to back it up to keep your data safe, and how to restore the device from backup when problems occur. Finally, you'll learn how to set up Remote Find and Wiping for your device in case you lose it.

UNDERSTANDING YOUR OPTIONS FOR LOADING AND SYNCING YOUR DEVICE

If you want to copy, move, or sync files between your Android device and your computer, your first decision is which management or sync app to use. Your choices depend on your computer's operating system and the Android device you're using.

> **NOTE** Google has designed Android to use the Internet as extensively as possible for setting up, syncing, and managing devices. Because of this approach, Google doesn't provide a desktop companion app for Android except for Android File Transfer for Mac, which you'll meet later in this chapter. By contrast, Apple offers iTunes as a one-stop means of syncing media files with your PC or Mac as well as providing the iCloud service as an online sync, backup, and restore option.

SETTING UP YOUR NEW DEVICE FROM YOUR OLD DEVICE WITH TAP & GO

If you're moving from one Android device to another Android device, look at the Tap & Go feature. Tap & Go enables you to copy your Google accounts, plus any apps and data you have backed up, from your current device to your new device. Both devices must have near-field communication (NFC) chips.

To use Tap & Go, power on the new device, select your language on the Welcome screen, and then connect the device to a Wi-Fi network. When the Tap & Go screen appears, unlock your current device and bring it back to back with the new device. You'll hear a tone when the NFC chips in the devices connect. Your new device then prompts you to check your other device.

On the other device, tap the OK button in the Copy Accounts and Data from This Device dialog box. The device then locks, and you must unlock it using your usual method—for example, by typing your PIN or password. Tap & Go then copies your data from your current device to your new device, displaying a progress readout as it does so.

CHOOSING THE RIGHT MANAGEMENT OR SYNC APP

Google doesn't provide an app for managing and syncing Android devices with Windows PCs. You can either access your device directly through File Explorer (in Windows 10 or Windows 8) or Windows Explorer (in earlier versions of Windows) or use a third-party app.

> **TIP**   If your computer runs Windows 10, you can use the built-in app called Phone Companion to sync items to your Android device. (Despite its name, Phone Companion works with tablets as well as phones.) See the section "Using Phone Companion in Windows 10," later in this chapter, for information about using Phone Companion.

Unlike Windows, OS X doesn't let you access an Android device's storage directly through the file system. Whereas Android devices show up in Windows' File Explorer like other drives, they don't appear in the Finder in OS X.

To enable you to access the file systems of Android devices on OS X, Google provides the free app called Android File Transfer. If you're using OS X with your Android device, Android File Transfer is a good place to start unless your device's manufacturer provides a desktop app.

Major Android manufacturers provide sync and management apps for Windows and for OS X. Here are three examples:

- **Samsung.** Samsung provides the Smart Switch app for managing its newer devices and the Kies app for managing older devices.
- **Motorola.** Motorola provides the Motorola Device Manager app for managing Motorola devices.
- **HTC.** HTC provides the HTC Manager app for managing HTC devices.

If your device's manufacturer provides a desktop app for managing your device, you'll probably want to start with that app because it will normally provide features tailored to that manufacturer's hardware and software. For example, Samsung Smart Switch includes features for backing up and restoring Samsung devices.

USING A THIRD-PARTY SYNC APP FOR WINDOWS OR OS X

If your device's manufacturer doesn't provide a desktop app, or if you don't find that app useful, you can go for an app from an independent developer instead. Of these, the most promising is doubleTwist, which you can download from the doubleTwist website, www.doubletwist.com. doubleTwist syncs your iTunes library, so it's great if you use iTunes to manage your music.

doubleTwist consists of a free desktop app that runs in Windows and the Mac and a free Android app that offers in-app purchases for extra features. The most compelling extra feature is AirSync, which enables you to sync music and videos with your iTunes library on your computer via Wi-Fi and to play music from your Android device to AirPlay devices such as Apple's AirPort Express wireless access point.

GETTING AND INSTALLING YOUR MANAGEMENT OR SYNC APP

After deciding which management or sync app you want to use, you need to get its distribution file and install it. In this section, you look at the general installation procedure in Windows, using one app as an example, and then go through how to download and install Android File Transfer on OS X.

INSTALLING A MANAGEMENT OR SYNC APP IN WINDOWS

After deciding which management or sync app to use, go to the manufacturer's website and download the latest version. In most cases, your browser gives you the choice of running the app or saving it; usually, it's best to save the app in case the installation fails and you need to launch it again. After the download completes, click the Run button to launch the installer.

> **TIP** Even if your device's manufacturer includes a CD containing an installation file of its management or sync app, you're better off downloading the app from the manufacturer's website because it is highly likely to be a newer version. Most of these apps check for updates and heavily encourage you to update them, so if you install a version from CD, you'll probably have to download and install the new version anyway almost immediately. Just make sure you're on the manufacturer's official website. Don't download a file from a third-party website because you run the risk that someone may have tampered with it.

> **NOTE** HTC devices usually have a distribution file of the HTC Manager app on an extra partition that appears when you connect the device to your computer. You can open this file to launch the installer, but in this case too, you'll usually be better off downloading the latest version of HTC Manager from the HTC website.

When you launch the installer, Windows usually displays the User Account Control dialog box (see the left screen in Figure 2.1) to make sure it's you who's running the software rather than a malicious process having launched it. Look at the Program Name readout and the Verified Publisher readout to make sure the software is genuine. You can also click the Show Details button to display the Program Location readout, which shows you where the program's installer is stored. In addition, the expanded dialog box displays a link for Show Information About This Publisher's Certificate, which you can click to find out more about the software publisher.

If you're satisfied that the program is genuine, click the Yes button to proceed.

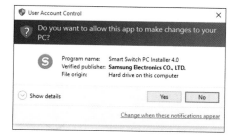 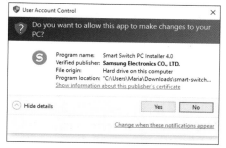

FIGURE 2.1

In the User Account Control dialog box (left), examine the Program Name readout and the Verified Publisher readout. You may want to click the Show Details button to display the location of the program file and a link for viewing the publisher's certificate (right).

After you have the installer running, the installation procedure is usually straightforward, but watch out for the installer offering to create desktop shortcuts, change settings, or install extra software. For example, the InstallShield Wizard for Samsung Smart Switch includes the Create Shortcut on Desktop check box (see Figure 2.2), which you'll need to uncheck if you don't want a Smart Switch shortcut cluttering up your desktop.

FIGURE 2.2

You may need to deselect options in the installer—for example, uncheck the Create Shortcut on Desktop box here unless you want a desktop shortcut for Smart Switch.

Some of the installers have an option for running the app on the final setup screen, which is handy. Otherwise, run the app as usual from the Start menu or the Start screen.

CHOOSING WHAT HAPPENS WHEN YOU CONNECT YOUR DEVICE TO WINDOWS

When you connect your device to Windows, the operating system finds and loads any driver needed to communicate with the device. Windows then prompts you to decide what to do with the device. The prompt varies depending on the version of Windows. For example, in Windows 10, you first see a pop-up message above the notification area. (See the left screen in Figure 2.3.) When you tap this message, you see the Choose What to Do with This Device window. (See the right screen in Figure 2.3.)

These are the choices you typically have:

- **Import Photos and Videos.** Click this button to import photos and videos from your device to your PC using the Photos app (or the other app identified).

- **Get Your Stuff on Your PC, Tablet, and Phone.** (Windows 10 only.) Click this button to launch Phone Companion, the Windows 10 app for syncing items to phones and tablets. See the section "Using Phone Companion in Windows 10," later in this chapter, for details.

- **Sync Digital Media Files to This Device.** Click this button to use Windows Media Player (or the other player identified) to sync music and video to the device.

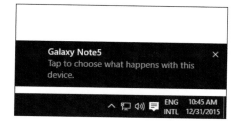

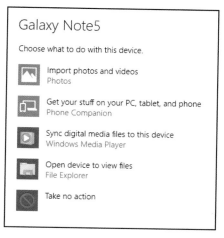

FIGURE 2.3

If Windows displays a pop-up message prompting you to choose what happens with the device (left), tap the message to display the Choose What to Do with This Device window (right).

- **Open Device to View Files.** Click this button to open a File Explorer window (or Windows Explorer window) showing the contents of the device. You can then copy files back and forth manually.

- **Take No Action.** Click this button to have Windows take no action with the device. You can then decide what to do each time you connect the device. For example, you may sometimes want to import photos and videos but other times use File Explorer or Windows Explorer to copy items back and forth.

INSTALLING ANDROID FILE TRANSFER ON OS X

Here's how to download and install Android File Transfer on OS X:

1. Open your web browser and go to www.android.com/filetransfer/.

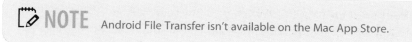

> **NOTE** Android File Transfer isn't available on the Mac App Store.

2. Click the Download Now button to download the disk image file containing the app.

3. If Safari (or whichever browser you're using) doesn't automatically mount the disk image on your Mac's file system and open a Finder window displaying the disk image's contents, click the Downloads icon on the Dock and then click the Android File Transfer disk image. The Android File Transfer disk image's icon appears on your desktop unless you have unchecked the External Disks box on the General tab in Finder Preferences.

> **NOTE** The name of the Android File Transfer disk image file varies, but it should be easy to identify. If it's the last file you downloaded, it'll be the file at the top or in the upper-left corner of the Downloads stack.

4. Drag the Android File Transfer icon to the Applications icon in the folder. OS X copies the app file.

5. Drag the Android File Transfer disk image's icon to the Trash to eject the disk image.

> **TIP** Ejecting the Android File Transfer disk image unmounts the disk image from your Mac's file system. The disk image file remains in your Downloads folder; you can delete it later if you don't want to keep it.

You can now launch Android File Transfer by clicking the Launchpad icon on the Dock and then clicking the Android File Transfer icon.

There's one complication you may run into at this point: OS X's Gatekeeper feature may block you from running Android File Transfer because it came from a source other than the Mac App Store. If this happens, follow these steps to permit the installation of apps from identified developers as well as from the Mac App Store:

1. Click the System Preferences icon on the Dock. If the icon doesn't appear there, click the Apple menu and then click System Preferences. The System Preferences window opens.

2. Click the Security & Privacy icon to display the Security & Privacy pane.

3. Click the lock icon in the lower-left corner, type your password (and an Administrator account name if necessary), and then click the Unlock button to unlock Security & Privacy preferences.

4. Click the Mac App Store and Identified Developers radio button (see Figure 2.4).

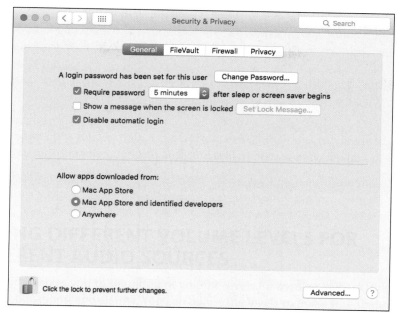

FIGURE 2.4
You may need to unlock Security & Privacy preferences and select the Mac App Store and Identified Developers radio button before you can launch Android File Transfer.

5. Run Android File Transfer by clicking the Launchpad icon on the Dock and then clicking the Android File Transfer icon.

6. Go back to the Security & Privacy pane and click the Mac App Store radio button again.

7. Click the Close button (the red button at the left end of the title bar) to close System Preferences.

USING YOUR MANAGEMENT OR SYNC APP

After installing your management or sync app, you can use it to manage your device or sync files between your device and your computer. Most management or sync apps also enable you to back up your device to your computer and restore it from the computer when things go wrong.

USING PHONE COMPANION IN WINDOWS 10

If you have Windows 10, you'll probably want to check out Phone Companion, the built-in app for syncing items back and forth. Phone Companion helps you set up your Android device to sync data automatically from your PC through your Microsoft account and OneDrive. Phone Companion also enables you to copy or move files manually back and forth between your PC and your Android device.

LAUNCHING PHONE COMPANION

When you connect your Android device to your PC, Windows 10 normally prompts you to decide what to do with the device. (Look back to Figure 2.3, earlier in this chapter.) You can launch Phone Companion by clicking the Get Your Stuff on Your PC, Tablet, and Phone button in the Choose What to Do with This Device window.

If you've already dismissed the Choose What to Do with This Device window, launch Phone Companion from the Start menu. Click the Start button, click All Apps, and then click Phone Companion.

Whichever way you open Phone Companion, you should see your Android device across the bottom of the window listing. (See Figure 2.5.) Click anywhere on this bar (you don't have to click the Show button) to display the information about your device (see Figure 2.6).

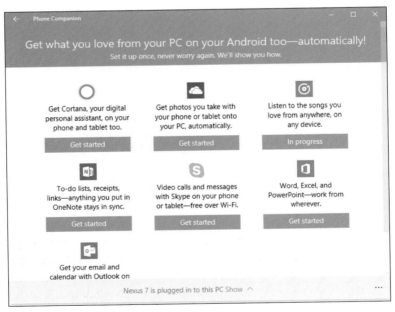

FIGURE 2.5

Click the Show button or anywhere on the bar at the bottom of the Phone Companion window to display the details of your Android device.

📝 **NOTE** If Phone Companion displays the prompt "To see more info, unlock your phone" even when your device is unlocked, first try restarting your device. If you still get this prompt after a restart, see if a new version of Phone Companion is available. If you have set USB on your device to Charging, open the Notification panel, tap the USB for Charging button, and then tap File Transfers in the Use USB For dialog box.

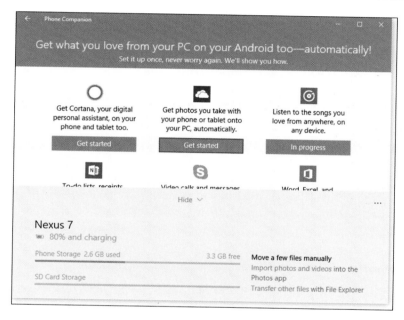

FIGURE 2.6

The pane at the bottom of the Phone Companion window shows your device's name, its battery percentage and charging status, and its amounts of storage and free space.

The details panel contains three buttons (or links, if you prefer) for taking actions: Move a Few Files Manually, Import Photos and Videos into the Photos App, and Transfer Other Files with File Explorer. We'll look at these actions a little later in this chapter. For now, let's examine how to set up the automatic syncing features.

Click the Hide button or anywhere on the bar on which it appears if you need to hide the details panel so you can see the rest of the Phone Companion window.

SETTING UP PHONE COMPANION TO SYNC THE ITEMS YOU WANT

The buttons in the main part of the Phone Companion window allow you to set up seven items as of this writing:

- **Cortana.** Cortana is Microsoft's personal-assistant technology, which Microsoft has now spread from Windows and Windows Phone to Android devices and Apple's iOS devices. Cortana competes with Google Now (not to mention competing with Apple's Siri), so if you're happy with Google Now, you might prefer not to install it on your Android device. But if you find Cortana useful on your PC, you may want to bring Cortana's capabilities to your Android device as well.

- **Photos.** Phone Companion helps you set up your Android device to automatically upload the photos you take on your device to your OneDrive account, which syncs with your Photos library in Windows. We'll use Photos as an example of how to use Phone Companion.

- **Music.** Phone Companion helps you set up syncing songs between your OneDrive Music folder and your Android device. It walks you through the process of moving your songs from your Music folder to your OneDrive Music folder. Windows then syncs the songs automatically via OneDrive. You then install the Groove app on your Android device, which enables your device to play back the songs by streaming them from OneDrive.

- **OneNote.** Phone Companion helps you install the OneNote app on your Android device and sign in to OneNote. You can then work with the OneNote notebooks you have stored online in your Microsoft account.

- **Skype.** Phone Companion walks you through installing the Skype app for Android and signing in using your Microsoft account. You can then make Skype calls from your Android device.

- **Word, Excel, and PowerPoint.** Phone Companion helps you install Microsoft Word, Microsoft Excel, and Microsoft PowerPoint apps on your Android device and sign in using your Microsoft account. You can then work with the documents, workbooks, and presentations you have stored online.

- **Email and Calendar.** Phone Companion walks you through installing the Outlook app on your Android device and signing into your Microsoft account. You can then access your email messages and your calendar events through the Outlook app.

The setup process for each of these seven items works in much the same way. As an example, here is a 15-step guide on how to set up the Photos feature.

1. Click the Get Started button for the Photos feature. The You're Signed into This PC with This Microsoft Account screen appears. (See Figure 2.7.)

FIGURE 2.7

On the *You're Signed into This PC with This Microsoft Account* screen, verify the Microsoft account you're using, and then click the Yes, This Is Me button.

2. Verify that the Microsoft account is the right one.

3. Click the Yes, This Is Me button. The next screen appears, such as the Get Photos onto Your PC with OneDrive for Android screen. (See Figure 2.8.)

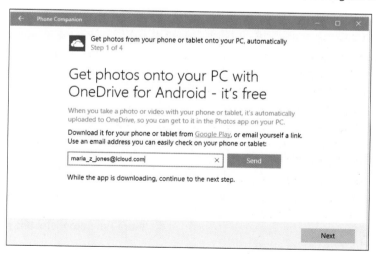

FIGURE 2.8

On the *Get Photos onto Your PC with OneDrive for Android* screen, you can send yourself a link to download the OneDrive for Android app, but it's usually simpler to go straight to the Play Store.

4. Read the instructions for getting OneDrive for Android. You can enter your email address in the box and click the Send button to send yourself a message with a download link, but this approach is unnecessarily convoluted.

5. Click the Next button to display the On Your Phone or Tablet, Sign In to OneDrive with This Account screen. (See Figure 2.9.)

FIGURE 2.9

When you reach the On Your Phone or Tablet, Sign In to OneDrive with This Account screen, switch to your Android device. Install the OneDrive for Android app, sign in to OneDrive, check the I'm Signed In to the OneDrive App on My Phone or Tablet check box, and click the Next button.

6. On your Android device, go to the Home screen and tap the Play Store icon to launch the Play Store app. Search for "OneDrive," install the app, and then tap the Open button to open it.

7. On the opening screen for OneDrive, tap the Sign In Now link to display the Sign In screen.

8. Type your Microsoft account name (your email address) and tap the arrow button. Another Sign In screen appears.

9. Type your password and tap the Sign In button. The Upload Your Photos and Videos screen appears.

10. Tap the OK button to tell the OneDrive app that you want to upload the photos and videos you shoot on your device.

11. Go back to Phone Companion on your PC and check the I'm Signed In to the OneDrive App on My Phone or Tablet box.

12. Click the Next button. The Make Sure Camera Upload Is On in OneDrive on Your Phone or Tablet screen appears. (See Figure 2.10.)

FIGURE 2.10

On the Make Sure Camera Upload Is On in OneDrive on Your Phone or Tablet screen, check the I Turned On Camera Upload in the OneDrive App on My Phone or Tablet box, and then click the Next button.

13. Check the I Turned On Camera Upload in the OneDrive App on My Phone or Tablet box.

14. Click the Next button. The Picture This—You're Done screen appears.

15. Click the Done button. The Phone Companion opening screen appears again so that you can start setting up another feature if you want.

> **TIP** After setting up a feature, it's a good idea to make sure it's working. For example, take a photo on your Android device, and make sure that it appears in Photos on your PC a few minutes later.

IMPORTING PHOTOS AND VIDEOS INTO THE PHOTOS APP

When you want to import photos or videos from your Android device to your PC, open Phone Companion, click the Show button (or anywhere on the bar that contains it) to display the details panel, and then click the Import Photos and Videos into the Photos App link.

Phone Companion launches the Photos app, which automatically scans your device's DCIM folder and displays the Select Items to Import dialog box. Check the box for each photo or video you want to import, and then click the Continue button. On the Start Importing from [Device] screen, you can click the Change Where They're Imported link to pick a different destination folder from that selected. You can check the Delete Imported Items from [Device] After Importing box if you want to delete the photos and videos from the device. Then click the Import button to import the items.

WHAT IS DCIM?

DCIM is the abbreviation for Digital Camera IMages. This is the standard folder that digital cameras and devices such as smart phones use for storing the pictures and videos you take.

TRANSFERRING OTHER FILES WITH FILE EXPLORER

When you want to copy or move files manually between your PC and your Android device, open Phone Companion, click the Show button (or anywhere on the bar that contains it) to display the details panel, and then click the Transfer Other Files with File Explorer link. Phone Companion opens a File Explorer window showing your device's storage. For any device, you'll see an Internal Storage drive that represents the device's built-in storage. If your device also has an SD card inserted, you'll see an SD Card drive as well.

Double-click the Internal Storage drive (or the SD Card drive, if appropriate) to display the folders it contains. You can then copy or move files to or from those folders by using standard Windows techniques. For example, you can open a second File Explorer window to the folder on your PC that contains the files you want to put on your Android device and then drag the files from there to the window showing the device's folders.

USING OTHER MANAGEMENT OR SYNC APPS IN WINDOWS

After you've installed your management or sync app in Windows, the app should launch automatically when you connect your device to your PC. If not, you can launch the app manually as usual—for example, by clicking its icon on the Start menu or the Start screen.

> **NOTE** For security, most management or sync apps require you to unlock your device before the app can control it.

Once the app is open, it connects your device automatically, and the controls appear for working with the device.

> **NOTE** If you connect multiple devices of types that the app can manage, you will need to click the device you want to work with.

The capabilities of management and sync apps vary widely, as do the apps' interfaces, so you'll need to explore your app to see what it's capable of. But here are a couple of quick examples:

■ Figure 2.11 shows Samsung's Smart Switch app running in Windows with a Galaxy Note phone connected. Smart Switch has three tabs—Backup, Restore, and Outlook Sync—whose purposes are easy to divine. Smart Switch does not provide features for syncing music libraries, photos and videos, and other information.

> **NOTE** If your management or sync app does not offer capabilities for syncing files, you can either use File Explorer or Windows Explorer to copy files manually or use Windows Media Player to sync media files.

FIGURE 2.11

Samsung's Smart Switch app enables you to back up your device, restore it from backup, or sync data with Outlook.

■ Figure 2.12 shows Samsung's Kies 3 app, also running in Windows and with a (different) Galaxy Note phone connected. Kies enables you to sync music, photos, videos, and story albums from your computer to your Samsung device. The figure shows how you add music to your device by clicking the Music item in the Library section of the left pane, checking the box for each song you want to transfer, and then clicking the Send to Device button on the toolbar. If the device has both internal and external memory, you get to choose which memory to use.

> **✓ TIP** Most management or sync apps include a setting for automatically checking for updates. If you will find this feature helpful, locate this setting in the Options or Preferences and turn it on.

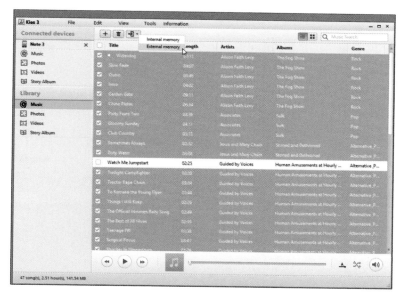

FIGURE 2.12

Samsung's Kies 3 app allows you to copy music, photos, videos, and story albums from your computer to your Android device.

USING ANDROID FILE TRANSFER ON OS X

After installing Android File Transfer on OS X, you can use the app to copy data between your Mac and your Android device.

When using Android File Transfer, unlock your Android device before you connect it to your Mac. Otherwise, Android File Transfer cannot access the device, and you must restart Android File Transfer after unlocking the device.

Android File Transfer on OS X provides a straightforward window (see Figure 2.13) for browsing your device's file system and managing files on it. These are the actions you'll need most often:

- **Copy files from your Mac to your device.** Drag the files from a Finder window to the appropriate folder in the Android File Transfer window.

- **Copy files from your device to your Mac.** Drag the files from their folder in the Android File Transfer window to a Finder window showing the destination folder.

- **Create a folder on your device.** Click the New Folder button in the upper-right corner, type the name for the folder, and then press Return.

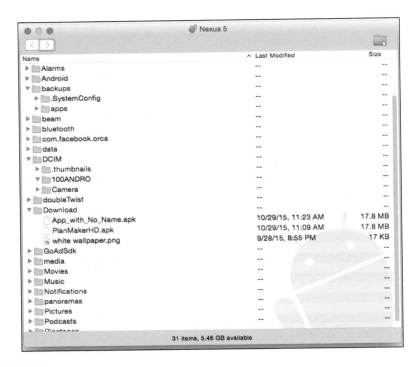

FIGURE 2.13

Android File Transfer enables you to browse the files on an Android device and copy files to it.

■ **Delete a file or folder from your device.** Ctrl+click the file or folder in the Android File Transfer window, click Delete on the contextual menu, and then click the Delete button in the confirmation dialog box that opens.

! **CAUTION** Android File Transfer has a 4GB size limit on files. This is seldom a problem unless you're heaving huge video files around, but it's worth knowing about.

LOADING FILES ON YOUR DEVICE

As you saw in the previous section, you can load files onto your device by using a sync app, by using Windows tools such as File Explorer (or Windows Explorer) and Windows Media Player, or by using Android File Transfer on OS X.

Alternatively, you can use other means of loading files on your device, such as these:

◼ **Load files using the SD card.** If your device has an SD card slot, you can use SD cards to load files onto your device or transfer files off it. Simply connect the SD card to a card reader attached to your computer (or another device that contains the files), copy the files to the SD card, and then reinsert it into your device.

> 📝 **NOTE** The convenience of loading files via SD card depends on your device's—and your device case's—ease of inserting and removing the SD card. If getting to the SD card involves surgery, you won't want to go switching SD cards unless you have to. But if you change SD cards in seconds (as you can do with the Samsung and Motorola phone models whose backs pull straight off), this is a great way of moving files to and from your device.

> ✅ **TIP** Using multiple SD cards is a great way to switch among having different sets of files on your device. For example, by carrying an SD card full of songs and another full of videos, you can switch between the two without having to skimp on either your music library or your movie library.

◼ **Load files using wireless connections.** You can use Wi-Fi, Bluetooth, or NFC to transfer files between your Android device and your computer or other device.

◼ **Load files using Google Drive.** Google Drive enables you to store your files securely on the Internet. You can upload files to your Google Drive account from your computer and download them to your device by using the Google Drive app—or vice versa.

◼ **Load files using Dropbox.** Like Google Drive, Dropbox enables you to store your files online and then download them to your device. If your device doesn't have the Dropbox app, you can install it for free from the Play Store.

◼ **Load files using OneDrive.** As you read earlier in this chapter, the Phone Companion app in Windows 10 helps you set up your Android device with the apps and details needed to sync songs, photos, notebooks, documents, and more through your OneDrive account. You can also use OneDrive to transfer files manually by uploading them from your computer and downloading them to your Android device.

■ **Transfer files using email.** When you need to transfer files individually and other means of sharing aren't convenient, email can be a great solution: Simply attach the file or files to an email message and send it to an account that you can access from your device. The main constraint is that most email servers limit messages to between 5MB and 10MB total. But if you keep any message to less than 5MB, including the overhead needed to encode the file attachments for transmission via email, the messages should transfer fine.

UPDATING, BACKING UP, AND RESTORING YOUR DEVICE

To keep your Android device running well, you should keep its software up to date with the latest versions that the manufacturer provides. To protect yourself against disaster, you should back up your device regularly so that you can restore from backup if necessary.

> ⌷◿ **NOTE**   Many manufacturers of Android devices customize each new release of Android for their devices. This development work takes time, so new versions of Android become available for different devices at different times. As you'd expect, the newest, most popular, and most expensive devices tend to get new versions of Android sooner than older devices do.

KEEPING YOUR DEVICE UPDATED

Android devices automatically check for software updates and download them when they are available.

Android then displays a notification such as "System Update Downloaded" on the Notifications panel to let you know that the update is ready for installation. Tap this notification to launch the installer for the update. If your device hasn't yet downloaded the update, the Notifications panel displays a notification such as "System Update Available," and you can tap the Download button to start downloading it. (See the left screen in Figure 2.14.)

The installer's screen summarizes the changes that the update brings. (See the right screen in Figure 2.14.) Tap the Restart & Install button when you're ready to proceed with the update.

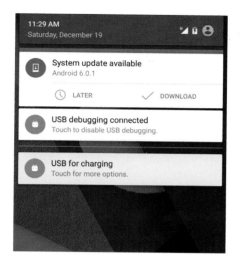
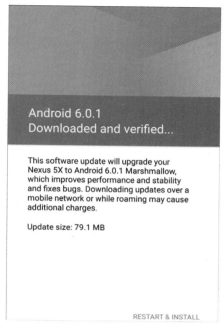

FIGURE 2.14

Tap the Download button on the System Update Available notification (left) to download an available update. Tap the Restart & Install button on the update screen (right) to restart your device and install the update.

CONTROLLING AUTOMATIC CHECKING FOR SOFTWARE UPDATES

Stock Android doesn't let you turn off automatic checking for software updates. Samsung's TouchWiz does, while HTC Sense enables you to turn off automatic downloading of updates. (The only way to turn off automatic checking in stock Android is to root your device, which this book doesn't cover.)

In TouchWiz on a Samsung device, open the Settings app, tap the About Device button, and then tap the Software Update button on the About Device screen. On the Software Update screen, set the Auto Update switch to Off. From the Software Update screen, you can tap the Update Now button to check for updates manually whether Auto Update is turned on or off.

In HTC Sense, open the Settings app, tap the About button to display the About screen, and then tap Software Updates. On the Software Updates screen, uncheck the Auto-Download System Updates box if you want to turn off automatic downloading. You can also uncheck the Auto-Update Apps box if you want to turn off automatic downloads and installation of apps. Note the "and installation" bit there: If you check the Auto-Update Apps box, HTC Sense not only downloads but also installs updates to system apps.

KEEPING YOUR APPS UPDATED

To keep your apps updated, you use the Play Store app like this:

1. Tap the Play Store icon on the Home screen or on the Apps screen. The Play Store app opens.

2. Tap the Navigation Panel button to display the navigation panel, and then tap the My Apps & Games button to display the My Apps & Games screen. (See Figure 2.15.)

3. Tap the Update All button to download and install all available updates.

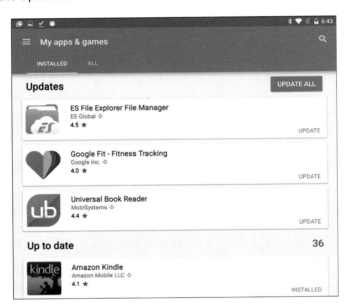

FIGURE 2.15

From the My Apps & Games screen in the Play Store app, you can tap the Update All button to apply all available updates at once, or tap an app's button to update that app individually.

> ☑ **TIP** Updating all your apps at once is usually the most convenient approach. But sometimes, such as when your device has a slow Internet connection or is using the cellular network (or both), you may prefer to update apps individually. In this case, tap the app's button in the Updates list to display the app's screen in the App Store, and then tap the Update button to download and apply the update.

RECOVERING FROM UPDATE OR RESTORE PROBLEMS

If a system update or a restore operation goes wrong, you may find your device doesn't start properly. For example, it may start to boot but then restart partway through the boot process.

If you run into this problem, you can perform a hard reset to recover from the problem. See the section "Performing a Hard Reset" in Chapter 3, "Customizing Your Device," for details on this procedure.

BACKING UP YOUR DEVICE

Most likely your Android device contains a treasure trove of valuable information. It's vital that you keep it backed so that you can recover your data if something goes wrong.

ASSESSING YOUR CHOICES OF BACKUP METHODS

Depending on your device and its manufacturer, and maybe on your computer setup, you have a choice of ways to back up your Android device. These are the options that you may have:

- **Back up to your Google account.** This is the easiest way to back up your essential data, including your app data, your Wi-Fi passwords, and your settings.

- **Back up to another online destination.** You can back up some or all the data on your device to a cloud backup service such as G Cloud (www.gcloudbackup.com). These services typically charge a subscription fee that varies depending on how much space you need.

! CAUTION Backing up to an online destination can be a great way to keep your data safe—with two main caveats. First, choose a service that will be around for the long haul; this may mean paying higher subscription fees than bargain-basement services charge. Second, backing up a full device's worth of data (say 32GB or 64GB) over a normal broadband connection will take a long time. This is a concern only on the first backup because after you have made a complete backup, the following backups are incremental, with each containing only the files that have changed since the previous backup.

- **Back up to your computer.** If you use an app such as Samsung's Smart Switch or HTC Manager to manage your device from your computer, you can back up specific items to your computer. This method works well but presupposes you have a computer and that you'll keep it safe enough, and in good enough condition, to be able to restore your device from it.
- **Back up to a USB On-The-Go drive.** If you want a compact solution that you can take with you anywhere, invest in a USB On-The-Go (OTG) drive and use an app such as ES File Explorer to copy files to it for backup.

☑ TIP Instead of a USB OTG drive, you can use a USB OTG cable and a regular drive. See the section "Connecting USB OTG Storage" in Chapter 1, "Getting Up to Speed with Android," for more information on this topic.

BACKING UP YOUR DEVICE TO YOUR GOOGLE ACCOUNT

If you have a stock Android device, the easiest solution is to back up your essential data to your Google account. This backup is set-and-forget and takes only moments to turn on.

☑ TIP Even if you use another form of backup, such as a management or sync app, you may want to back up essential data to your Google account for belt-and-braces security.

Here's how to set your device to back up to your Google account:

1. Open the Settings app.
2. Tap the Backup & Reset button to display the Backup & Reset screen. (See the left screen in Figure 2.16.)

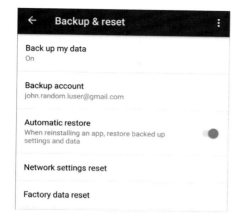

FIGURE 2.16

On the Backup & Reset screen in the Settings app (left), specify your backup account and set the Back Up My Data switch to On.

3. Tap the Back Up My Data button to display the Back Up My Data screen. (See the right screen in Figure 2.16.)

4. Tap the arrow button or the Back button below the screen to return to the Backup & Reset screen.

5. If the Backup Account button shows the wrong Google account, tap the button, and then tap the right account in the Set Backup Account dialog box.

> **NOTE** In the Set Backup Account dialog box, you can tap the Add Account button to use another account for backup that is not currently set up on your device.

6. Set the Automatic Restore switch to On if you want Android to automatically restore backed-up settings and data when you restore an app to your device. This setting is usually helpful.

> **NOTE** Backing up your device to your Google account doesn't back up your apps, but it does back up details about them. When you restore your data, you can download all your apps again from the Play Store by using the My Apps list in the Play Store app.

BACKING UP YOUR DEVICE USING A MANAGEMENT OR SYNC APP

Most management or sync apps include features for backing up your device to your computer and restoring it afterward. The details vary depending on the app. As an example, here is what you do with Samsung's Smart Switch app:

1. Connect your device to your computer.

2. Launch Smart Switch if it doesn't launch automatically. Your device appears in the Smart Switch window.

3. Click the Backup button. Smart Switch starts backing up your device. (See Figure 2.17.)

FIGURE 2.17

Click the Backup button in the Smart Switch window to start backing up your Samsung device.

4. When the Backing Up Data Finished screen appears, you can click the Check Backup Items to display the Check Backup Items screen, on which you can verify that Smart Switch has backed up all the items you care about.

5. Whether you displayed the Check Backup Items screen or not, click the Confirm button.

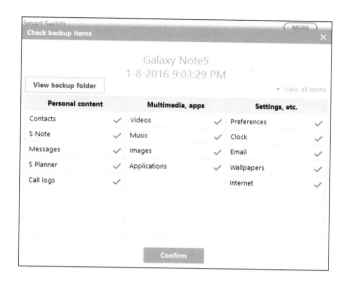

FIGURE 2.18

In Smart Switch, you can display the Check Backup Items screen to verify that the backup has completed satisfactorily.

RESTORING YOUR DEVICE

After things go wrong, you can restore your device from your last backup to get it back to its previous state (or as near as possible).

RESTORING YOUR DEVICE FROM A GOOGLE BACKUP

To restore your device from a Google backup, reset the device as explained in the section "Performing a Hard Reset" in Chapter 3.

> **TIP** You can also use your backup from one device to restore your data to another device. So if you drop your phone onto an unforgiving surface or into too much water, you can set up your new phone (in its bulletproof and waterproof case) by restoring your data onto it from the latest backup.

When your device restarts, tap the Enter Your Email button on the Add Your Account screen and tap the Next button. On the next screen, type your password and tap the Next button. On the Sign In screen, tap the Accept button.

When the Google Services screen appears, check the Automatically Back Up Device Data box and tap the Next button. Follow through the process of setting up a

PIN, password, or pattern to protect your device. Then, on the Get Your Apps & Data screen, tap the Restore from This Backup pop-up menu, tap the appropriate backup in the Restore From dialog box, and tap the Done button. Tap the Also Include pop-up menu to display the All Apps dialog box, uncheck the box for any app you don't want to restore, and then tap the Done button.

Android then downloads the backup you chose and installs it on your device with the apps you chose to include.

RESTORING DEVICES WITH A MANAGEMENT OR SYNC APP

If you've backed up your device using a management or sync app, you can restore it by using the Restore functionality. You'll normally find the controls for restore near those for backup.

For example, here's how to restore a Samsung device that you've backed up with Smart Switch:

1. Connect your device to your computer.

2. Launch Smart Switch if it doesn't launch automatically. Your device appears in the Smart Switch window.

3. Click the Restore button. The Restore screen appears. (See Figure 2.19.)

FIGURE 2.19

In Smart Switch, you can click the Restore Now button to restore completely using the latest backup file, or you can click the Select a Different Backup button to choose a different backup file or perform a partial restore.

4. If you want to perform a full restore using the last backup file, click the Restore button and go to step 8. If you want to choose which backup file to use, or if you want to perform a partial restore, click the Select a Different Backup button to display the Select a Backup to Restore screen. (See Figure 2.20.)

FIGURE 2.20

On the Select a Backup to Restore screen in Smart Switch, select the backup file, choose which items to restore, and then click the OK button.

5. At the top of the Select a Backup to Restore screen, select the backup you want to use.

6. In the lower part of the screen, uncheck the box for each item you do not want to restore. (Smart Switch checks all the boxes by default.)

7. Click the OK button to start restoring the data. When the restore operation finishes, Smart Switch displays the message "The backup data has been restored to your device."

8. Click the Confirm button. You can then disconnect your device from your computer and verify that the data is present and correct.

USING REMOTE LOCK AND WIPING

Being portable, valuable, and highly covetable, your Android device makes a tempting target for those with light fingers and loose morals. And even if you manage to keep your device safe from others, you may manage to lose it yourself.

> ✅ **TIP**   Android automatically sets up your device so that you can find or lock your device if you mislay it, or you can wipe it if someone else takes it.

> ❗ **CAUTION**   Remotely erasing your device may not be able to wipe the content of the SD card (if your device has one). In any case, someone who has grabbed your device can remove the SD card. So it's best to put any valuable or sensitive data on the device's main storage rather than on the SD card.

If your device goes missing, you can remotely lock and wipe it by doing the following:

1. Open a web browser on your computer or on another device that you have. These instructions are for a computer, but you can follow them easily enough on a device.

2. Go to the Android Device Manager website, www.google.com/android/devicemanager.

3. Log in using the Google account you use on your device.

4. On the Welcome to Android Device Manager screen, click the Accept button. Android Device Manager displays a map showing the location of your device. (See Figure 2.21.)

> 📝 **NOTE**   If you have multiple devices registered to this account, click the pop-up menu showing the first device's name, and then click the device you want to locate.

5. If you want to make your device ring, click the Ring button, and then click the Ring button again in the Ring Device dialog box that opens.

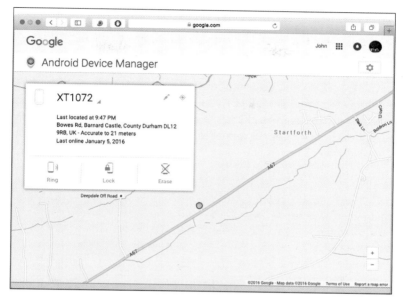

FIGURE 2.21
Android Device Manager locates your device and displays the location on a map.

> ✅ **TIP** Ringing a device is good both for finding the device yourself if the map shows that you've misplaced it at home or for causing someone else to pick it up if you've left it somewhere else. If the device is somewhere else, it's best to lock the device before ringing it.

> 🗒 **NOTE** Using the Ring feature makes the device ring at full volume for five minutes or until someone presses the Power button to stop the ringing.

6. To lock the device, click the Lock button, and then enter a new password, a recovery message, and a phone number in the New Lock Screen dialog box that opens. (See Figure 2.22.) The new password is compulsory. The recovery message and phone number are optional but are important if you want whoever finds your phone to contact you about returning it.

7. If you've lost hope of recovering your device, click the Erase button to display the Erase All Data dialog box and then click the Erase button. (See Figure 2.23.)

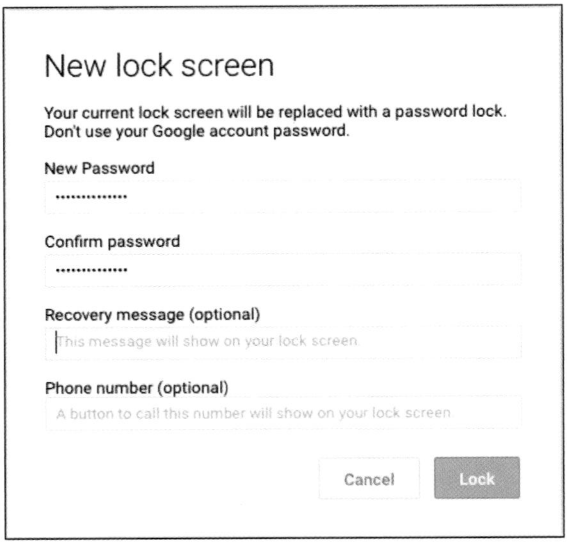

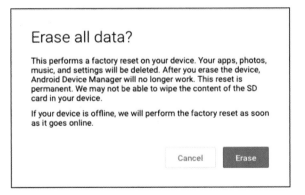

FIGURE 2.22

When locking your device remotely, you must specify a new password in the New Lock Screen dialog box. You can also enter a recovery message and a contact phone number.

FIGURE 2.23

Click the Erase button if there's no hope of getting your device back and you want to erase its data.

> **NOTE** The Erase feature performs a factory reset on the device to erase the data. If the device is online when you give the command, the reset happens almost immediately. If the device is offline, the factory reset happens as soon as it goes back online.

3

CUSTOMIZING YOUR DEVICE

In this chapter, you'll learn to customize your Android device. You'll start with the Home screens because setting these up the way you prefer can make a huge difference in how you use your phone or tablet.

Android gives you access to a wide range of settings, enabling you to configure your device to work the way you prefer. You can access most of these settings through the Settings app.

SETTING UP YOUR HOME SCREENS

Your Home screens are your base camp for getting things done in Android, so you will want to make them as useful as possible. This means adding the icons and widgets you use the most and arranging them into your preferred order. You may also want to add Home screens (or remove existing ones) and change the wallpaper.

TIP   This section explains how to customize the Home screens using stock Android. If your device has a skin, you may need to use different techniques. If you have a Samsung device, see Chapter 14, "Using Samsung TouchWiz," for instructions on customizing the Home screens on the Samsung TouchWiz skin.

The way you customize Home screens depends on the version of Android and the launcher it is running.

NOTE   This chapter focuses on Marshmallow (Android 6) and Lollipop (Android 5) with Google Now Launcher. This is the default launcher for these versions of Android. However, if you have an older device that you have upgraded to Lollipop, you may need to install the Google Now Launcher and set it to be the default launcher. See the section "Using a Different Launcher," later in this chapter, for instructions on changing launchers.

ADDING AND REMOVING HOME SCREENS

To give yourself space for your icons and widgets, you can create extra Home screens. If you no longer need a Home screen, you can remove it.

NOTE   Some versions of Android with certain launchers provide a set number of Home screens and don't let you add or delete Home screens. If your version of Android restricts you in this way, consider installing a third-party launcher to enable yourself to add and delete Home screens.

Google Now Launcher makes it easy to add Home screens. Follow these steps:

1. Swipe left one or more times to display the last Home screen (the one on the right).
2. Tap and hold an icon to make it mobile, and then drag it to the right edge of the screen. Android automatically creates another Home screen.
3. Release the icon.

TIP   You can create further Home screens in the same way. Before you do, you must put at least one more icon on the new Home screen you've just created so that there will be at least one icon left on that Home screen when you drag an icon to create another Home screen.

To remove a Home screen with Google Now Launcher, you remove all the icons from it. Android then gets rid of the surplus Home screen automatically.

ADDING APPS TO YOUR HOME SCREENS

You can run any app from the Apps screen, but you'll probably want to put the apps you use most on your first Home screen for quick access.

Here's how to add an app's icon to a Home screen:

1. On the Home screen, tap the Apps icon to display the Apps screen.

2. Tap and hold the icon for the app you want to add to the Home screen. Thumbnails of the Home screens appear.

3. Drag the icon to the destination Home screen, position it where you want it, and then drop it.

> **NOTE** If you need to move the app's icon again on the Home screen, tap the icon and hold down until it becomes mobile, drag it to the new location, and then drop it.

ADDING WIDGETS TO YOUR HOME SCREENS

You can also add widgets, tiny apps that display specific information, to your Home screens. Android comes with an extensive selection of widgets built in. If you need widgets beyond these, you can find many more on the Play Store and other online sites.

Here's how to add a widget to a Home screen with Google Now Launcher:

1. Tap and hold open space on the Home screen to display the customization controls. (See the left screen in Figure 3.1.)

2. Tap the Widgets button to display the Widgets screen. (See the right screen in Figure 3.1.)

3. Swipe up until you find the widget you want to add. You may also need to swipe left to see all the widgets available for a particular app.

FIGURE 3.1

Tap and hold open space on the Home screen to display the customization controls (left), and then tap the Widgets button to display the Widgets screen (right).

4. Tap and hold the widget to pick it up. The Home screens then appear as thumbnails. (See the left screen in Figure 3.2.)

> **NOTE** Each widget has its size to the right of its name, such as 1×1 for the Contacts widget for Google Contacts, 3×3 for the Gmail widget, and 4×1 for the Drive widget. You can use these sizes to judge where the widgets will fit on your Home screens.

5. Drag the widget to where you want it to appear, and then drop it.

6. If the widget displays any configuration options, choose suitable settings. For example, when you add the Gmail widget to a Home screen, you get to choose which folder to display in the widget. (See the right screen in Figure 3.2.)

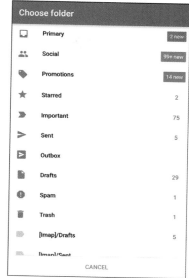

FIGURE 3.2

When the Home screen thumbnails appear (left), drag the widget to the appropriate Home screen. For some widgets, you then must choose the content to display, such as choosing the folder for the Gmail widget (right).

ADDING WEB ADDRESSES TO YOUR HOME SCREENS

If you need to be able to quickly access particular websites, you can add their addresses to your Home screens. Follow these steps:

1. Open the Chrome browser and go to the web page or website.

2. Tap the Menu button to open the menu.

3. Tap the Add to Home Screen button to display the Add to Home Screen dialog box.

4. Either accept the default name for the icon or type a descriptive name that will enable you to identify it. Often, you'll need to shorten the name to make it useful.

5. Tap the Add button. Android adds the icon to your Home screen. You can then tap and hold it and move it to another location if you want.

ORGANIZING HOME SCREEN ITEMS INTO FOLDERS

Your device's Home screens provide enough space for an almost infinite number of icons, but you'll probably need to keep them organized in a human-friendly way. To organize your icons, you can create folders either on the Home screens themselves or in the Favorites tray.

Here's how to create a folder:

1. Navigate to the Home screen that contains the icons. You can drag icons from one screen to another, but it's easier to start with them on the same screen.

2. Tap and hold an icon until it becomes mobile.

3. Drag the icon on top of another icon you want to put in the same folder. Android puts the two icons in a folder and assigns it the default name *Unnamed Folder*.

> **NOTE** When you drag one icon on top of another icon, a highlighted circle appears behind the second icon to show that the icon is in the right place. If you miss the target icon, it moves out of the way on the assumption that you are rearranging the icons rather than creating a folder.

4. Tap the folder to open it.

5. Tap the folder's default name (*Unnamed Folder*) and then type the name you want to give it.

6. Tap the check-mark button on the keyboard or tap outside the folder's name to apply the name.

> **TIP** To take an icon out of a folder, tap the folder to open it. Tap and hold the icon until it becomes mobile, and then drag it out of the folder to where you want it on the Home screen. To delete a folder, remove all its icons; when only one icon is left, the folder disappears, and that icon moves to the Home screen.

ADDING DROPBOX FOLDERS TO YOUR HOME SCREENS

If you've installed the Dropbox app on your device, you may want to give yourself an easy way to access key folders. To do so, add one or more instances of the Dropbox widget to your Home screen using the technique explained earlier in this chapter. When you add the widget, Android prompts you to choose the folder that the widget will open. Tap the appropriate folder, and then tap the Create Shortcut button. Android gives the widget the name of the folder.

REPOSITIONING ITEMS ON YOUR HOME SCREENS

To reposition an item on a Home screen, tap and hold it until it becomes mobile, and then drag it to where you want to place it.

REMOVING ITEMS FROM YOUR HOME SCREENS

To remove an item from a Home screen, tap and hold the item's icon until the Remove button appears at the top of the screen. Drag the icon to the Remove button and drop it there.

NOTE If the app you tap, hold, and drag on the Home screen is an app you've installed, the Uninstall button appears to the right of the Remove button. You can uninstall the app by dragging it to the Uninstall button and then tapping the OK button in the confirmation dialog box that opens.

REARRANGING YOUR HOME SCREENS

To rearrange your Home screens with Google Now Launcher, open the Home screens for customization, and then tap and hold the thumbnail for the Home screen you want to move. When it becomes mobile, drag it to its destination and drop it there.

SETTING THE WALLPAPER

To change the overall look of your Home screens, you can change the wallpaper. Android comes with a set of colorful wallpapers, and you can download other wallpapers to add variety. You can also use a photo of your own.

NOTE Each Home screen uses the same wallpaper on stock Android. Some skins enable you to use different wallpapers on different Home screens.

> **✓ TIP** The live wallpapers include motion, which can make the Home screens look more entertaining when you're not working in an app. However, because they take up more processing power, you should avoid them if you want maximum performance or maximum runtime on the battery.

Follow these steps to set the wallpaper with Google Now Launcher:

1. Tap and hold open space to open the Home screen for customization.
2. Tap the Wallpapers button to display the Wallpapers screen.
3. Tap the My Photos button if you want to use one of your own images for the wallpaper; when you find the image, tap it to preview it. Otherwise, scroll the list of wallpapers and tap the one you want to preview.
4. When you've selected the wallpaper you want, tap the Set Wallpaper button to apply it.

> **✓ TIP** You can find vast numbers of wallpapers on both the Play Store and on the Web. For best results, make sure you get wallpapers of the right resolution for your device—for example, 1080×1920 for a device such as the Nexus 5X. If you're not sure of your device's resolution, look it up online.

> **! CAUTION** Before downloading a wallpapers app from the Play Store, read user reviews to determine its quality. If you decide to install it, carefully review the permissions it requires. If it requires permissions it shouldn't need, such as accessing your contacts, cancel the installation.

USING A DIFFERENT LAUNCHER

A *launcher* is an app that enables you to launch other apps. The launcher controls the way your device's Home screen and other main screens appear, including any live widgets you place on them.

Android includes a default launcher that runs by default and which you summon each time you press the Home button. But you can install different launchers to change the way Android looks and acts on your device.

CHOOSING A LAUNCHER

If you want to change your launcher, you have plenty of choices because developers have built many different launchers. You can find various launchers by opening the Play Store app, tapping the Apps button, and then searching for *launcher*.

Here are three of the top launchers at this writing:

- **Google Now Launcher.** Google Now Launcher is a launcher developed by Google that enables you to upgrade the launcher functionality on devices running new versions of Android. Stock versions of both Marshmallow and Lollipop come with Google Now Launcher as the standard launcher, but you also can try running it on skinned versions of Android. Google Now Launcher is free.

- **Nova Launcher.** Nova Launcher is a slick launcher that makes substantial changes to the Android user interface. The basic version of Nova Launcher is free and provides a slew of customization features, but the Prime version (which costs $4.99) has even more, including the use of gestures on the Home screens. With Nova Launcher, you can even put small horizontal widgets in the app drawer if you find that helpful. The left screen in Figure 3.3 shows the main Nova Settings screen for Nova Launcher, which gives you an idea of what you can customize: the desktop, the app and widget drawers, the dock, the folders, the look and feel of the launcher, the gestures and inputs, and the unread count badges (a Prime feature).

- **Go Launcher.** Go Launcher offers a range of customizations, including themes that dramatically change the look of Android. Some themes are free; others you must pay for. Go Launcher includes shortcuts to many recommended apps, some of which are free. The right screen in Figure 3.3 shows the Effect panel for customizing Go Launcher. You'll probably want to start with the free version of Go Launcher; if you like it, consider upgrading to Go Launcher Prime, which costs $5.99 and offers features such as removing ads, using a side dock to switch among running tasks, and a security lock that enables you to lock specific apps and settings.

! CAUTION   A launcher typically needs many permissions to run successfully. For safety, it is best to avoid launchers from sources other than the Play Store unless you are certain of their provenance, integrity, and coding.

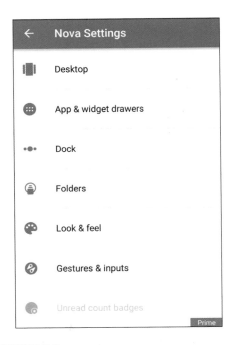 

FIGURE 3.3

From the Nova Settings screen (left), you can configure many areas of Nova Launcher. Go Launcher (right) also offers many settings, but its interface is completely different.

INSTALLING A LAUNCHER

To install a launcher, you download it from the Play Store like any other app. When the download completes, open the launcher by tapping the Open button on the app's screen in the Play Store app or by tapping the launcher's icon on the Apps screen.

Some launchers walk you through a setup routine on first run. For example, Nova Launcher prompts you to import items from your existing launcher, saving you the trouble of rebuilding your existing Home screens for the new launcher. If the launcher cannot import widgets, you will need to add them manually.

After you finish any setup routine, the launcher displays your Home screen in all its transformed glory (or otherwise), and you can start exploring the launcher.

SWITCHING AMONG LAUNCHERS

After installing multiple launchers, you can switch among them as needed by following these steps:

1. Open the Settings app and navigate to the Device section (shown on the left in Figure 3.4).

2. Tap the Home button in the Device section to display the Home screen. (See the right screen in Figure 3.4.)

FIGURE 3.4

Use the Home screen in the Settings app to choose your default launcher. You can also delete any launcher you no longer want.

> **NOTE** The Home button appears in the Device section of the Settings screen only when multiple launchers are installed on your device. If your device has only Google Now Launcher, the Home button doesn't appear because you don't need it.

3. Tap the launcher you want to make the new default, selecting its radio button.

4. Tap the Home button. The Home screen appears, showing any customizations that the launcher makes automatically.

You can then use the launcher's controls to make further customizations. For example, to delete a launcher on Nova Launcher, tap the Delete button (the trash can) on the right of its button on the Home screen in the Settings app.

MAKING NO LAUNCHER THE DEFAULT

When you're experimenting with launchers, you may want to try making no launcher the default so that you can easily switch among the launchers. By removing your default launcher, you can make Android display the Select a Home App dialog box each time you tap the Home button, allowing you to choose the launcher you want to use next.

Here's how to remove your default launcher:

1. Open the Settings app.

2. Tap the Apps button in the Device section to display the Apps screen.

3. On Lollipop, swipe left twice to display the All screen. (If the launcher is one you've downloaded, you can use the Downloaded screen instead.)

4. Scroll down and find the launcher that's currently running. This example uses Nova Launcher.

5. Tap the launcher to display its App Info screen.

6. On Marshmallow, tap the Open by Default button to display the Open by Default screen (shown on the left in Figure 3.5).

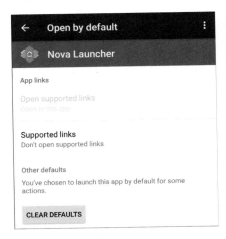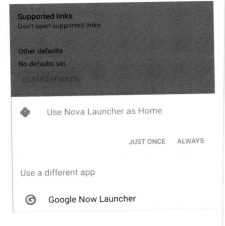

FIGURE 3.5

Tap the Clear Defaults button on the Open by Default screen in Marshmallow (left) or the App Info screen in Lollipop to clear your default launcher. When you tap the Home button, you can then choose which launcher to use (right).

7. Tap the Clear Defaults button. There's normally no response to this move except for a quick blink of the button, but if you see a confirmation dialog box, tap the OK button or its functional equivalent to confirm you want to clear the default launcher.

8. Tap the Home button. Because you've cleared the defaults, an untitled dialog box opens prompting you to choose a launcher. The right screen in Figure 3.5 is an example of this dialog box. The launcher you've just cleared—in this case, Nova Launcher—appears at the top, with a Just Once button and an Always button below it. The lower section of the dialog box shows the Use a Different App list, which contains your other launchers.

9. Tap the button for the launcher you want to use. In this example, you'd tap Google Now Launcher to switch to the Google Now Launcher. Because you're not tapping an Always button, this is only a temporary switch, so each time you tap the Home button, the dialog box appears again.

When you decide which launcher you want to use, tap the Home button to display the dialog box for choosing the launcher. If the launcher you want appears at the top of the dialog box, tap the Always button to make the launcher the default option. If not, tap the launcher in the Use a Different App list; then tap the Home button again to display the dialog box again, this time with the launcher you just tapped at the top. Now tap the Always button to set the default.

> **NOTE** The rest of this book assumes that you are using Google Now Launcher because this is the default launcher for stock Marshmallow and Lollipop.
>
> To set your default launcher on Samsung TouchWiz, open the Settings app, tap Applications to display the Applications screen, and then tap Default Applications to display the Default Applications screen. In the Set Defaults section, tap the Home button to display the settings screen called Home, tap the radio button for the launcher you want to use, and then press the Home button.

CONFIGURING INPUT OPTIONS

Android supports different input options to enable you to get text into your device using your preferred language and a keyboard that suits your needs. You can also input text using your voice with the Google Voice Typing feature.

To set up your input options, you work on the Language & Input screen in the Settings app. (See the left screen in Figure 3.6.) To display this screen, open the Settings app and tap the Language & Input button in the Personal section.

First, make sure the Language button at the top shows the language you want to use, such as English (United States). If not, tap this button to display the Language screen and then tap the correct language. You can tap the Search icon and search for the language if necessary.

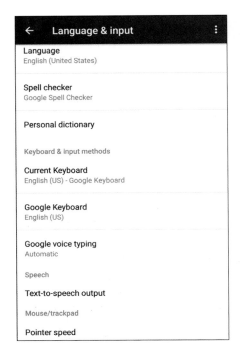
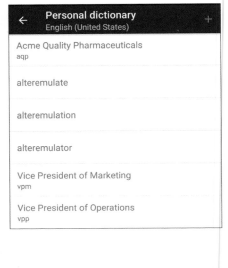

FIGURE 3.6

Use the Language & Input screen (left) to set your input language and configure input options. On the Personal Dictionary screen, you can set up text shortcuts or add words you don't want the spell checker to query.

Next, tap the Spell Checker button to display the Spell Checker screen. Here, you can set the switch at the top to On or Off to enable or disable spell checking. If you set the switch to On, you can also take three other actions:

- **Change the language.** Tap the Language button to set the language for spell checking. The default setting, Use System Language, works well in many cases.

- **Choose which spell checker to use.** If multiple radio buttons appear, tap the spell checker you want to use. If the only radio button is Google Spell Checker, the choice is made for you.

- **Configure the spell checker.** If the spell checker you use has a Settings button (the gear icon), tap this icon to display the Settings screen for the spell checker. You can then enable or disable any options as needed. For example, on the Google Spell Checker Settings screen, you can set the Look Up Contact Names switch to On if you want the spell checker to be able to look up names in your contact list to get them right.

Also at the top of the Language & Input screen, you can tap the Personal Dictionary button to display the Personal Dictionary screen. (See the right screen in Figure 3.6.) Here, you can tap the Add (+) button in the upper-right corner to add a text shortcut or a custom spelling to your personal dictionary. Alternatively, tap an existing entry to edit its contents or to delete it.

> **TIP** The Personal Dictionary has two features. First, you can create short-cuts to enable you to enter text quickly and accurately; for example, you might create a shortcut of **vpm** to enter **Vice President of Marketing** quickly. Second, you can add a word to stop the spell checker from querying it.

Next, in the Keyboard & Input Methods section, set up the keyboards and other input methods you want to use on your device. Here's what you can do:

■ **Change the current keyboard.** Tap the Current Keyboard button to display the Change Keyboard dialog box, and then tap the radio button for the keyboard you want to use. If the keyboard you want doesn't appear, tap the Choose Keyboards button to display the Language & Input screen, and then set the switch to On for each keyboard you want to have available. Chapter 1, "Getting Up to Speed with Android," discusses some alternative keyboards you may want to try on your device.

> **NOTE** The Google Keyboard is normally the default keyboard, so its switch will be set to On unless you select a different keyboard. Google Voice Typing enables you to enter text by tapping the microphone button on the right side of the suggestion strip above the keyboard and then speaking into your device's microphone (or an attached microphone). Make sure the Google Voice Typing switch is set to On if you want to be able to use this feature.

■ **Configure a keyboard.** Tap the keyboard's button to display its Settings screen, and then choose the settings you want. For example, the left screen in Figure 3.7 shows the Google Keyboard Settings screen, where you can set your input language (such as U.S. English), set preferences (such as auto-capitalization and vibration), configure text correction (see the right screen in Figure 3.7), and choose other options. Chapter 1 explains your choices on the Google Keyboard Settings screen.

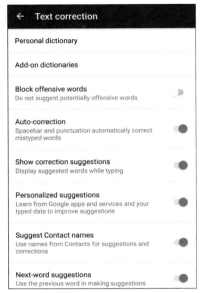

FIGURE 3.7

Choose options for a keyboard on its Settings screen, such as the Google Keyboard Settings screen (left), and the screens to which it gives access, such as the Text Correction screen (right).

CHANGING KEYBOARDS QUICKLY

You can change keyboards quickly from within an app that accepts text input. With the keyboard displayed, tap and hold the key to the left of the spacebar to display the Change Keyboard dialog box, and then tap the radio button for the keyboard you want. If the keyboard doesn't appear in the Change Keyboard dialog box, tap the Choose Keyboards button to go to the Language & Input screen, where you can add it.

CONFIGURING THE LOCK SCREEN

The lock screen is the screen that appears when you start your device or when you wake your device after sleep. You can choose different lock strengths or even turn off locking altogether; you can also configure the Smart Lock feature to allow you to easily unlock your device. You can display your owner information (or other information) on the lock screen to help someone who finds your device return it to you.

TAKING ACTIONS FROM THE LOCK SCREEN

By default, the lock screen in stock Android allows you to unlock your device, make an emergency call (swipe up and then tap the Emergency button), or open the Camera app (swipe the Camera icon up or to the left). However, because many manufacturers customize the lock screen, you may find that your device's lock screen offers more functionality, such as widgets for keeping on top of your communications.

On stock Marshmallow with some Nexus models, you can also press the Power button twice to open the Camera app quickly without unlocking your device. If this setting doesn't work, choose Settings, Display and then set the Press Power Button Twice for Camera switch to On. If this setting doesn't appear, your device doesn't support it.

CHOOSING THE BEST LOCKING METHOD

To keep your data safe, lock your device. Android offers four ways to unlock the screen, but only two are worth using if your device contains any personal or sensitive information, as almost all devices do. These are the four unlock methods:

- **Swipe.** You tap the lock icon on the lock screen and swipe your finger across the screen to unlock your device. Swipe provides no security at all, but it does prevent your device from becoming unlocked by accident in your pocket or bag.

- **Pattern.** You draw a pattern on a nine-dot grid on the screen to unlock your device. A pattern is useful only for light security. You can draw a complex pattern to make this harder for a determined attacker to break, but the result may be more difficult for you to use than a PIN or password.

- **PIN.** You type in a numeric personal identification number (PIN) and tap the Enter button to unlock your device. PIN is a good choice for medium security. The PIN must be at least four digits long (giving 10,000 possible combinations), but it is sensible to use eight digits (10,000,000 combinations) or more.

> **NOTE** If you enter the wrong PIN or password five times in succession, Android makes you wait 30 seconds before trying again. This delay is to make it awkward for someone to guess your PIN or password—for example, by entering the names of your family, friends, or pets. It also helps delay an attacker breaking your PIN by "brute force," simply entering every possible PIN value in turn until stumbling on the correct one.

- **Password.** You type in a password using any characters—letters, numbers, or symbols—but containing at least one letter. Password is the only choice for serious security on your device. Android requires the password to be at least four characters long, but you should consider eight characters a minimum to secure your device effectively. The longer the password, the harder it is for an attacker to break by brute force.

! CAUTION Even a strong password may not protect your device against professional intrusion. Some law-enforcement agencies have automated tools for brute-force attacks on iOS devices (the iPhone, iPad, and iPod touch). These tools cut the device's power after a failed PIN attempt to avoid triggering the delay mechanism. It is likely that agencies have similar tools for cracking Android devices.

SETTING UP LOCKING ON YOUR DEVICE

Here's how to set up locking on your device:

1. Open the Settings app.
2. Tap the Security button in the Personal section to display the Security screen.

NOTE The screen locking settings may be in a different location on your device, such as a screen called Lock Screen or Security & Screen Lock.

3. Tap the Screen Lock button in the Screen Security section to display the Choose Screen Lock screen. If you have already applied a lock, you will need to use the unlocking method to proceed. For example, type your PIN and tap the Next button or the right-arrow button.
4. Tap the unlock method you want to use, and then follow through any screens that appear. For example, if you tap the Password button, you must type a password and then confirm it.

NOTE On Marshmallow, when you tap the Pattern button, the PIN button, or the Password button on the Choose Screen Lock screen, the Secure Start-Up screen appears, offering to apply further protection by requiring your password before the device starts. Tap the Require Password to Start Device radio button if you want to implement this security mechanism, which is a good idea. Otherwise, tap the No Thanks radio button. Either way, tap the Continue button to proceed.

5. Back on the Security screen, tap the Automatically Lock button to display the Automatically Lock dialog box, and then tap the button for the delay between the device going to sleep and the screen locking. The best choice is Immediately, but you may want to have a short delay, such as 5 Seconds or 15 Seconds, if you find yourself needing to wake your device soon after you put it to sleep.

6. Also on the Security screen, set the Power Button Instantly Locks switch to On so that you can lock your device quickly by pressing the Power button.

Locking is now set up. To try it, press the Power button once to lock your device, press the Power button again to wake it, and then use the unlock method to unlock the device.

SETTING UP SMART LOCK

Android's Smart Lock feature allows you to set up other ways of unlocking your device than your pattern, PIN, password, or fingerprint. As of this writing, Smart Lock offers five smart ways to keep your device unlocked or unlock it automatically:

- **Trusted Devices.** You can specify one or more trusted devices whose presence allows your device to remain unlocked. Trusted devices use either NFC or Bluetooth. For example, if you wear a Bluetooth-capable watch, you can use that as a trusted device.

- **Trusted Places.** You can specify one or more trusted places—map locations—in which your device remains unlocked. For example, you can set up your home as a trusted place.

- **Trusted Face.** You can set up your device to unlock when its screenside camera detects you gazing lovingly at it.

- **Trusted Voice.** You can set up your device to unlock when it hears a voice that matches the voice model you set up.

- **On-Body Detection.** You can set up your device to remain unlocked while it detects you are holding it or carrying it.

UNDERSTANDING THE PITFALLS OF SMART LOCK

If you use your Android device extensively but want to keep your data safe, you'll need to unlock your device many times per day. Unlocking is vital for security, but it reduces your productivity by increasing the time it takes to start interacting with your phone or tablet.

Smart Lock is a great idea for helping overcome users' understandable reluctance to keep typing in a PIN or a complex passcode each time their device has locked. As explained in the main text, Smart Lock offers three smart tests for keeping your device unlocked (Trusted Devices, Trusted Places, and On-Body Detection) and two smart means of unlocking your device quickly and almost effortlessly (Trusted Face and Trusted Voice).

Unfortunately, all these five Smart Lock approaches have security problems—especially the three stay-unlocked methods.

A malefactor can defeat the Trusted Devices feature by removing a trusted device along with your Android device. To defeat the On-Body Detection feature, an attacker need only remove your Android device from your hand or take your purse (with your phone in it) from your shoulder.

Trusted Places is even worse. If you make home a trusted place, any of your family can use your Android device the moment you turn your back. If you make work a trusted place, any colleague can filch your device and start using it.

The two smart-unlock methods, Trusted Face and Trusted Voice, are better—but even so, you may not want to use them. With Trusted Face, someone who looks like you to the camera and its algorithms may be able to unlock your device. (A picture of you shouldn't work because Trusted Face includes a "liveness check" that makes sure the face's eyes blink.) Similarly, Trusted Voice is open to attacks using either similar voices or recordings of your voice.

Setting up Smart Lock is straightforward. Choose Settings, Security, Smart Lock to display the Smart Lock screen. (See the left screen in Figure 3.8.) You'll need to enter your password, PIN, or pattern to prove you're you.

Next, tap the button for the Smart Lock method you want to set up, and follow the prompts on the screens that appear. Here are brief notes on the Smart Lock methods:

- **Trusted Devices.** On the Trusted Devices screen (see the right screen in Figure 3.8), tap the Add Trusted Device button. On the Choose Device Type screen, tap the Bluetooth button or the NFC button, as appropriate.

For Bluetooth, you then select the device on the Choose Device screen. For NFC, you bring the NFC tag or device to within striking distance of the NFC chip in your Android device. Usually, you'll hear a bleep when the NFC chips connect.

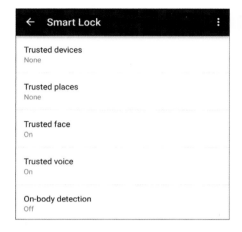
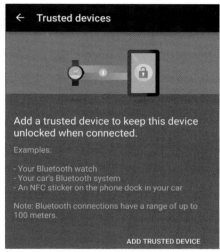

FIGURE 3.8

On the Smart Lock screen (left), tap the Smart Lock method you want to set up. Then use the screen that appears, such as the Trusted Devices screen (right), to configure the Smart Lock method.

- **Trusted Places.** On the Trusted Places screen, tap the place if it already appears. Otherwise, tap the Add Trusted Place button and then use the Pick a Place screen to select the place; Android suggests your current location, but you can move the location as needed.

- **Trusted Face.** On the Add a Trusted Face screen (in Marshmallow) or the About Trusted Face screen (in Lollipop), read the warnings and then tap the Set Up button. On the next screen, which is called Add a Trusted Face in both Marshmallow and Lollipop, tap the Next button, and then position your face in the dotted frame onscreen and wait while Android recognizes it.

> **TIP** After setting up Trusted Face, tap the Improve Face Matching button on the Trusted Face screen and go through the procedure a few more times to teach Android how your face looks from different angles, with or without glasses or makeup, or shaven and unshaven.

- **Trusted Voice.** On the Settings screen that appears, set the Always On switch (on Marshmallow) or the From Any Screen switch (on Lollipop) to On if it is set to Off. You can then set the Trusted Voice switch to On; you'll need to enter your pattern, password, or PIN, too.

- **On-Body Detection.** On the On-Body Detection screen, set the switch to On, and then tap the Continue button in the Keep in Mind dialog box that opens and warns you that someone else might be able to grab your device from you without causing automatic locking to take place.

> **TIP** After setting up your Smart Lock method or methods, test them to make sure they work as you expect them to.

PUTTING A MESSAGE OR OWNER INFORMATION ON THE LOCK SCREEN

You can display a message or your owner information on the lock screen. This works a little differently in Marshmallow than in Lollipop:

- **Marshmallow.** Choose Settings, Security, Lock Screen Message to open the Lock Screen Message dialog box. Type the message you want to display, tapping the Enter key as needed to create new lines, and then tap the Save button.

- **Lollipop.** Choose Settings, Security, Owner Info to display the Owner Info screen. Check the Show Owner Info on Lock Screen box, and then type the text you want to display.

> **CAUTION** Any information you display on the lock screen is accessible to anybody who can pick up your device and press the Power button. So you'll need to balance your desire for instant access to information against your need to keep that information private.

UNLOCKING YOUR DEVICE WITH YOUR FINGERPRINT

If your device has a fingerprint scanner, you can set up one of more of your fingertips as an easy way of unlocking your device.

On those Google Nexus models that have fingerprint scanners, such as the Nexus 6P and the Nexus 5X, the fingerprint-unlock feature is called Nexus Imprint. To set it up, choose Settings, Security, Nexus Imprint; enter your PIN, pattern, or password to authenticate yourself; and then tap the Add Fingerprint button on the Nexus Imprint screen to start the process of adding a fingerprint. When you reach the Fingerprint Added screen, you can tap the Add Another button to add another finger.

The Nexus Imprint assigns the first fingerprint the default name Finger 1. When you finish adding fingerprints and return to the Nexus Imprint screen, you can tap a Finger button to open a dialog box that enables you to either add a more useful name (such as Right Index Finger) or delete the fingerprint.

> **TIP** Normally, it's a good idea to add multiple fingerprints so that you can unlock your device using either hand. If the fingerprint scanner is on the front of the device, you may want to add your thumbs as well.

Other manufacturers give different names to the fingerprint-unlocking feature on their devices and put them in different areas of the Settings app, so you may need to search for them. For example, on Samsung devices that have fingerprint readers, such as the Galaxy Note 5, choose Settings, Lock Screen and Security, Fingerprints to display the Fingerprints screen, and then tap the Add Fingerprint button.

CONFIGURING LOCK-SCREEN NOTIFICATIONS

Android enables you to choose whether to display notifications on the lock screen. Displaying notifications on the lock screen can be a time-saver, but it also risks exposing notifications to people you'd rather didn't see them. So Android gives you another choice: You can display notifications but hide any content that might be sensitive.

To configure lock-screen notifications, choose Settings, Sound & Notification. On the Sound & Notification screen, tap the When Device Is Locked button, and then tap the appropriate option in the pop-up menu: Show All Notification Content, Hide Sensitive Notification Content, or Don't Show Notifications at All.

> **NOTE** On a tablet running Marshmallow, the Hide Sensitive Notification Content option might not be available.

CHOOSING LOCATION SETTINGS TO PROTECT YOUR PRIVACY

Carrying a cell phone is like carrying a beacon that constantly tracks your location, and even a Wi-Fi–only tablet keeps track of your whereabouts so that it can provide map information and other location-dependent data. Besides, electronics devices are exposed to snooping, so it's essential to choose privacy settings that suit your needs.

Here's how to choose location settings:

1. Open the Settings app.

2. In the Personal section, tap the Location button to display the Location screen. (See the left screen in Figure 3.9.)

3. Set the Location switch to the On position to use location tracking.

4. Tap the Mode button to display the Location Mode screen. (See the right screen in Figure 3.9.)

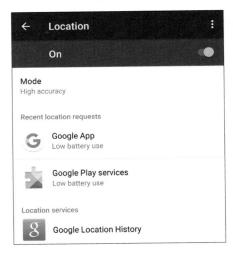
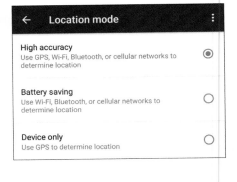

FIGURE 3.9

On the Location screen (left), you can turn location tracking On or Off, choose which mode to use, and configure Location Services. On the Location Mode screen, choose how you want Android to track your device's location.

5. Tap the button for the location mode you want to use: High Accuracy, Battery Saving, or Device Only.

6. Tap the arrow button or the Back button below the screen to return to the Location screen.

7. Review the apps and services in the Recent Location Requests list to make sure that all are apps you want to use location services.

8. In the Location Services list, tap Google Location History to display the Location History screen. (See the left screen in Figure 3.10.)

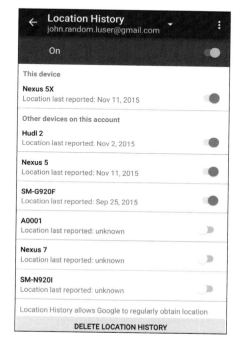
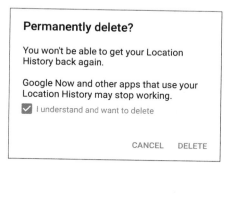

FIGURE 3.10

From the Location History screen (left), you can pause location history tracking or turn it off for a device. To delete your location history, tap the Delete Location History button and then tap the Delete button in the Permanently Delete dialog box (right).

> **TIP** If you have set up multiple Google accounts on your device, make sure the Location History screen is showing the account you want to configure. You can switch accounts by using the pop-up menu at the top of the screen.

9. If you want to pause location history, set the switch at the top of the Location History screen to Off, and then tap the OK button in the Pause Location History dialog box that opens.

10. Look at the devices shown on the Location History screen. You can set the switch for a device to Off to turn off location history for that device.

11. If you want to delete all the location history entries for this Google account, tap the Delete Location History button at the bottom of the Location History screen. In the Permanently Delete? dialog box that appears (see the right screen in Figure 3.10), check the I Understand and Want to Delete box, and then tap the Delete button.

> **! CAUTION** Deleting your location history entries may stop apps that use your location history from working. Google Now is the app most likely to be affected, but other apps also can be affected.

ENCRYPTING YOUR DEVICE

To protect your device against unauthorized access if you lose it, you can encrypt its contents. Encryption deliberately scrambles the content using an encryption key, leaving the content unreadable without the key to decrypt it.

MOST MARSHMALLOW DEVICES HAVE MANDATORY ENCRYPTION

If your device came with Marshmallow installed, chances are that it is already encrypted. In Marshmallow, Google made encryption mandatory for all new Android devices that meet certain technical and performance criteria, so unless your device doesn't meet them, it should be encrypted. But if you have upgraded your device from Lollipop to Marshmallow, you should check that encryption has been applied. And if your device is still running Lollipop, you should apply encryption if you haven't already done so.

To check whether your device is encrypted, choose Settings, Security and then look at the Encryption section of the Security screen. If the Encrypt Phone button or Encrypt Tablet button has an Encrypted readout, you're all set. If not, you can encrypt your device as explained in this section.

> **NOTE** Encryption can take an hour or more, depending on the amount of data your device contains and its processor speed; and if encryption fails to complete, your data may get corrupted. So Android ensures enough power is available by making the encryption controls unavailable unless the device's battery is fully charged *and* the device is connected to a power supply.

For the encryption to work, you must set a lock screen PIN or password to prevent others from unlocking your device. If you've already set a PIN or password, you're good to go; if not, go back to the section "Setting Up Locking on Your Device," earlier in this chapter, and set one or the other.

UNDERSTANDING THE DISADVANTAGES OF ENCRYPTION

Encryption has three disadvantages you should understand before you encrypt your device.

First, your device must decrypt data to present it to you, so it may run more slowly. Depending on the device's hardware, the difference may not be noticeable, but it may be enough to be annoying. This is why Google included performance criteria rather than making encryption mandatory for *all* Marshmallow devices.

Second, on Lollipop, you must enter your PIN or password to decrypt the storage each time you restart the device. On Marshmallow, you can choose whether to require the PIN or password at startup. (This feature is called Secure Start-Up.) This is easy enough, but it makes an extra step between booting your device and getting to use it.

Third, the only way to remove encryption is by restoring your device to factory settings. Doing this removes all your data and apps from the device, so you have to set it up again from scratch.

For a device that has multiple user accounts set up, there's a fourth disadvantage: Even if you encrypt the device from your owner account, the other accounts remain unencrypted and aren't required to set a PIN or passcode. This raises the possibility that an attacker can use the other accounts to attack your data.

> **! CAUTION**   Android's encryption is strong enough to prevent civilian attackers from unencrypting it. However, you should assume that law-enforcement agencies and government security agencies have tools powerful enough to crack the encryption without breaking a serious sweat.

ENCRYPTING THE DATA ON YOUR DEVICE

Here's how to encrypt your device:

1. Fully charge the battery, and leave the device connected to power.
2. Open the Settings app.

3. Tap the Security button in the Personal section to display the Security screen.

> **✎ NOTE** Depending on your device, the encryption settings may be in a different location. If you can't find them, search for "encrypt."

4. Tap the Encrypt Phone button or the Encrypt Tablet button (whichever one appears). The Encrypt Phone screen or the Encrypt Tablet screen appears. (Some devices have the Encrypt Device button and Encrypt Device screen instead.)

5. Read the information and then tap the Encrypt Phone button or the Encrypt Tablet button. The Confirm Your PIN screen or Confirm Your Password screen appears.

> **✎ NOTE** If your device doesn't have a PIN or password set, the No Lock Screen PIN or Password dialog box opens, telling you that you need to set a PIN or password. Turn back to the section "Setting Up Locking on Your Device," earlier in this chapter, and return when you have set a PIN or password.

6. Type your PIN or password.

7. Tap the Continue button. The Encrypt screen appears, warning you that encryption is irreversible and that your device will restart several times during the encryption process.

8. Tap the Encrypt Phone button or the Encrypt Tablet button. Android starts the encryption process. You'll see the Encrypting screen with a progress readout as it works.

9. When the Type Password to Decrypt Storage prompt appears, type your PIN or password and tap the Done button on the keyboard. Android then decrypts your data, the lock screen appears, and you can type your PIN or password (again) to unlock the device as usual.

> **✎ NOTE** If you have a PIN rather than a password, don't worry that the Type Password to Decrypt Storage prompt asks for a password. Type in your PIN, and all will be well.

> **TIP** If encryption fails on a tablet that has multiple user accounts set up, try updating to the latest version of Android before encrypting the tablet.

DECRYPTING THE DATA ON YOUR DEVICE

The only way to decrypt the data on your device is to perform a factory data reset. This move wipes all your apps and data off your device and restores it to its original settings.

> **! CAUTION** Back up your device's data to your computer or to an online account—or, better, to both—before performing a factory data reset.

> **TIP** You may want to perform a factory data reset before selling your phone or tablet or giving it to someone else.

Here's how to perform a factory data reset:

1. Open the Settings app.
2. Tap the Backup & Reset button in the Personal section to display the Backup & Reset screen.
3. Tap the Factory Data Reset button. The Factory Data Reset screen appears. (See the left screen in Figure 3.11.)
4. The Confirm Your PIN screen or Confirm Your Password screen appears.
5. Type your PIN or password.
6. Tap the Continue button. The Reset screen appears, displaying a final, excited warning. (See the right screen in Figure 3.11.)
7. Tap the Erase Everything button. The Power Off dialog box opens for a few seconds. The device then shuts down and restarts. The Erasing screen appears while Android erases the data.

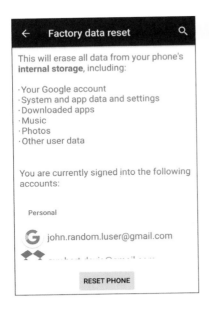

FIGURE 3.11

On the Factory Data Reset screen (left), tap the Reset Phone button or Reset Tablet button. On the Reset screen (right), tap the Erase Everything button.

Android then resets the operating system to factory defaults and displays the Welcome screen. You can then set up your device again as you did when you first got it.

> **TIP** The quickest and easiest way to get your device up and running again is to restore data from your Google account to it. Tap the Yes button on the Got Google screen, and then type your email address and password on the Sign In screen. When the Google Services screen appears, check the box called "Back Up Your Data to a Google Account. Restore Previous Backups to This Device."

PERFORMING A HARD RESET

In addition to the factory data reset explained in the previous section, there's another type of reset called a *hard reset*. A hard reset is a move you typically perform when your device won't start correctly; for example, it crashes while loading Android.

FIND SPECIFIC INSTRUCTIONS FOR YOUR DEVICE BEFORE PERFORMING A HARD RESET

Exactly how you perform a hard reset depends on the device you're using and the version of Android it's running. This section gives you the general steps needed, but before performing them, you should search online to find the different key presses or commands your device and version of Android need. Search for the device's name and *hard reset*.

Here's an example of how to perform a hard reset. These instructions are specifically for the Nexus 5X running stock Marshmallow.

1. Power down your phone or tablet. Press and hold the Power button until the Power dialog box opens, and then tap the Power Off button in the dialog box that opens.

NOTE If the Power dialog box doesn't appear because your device is frozen, keep holding down the Power button until the device turns off.

2. Hold down the Volume Up button, the Volume Down button, and the Power button for several seconds. Your device turns on and displays a picture of an Android lying on its back with its cover open for maintenance. Release the buttons.

TIP Different devices use different combinations of hardware buttons to perform a hard reset. If the combination given here doesn't work for your device, search online for the device's name and *recovery buttons*.

3. Press the Volume Up button or the Volume Down button one or more times until the Recovery Mode button appears at the top of the screen.

4. Press the Power button to give the Recovery Mode command. Your device restarts and displays another screen showing an Android lying on its back, cover open for maintenance, a red triangle with an exclamation point, and the message "No Command."

5. Press and hold the Power button and then press the Volume Up button. The Android Recovery screen appears.

6. Press the Volume Up button or the Volume Down button to select the Wipe Data/Factory Reset command on the menu.

7. Press the Power button to give the command. A confirmation screen appears because this is a drastic move.

8. Press the Volume Up button or the Volume Down button to select the Yes – Erase All User Data command.

9. Press the Power button to give the command. Android erases the data, restarts, and displays the Welcome screen. You can then set up the device from scratch.

4

CONNECTING TO NETWORKS AND DEVICES

To get the most out of your Android device, you'll want to connect it to wireless networks as often as possible, and to cellular networks if it is a phone or has cellular capability. You'll likely also want to connect it to Bluetooth devices, such as keyboards or headphones, to make full use of its features. You may also want to connect your device to a virtual private network, or VPN, to establish a secure connection to a server across the Internet.

USING AIRPLANE MODE

Android's Airplane mode feature turns off all your device's wireless communications. Airplane mode is primarily designed for those times when you're in an airplane and FAA regulation or crew intransigence forbids you from using wireless communications. But you can also use Airplane mode at any time to save power.

To turn on Airplane mode, open the Quick Settings panel and tap the Airplane Mode icon, changing the icon from an outline to solid white. A white airplane icon appears near the right end of the status bar, just to the left of the battery icon, to remind you that Airplane mode is on.

To turn off Airplane mode, open the Quick Settings panel and tap the Airplane Mode icon again.

> **☑ TIP**   You can also turn Airplane mode on or off by opening the Settings app, tapping the More button in the Wireless & Networks section, and then setting the Airplane Mode switch on the More screen to On or Off. Usually, though, it's easier to use the icon on the Quick Settings panel. On some skinned devices, you may find an Airplane Mode switch directly on the Settings screen, which is handy.

While Airplane mode is on, you can turn on Wi-Fi and establish connections to wireless networks if necessary. You can also turn on Bluetooth so that you can use Bluetooth devices.

> **☑ TIP**   Turning on Airplane mode generally enables your device to charge faster.

TAKING CONTROL OF CELLULAR CONNECTIONS

If your Android device is a phone or a cellular-capable tablet, you'll want to manage its cellular connections. This means using data roaming deliberately rather than by accident to avoid extra charges, making sure you keep within your data plan (likewise), and switching between 3G and 4G networks as needed to maintain connectivity.

DISPLAYING THE CELLULAR NETWORK SETTINGS SCREEN

Most of the settings you need for controlling your cellular connection are on the Cellular Network Settings screen. (See the left screen in Figure 4.1.) To reach this screen, open the Settings app, tap the More button in the Wireless & Networks area, and then tap the Cellular Networks button on the More screen.

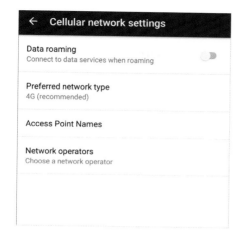
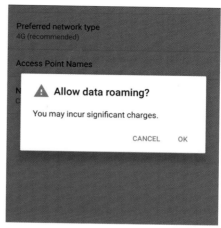

FIGURE 4.1

From the Cellular Network Settings screen (left), you can control data roaming and select your preferred network type. The Allow Data Roaming dialog box (right) warns you that data roaming may hit you in the pocketbook.

ENABLING AND DISABLING DATA ROAMING

On the Cellular Network Settings screen, set the Data Roaming switch to On if you want to allow your device to transfer data when it's connected to other carriers' cellular networks.

UNDERSTANDING THE DIFFERENCE BETWEEN CELLULAR DATA AND DATA ROAMING

Cellular data is data your device transfers over the cellular network when connected to your regular carrier—for example, getting your email. This data normally counts against the data allowance in your cellular plan. (I say "normally" because there are various exceptions, such as carriers that exempt their favored music or video services to encourage you to use those services instead of their competitors.) To manage your cellular data usage in Lollipop and Marshmallow, you work on the Data Usage screen, which you'll meet in the section "Keeping Within Your Data Plan," a little later in this chapter.

If you go outside your carrier's area, especially if you go outside the country, you may need to connect to another carrier to get your device working. This is *data roaming*—transferring data across a cellular connection when connected to another carrier's cellular network. Data roaming usually costs extra money, so normally you'll want to keep the Data Roaming screen on the Cellular Network Settings screen set to Off to make sure your device isn't using data roaming when it shouldn't be.

NOTE Your device may show a different name for the data roaming control, such as the Global Data Roaming Access check box.

CAUTION Connecting to another carrier's network can be expensive for calls, so check the cost first. Double-check the costs for data roaming because they can be exorbitant. Some carriers have the grace to warn you (usually by sending a text message) when you cross country borders and start roaming; some even point out what roaming will cost you. But don't rely on such warnings.

When you set the Data Roaming switch to On, the Allow Data Roaming dialog box (refer to the right screen in Figure 4.1) opens to warn you that you may incur significant charges. Tap the OK button if you're sure you want to use roaming.

NOTE Depending on your carrier, you may see a different dialog box than the Allow Data Roaming dialog box when you set the Data Roaming switch to On. For example, you may see a dialog box asking whether you want to allow roaming access just for this trip or for all trips.

TIP When using data roaming, transfer as little data as possible. Downloading movies or TV shows is obviously unwise, but you should also watch out for other data hogs, such as streaming audio and email attachments. Instead of streaming audio, put your music on your device for when you travel. For email, reduce the sync frequency or set it to never sync, checking manually for messages when necessary—and preferably when your device has a Wi-Fi connection rather than a cellular connection.

CHOOSING AMONG CELLULAR NETWORK TYPES

Depending on your location and your carrier, you may have multiple types of cellular networks available. For example, you may be able to choose between 3G and 4G networks; or you may have a choice among Global, LTE/CDMA, and GSM/UMTS networks.

In this case, you should tell your device which you want to use. Tap the Preferred Network Type button on the Cellular Network Settings screen to display the Preferred Network Type dialog box, and then tap the appropriate radio button.

CONFIGURING A NEW ACCESS POINT

Cellular devices connect to a carrier's network through access points. The Access Point Names (APN) setting on your device controls which access point your device uses.

Normally, your device's SIM card causes the device to connect to the right APN, so you don't need to change the setting. But in special circumstances you may need to specify the APN for your device. To do so, tap the Access Point Names button on the Cellular Network Settings screen, and then work on the APNs screen. Here you can take the following actions:

- **Switch among existing APNs.** If the APNs screen already has multiple APNs, tap the radio button for the APN you want to use. For example, your carrier may provide an APN for regular cellular use and an APN for hotspot use.

- **Edit an existing APN.** Tap the APN to display the Edit Access Point screen, and then make the changes needed.

- **Add a new APN.** Tap the Add (+) button to display the Edit Access Point screen, and then type in the information for the APN. When you finish, tap the Menu button, and then tap Save on the menu.

 NOTE Some carriers suppress the Add a New VPN command.

TIP If you mess up your APN settings, you can easily reset them to their defaults. Tap the Menu button on the APNs screen, and then tap Reset to Default on the menu.

CONNECTING TO A DIFFERENT CARRIER

To connect to a different carrier, tap the Network Operators button on the Cellular Network Settings screen. The Available Networks screen appears, and Android automatically searches for carriers. You can then tap the carrier to which you want to connect.

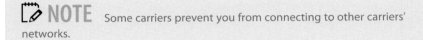

NOTE Some carriers prevent you from connecting to other carriers' networks.

To return to your normal carrier, tap the Choose Automatically button on the Available Networks screen.

KEEPING WITHIN YOUR DATA PLAN

Android includes a Data Usage tool to help you keep within your data plan and not overrun your mobile data limit. On most devices, you can set a limit for your data usage and set a warning level to let yourself know you're approaching the cutoff point.

Open the Settings app and tap the Data Usage button in the Wireless & Network section to display the Data Usage screen. (See the left screen in Figure 4.2.)

Here you can set the Cellular Data switch to On or Off to control cellular data as a whole. Normally, you want to leave it On unless you've run out of data plan.

SETTING A WARNING LEVEL AND A LIMIT

To set a limit for data usage, set the Set Mobile Data Limit switch to On, tap the OK button in the Limiting Data Usage dialog box that opens, and then drag the red bar up or down the diagram to set the limit. Drag the gray bar up or down to set the warning level.

Tap the Usage Cycle pop-up menu and choose the dates to use for the billing cycle. You can either tap one of the suggested date ranges on the pop-up menu or tap Change Cycle and set the appropriate date in the Usage Cycle Reset Date dialog box.

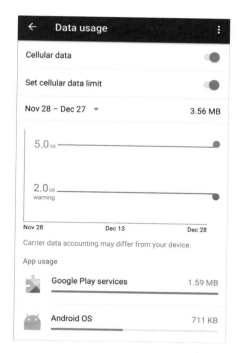
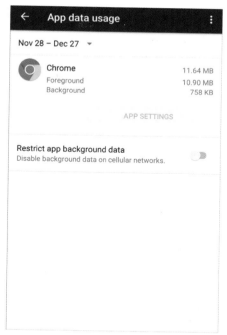

FIGURE 4.2

On the Data Usage screen (left), you can enable and disable cellular data and set your data limit and warning levels. On the App Data Usage screen (right), you can set the Restrict App Background Data switch to On to prevent the app from using mobile data when it is in the background.

IDENTIFYING DATA HOGS

Look at the App Usage list at the bottom of the Data Usage screen to identify data hogs. The list shows the apps, services, and hardware in descending order of appetite, so you can easily see which of them have been greediest.

Tap an app to display that app's App Data Usage screen. The right screen in Figure 4.2 shows an example for the Chrome app. Use the Usage Cycle pop-up menu at the top of the screen to specify the dates you want to review. You can then look at the Foreground readout and Background readout to see how the app has been using data.

If you don't want the app to use mobile data when it's in the background, set the Restrict Background Data switch to On.

If the App Settings button on the App Data Usage screen is available, you can tap it to go to the app to choose settings for it. This should take you to the app's Settings screen, but some apps display the main screen instead; if so, open the navigation panel and tap the Settings button to display the Settings screen.

WORKING WITH THE DATA USAGE SCREEN'S MENU

The menu on the main Data Usage screen (see the left screen in Figure 4.3) contains several key commands for managing your data usage:

- **Restrict Background Data.** Check this box to prevent all apps and services from using mobile data when they're in the background. Android displays the Restrict Background Data dialog box to warn you that restricting background data prevents some apps and services from working unless they have a Wi-Fi connection. Tap the OK button if you want to proceed.

- **Show Wi-Fi/Hide Wi-Fi.** Tap this button to display Wi-Fi data usage on a separate tab. Being able to check Wi-Fi usage is useful if you're on a metered Wi-Fi connection (such as at a hotel) or if you suspect an app of hogging Wi-Fi bandwidth. Otherwise, if you're on an all-you-can-eat Wi-Fi connection, you probably don't care how much data you're shifting over it. Tap the Hide Wi-Fi button on the menu when you want to hide the Wi-Fi tab again.

- **Network Restrictions.** Tap this button to display the Network Restrictions screen (see the right screen in Figure 4.3), and then set the switch to On for each Wi-Fi network that is a metered network rather than a regular wireless network. You can then restrict apps in the background from using the metered networks.

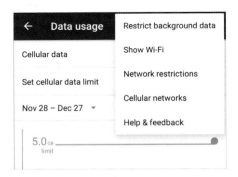
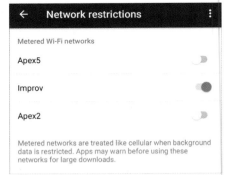

FIGURE 4.3

Use the menu on the Data Usage screen (left) to manage your data usage. On the Network Restrictions screen (right), set the switch to On for any Wi-Fi network that is metered and that you want to restrict.

> **TIP** The other difference that marking metered networks makes is that when your device is connected to a known metered network, apps may also warn you before downloading large files.

- **Cellular Networks.** Tap this button to display the Cellular Network Settings screen, on which you can configure data roaming, your preferred network type, access point names, and network operators.

- **Help & Feedback.** Tap this button to display the Help screen, which provides a Popular list of questions, a Search box for searching for other help, and a Send Feedback button for giving your feedback.

MANAGING YOUR WI-FI CONNECTIONS

Even if you have a cellular device with a generous data plan, Wi-Fi tends to be essential to getting the most out of your device. In this section, you learn how to find and identify networks; connect to them using passwords, Wi-Fi Protected Setup, and Wi-Fi Direct; install digital certificates; whitelist your device; configure IP settings; connect through a proxy server; and more.

TURNING WI-FI ON AND OFF

You can quickly turn Wi-Fi on or off by opening the Quick Settings panel and tapping the Wi-Fi icon. When Wi-Fi is off, this icon shows the text "Wi-Fi"; when Wi-Fi is on and your device has connected to a wireless network, the icon shows three pieces of information. (See the left screen in Figure 4.4.)

- The network's name under the icon (abbreviated if necessary).

- The connection's strength—the larger the white beam, the stronger the connection.

- Whether the connection is transferring data. An up arrow indicates data going to the server, while a down arrow indicates data coming to your device.

To switch networks, tap the pop-up button to the right of the current network's name. The Wi-Fi Quick Settings panel appears. (See the right screen in Figure 4.4.) Here, you can tap the network you want to start using; set the Wi-Fi switch at the top to On or Off, as needed; or tap the More Settings button to display the Wi-Fi screen, where you can choose further settings.

FIGURE 4.4

The Wi-Fi icon on the Quick Settings panel (left) shows the current Wi-Fi network's name, strength, and whether it is transferring data upstream or downstream. Tap the pop-up button to display the Wi-Fi Quick Settings panel (right).

> ☑ **TIP** Instead of using the icon on the Quick Settings panel to turn Wi-Fi on or off, you can set the switch on the Wi-Fi screen.

When you turn Wi-Fi on, Android checks to see if any of the Wi-Fi networks to which you've previously connected your device are available. If a network is available, Android connects to it.

> ☑ **TIP** For instant access to the Wi-Fi screen, create a Settings shortcut to it on the Home screen.

CONNECTING TO WI-FI NETWORKS

To choose which Wi-Fi network your Android device connects to, open the Wi-Fi screen in one of these ways:

- Open the Settings app and tap the Wi-Fi button on the Settings screen.
- Tap the Wi-Fi pop-up button on the Quick Settings panel, and then tap the More Settings button on the Wi-Fi Quick Settings panel.

If the Wi-Fi switch on the Wi-Fi screen is set to Off, set it to On. Android then searches for available networks and displays a list of them. If a network to which you've previously connected is available, Android connects to it.

If no such network is available, or if you want to connect to a different network, tap it on the Wi-Fi screen. If the network requires a password, Android displays a dialog box (whose title bar bears the network's name) to prompt you for it. (See the left screen in Figure 4.5.) Type the password—check the Show Password box if you need to see what you're typing—and then tap the Connect button to connect.

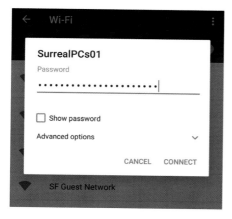

FIGURE 4.5

Android prompts you to enter the password for the wireless network you're trying to join (left). When you need to connect to a closed network, enter its name and details in the Add Network dialog box (right).

TIP If the Wi-Fi network you're expecting to see doesn't appear on the Wi-Fi screen, tap the Menu button and then tap Refresh on the menu to force another scan. If the network still doesn't appear, you may need to provide the network name; see the next section for details.

Each Wi-Fi network has a network name to identify it. The administrator assigns the name when setting up the network. The name contains alphanumeric characters—letters and numbers—and has a maximum length of 32 characters.

NOTE The technical term for a wireless network's name is *service set identifier*, or *SSID*.

When setting up a Wi-Fi network, the administrator can decide whether to have the router broadcast the network's name—as networks normally do—or whether to create a *closed* network that doesn't broadcast its name.

NOTE Creating a closed network is one of the security measures an administrator can take for a wireless network. It is only moderately effective: Casual intruders may miss the network, but anyone with a Wi-Fi scanner can still detect the network.

CONNECTING TO A CLOSED NETWORK

To connect to a closed network, you need to provide the network name as well as the password or other security measure. Tap the Menu button and then tap Add Network on the menu to display the Add Network dialog box. (Refer to the right screen in Figure 4.5.) Then enter the details and tap the Save button.

NOTE SSIDs are case sensitive, so use the exact case.

TIP You can also use the Add Network dialog box to add an open network that is not currently in range.

After adding the closed network to the list on the Wi-Fi screen, you can tap the network to connect to it.

WORKING ON THE ADVANCED WI-FI SCREEN

The Wi-Fi screen gives you access to the essential settings for configuring Wi-Fi networks, but to take full control of Wi-Fi, you need to configure advanced settings. Tap the Menu button on the Wi-Fi screen to open the menu, and then tap Advanced to display the Advanced Wi-Fi screen. (See the left screen in Figure 4.6.)

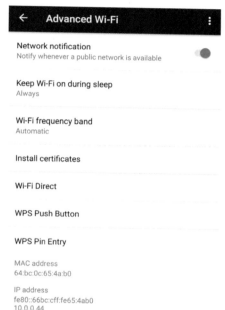 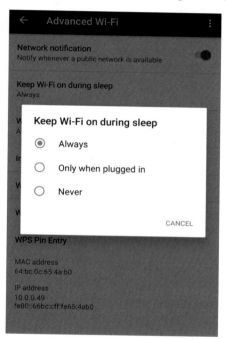

FIGURE 4.6

From the Advanced Wi-Fi screen (left), you can configure network notification, sleep (right), and frequency band settings.

CONFIGURING NETWORK NOTIFICATION, SLEEP, AND FREQUENCY BAND

At the top of the Advanced Wi-Fi screen, you can configure the following three settings:

- **Network Notification.** Set this switch to On to have Android notify you when an open network is available. Some devices call this Wi-Fi Notifications rather than Network Notification.

■ **Keep Wi-Fi On During Sleep.** Tap this button to display the Keep Wi-Fi On During Sleep dialog box, and then tap the Always radio button, the Only When Plugged In radio button, or the Never radio button.

> **! CAUTION** Selecting the Never radio button in the Keep Wi-Fi On During Sleep dialog box on a phone or cellular-capable tablet increases your data usage because apps use the cellular connection to check for data. Normally, it's best to choose Only When Plugged In if you need to conserve battery power. Choose Always if having the latest data available is more important than battery power.

■ **Wi-Fi Frequency Band.** To control which frequency band your device uses, tap this button, and then tap the appropriate radio button in the Wi-Fi Frequency Band dialog box: Automatic, 5 GHz Only, or 2.4 GHz Only. Normally, you'd choose Automatic to give your device more flexibility, but you may sometimes need to prefer one frequency band over another. For example, you might need to choose 2.4 GHz Only if you keep the 5 GHz frequency band for your other devices; or you might need to choose 5 GHz Only if interference from your neighbors' microwave ovens and baby monitors swamps the 2.4 GHz band in your dwelling.

> **NOTE** You can also make Android forget a wireless network. See the section "Forgetting a Network," later in this chapter.

INSTALLING DIGITAL CERTIFICATES

For some connections, you may need to use a digital certificate to authenticate your device to a server. A digital certificate is a unit of encrypted code that you install on your device and tell it to use for specific tasks.

You can install a digital certificate either from an email message or from a folder on your device. You start the installation process in different ways, but the rest of the process is the same.

> **NOTE** If you have saved a digital certificate in a file, you can start installing it by tapping the Install Certificates button on the Advanced Wi-Fi screen: Select the location, such as the Downloads folder in the Open From panel, and then tap the certificate file.

In general, however, it's usually easier to start installing the certificate from either the Security screen in the Settings app or from an email message that has the certificate attached.

To start installing a digital certificate from an email message, tap the attachment button for the digital certificate in the message. The Extract Certificate dialog box opens. (See the left screen in Figure 4.7.)

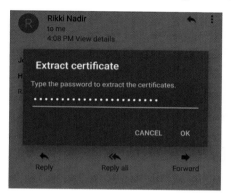 

FIGURE 4.7

In the Extract Certificate dialog box (left), type the password for the certificate. In the Name the Certificate dialog box (right), type a descriptive name for the certificate and specify what you will use it for.

☑ **TIP** If you receive a digital certificate in an email message but you don't want to install it now, tap the Download button (the downward arrow pointing to a horizontal line) on the attachment to save the file to your Downloads folder.

To start installing a digital certificate from a folder, follow these steps:

1. Open the Settings app.
2. Tap the Security button in the Personal section to display the Settings screen.

📝 **NOTE** You may need to tap a different button on your device, such as Security & Screen Lock. The button for installing digital certificates from the SD card may also have a different name (such as Install from SD Card), but you should have no trouble finding it.

3. Tap the Install from Storage button in the Credential Storage section. The Open From panel appears.

4. Navigate to the folder that contains the certificate. For example, if you've saved the certificate file to the Downloads folder, tap the Downloads button in the Open From panel.

5. Tap the certificate file. The Extract Certificate dialog box opens.

In the Extract Certificate dialog box, type the password for the certificate. Normally, you need to find this out from the person who sent you the certificate.

Tap the OK button, and the Name the Certificate dialog box opens. (See the right screen in Figure 4.7.) Type a descriptive name in the Certificate Name box so that you can easily distinguish this certificate from any others on your device. Then tap the Credential Use pop-up menu and tap the appropriate button:

- **VPN and Apps.** Tap this button to make this digital certificate available for connecting to VPN servers or for use in apps (such as for connecting to an Exchange Server system).

- **Wi-Fi.** Tap this button to make this digital certificate available for connecting to Wi-Fi networks.

Tap the OK button to close the Name the Certificate dialog box. Android installs the certificate and briefly displays a readout saying that it has been installed.

USING WI-FI DIRECT

Wi-Fi Direct is a Wi-Fi standard for connecting two devices without using an access point, enabling you to share files between the devices or share one device's Internet connection with the other. Wi-Fi Direct uses Wi-Fi Protected Setup (WPS) to negotiate the link between the devices.

> **! CAUTION** Only some Android devices support Wi-Fi Direct. If the Wi-Fi Direct item doesn't appear on the Advanced Wi-Fi screen in Settings, your device doesn't support Wi-Fi Direct.

Here's how to establish a connection using Wi-Fi Direct:

1. On the Advanced Wi-Fi screen on each device, tap the Wi-Fi Direct button. The Settings screen for Wi-Fi Direct appears (see the left screen in Figure 4.8), displaying a list of peer devices and a list of remembered groups (of which there may not be any).

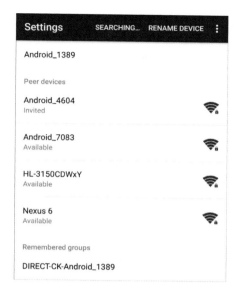
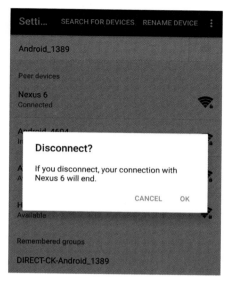

FIGURE 4.8

On the Settings screen for Wi-Fi Direct (left), tap the device to which you want to connect. When you finish using Wi-Fi Direct, tap the connected device and then tap the OK button in the Disconnect dialog box (right).

> **TIP** If the Wi-Fi Direct screen shows a generic name (such as Android_4604) for your device, tap the Rename Device button, type a descriptive name (such as Nexus 6), and then tap the OK button. If the Rename Device button doesn't appear on your device, tap the Menu button and then tap Configure Device to reach a screen that enables you to rename the device.

2. Tap the device to which you want to connect. The word *Invited* appears under the device's name while Wi-Fi Direct waits for the user of the other device to accept the invitation to connect.

3. After Wi-Fi Direct establishes the connection, the word *Connected* appears under the device's name in the Peer Devices list. You can now transfer files as needed between the devices.

4. When you are ready to stop using Wi-Fi Direct, tap the connection. The Disconnect dialog box opens.

5. Tap the OK button.

TROUBLESHOOTING WI-FI DIRECT CONNECTIONS

Wi-Fi Direct is great when it works, but often it doesn't. You may find that the target device doesn't appear on the Wi-Fi Direct screen, even though it's physically right next to your device, it has Wi-Fi enabled, the Settings screen for Wi-Fi Direct is displayed, and your device appears in its Peer Devices list. Or you may find that the device is listed, but when you tap it, Wi-Fi Direct fails to establish a connection. Or Wi-Fi Direct may connect, but your device doesn't enable you to transfer the file type you want to.

If you're having trouble with Wi-Fi Direct, tap the Back button below the screen to return from the Settings screen for Wi-Fi Direct to the Advanced Wi-Fi screen. Turn Wi-Fi off, wait a few seconds, turn it back on, and then tap the Wi-Fi Direct button again to display the Settings screen for Wi-Fi Direct once more. If Wi-Fi Direct still isn't working, try turning off your device and then restarting it.

At this point, you'll probably want to turn to a different means of connection. NFC and Bluetooth are both options, but if you need to transfer large files, you'll do better with an app such as SuperBeam or HitcherNet. Each offers a limited free version to persuade you to pay for an upgrade. For example, SuperBeam plays ads at you until you pay the premium for the Pro version, which offers extra features and no ads.

SETTING UP A NETWORK USING WI-FI PROTECTED SETUP

Some Wi-Fi routers include a feature called Wi-Fi Protected Setup (WPS) to help you set up networks securely. If your router includes WPS, and you have direct access to the router, you can set up the wireless network easily on your Android device. Android supports two types of WPS:

- **WPS.** You press a hardware button on your Wi-Fi router to permit the connection.
- **WPS PIN Entry.** You enter a PIN in your Wi-Fi router's configuration interface to permit the connection.

> **NOTE** WPS is mostly used by Wi-Fi routers designed for the home market. It is a moderately secure way of establishing a connection to a Wi-Fi network.

To connect via WPS, tap WPS Push Button on the Advanced Wi-Fi screen. The WPS Push Button Setup dialog box opens, commanding you to press the WPS button on your router. Obey, and WPS sets up the network for you.

To connect via WPS PIN Entry, tap the WPS Pin Entry button on the Advanced Wi-Fi screen. The WPS PIN Entry dialog box opens, showing the PIN you need to enter on your Wi-Fi router (usually through a browser-based configuration utility). After you enter the PIN correctly, your device can connect to the network.

WHITELISTING YOUR DEVICE ON A WI-FI NETWORK

Some Wi-Fi networks use whitelists to determine which devices are allowed to connect to them. A whitelist is a list of approved MAC addresses on devices.

> **NOTE** MAC is the abbreviation for Media Access Control. A MAC address is a unique hexadecimal identifier (such as f8:a9:d0:73;c4:dd) burned into the network hardware of a device such as the wireless network interface on your Android device. MAC addresses are not directly related to Apple's Mac computers, although each network interface on a Mac has its unique MAC address.

You can find your device's MAC address in two places:

- **The MAC Address readout on the Advanced Wi-Fi screen.** Open the Settings app, tap the Wi-Fi button, tap the Menu button, and then tap Advanced on the menu.

- **The Wi-Fi MAC Address readout on the Status screen or in the Status dialog box.** Open the Settings app, tap the About Phone button or the About Tablet button (or the About Device button on some devices), and then tap the Status button.

> **CAUTION** If you're administering a wireless network, a whitelist of MAC addresses is a useful security measure for preventing unauthorized devices from connecting. But it's not foolproof because software can *spoof* (fake) an authorized MAC address that an attacker has grabbed using a network sniffer tool.

Of these two places to find your device's MAC address, the Status screen is the more helpful because it enables you to copy the MAC address. Tap and hold the Wi-Fi MAC Address button until the message "Text copied to clipboard" appears.

You can then go to another app and paste in the address—for example, you might paste it into a Gmail message so you can send it to your network's administrator for whitelisting.

CONFIGURING IP SETTINGS MANUALLY

To connect to a wireless network, your device must have suitable Internet Protocol (IP) settings: the IP address, the gateway address, the network prefix length, and the DNS server addresses. Typically, the device receives these settings automatically from the network, but you can also set them manually if necessary.

Most Wi-Fi networks use Dynamic Host Configuration Protocol (DHCP), a protocol in which a DHCP server or DHCP allocator automatically provides IP addresses and network configuration information to devices that connect. DHCP is an efficient way of sharing available IP addresses among devices, so it's widely used. But some networks use static IP addresses instead, assigning a particular address to each device. For such networks, you must configure your device's IP settings manually.

You can configure IP settings either when setting up the network in the first place (tap the network on the Wi-Fi screen) or afterward by tapping and holding the network's button on the Wi-Fi screen and then tapping the Modify Network button on the pop-up menu. Either way, you work in the dialog box for the network. This dialog box's title bar shows the network's name.

Tap the Advanced Options button, and the dialog box expands to show the Proxy controls and the IP Settings controls.

You'll meet the Proxy controls in the next section. For now, tap the IP Settings pop-up menu and then tap Static instead of DHCP. The dialog box expands again (see the left screen in Figure 4.9) to reveal the following fields for you to fill in:

- **IP address.** Type the static IP address for your device.

> **NOTE** Normally, you'll be using an IPv4 address, which consists of four groups of numbers in the 0–255 range, separated by periods—for example, 192.168.1.44 or 10.0.0.250. If you're connecting to an IPv6 network, the address consists of six hexadecimal groups separated by colons—for example, fe80:0000:faa9:d0fe:fe72:c4dd. If a group consists of zeros, you can collapse it to nothing, simply putting a pair of colons to indicate where it would be. For example, the previous address can also be written fe80::faa9:d0fe:fe72:c4dd, with the group of zeros removed.

- **Gateway.** Type the IP address of the network gateway or router.
- **Network Prefix Length.** Leave the default setting, 24, unchanged for IPv4 networks. For IPv6 networks, type the length the administrator has specified, such as 64.

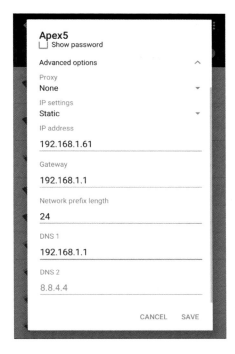
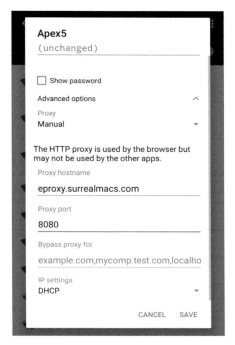

FIGURE 4.9

Choose Static in the IP Settings pop-up menu if you need to enter a static IP address and other network information (left). Choose Manual in the Proxy pop-up menu to display the fields for configuring a Wi-Fi connection to use a proxy server (right).

> **TIP** The Network Prefix Length setting replaces the subnet mask setting (such as 255.255.255.0) that was previously used for IPv4 networks.

- **DNS 1.** Type the IP address of the first DNS server your administrator or ISP has given you, or use Google's primary DNS server, 8.8.8.8.

- **DNS 2.** Type the IP address of the second DNS server your administrator or ISP has given you, or use Google's secondary DNS server, 8.8.4.4.

Tap the Save button after you make your choices.

CONNECTING THROUGH A PROXY SERVER

Instead of directly connecting to websites, your device can connect through a proxy server. This server fulfills network requests for your device, either by providing data that the server has previously cached or by relaying the requests to a suitable server. For example, instead of requesting a web page directly from the web server, your device requests it from the proxy server. The proxy server either delivers the web page from its cache, quickly providing the data and reducing Internet use, or requests the web page from the web server and passes it along to your device.

 TIP Normally, you'd connect through a proxy server in a corporate or organizational setting, where the proxy server not only caches data but also prevents access to blocked sites. You can also connect through a proxy server with the aim of disguising the location where the network requests are coming from.

To set up a Wi-Fi connection to use a proxy server, follow these steps:

1. On the Wi-Fi screen, tap and hold the Wi-Fi connection, and then tap the Modify Network button on the pop-up menu to open the configuration dialog box for the network.

NOTE You can also set up a proxy connection when first connecting to a Wi-Fi network.

2. Tap Advanced Options button. The dialog box expands to show the Proxy controls and the IP Settings controls.

3. Tap the Proxy pop-up menu and then tap Manual instead of None on the menu. The proxy settings appear. (See the right screen in Figure 4.9.)

NOTE If you need to use a proxy service that automatically configures the proxy settings depending on the network to which your device is connected, choose Proxy Auto-Config in the Proxy pop-up menu. Then tap the PAC URL box and type the address of the proxy server and configuration file, such as https://www.surrealmacs.com/proxy.pac.

4. Type the proxy server's hostname (such as eproxy.surrealmacs.com) or IP address (such as 208.42.68.13) in the Proxy Hostname box.

5. Type the port number in the Proxy Port box. The default port is 8080.

6. In the Bypass Proxy For box, type any domains or hosts that you want your device to access without the requests going through the proxy server.

7. Tap the Save button to close the dialog box and save the changes.

IMPROVING YOUR WI-FI CONNECTIONS

By this point, your Android device should be establishing connections to the Wi-Fi networks you want to use. But what if the connections aren't working as well as you need them to?

First, if your device keeps dropping the connection and then having to reestablish it, try turning Wi-Fi off and back on again. If that doesn't help, try powering down your device and restarting it. Restarting is tedious if you're in a hurry, but it can clear up any number of niggling problems.

If the connection is still problematic, and it's a network that you administer, restart the wireless router.

Second, look at the connection's status to see if anything is obviously wrong. Open the Wi-Fi screen in the Settings app and tap the button for the network to which your device has connected. In the dialog box that opens (see the left screen in Figure 4.10), look at the Signal Strength readout. This readout uses plain English terms—Excellent, Good, Fair, Poor, and Out of Range—to indicate the connection's strength or lack thereof. If the Signal Strength is Poor, you may want to try another wireless network instead if one is available.

Look also at the Link Speed readout. If the speed is lower than usual, try dropping the connection and then reconnecting. The easiest way to drop the connection is to set the Wi-Fi switch to Off for a moment and then set it back to On.

> **NOTE** Android usually connects at the highest link speed possible. But if you establish the connection when your device is relatively far from the wireless access point and the signal is correspondingly weak, you may get a low link speed that persists even when you move your device closer to the wireless access point. If this happens, drop the connection and reconnect to try to get a higher link speed.

Third, you may need to change channels to get a decent connection. A wireless network can use any of a variety of channels, which the administrator can choose using whatever configuration utility the wireless access point provides. If many of the wireless networks in your immediate vicinity use the same channels, you may get lower throughput.

 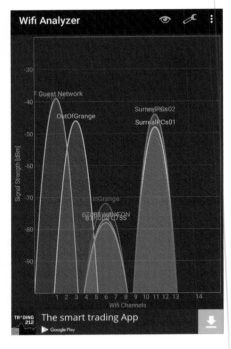

FIGURE 4.10

Look at the Signal Strength readout and Link Speed readout to identify anything obviously wrong with a Wi-Fi connection (left). You can use a Wi-Fi analyzer app, such as Wifi Analyzer (right), to see which channels are busiest.

To see which network is using which channels, you can install a Wi-Fi analyzer app or Wi-Fi stumbler app from the Play Store. Many are available with different features, but most show you the available networks, their relative signal strength, and the channels they are using. Armed with this information, you can set your wireless network to avoid the channels your neighbors are using. The right screen in Figure 4.10 shows the Wifi Analyzer app in action.

> ✅ **TIP**   A Wi-Fi analyzer app or Wi-Fi stumbler app is also useful for locating available wireless networks when you need to get online.

FORGETTING A NETWORK

When you no longer want to use a particular network, you can tell your device to forget it. Tap the network's button on the Wi-Fi screen to display the dialog box for the network, and then tap the Forget button.

NOTE You can also tap and hold the network on the Wi-Fi screen and then tap Forget Network on the pop-up menu.

TIP If your device cannot connect to a network to which it has successfully connected before, forget the network and then rejoin it, entering the password again.

SHARING YOUR DEVICE'S INTERNET CONNECTION

If you have a phone or a cellular-capable tablet, you can share your cellular Internet connection with your computer or other devices. You have three options for sharing:

- **USB Tethering.** Connect your device to your computer via USB and enable the computer to use the device's Internet connection across the USB cable.
- **Portable Wi-Fi Hotspot or Mobile Hotspot.** Share your device's Internet connection via Wi-Fi with multiple devices.
- **Bluetooth Tethering.** Share your device's Internet connection via Bluetooth with other devices. See the section "Sharing an Internet Connection via Bluetooth Tethering," later in this chapter.

NOTE Some cellular providers disable the Portable Wi-Fi Hotspot feature unless you pay an extra fee for it.

To control sharing, you use the Tethering & Portable Hotspot screen (see the left screen in Figure 4.11). To display this screen, open the Settings app, tap the More button in the Wireless & Networks section, and then tap the Tethering & Portable Hotspot button on the More screen.

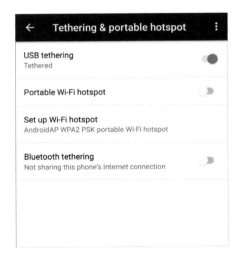

FIGURE 4.11

From the Tethering & Portable Hotspot screen (left), you can set up USB tethering, portable Wi-Fi hotspot, or Bluetooth tethering. In the Set Up Wi-Fi Hotspot dialog box (right), name your hotspot and choose the security type.

> **! CAUTION**   Sharing your device's cellular connection puts more stress on the device and may cause it to wear out sooner. For this reason, you may decide to use Internet sharing only when absolutely necessary rather than every day.

SHARING THE INTERNET CONNECTION VIA USB TETHERING

To share your device's Internet connection via USB sharing, connect your device to your computer via USB and then set the USB Tethering switch to On. The readout saying "USB connected, check to tether" changes to "Tethered."

> **☑ TIP**   Windows normally picks up the tethered connection immediately without your intervention. On the Mac, you may need to select the tethered network interface manually: Click the Apple menu and click System Preferences, and then click Network in the System Preferences window. In the Network pane, click your device's name in the list of network interfaces, and then click the Apply button.

SHARING THE INTERNET CONNECTION VIA PORTABLE WI-FI HOTSPOT

To share your device's Internet connection via Portable Wi-Fi Hotspot, first set up the hotspot. Tap the Set Up Wi-Fi Hotspot button on the Tethering & Portable Hotspot screen and choose suitable settings in the Set Up Wi-Fi Hotspot dialog box. (Refer to the right screen in Figure 4.11.)

■ **Network Name.** Type a name that you can easily identify from other nearby Wi-Fi hotspots. Many people leave the default name, AndroidAP, so it's a good idea to change the name.

> **NOTE** Instead of Android AP as the default hotspot name, some carriers put the phone's model number followed by a random number.

■ **Security.** Tap this pop-up menu and choose WPA2 PSK.

> **NOTE** The Security pop-up menu offers only two choices: WPA2 PSK and None. Don't use None because any device within Wi-Fi range will be able to use your hotspot.

■ **Password.** Type the password for the connection. Use at least 8 characters for the password, and preferably 12–20 characters. (If you choose None in the Security pop-up menu, the Password field disappears.)

■ **Select AP Band.** If this pop-up menu appears, tap it and then tap 2.4 GHz Band or 5 GHz Band, as needed. Generally, the 5 GHz band is less busy than the 2.4 GHz band, so it is a good choice as long as all the devices that need to connect to the hotspot are capable of 5 GHz.

> **! CAUTION** Sharing your Internet connection via Portable Wi-Fi Hotspot can eat through your data plan at high speed. Use the Data Usage screen in the Settings app to monitor how much data your device has used and how much remains.

Tap the Save button to close the Set Up Wi-Fi Hotspot dialog box, and your hotspot is ready for use. Set the Portable Wi-Fi Hotspot switch on the Tethering & Portable Hotspot screen to On to turn on the hotspot. Computers and devices can then connect to the hotspot using the same techniques as for any other wireless network.

> **NOTE** The maximum number of simultaneous connections for the hotspot depends on the device but is usually between three and eight. Android doesn't indicate how many clients have connected to the hotspot, so it can be hard to tell how much use it's getting.

While the hotspot is active, the hotspot icon appears on the status bar to the left of the Bluetooth icon as a reminder. To turn off the hotspot, either open the Notification panel and tap the Hotspot icon or display the Tethering & Portable Hotspot screen in the Settings app and set the Portable Wi-Fi Hotspot switch to Off.

CONNECTING BLUETOOTH DEVICES

Most Android devices include Bluetooth capabilities, enabling you to wirelessly connect a variety of devices through the Bluetooth protocol. For example, you can connect Bluetooth headphones to listen to music comfortably or connect a Bluetooth keyboard so that you can enter text at full speed in documents. If your device is a phone or a cellular-capable tablet, you can also use Bluetooth to share its Internet connection with other devices.

The first time you connect a Bluetooth device, you must pair it with your Android device. After pairing the devices, you can subsequently connect them quickly and easily.

PAIRING A BLUETOOTH DEVICE WITH YOUR ANDROID DEVICE

Here's how to pair a Bluetooth device with your Android device:

1. Open the Settings app.
2. Tap the Bluetooth button to display the Bluetooth screen.
3. Set the switch at the top to On to enable Bluetooth.
4. Turn on the Bluetooth device and make it visible via Bluetooth.

> **NOTE** To make a device visible, you may need to press a dedicated button or press its other control buttons in combination. Typically, the device indicates that it is visible—for example, by flashing lights of different colors or emitting beeps—so you'll know when you've got it right.

5. If the Bluetooth device doesn't appear in the Available Devices list on your Android device (see the left screen in Figure 4.12), tap the Menu button and then tap Refresh on the menu.

6. If the Bluetooth Pairing Request dialog box opens (see the right screen in Figure 4.12), type the code shown and press Enter or Return.

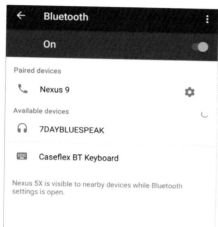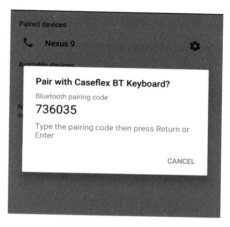

FIGURE 4.12

Tap the Bluetooth device's button in the Available Devices list (left) to start pairing it with your Android device. If the Pair With dialog box appears, type the Bluetooth pairing code and press Enter or Return on the keyboard.

7. When the pairing is complete, the Bluetooth device appears in the Paired Devices list. Tap the Settings button (the gear icon) to display the Paired Devices dialog box. (See the left screen in Figure 4.13.)

8. If you want to rename the device, tap the Name field, type a descriptive name in place of the default name, and then tap the OK button.

> **NOTE** In the Paired Devices dialog box, you can uncheck the device's box in the Profiles list to stop using a device for the purpose shown. For example, Android lists a keyboard as an input device. You can uncheck the box to stop using the keyboard for input temporarily without disconnecting it.

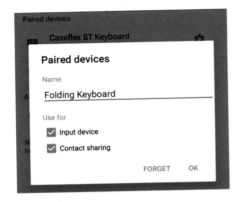

FIGURE 4.13

Use the Paired Devices dialog box (left) to rename a Bluetooth device, unpair it, or turn off its profile. To disconnect a device, tap it on the Bluetooth screen, and then tap the OK button in the Disconnect dialog box (right).

> **TIP** When you're not using Bluetooth, turn it off to save battery power and to prevent other devices from trying to connect to your device via Bluetooth. The quickest way to turn Bluetooth on and off is by opening the Quick Settings panel and then tapping the Bluetooth icon.

When you want to stop using a Bluetooth device, disconnect it. Tap the device's button on the Bluetooth screen to display the Disconnect dialog box (see the right screen in Figure 4.13) and then tap the OK button.

TRANSFERRING FILES TO ANOTHER DEVICE VIA BLUETOOTH

You can transfer files to another device via Bluetooth by using the Share feature.

1. Open the app that owns the files.

2. Select the files. The way you do this depends on the app, but in many apps, you can turn on Selection mode by tapping and holding a file.

3. Give the Share command. This also depends on the app, but in many apps you can either tap the Share button on the toolbar or tap the Bluetooth button on the toolbar.

4. In the Share Via dialog box, tap Bluetooth to display the Choose Bluetooth Device screen.

5. Tap the device to which you want to send the files.

The target device then receives a prompt about the files. If the user accepts the file, Android transfers it.

When another device tries to transfer a file to your device via Bluetooth, your device displays an Incoming File message for a few moments. (See the left screen in Figure 4.14.) Tap the message to display the Accept Incoming File dialog box (see the right screen in Figure 4.14), and then tap the Accept button or the Decline button, as appropriate. You can then go to the file by tapping the Bluetooth Share: Received File notification in the Notifications panel or by tapping the Menu button on the Bluetooth screen and then tapping Show Received Files on the menu.

 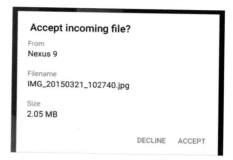

FIGURE 4.14

Tap the Incoming File message (left) for a Bluetooth file transfer to display the Accept Incoming File dialog box (right), in which you can tap the Accept button or the Decline button.

SHARING AN INTERNET CONNECTION VIA BLUETOOTH TETHERING

As you learned earlier in this chapter, the Tethering & Portable Hotspot screen (look back to Figure 4.11) includes a Bluetooth Tethering switch. By setting this switch to On, you can share your device's Internet connection via Bluetooth—after pairing the device that will share the connection and enabling Internet access in its Bluetooth settings.

PAIRING TWO ANDROID DEVICES

To pair another Android device with your device, open the Settings app, display the Bluetooth screen on each device, and make sure the switch at the top of the screen is set to On.

NOTE Displaying the Bluetooth screen with Bluetooth enabled makes a device visible to other Bluetooth-enabled devices that are within range.

In the Available Devices list, tap the button for the device you want to pair. Each device displays a dialog box to confirm the pairing request. In Lollipop, this is the Bluetooth Pairing Request dialog box (see the left screen in Figure 4.15); in Marshmallow, the dialog box is called Pair With and the device's name (see the right screen in Figure 4.15).

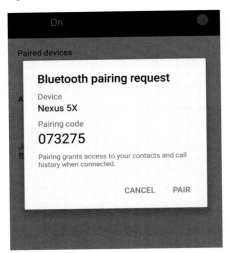
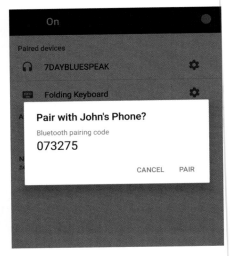

FIGURE 4.15
When pairing Android devices, verify that the pairing code in the Bluetooth Pairing Request dialog box in Lollipop (left) or the Pair With dialog box in Marshmallow (right) is the same on each device.

TIP You can change your device's Bluetooth name by tapping the Menu button, tapping Rename This Device on the menu, typing the new name in the Rename This Device dialog box, and then tapping the Rename button.

Verify that both dialog boxes show the same pairing code, and then tap the Pair button in each dialog box. Android establishes the connection, and each device appears in the Paired Devices list on the other device.

TIP   After pairing devices, you can quickly reestablish a connection to a paired Bluetooth device by using the Quick Settings panel for Bluetooth. To display this panel, open the Quick Settings panel, and then tap the pop-up button to the right of the Bluetooth label. You can then tap the device to which you want to connect or tap the More Settings button to display the Bluetooth screen in the Settings app.

SET ONE PAIRED DEVICE TO USE THE OTHER DEVICE'S INTERNET CONNECTION

Now that you've paired the devices, you need to enable Internet access for the device that will use the shared Internet connection.

On this device, tap the Settings button to the right of the device's name in the Paired Devices list on the Bluetooth screen. In the Paired Devices dialog box that opens, check the Internet Access box in the Use For list, and then tap the OK button. On the Paired Bluetooth Device screen that appears, check the Internet Access box in the Profiles list. You can then use the Internet connection.

NOTE   Android turns off Internet access automatically when the device locks.

USING VPNS

Virtual private networking (VPN) enables you to create a secure connection to a server across an insecure network. You'd typically use a virtual private network (also abbreviated VPN) for connecting across the Internet to a work network.

TIP   Here are two more uses for VPN. First, when you connect to a Wi-Fi hotspot, you can use a VPN to secure your Internet traffic against snooping. Second, you can use a VPN if you need to make your device appear to be in a different location than it actually is. For example, if you subscribe to a U.S.-based media service, you may not be able to access it when you travel abroad. But by connecting to a VPN server within the United States, you can make your computer appear to be in the country, enabling you to use the service. Leading VPN services include IPVanish (www.ipvanish.com), StrongVPN (www.strongvpn.com), and CyberGhost VPN (www.cyberghostvpn.com).

SETTING UP A VPN CONNECTION

To set up a VPN connection on your Android device, you need to know the following:

- **VPN type.** This can be PPTP, L2TP/IPSec PSK, L2TP IPSec RSA, IPSec Xauth PSK, IPSec Xauth RSA, or IPSec Hybrid RSA.

- **Server address.** This can be a server name (such as vpnserv.notionalpress. com) or an IP address (such as 209.14.241.1).

- **L2TP secret.** This is a text string used for securing some L2TP connections.

- **IPSec identifier.** This is a text string used for some IPSec connections.

- **IPSec preshared key.** This is a text string used for some IPSec connections.

> **NOTE** For some types of VPN, you may also need to provide a digital certificate. See the section "Installing Digital Certificates," earlier in this chapter, for instructions on installing a digital certificate.

Ask the VPN's administrator for this information. Ask also for your username and password for the VPN connection. You don't need these for setting up the connection, but you need them when you connect.

Armed with the right information, follow these steps to set up the VPN on your device:

1. Open the Settings app.

2. Tap the More button in the Wireless & Networks section to display the More screen.

3. Tap the VPN button to display the VPN screen.

4. Tap the + button to open the Edit VPN Profile dialog box. (See the left screen in Figure 4.16.)

5. Type a descriptive name in the Name box.

6. Tap the Type pop-up menu and select the type, such as L2TP/IPSec PSK. The Edit VPN Profile dialog box changes to display fields for the information required.

7. Fill in the other information required for the VPN using the data the administrator has given you.

FIGURE 4.16

In the Edit VPN Profile dialog box (left), select the VPN type and enter its details. In the Connect To dialog box (right), type your credentials and check the Save Account Information box if you want to store them for future use.

> **NOTE** If you need to fill in DNS search domains, DNS servers, or forwarding routes, check the Show Advanced Options box to reveal the fields in which you can enter this information.

8. Tap the Save button. The VPN appears on the VPN screen.

CONNECTING VIA THE VPN

After you've set up a VPN connection, you can connect via the VPN using the following steps:

1. Tap the VPN's button on the VPN screen. The Connect To dialog box opens (refer to the right screen in Figure 4.16), showing the VPN's name (for example, Connect to Work for a VPN called "Work").

2. Type your username and password.

3. Check the Save Account Information box if you want to save your username and password so you don't have to type them next time.

4. Tap the Connect button. Android connects to the server and displays the readout "Connected" under the connection's name. The VPN icon appears in the status bar. (See the left screen in Figure 4.17.)

VPN icon

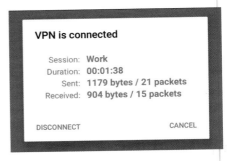

FIGURE 4.17
When the VPN is connected, the VPN icon appears in the status bar as a reminder (left). Tap the Disconnect button in the VPN Is Connected dialog box (right) when you're ready to disconnect the VPN.

After connecting, you can work across the VPN connection in much the same way as a local network connection. Normally, the speeds are much slower across the VPN, so you may need to be patient while transferring data.

When you're ready to stop using the VPN, tap its button on the VPN screen or on the Notifications panel. The VPN Is Connected dialog box opens (see the right screen in Figure 4.17), and you can tap the Disconnect button to disconnect the connection.

NOTE If your device changes its Internet connection from Wi-Fi to cellular or vice versa while you are using a VPN connection, Android disconnects the VPN automatically as a safety measure. If you cannot reconnect the VPN over the new means of connection, restart your device.

INSTALLING, RUNNING, AND MANAGING APPS

In this chapter, you learn how to install, run, and manage apps on your Android device. Along the way, you learn how to install apps from the Play Store, how to sideload apps from other sources, and how to force apps to stop when they misbehave.

GETTING APP INSTALLATION RIGHT

In this section, we'll look first at how to evaluate permissions when installing apps. We'll then go over your options for getting your money back if you pay for an app that doesn't live up to its claims.

As I'm sure you know, the main source for apps for Android devices is Google's Play Store. By launching the Play Store app from its icon on your device's Home screen or Apps screen, you can visit the Play Store and browse or

search through the hundreds of thousands of apps approved by Google for Android devices.

After you've found the app you want to install, you can install it by tapping the Install button (if the app is free) or the Price button (if it is not).

EVALUATING PERMISSIONS WHEN INSTALLING APPS

The key question during installation is which permissions the app needs. Don't just "click through" this step by tapping the Accept button; instead, read the list of permissions, and make sure they fit the app and what you understand it to do.

There are no hard-and-fast rules for what you should allow and what you should refuse because everything depends on the app and what it does. For example, a social-media app such as Snapchat will need access to your contacts and calendar, location, photos, camera and microphone, and so on if it is going to revolutionize your social life, so you would accept the permissions if you wanted to install the app. By contrast, if a spreadsheet app requested the same permissions, you should run for the hills.

The left screen in Figure 5.1 shows the permissions list for Snapchat. You can tap any of the headings, such as the In-App Purchases heading or the Identity heading, to display brief details. (See the right screen in Figure 5.1.)

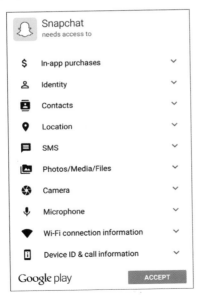
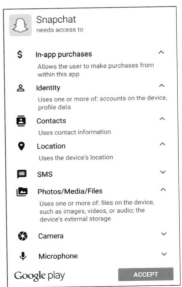

FIGURE 5.1

Verify that the list of permissions requested (left) is appropriate to the app. You can tap any heading to display brief details about the permission (right).

After you've tapped the Accept button, the installation proceeds. After the app is installed, you can run it easily by tapping the Open button on its screen in the Play Store app. If you've displayed other screens elsewhere in the meantime, you can also launch the app from its Successfully Installed notification in the Notifications panel, or simply launch the app from the Apps screen as usual.

GETTING A REFUND ON AN APP

If you buy an app and decide you don't want to keep it—or you realize that you bought the wrong app—you can get a refund for it. Within two hours of making the purchase, return to the app's screen in the Play Store app and tap the Refund button.

> **☑ TIP**   After two hours, you may still be able to get a refund. Open your web browser, go to the Play Store (play.google.com), and then sign in. Tap or click the Settings icon (the gear icon) and then tap or click My Account. Tap or click the Menu button (the three vertical dots) in the row for the purchased item and select Report a Problem. In the Report a Problem dialog box, open the pop-up menu and select the most appropriate reason, such as Purchase Is Defective or Doesn't Work as Advertised. Type an explanation in the Please Describe Your Issue text box and click or tap the Submit button.

CONFIGURING YOUR PLAY STORE ACCOUNT

To make the Play Store app work the way you prefer and to avoid getting unwanted notifications about updates to apps and games, spend a few minutes configuring your Play Store account. Open the Play Store app by tapping its icon on the Home screen or on the Apps screen; then tap the menu-panel button in the upper-left corner (the button with three horizontal lines) and tap Settings on the menu panel to display the Settings screen. The left screen in Figure 5.2 shows the upper part of the Settings screen on a phone, and the right screen shows the lower part.

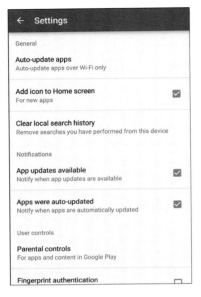
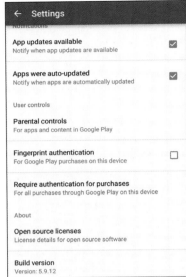

FIGURE 5.2
Use the Settings screen to configure the Play Store app to work your way.

The General area of the Settings screen contains three settings:

■ **Auto-Update Apps.** Tap this button to display the Auto-Update Apps dialog box, and then tap the appropriate radio button: Do Not Auto-Update Apps; Auto-Update Apps at Any Time. Data Charges May Apply; or Auto-Update Apps over Wi-Fi Only.

> **TIP** Auto-Update Apps over Wi-Fi Only is usually the best choice in the Auto-Update Apps dialog box. Unless you have an unlimited data plan, it's a mistake to update apps over the cellular connection.

■ **Add Icon to Home Screen.** Check this box if you want each new app to add an icon to the Home screen. Usually, it's best to uncheck this box, run most apps from the Apps screen, and add to the Home screen only icons for those apps you use the most.

■ **Clear Local Search History.** Tap this button to clear the history of the searches you've performed on the App Store. When you tap this button, no dialog box opens and no confirmation readout appears.

The Notifications area of the Settings screen contains two settings:

- **App Updates Available.** Check this box if you want the Play Store app to notify you when app updates are available. This notification is usually helpful unless you have so many apps that you get an avalanche of notifications.

- **Apps Were Auto-Updated.** Check this box if you want the Play Store app to notify you after it has automatically updated apps. This notification, too, is usually helpful.

The User Controls area of the Settings screen contains three settings, the second of which appears only if your device has a fingerprint scanner:

- **Parental Controls.** To implement parental controls, tap this button. On the Parental Controls screen, set the switch at the top to On, and then type a four-digit PIN in the Create Content PIN dialog box that opens. Tap the OK button, type the PIN again in the Confirm PIN dialog box, and tap the OK button again. The Parental Controls screen then appears again with its controls enabled. (See the left screen in Figure 5.3.) You can tap the Apps & Games button, the Movies button, or the TV button to display the Allow Up To dialog box for that category, and then tap the maximum rating you will permit. The right screen in Figure 5.3 shows the Allow Up To dialog box for TV. You can also check the Books box to restrict books that are marked as sexually explicit, or check the Music box to restrict music that is marked as explicit. Tap the Back button when you finish using the Parental Controls screen.

- **Fingerprint Authentication.** Check this box if you want to enable using your fingerprint to authenticate purchases on Google Play. As you'd imagine, this button appears only if your device has a fingerprint scanner.

- **Require Authentication for Purchases.** Tap this button to display the Require Authentication dialog box, and then tap the appropriate radio button: For All Purchases Through Google Play on This Device, Every 30 Minutes, or Never.

> **! CAUTION** Don't choose the Never radio button in the Require Authentication dialog box, especially if you ever let other people use your device. It's best to choose the For All Purchases Through Google Play on This Device radio button for security, but you may prefer to choose the Every 30 Minutes radio button if you allow yourself to go on app-shopping sprees.

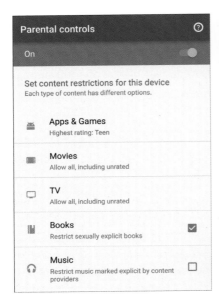
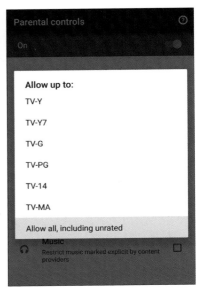

FIGURE 5.3

Set the switch at the top of the Parental Controls screen to On (left). You can then tap Apps & Games, Movies, or TV to display the Allow Up To dialog box (right), and check or uncheck the Books box and the Music box as needed.

> **NOTE** In the About section at the bottom of the Settings screen for the Play Store app, you can tap the Open Source Licenses button to display details of the open-source licenses the app uses. You can also tap the Build Version button to check whether the Play Store app itself is up to date; the app displays a message box saying "Google Play Store is up to date."

SIDELOADING APPS

When you want to install an app that isn't available on the Play Store, you can *sideload* it. Sideloading is a manual installation technique in which you get the app in a distribution file called a package file (which uses the .apk file format), copy the package file to your device, and then install the app. You may need to change a security setting to enable sideloading.

INSTALLING A FILE MANAGER

To sideload apps, you need to use a file-management app such as ES File Explorer or ASTRO File Manager. If you already have such an app installed, you're ready to begin. If not, open the Play Store app and install a file-management app. This section shows screens from ES File Explorer, which is free and works well.

GETTING THE PACKAGE FILE FOR THE APP

Next, you need the package file containing the app you want to load. These are the three main ways of getting the package file:

- **Download the package file from the Internet.** You can find many Android package files in online repositories. Some of the files are shared illegally, and some may contain malware as well as the apps, so you need to be careful.

- **Get the package file from a company or organization.** If your company or organization provides an Android app, the website may provide it for download, or an administrator may provide it on a physical device such as a USB On-the-Go drive.

- **Get the package file from another device.** If you already have the app on another device, you can create a package file containing the app.

How you create a package file depends on the file-management app you're using, but here's an example using ES File Explorer:

1. Open ES File Explorer.

2. Tap the menu-panel button in the upper-left corner to display the menu panel.

3. Tap APP in the Library section to display the User Apps folder. This folder contains the apps you've installed on your device.

> **! CAUTION** Don't tap APP in the Favorites section instead of the Library section. Tapping APP in the Favorites section takes you to the Play Store instead.

4. Tap and hold the icon for the first app you want to package. ES File Explorer turns on selection mode and checks the box on the icon.

5. Tap to check the box for any other app you want to package (see Figure 5.4).

Backup

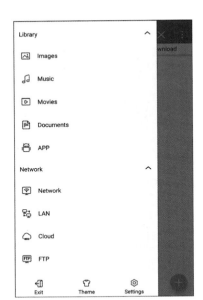
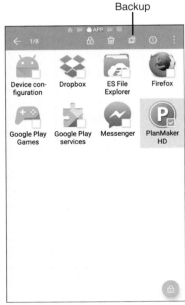

FIGURE 5.4

In ES File Explorer, check the box for each app you want to package, and then tap the Backup button.

6. Tap the Backup button at the top of the screen on a phone or at the bottom of the screen on a tablet. The message "Backup application successfully" appears briefly.

You can now navigate to the /sdcard/backups/apps/ folder to locate the package file and copy it to the device on which you want to install it. You can copy the package file in any convenient way, such as these:

■ **Bluetooth.** Transfer the file using Bluetooth, as discussed in Chapter 4, "Connecting to Networks and Devices."

■ **USB On-the-Go.** Connect a USB On-the-Go memory stick to the source device and copy the file to the memory stick. Then connect the memory stick to the destination device and copy the file across.

■ **Dropbox or a similar service.** Upload the file to your Dropbox account from the source device and then download it to the destination device.

■ **Email.** If the file is small enough to go through email servers, you can simply send the file to an account that's set up on the destination device.

TIP If you need an easier way to transfer a file from one Android device to another, install the app called File Beam (Touch to Send) written by Mohammad Abu-Garbeyyeh. This app enables you to transfer pretty much any file type, including .apk files, through Near Field Communication (NFC). You select the file in an app such as ES File Explorer, give the Share command, and then tap Beam File in the Share Via panel. Your device then prompts you to bring the devices back to back so that the NFC chips identify each other. You then tap the Touch to Beam prompt, and your device sends the file.

SETTING ANDROID TO ALLOW APPS FROM UNKNOWN SOURCES

Android has a security mechanism that prevents you from installing apps from what it calls "unknown sources"—in other words, from anywhere other than the Play Store. Follow these steps to allow yourself to sideload apps:

1. Open the Settings app.

2. Tap the Security button to display the Security screen. On some devices, you'll need to use a different screen, such as Security & Screen Lock.

3. In the Device Administration section, set the Unknown Sources switch to On. (See the left screen in Figure 5.5.) A warning dialog box opens. (See the right screen in Figure 5.5.)

4. Tap the OK button.

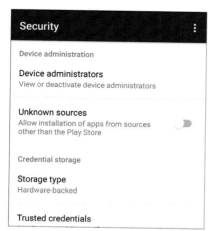

FIGURE 5.5

When you set the Unknown Sources switch on the Security screen (left) to On, Android displays a dialog box (right) warning you that apps may attack your device and data.

SIDELOADING THE APP

You can now sideload the app on your device. To start the installation, tap the package file to open it. For example, if you have copied the file to a folder, open your file-management app to that folder and tap the file, and then tap the Install button in the Properties dialog box. (See the left screen in Figure 5.6.) If you have received the app attached to an email message, tap the attachment file in the Email app.

> **NOTE** If the Install Blocked dialog box opens at this point, you need to allow apps from unknown sources. Tap the Settings button to display the Security screen, and then set the Unknown Sources switch to On.

Android displays a screen showing the app's name at the top. The Privacy list and the Device Access list show the permissions that the app requires. (See the right screen in Figure 5.6.)

FIGURE 5.6

You can begin the sideloading process by tapping the app's package file in a file-management app and then tapping Install (left). Review the permissions in the Privacy list and the Device Access list before tapping the second Install button (right).

Review the permissions and tap the Install button if you want to proceed. When the installation is complete, you can run the app from the Apps screen like any other app.

RUNNING APPS

After installing an app, you can run it from the Apps screen. If you will need to run the app frequently, create a shortcut for it on the Home screen. Or, if you checked the Add Icon to Home Screen box on the Settings screen for the Play Store app, the app will already appear on the Home screen.

If you have a keyboard attached, you can run apps by using the keyboard shortcuts shown in Table 5.1.

Table 5.1   Keyboard Shortcuts for Running Apps

Keyboard Shortcut	Opens This App
Search+B	Default browser (for example, Chrome)
Search+C	Contacts
Search+E	Email app
Search+G	Gmail
Search+I	Calendar
Search+M	Maps
Search+P	Music
Search+S	Messages
Search+Y	YouTube

WORKING WITH THE OVERVIEW SCREEN

Android displays each app full screen, so you can work with only one app at a time. However, you can quickly switch from one app to another by using the Overview screen. This screen also enables you to close an app or display its App Info screen.

> **NOTE** Some Android skins include the ability to display multiple windows at the same time. For example, Samsung's TouchWiz skin includes the Multi-Window feature, which works on both phones and tablets. Because of the amount of screen real estate involved, multiple windows tend to be more useful on tablets than on phones.

SWITCHING APPS WITH THE OVERVIEW SCREEN

To switch apps, tap the Overview button. The Overview screen appears (see Figure 5.7), showing a thumbnail of each open window. The most recent windows are the ones at the bottom of the list, which is the part of the list that appears on the screen at first. Swipe or drag down to scroll the list so that you see other windows.

> **NOTE** On a phone, the Chrome browser enables you to display your open tabs either on the Overview screen or in its built-in tab browser. The default setting is for the tabs to appear on the Overview screen. See the section "Choosing Whether to Merge Tabs and Apps on a Phone" in Chapter 8, "Browsing with Chrome," for details on changing this setting.

When you find the window you want to display, tap its thumbnail.

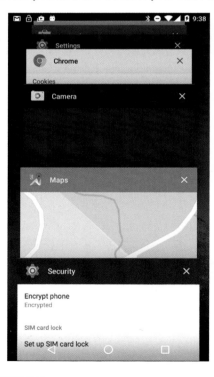 

FIGURE 5.7

From the Overview screen (left), you can tap the app you want to view. To close an app, tap its × button or swipe it left or right off the screen (right).

CLOSING AN APP FROM THE OVERVIEW SCREEN

You can close an app from the Overview screen by swiping it off the list to the left (see the right screen in Figure 5.7) or to the right, whichever you find more convenient. Alternatively, tap its × button.

PINNING AN APP TO THE SCREEN

When you need to let someone else briefly use your Android device, you can pin an app to the screen. Pinning keeps that app fixed to the screen, preventing the person to whom you hand your device from using any other apps.

ENABLING SCREEN PINNING

Before you can use screen pinning, you must enable the feature. To do so, open the Settings app, tap Security, tap Screen Pinning, and then set the switch at the top of the Screen Pinning screen to On.

Once you've set the main switch, the Ask for PIN Before Unpinning switch appears. You can set this switch to On to make your device require you to enter the PIN to unpin the pinned app. Normally, you'll want to set this switch to On because otherwise anybody can turn off screen pinning and get busy with your other apps.

PINNING AND UNPINNING AN APP

With screen pinning enabled, you can pin an app like this:

1. Make active the app you want to pin. Launch the app if it's not already running, or use the Overview screen to switch to the app if it is running.

2. Tap the Overview button to display the Overview screen.

3. Pull up the thumbnail for the front app (the app at the bottom of the Overview screen) and tap the pin in its lower-right corner. A readout saying "Screen pinned" appears briefly to let you know that you've pinned the screen.

4. Hand the device to the person who needs to use it.

5. When you get the device back, tap and hold the Back button and the Overview button together until the lock screen appears.

6. Unlock your device as usual—for example, by entering the PIN or applying one of your registered fingers to the fingerprint scanner.

> **NOTE** If you set the Ask for PIN Before Unpinning switch to Off, tap and hold the Back button and the Overview button until the readout saying "Screen unpinned" appears.

> **TIP** Screen pinning is a great feature, but you may sometimes need to go beyond it. If you need to prevent other people who use your device from running particular apps or using certain features on it, try the AppLock app from DoMobile Lab. This app enables you to choose which items to lock, so if you share your device with other people, you can prevent them from using apps and features without entering the AppLock password.

OPENING THE APP INFO SCREEN FOR AN APP

When you need to force an app to stop, or you need to uninstall an app, you use the App Info screen for that app. You can display the App Info screen by following these steps:

1. Open the Settings app.
2. Tap the Apps button to display the Apps screen.
3. Tap the button for the app.

> **NOTE** In Marshmallow, the Apps screen shows a single alphabetical list of apps. In Lollipop, the Apps screen has three tabs: Downloaded, Running, and All. Swipe left or right to display the tab you need, and then tap the button for the app.

As you can see in Figure 5.8, the App Info screen is different in Marshmallow (left screen) than in Lollipop (right screen). Whereas Lollipop packs all the controls onto a single screen (which is much longer than just the part shown here), Marshmallow shows a handful of buttons that summarize the settings; by tapping these buttons, you can display screens that contain more information and controls for making changes.

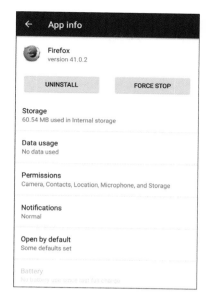
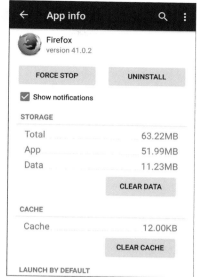

FIGURE 5.8

The App Info screen in Marshmallow (left) is laid out in a substantially different way from the App Info screen in Lollipop (right).

WHICH APPS ARE PERFORMANCE KILLERS?

If you find your Android device's performance is disappointing, or that runtime on the battery is shorter than expected, examine the apps you're using and try to identify those that drain performance and battery life.

By their nature, social-media apps tend to be resource hungry, needing to keep up to date with what's happening online. So start by looking at apps such as Facebook, Twitter, Instagram, and Snapchat. The *Android App Performance Report* for the second quarter of 2015 by AVG Technologies, a leading antivirus company, identified Snapchat as the app with the highest overall performance drain on Android devices. This perhaps isn't surprising, given that Snapchat can use not only Wi-Fi, cellular, and GPS functionality but also the camera functionality while it runs. But if you're looking for a place to start improving your device's performance, and you run Snapchat, try stopping the app.

That same report also found that Tumblr used more traffic than Netflix (video streaming) and Spotify (music streaming) put together. So if you run Tumblr and you find your data allowance mysteriously disappears, try stopping Tumblr. Similarly, Facebook Pages Manager can take up a lot of storage on your device.

Social-media apps are obvious culprits, but updates apps, which tend to run under the radar, can also sap performance and battery life. On any Android device, look to see whether Google Play updates have been consuming large amounts of battery power. And on a Samsung device, check the com.sec. android.fwupgrade service (which gets updates via Wi-Fi) and the Security Policy Update service, which can also be greedy. You may find it better to check manually for updates and apply any that are available to avoid having these services running extensively.

FORCING AN APP TO STOP

If an app stops responding to the touchscreen, you can force it to stop. To do so, display the App Info screen for the app and then tap the Force Stop button. In the Force Stop dialog box that opens, warning you that force stopping an app may cause it to misbehave, tap the OK button.

CLEARING AN APP'S CACHE, DATA, OR DEFAULTS

If an app starts acting oddly, you may need to clear its cache or its data. If you have set it to be the default app for a particular action or file type, you can clear its defaults when you need to use another app for those purposes.

You can take all these actions from the App Info screen for an app:

- **Clear Data.** In Marshmallow, first tap the Storage button to display the Storage screen. Tap the Clear Data button, and then tap the OK button in the Delete App Data dialog box that opens to delete all the app's data, including any accounts you have set up in the app.

- **Clear Cache.** In Marshmallow, first tap the Storage button to display the Storage screen. Tap the Clear Cache button to delete all the data that the app has cached. You'd normally want to do this if the cached data appears to have become corrupted and is making the app unstable or if you suspect the cache of containing sensitive data that you want to get rid of.

- **Clear Defaults.** In Marshmallow, first tap the Open by Default button to display the Open by Default screen. Tap the Clear Defaults button to clear any default settings associated with the app. For example, if you've installed a Home screen launcher and made it the default, tapping the Clear Defaults button stops the launcher from running when you press the Home button. Instead, you can choose the launcher you want, and you can decide whether to make it the new default.

> **TIP** If you need to clear the cached data from all your apps, you don't need to go through them one by one. Instead, open the Settings app, tap the Storage & USB button on Marshmallow or the Storage button on Lollipop, and then tap the Cached Data button. In the Clear Cached Data dialog box, tap the OK button, and Android wipes out all the data that apps have cached.

UNINSTALLING APPS

When you no longer need an app, you can uninstall it. Here's how:

1. Open the App Info screen for the app.
2. Tap the Uninstall button. A confirmation dialog box opens, with its title bar showing the app's name.
3. Tap the OK button.

> **TIP** After uninstalling an app, you can reinstall it easily from the My Apps list in the Play Store app.

> **NOTE** You can't uninstall the apps built into Android. Instead, you can tap the Disable button on the App Info screen for the app. In the Disable Built-In App dialog box that opens, tap the OK button. If you need to enable the app again, tap the Enable button that then appears on the App Info screen.

REBOOTING INTO SAFE MODE

If your device becomes unstable and crashes when you restart it, you can boot into Safe mode to prevent third-party apps from loading.

Here's how to reboot into Safe mode:

1. Press and hold the Power button until the Power Off dialog box opens.
2. Tap and hold the Power Off button until the Reboot to Safe Mode dialog box opens. (See the left screen in Figure 5.9.)
3. Tap the OK button.

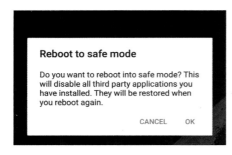

Reset app preferences?

This will reset all preferences for:

· Disabled apps
· Disabled app notifications
· Default applications for actions
· Background data restrictions for apps
· Any permission restrictions

You will not lose any app data.

CANCEL   RESET APPS

FIGURE 5.9

You can reboot into Safe mode (left) to disable third-party apps that may be making your device unstable. You can reset app preferences (right) to reset the preferences for all the apps on your device.

TIP If the method for rebooting into Safe mode doesn't work for your device, turn it off and then hold down the Up volume button while you restart it.

After your device restarts, the words "Safe mode" appear in the lower-left corner of the screen so you can't forget Safe mode is on. You can then uninstall apps as needed.

To leave Safe mode, power your device off as normal, and then power it back on.

RESETTING APP PREFERENCES

When you need to return the settings on all your apps to their default state, you can reset your device's app preferences. Normally, you'd do this either if configuration changes you've made have rendered your device unstable and you can't work out which change caused the problem or if you want to be able to choose your default apps for particular tasks again.

Here's how to reset app preferences:

1. Open the Settings app.

2. Tap the Apps button to display the Apps screen.

3. Tap the Menu button and then tap Reset App Preferences on the menu. The Reset App Preferences dialog box opens. (Refer to the right screen in Figure 5.9.)

4. Tap the Reset Apps button.

SHOULD YOU USE A TASK-KILLER APP?

As you know, your device uses random access memory (RAM) to store the apps you're running. Your device has a fixed amount of RAM, typically ranging from 1GB for a low-end device to 3GB or 4GB for a powerhouse. The more RAM, the more apps you can run at once.

You can find task-killer apps for Android—apps that enable you to kill (in other words, close) apps that are running in the background. The idea is to reclaim memory by removing apps from it, making more memory available to the apps you're actually using.

Killing apps like this makes sense on the face of it, but it's seldom if ever necessary. Android is pretty smart about managing memory and is designed to keep apps running in the background. When you display the Home screen or jump to another app, Android pauses the app you've just left unless it's doing something that needs to continue, such as playing music or downloading the Library of Congress. Android keeps the app in memory, so your device can display the app almost instantly when you go back to it.

If you use a task killer to close the app, you do free up some memory. But if the app interprets its killing as an error having occurred, the app may restart automatically, taking up memory again and consuming processor cycles to load.

The other point to bear in mind is that Android is designed to use memory efficiently. This means using as much of the memory as possible as much of the time, not trying to keep memory free for use in the future. So if you look at a breakdown of the memory your apps are using, you'll probably see that the memory is full. That's not a problem; it's how it should be.

A task-killer app can be useful if an app keeps crashing, but normally you can close such an app using Android's regular tools, as discussed earlier in this chapter. You should then remove the problem app from your device.

TAKING GMAIL TO THE PRO LEVEL

Your Android device gives you access to your email everywhere you go via the Gmail app. Your first move in this chapter is to get all your email accounts set up on your device. Your second move is to configure all those accounts to work the way you prefer and to fully exploit the features that the Gmail app offers.

After that, you'll put those features into use triaging and reading your messages, writing messages and managing your mail, and dealing with spam and problem senders. You'll also learn how to search for messages using advanced search operators and how to set up 2-Step Verification to protect your Google account.

UNDERSTANDING THE GMAIL APP AND THE EMAIL APP

In stock Lollipop and Marshmallow, the Gmail app is Android's primary email app. The Gmail app can access all standard types of email accounts, including Google Gmail and Google Apps, Yahoo! Mail, Microsoft Outlook and Hotmail, and Microsoft Exchange Server.

The Gmail app that came with earlier versions of Android, up to KitKat (4.4), worked only for Gmail and Google Apps accounts. For other types of email accounts, you used the Email app, which could access all standard account types other than Gmail and Google Apps.

So far, so straightforward: If your device is running Lollipop or Marshmallow, you should be using the Gmail app rather than the Email app for all your email accounts. But there's a complication: Some skinned versions of Lollipop and Marshmallow still use the Email app for accessing certain types of accounts, such as Exchange. Other versions of Lollipop include a stub version of the Email app that simply displays a screen telling you to use the Gmail app instead.

If you go to set up an email account in the Gmail app and find that the account type isn't available, use the Email app instead. This book doesn't cover the Email app, but you'll find it mostly straightforward to use.

SETTING UP YOUR EMAIL ACCOUNTS

Normally, you'll have set up your primary Gmail account while setting up your device for the first time. Now is the time to set up any other Gmail or Google Apps accounts you have, plus your other types of email accounts. You start the setup process for each type of account in the same way, but after that the details vary, so we'll look at the different account types separately.

GATHERING THE INFORMATION NEEDED TO SET UP AN EMAIL ACCOUNT

Before starting to set up your email account, make sure you have the information you need. It's better to have all the information available and not need all of it when the Gmail app detects some of the details than to have to give up partway through and find out the missing pieces of information.

GETTING THE INFORMATION NEEDED FOR A GOOGLE ACCOUNT

For a Gmail account or a Google Apps account, you need only your email address and password. If you have enabled 2-Step Verification on the account, you need access to the device or account you've chosen to use for verification.

> **NOTE** See the section "Setting Up 2-Step Verification for Your Google Account," toward the end of this chapter, for details on 2-Step Verification.

GETTING THE INFORMATION NEEDED FOR A PERSONAL ACCOUNT

For what the Gmail app calls a "personal" account, you may need various other pieces of information beyond your email address and password. Table 6.1 explains the information you may need, with examples of what each item looks like.

Table 6.1   Information for Setting Up an Email Account

Information	Example	Notes
Email address	csmith@notionalpress.com	
Password	h18Det2!cab0os	The password is case sensitive.
Incoming mail server	imap.notionalpress.com pop.notionalpress.com	The address has periods but no @ sign.
Outgoing mail server	imap.notionalpress.com smtp.notionalpress.com	The address has periods but no @ sign.
Port for incoming mail	110	The port used depends on the mail server type and the security type.
Security type for incoming mail	None SSL/TLS SSL/TLS (Accept All Certificates) STARTTLS STARTTLS (Accept All Certificates)	Most mail servers use SSL/TLS.
Port for outgoing mail	587	The port used depends on the mail server type and the security type.
Security type for outgoing mail	None SSL/TLS SSL/TLS (Accept All Certificates) STARTTLS STARTTLS (Accept All Certificates)	Most mail servers use SSL/TLS.

UNDERSTANDING POP3, IMAP, SMTP, AND EXCHANGE

POP3, IMAP, SMTP, and Exchange are four technologies widely used for mail servers. POP3 and IMAP are protocols that email clients (such as the Gmail app on your Android device) use to communicate with incoming mail servers—the servers from which you receive your messages. SMTP is a protocol used for many outgoing mail servers—the servers that send your messages for you. Exchange is Microsoft's Exchange Server technology for email, scheduling, and calendars.

POP is the acronym for Post Office Protocol, and POP3 is version 3 of Post Office Protocol. IMAP is the acronym for Internet Mail Access Protocol, a newer protocol than POP3. SMTP is the abbreviation for Simple Mail Transfer Protocol, a protocol for sending mail.

The main difference between POP3 and IMAP is that POP3 is mostly designed to download your messages to your email client, removing them from the server, whereas IMAP is designed to enable you to view and manage your messages on the server without downloading them to your email client.

The advantage of IMAP is that, with your messages on the server, you can view and manage them from multiple devices. So if you view a message using your Android device, the message is marked as having been read in your laptop computer's mailbox as well. And if you delete a message on your laptop, it disappears from your Android device's mailbox, too.

Your email provider will tell you which account type—POP3, IMAP, or Exchange—to specify when setting up your account. If your email provider gives you the choice between POP3 and IMAP, you'll normally want to choose IMAP for your Android device so that you can access your messages on other computers and devices as well.

GETTING THE INFORMATION NEEDED FOR AN EXCHANGE SERVER ACCOUNT

Before trying to set up your Exchange Server account on your device, make sure you have all the information required. Table 6.2 shows the details. Normally, you need to get the information from the Exchange Server administrator.

Table 6.2 Information for Setting Up an Exchange Server Account

Information	Example	Notes
Email address	csmith@surrealmacs.com	
Password	G43s9PiaPT!	The password is case sensitive.
Domain	CORP	Ask an administrator what the domain is and whether you need to use it.
Security type	SSL/TLS	See Table 6.1 and the sidebar "Understanding Security Types for Email Accounts," below, for an explanation of security types.
Client certificate	N/A	Some systems require a digital certificate file provided by an administrator for authentication.
Port	443	The port used depends on the security type.

> **TIP** Using the right domain can be crucial to getting your Exchange Server account to work. Exchange Server systems tend to be complex, and it is hard to guess the domain name. What's especially awkward is that you may not need to enter a domain name at all, but usually only the administrator can tell you whether or not to enter it.

UNDERSTANDING SECURITY TYPES FOR EMAIL ACCOUNTS

When manually setting up an email account , you need to specify the security type used to secure the connection. Normally, you must choose the right security type to make the email account work at all.

The Gmail app offers these five security types:

- **None.** This option transmits all data using plain text. You may occasionally need to use this option to check whether an email account is functional. If so, change the security type and password immediately afterward.

- **SSL/TLS.** Secure Sockets Layer (SSL) and Transport Layer Security (TLS) are widely used protocols for securing communications between a computer or a device and a server. TLS is based on SSL and is more secure than SSL. SSL and TLS use digital certificates to secure the connection and check that the certificates are valid and issued by a trusted certificate authority (CA). This is the security type you will normally use for an email account.

- **SSL/TLS (Accept All Certificates).** This security type uses SSL and TLS but accepts any digital certificate instead of rejecting certificates that are invalid, out of date, issued by an untrusted CA, or self-signed. (Developers use self-signed certificates for testing code.) You may need to use this security type for some accounts, but accepting all certificates is generally unsafe.

- **STARTTLS.** STARTTLS is a protocol extension that can upgrade an existing insecure connection to a secure connection without changing the port used (as would normally happen). STARTTLS enables servers to make better use of their ports. Despite its name, STARTTLS can use SSL instead of TLS for the secure connection.

- **STARTTLS (Accept All Certificates).** As with SSL/TLS (Accept All Certificates), this security type uses STARTTLS but accepts any digital certificate instead of rejecting certificates that would normally be unacceptable. You may need to use this security type for some accounts or for testing, but accepting all certificates is generally unsafe.

DISPLAYING THE SET UP EMAIL SCREEN

To add an email account to the Gmail app, first display the Set Up Email screen.

> **NOTE** For clarity, this chapter uses "the Gmail app" to refer to the Gmail app, and "Gmail" to refer to the Gmail service.

Follow these steps:

1. Open the Gmail app by tapping its icon on the Home screen or the Apps screen.

2. Tap the Navigation Panel button or swipe right from the left side of the screen to open the navigation panel. (See the left screen in Figure 6.1.) At first, the navigation panel displays a list of mailboxes, with the Settings button and the Help & Feedback button below them.

3. Tap at the top of the navigation panel—where your account picture and the account name appear—to display the account-management commands. (See the right screen in Figure 6.1.)

4. Tap the Add Account button to display the Set Up Email screen.

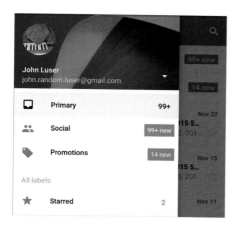 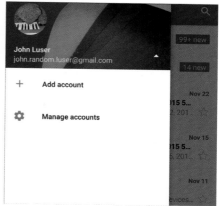

FIGURE 6.1

Tap the Navigation Panel button to display the navigation panel (left), and then tap the colorful area at the top to display the account-management commands (right).

ANOTHER WAY TO START SETTING UP AN EMAIL ACCOUNT

You can also start the process of setting up an email account in the Settings app. Open the Settings app from the Apps screen or the Notifications panel as usual, go to the Personal section, and then tap the Accounts button to display the Accounts screen. Tap the Add Account button to display the Add an Account screen, and then tap the button for the account type: Exchange, Google, Personal (IMAP), or Personal (POP3).

ADDING A GOOGLE ACCOUNT

From the Set Up Email screen (see the left screen in Figure 6.2), take the following steps to set up a Gmail account or Google Apps account. This example uses a Gmail account.

1. Tap the Google option button.

2. Tap the Next button to display the Add Your Account screen (shown on the right in Figure 6.2).

> **NOTE** On Marshmallow, you may have to enter your password before you can add a Google account.

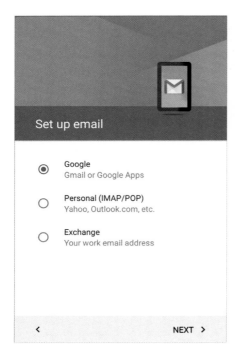 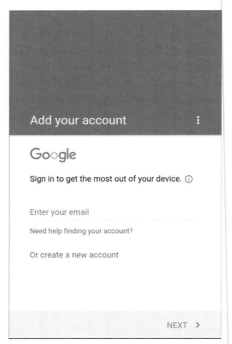

FIGURE 6.2

On the Set Up Email screen (left), tap the Google option button and then tap the Next button. On the Add Your Account screen (right), enter your email address and tap the Next button again.

3. Tap the Enter Your Email field and type your email address.

> **TIP** If the address you're typing in the Enter Your Email field is a Gmail address, you can omit the "@gmail.com" part of the address. Android fills that in for you automatically.

4. Tap the Next button. Android displays a screen prompting you for your password.
5. Type your password.
6. Tap the Next button.
7. Review the Terms of Service and Privacy Policy, and then tap the Accept button if you want to proceed.

Android finishes setting up the account, which appears on the navigation panel in the Gmail app.

ADDING A PERSONAL ACCOUNT

From the Set Up Email screen, take the following steps to set up a personal email account. There are a lot of steps to take, but it is fairly straightforward.

1. Tap the Personal (IMAP/POP) option button.

2. Tap the Next button to display the Add Your Email Address screen. (See the left screen in Figure 6.3.)

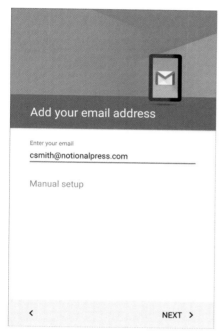 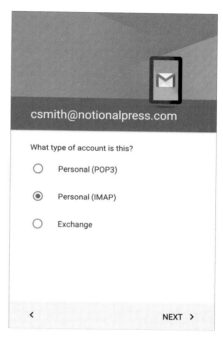

FIGURE 6.3

On the Add Your Email Address screen (left), you can tap the Next button to try automatic setup or tap the Manual Setup button to retain full control of the configuration. Either way, you must specify the type of account on the What Type of Account Is This screen (right).

3. Tap the Enter Your Email field and type or paste in your email address.

4. Tap the Next button if you want the Gmail app to try to set up the account automatically. Otherwise, tap the Manual Setup button. Whichever button you tap, the What Type of Account Is This screen appears. (See the right screen in Figure 6.3.)

5. Tap the POP3 button, the IMAP button, or the Exchange button, as appropriate. See the sidebar titled "Understanding POP3, IMAP, SMTP, and Exchange" earlier in this chapter for an explanation of these terms.

6. Tap the Next button. A screen appears prompting you for your password.

7. Type your password. You can check the Show Password box if you want to see what you're typing.

8. Tap the Next button. If you're using automatic setup, and it works, go to step 16. If you're using manual setup, the Incoming Server Settings screen appears. (See the left screen in Figure 6.4.)

9. Type the server name, such as imap.notionalpress.com, in the Server box.

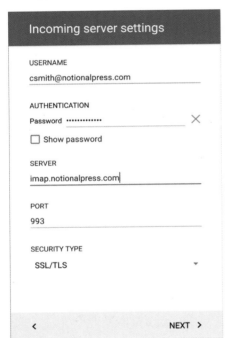

FIGURE 6.4

On the Incoming Server Settings screen (left), enter the server address, choose the security type, and correct the port if necessary. On the Outgoing Server Settings screen (right), specify the outgoing server address, security type, port, and whether to sign in.

NOTE The Account Setup screens that appear after this point differ for the different account types. This section shows the IMAP screens and explains the differences in the POP3 screens. You'll learn how to set up an Exchange account in the next main section.

10. Tap the Security Type pop-up menu and choose the security type: None, SSL/TLS, SSL/TLS (Accept All Certificates), STARTTLS, or STARTTLS (Accept All Certificates). The Gmail app enters the normal port for that security type in the Port box.

> **NOTE** Look back to the sidebar titled "Understanding Security Types for Email Accounts" earlier in this chapter for an explanation of the security types.

> **! CAUTION** Avoid using the None security type or either of the Accept All Certificates security types. In most cases you should use the SSL/TLS security type.

11. If your email provider has told you to use a different port than the Gmail app has chosen, type the port number in the Port box. Table 6.3 explains the ports normally used by mail servers.

Table 6.3 Standard Ports for Email Servers

Server Type	Security Type	Port
POP3	None	110
POP3	SSL/TLS	995
POP3	STARTTLS	110 (starts insecure)
IMAP	None	143
IMAP	SSL/TLS	993
IMAP	STARTTLS	143 (starts insecure)
SMTP	None	25
		587
SMTP	SSL	465
SMTP	TLS	587

> **NOTE** For a POP3 server, tap the Delete Email from Server pop-up menu and then tap the Never button or the When I Delete from Inbox button, as appropriate.

12. Tap the Next button. The Gmail app checks the incoming server and makes sure the account name, password, and security type are valid. If so, the Outgoing Server Settings screen (see the right screen in Figure 6.4) appears for you to set up the outgoing mail server.

> **TIP** If the Couldn't Finish dialog box appears after you tap the Next button, it usually means that the information you've provided is wrong. Tap the Edit Details button to return to the screen you were on, verify each piece of information, and correct any mistakes. If you get the same error again, check that your Internet connection is working. For example, tap the Home button, tap the Chrome icon, and verify that Chrome can load a website.

13. Enter the outgoing server's address, such as smtp.notionalpress.com, in the Outgoing Server box.

> **NOTE** The Gmail app automatically fills the SMTP Server box on the Account Setup screen for the outgoing mail server with a name derived from the incoming mail server name you provided. If your email provider uses a different name, you need to edit the suggested name.

14. Tap the Security Type pop-up menu and then tap the security type: None, SSL/TLS, SSL/TLS (Accept All Certificates), STARTTLS, or STARTTLS (Accept All Certificates). The Gmail app enters the normal port for that security type in the Port box.

15. If your email provider has told you to use a different port than the Gmail app has chosen, type the port number in the Port box. Refer to Table 6.3 for details of the normal ports.

16. If your email provider requires you to sign in to send messages, check the Require Signin box and enter the appropriate username and password in the Username field and the Authentication field.

> **TIP** Your sign-in username may be different from your email address; for example, it may be the portion of your email address before the @ sign (such as csmith for the email address csmith@notionalpress.com). If in doubt, ask your email provider.

17. Tap the Next button. The Gmail app tries to validate your SMTP settings. If it succeeds, the Account Options screen appears. (See the left screen in Figure 6.5.)

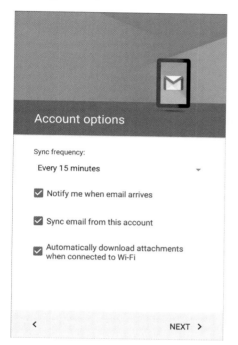

FIGURE 6.5

On the Account Options screen (left), choose how frequently to check for email, whether to receive notifications, and whether to sync email. On the Your Account Is Set Up and Email Is on Its Way screen (right), give the email account a descriptive name and enter your name the way you want it to appear on messages you send.

> **TIP** As with the incoming server, if the Couldn't Finish dialog box appears after you tap the Next button on the Account Setup screen for the outgoing server, it normally means that the information you've provided is wrong. Tap the Edit Details button, verify each piece of information, and correct any mistakes.

18. Tap the Sync Frequency pop-up menu and then tap the frequency with which to check for new messages: Never, Every 15 Minutes, Every 30 Minutes, or Every Hour.

19. Check the Notify Me When Email Arrives box if you want the Gmail app to display a notification when new messages arrive. If new messages arrive in a batch, the app displays a single notification for the batch rather than a separate notification for each message.

20. Check the Sync Email from This Account box to make the Gmail app sync this account. Normally, you'll want to do this.

21. Check the Automatically Download Attachments When Connected to Wi-Fi box if you want the mail app to download attachments automatically when your device has a Wi-Fi connection instead of a cellular connection. This setting is usually handy unless you often receive large attachments that you don't want to download.

22. Tap the Next button. The Your Account Is Set Up and Email Is on Its Way screen appears. (See the right screen in Figure 6.5.)

23. In the Account Name (Optional) box, type a descriptive name for the account. This name is to help you distinguish this account from your other accounts; the more accounts you have, the more important it is to have easily distinguishable names.

24. In the Your Name box, type your name the way you want it to appear on messages you send. For example, you may want your full name to appear, including your middle initial.

25. Finally, tap the Next button. The Gmail app appears again, and you can start using the account you've just added.

ADDING AN EXCHANGE SERVER ACCOUNT

Setting up an Exchange Server account in the Gmail app works in largely the same way as setting up another account, but you have to jump through several more hoops to set it up. The Gmail app can set up some Exchange Server accounts automatically with just the email account name and password, but for others, you need to fill in the server and domain details.

> **! CAUTION** Setting up an Exchange Server account on your Android device requires you to give the Exchange administrator permission to administer your device remotely. The administrator can take a range of actions on your device, up to and including remotely wiping it of all its content. Normally, the administrator doesn't wipe your device unless it goes missing, presumed stolen; however, the administrator *can* wipe the device any time, either intentionally or by accident.

If your Android device is one that your company or organization has supplied, this is fine, but you should either avoid storing any personal files on the device or make sure that you have backups of all your personal files elsewhere in case an administrator nukes the device.

If your company or organization allows you to bring your own device (BYOD) to work and set it up to access your Exchange Server account, you need to decide whether having access to your Exchange data is worth the potential loss of your personal data.

From the Set Up Email screen, take the following steps to set up an Exchange Server account:

1. Tap the Exchange option button.

2. Tap the Next button. The Add Your Email Address screen appears.

3. Type or paste your email address in the Enter Your Email field.

4. Tap the Next button if you want the Gmail app to try to set up the account automatically. Otherwise, tap the Manual Setup button. Whichever button you tap, the What Type of Account Is This screen appears.

TIP Exchange Server setups can be complex, but the Gmail app is good at detecting server settings, so you may want to try automatic setup.

5. Tap the Exchange option button. (Yes, this step is redundant because you've already specified the account type in step 1. Perhaps this step will disappear in an updated version of Android.)

6. Tap the Next button. A screen appears prompting you to enter your password or provide a client certificate.

7. Tap the Password field and type your password.

NOTE If your Exchange Server administrator has given you a digital certificate to use for authentication, tap the Select button to the right of the Client Certificate readout. In the Choose Certificate dialog box that opens, tap the certificate you want to use, and then tap the Allow button. The Client Certificate readout then displays the certificate's name.

8. Tap the Next button. If you're using automatic setup, the Gmail app tries its luck with your settings at this point, attempting to detect the server settings needed for the account. If it succeeds, the Remote Security Administration dialog box opens, and you can continue with step 13; if it fails, you'll get an error message, and you'll need to choose settings manually. If you're using manual setup, the Incoming Server Settings screen appears; continue with the following steps.

> ☑ **TIP**   For some systems, you may need to enter in the Username box the domain followed by a backslash and your full email address. For example, if your email address is john@surrealmacs.com, you would enter **surrealmacs.com\ john@surrealmacs.com**. This looks awkward, especially if it's too long to fit in the Domain\Username text box, but it is correct and it does work.

9. Edit the server name in the Server box if necessary.

10. Tap the Security Type pop-up menu and then tap the security type: None, SSL/TLS, or SSL/TLS (Accept All Certificates). The mail app enters the normal port for that security type in the Port box.

> ❗ **CAUTION**   Normally, you will use the SSL/TLS security type. Don't use the SSL/TLS (Accept All Certificates) security type, much less the None "security" type.

11. If your Exchange Server administrator has told you to use a different port than the one the Gmail app has chosen, type the port number in the Port box.

> ☑ **TIP**   Exchange Server normally uses port 443 for SSL/TLS and port 80 for no security. These are standard web ports (port 443 for https, giving secure access, and port 80 for open access) because your device is accessing the Exchange Server across the Web.

12. Tap the Next button. The Gmail app attempts to validate the server settings. If it succeeds, the Remote Security Administration dialog box opens. (See the left screen in Figure 6.6.)

13. Tap the OK button. The Gmail app displays the Account Options screen. (See the right screen in Figure 6.6.)

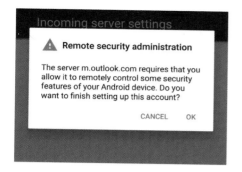

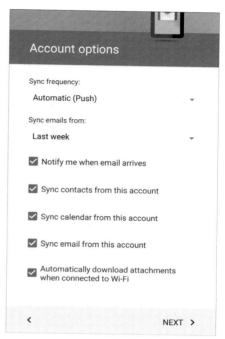

FIGURE 6.6

In the Remote Security Administration dialog box (left), tap the OK button if you want to proceed with setting up the Exchange Server account. On the Account Options screen (right), choose how often to check email, whether to receive notifications for messages, and which items to sync.

14. Tap the Inbox Checking Frequency pop-up menu and then tap the frequency with which to check for new messages: Automatic (Push), Never, Every 5 Minutes, Every 10 Minutes, Every 15 Minutes, Every 30 Minutes, or Every Hour.

> **TIP** The Automatic (Push) setting for Inbox Checking Frequency causes the mail server to "push" new messages to your device as soon as they arrive instead of waiting for the device to check for new messages. Choose Push to get your messages more quickly at the cost of some battery power.

15. Tap the Sync Emails From pop-up menu and choose what to sync: Last Day, Last Three Days, Last Week, Last Two Weeks, Last Month, or All.

16. Check the Notify Me When Email Arrives box if you want the Gmail app to display a notification when new messages arrive. If new messages arrive in a batch, the app displays a single notification for the batch rather than a separate notification for each message.

17. Check the Sync Contacts from This Account box if you want to sync your contacts to your device. Syncing the contacts is usually helpful.

18. Check the Sync Calendar from This Account box if you want to sync your Exchange Server calendar appointments to your device. This, too, is usually helpful.

19. Check the Sync Email from This Account box to make the Gmail app sync this account. Normally, you'll want to do this.

20. Check the Automatically Download Attachments When Connected to Wi-Fi box if you want the Gmail app to download attachments automatically when your device has a Wi-Fi connection instead of a cellular connection. This setting is usually handy unless you often receive large attachments that you don't want to download.

21. Tap the Next button. The Activate Device Administrator screen appears. (See the left screen in Figure 6.7.)

22. Read the details of what the administrator can do: Erase All Data, Set Password Rules, Monitor Screen-Unlock Attempts, Set Storage Encryption, and so on.

23. Tap the Activate button if you want to proceed. The mail app activates the device administrator. The Your Account Is Set Up and Email Is on Its Way screen appears. (See the right screen in Figure 6.7.)

24. In the Account Name (Optional) field, type a descriptive name for the account. The default setting is your email address, but you will likely want to improve on this.

> **NOTE** As of this writing, the Displayed on Sent Messages label appears on the Your Account Is Set Up and Email Is on Its Way screen, but there is no field for entering your name the way you want it to appear on outgoing messages.

25. Finally, tap the Next button. The Gmail app appears again, and you can start using your Exchange account in it.

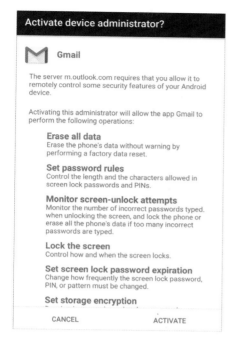

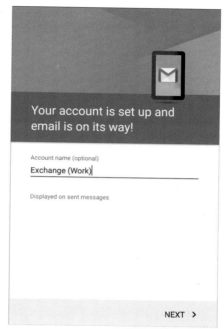

FIGURE 6.7

On the Activate Device Administrator screen (left), read the changes an administrator can make to your device remotely. Tap the Activate button if you still want to set up your Exchange Server account. On the Your Account Is Set Up and Email Is on Its Way screen, give your Exchange account a descriptive name.

CONFIGURING GMAIL AND YOUR ACCOUNTS TO WORK YOUR WAY

The Gmail app provides a variety of settings that you can configure to make the app itself and your email accounts work the way you prefer. To get started with configuration, open the navigation panel and tap the Settings button to display the Settings screen. As you can see in the left screen in Figure 6.8, this screen contains a General Settings button and a button for each of the accounts you have set up, enabling you to configure each account separately.

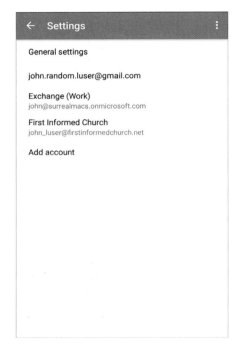
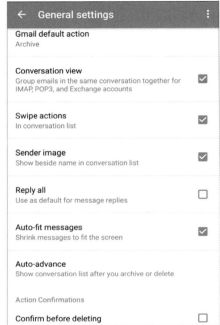

FIGURE 6.8

The Settings screen (left) gives you access to general settings and to each email account you have configured. The General Settings screen (right) enables you to choose Gmail-wide settings such as Archive & Delete, Auto-Advance, and Action Confirmations.

CHOOSING GENERAL SETTINGS

Normally, you'll want to start by tapping the General Settings button to display the General Settings screen so that you can choose options for how the Gmail app works overall.

CHOOSING THE GMAIL DEFAULT ACTION

Gmail gives you all the space you need to keep all your messages indefinitely and encourages you to archive your old messages instead of deleting them. Some people think keeping all their old messages is a good idea, whereas others prefer to keep only important messages. Depending on which you prefer, you can set the Gmail app to use the archive action or the delete action as the default action. To choose which actions appear, tap the Gmail Default Action button. In the Default Action dialog box that opens, tap the Archive option button or the Delete option button.

CHOOSING CONVERSATION VIEW AND SWIPE ACTIONS SETTINGS

Check the Conversation View box if you want the Gmail app to automatically group messages that belong to the same conversation. Grouping the messages makes it easier to see all the related messages, so you may find it helpful. This setting works for IMAP, POP3, and Exchange accounts, but not for other account types.

Check the Swipe Actions box if you want to be able to use swipe actions in the conversation list. You can swipe either left or right to perform the default action you set for Gmail—either archiving or deleting the message you swipe.

CHOOSING SENDER IMAGE, REPLY ALL, AND AUTO-FIT MESSAGES SETTINGS

Check the Sender Image box if you want the sender image to appear to the left of the sender's name in the conversation list. The sender image shows the sender's photo if it's available in your contacts; otherwise, it displays the first letter of the sender's name. You can tap the sender image to select a message quickly.

Check the Reply All box if you want to use Reply All as the default action for replying to messages that have multiple recipients.

> **! CAUTION** Check the Reply All box only if you're required to include all recipients in your replies. Some companies and organizations require this. Otherwise, use Reply All manually and sparingly to minimize unnecessary emails.

Check the Auto-Fit Messages box if you want the Gmail app to automatically shrink messages to fit on your device's screen. This setting is usually helpful unless it makes the messages too small to read.

CONFIGURING AUTO-ADVANCE

The Auto-Advance feature enables you to control what the Gmail app displays next when you deal with a message by archiving or deleting it. Your choices are to display the next newer item, display the next older item, or return to the conversation list so that you can pick the next item you want to deal with. What to choose here depends on the messages you receive and the way you prefer to work with them.

Tap the Auto-Advance button to display the Advance To dialog box, and then tap the Newer radio button, the Older radio button, or the Conversation List radio button, depending on which you want.

CHOOSING ACTION CONFIRMATIONS

In the Action Confirmations section of the General Settings screen, you can check or uncheck the Confirm Before Deleting box, the Confirm Before Archiving box, or the Confirm Before Sending box to control which actions the Gmail app confirms and which it doesn't.

> **✓ TIP** Action confirmations can be useful if you use your device in a moving or busy environment, such as on public transit. If you're stationary and have a sure touch, you may prefer to turn confirmations off.

After you finish on the General Settings screen, tap the arrow button or the Back button below the screen to return to the Settings screen.

Apart from the General settings, Gmail's remaining settings are account-specific, so you can set them differently for your various accounts if you need to. The settings available are different for Google accounts, personal (IMAP and POP) accounts, and Exchange accounts, so we'll look at them separately.

CONFIGURING SETTINGS FOR A GOOGLE ACCOUNT

To configure a Google account, tap the account's button on the Settings screen. The account's settings screen appears, showing the account's name at the top. (See the left and right screens in Figure 6.9.)

CONFIGURING YOUR INBOX

Your first choice on an account settings screen is the Inbox type. You can configure it either as a Default Inbox or as a Priority Inbox. Here's what those terms mean:

- **Default Inbox.** A Default Inbox gives you a choice of categories into which you can have it organize your messages. Table 6.4 explains the categories. The Primary category always appears, but you can choose which of the other categories to display.

- **Priority Inbox.** A Priority Inbox gives you a way to separate your most important messages from the rest. Gmail assesses your incoming messages, decides which are important, and places those in the Priority Inbox.

> **✎ NOTE** You can train Gmail to recognize important messages for your Priority Inbox. You'll learn how to do this later in this chapter.

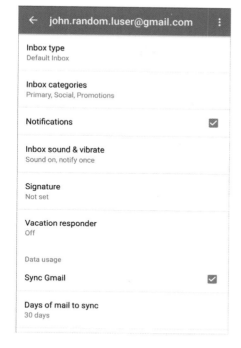
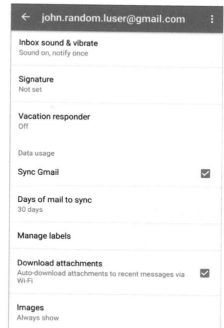

FIGURE 6.9

The account-specific settings screen enables you to configure your Inbox, notifications, sync options, labels, and more.

Table 6.4 Categories in the Default Inbox

Category	Receives These Messages
Primary	Personal messages, such as from your family and friends; messages that don't fit the other categories you're using; and messages you mark with a star
Social	Messages from your social networks, gaming networks, media-sharing sites, and the like
Promotions	Marketing messages, such as messages containing special offers
Updates	Receipts, bills, statements, and updates
Forums	Messages from mailing lists or online groups to which you subscribe

To choose which categories to use in your Default Inbox, tap the Inbox Categories button and then check or uncheck the boxes on the Inbox Categories screen. (See the left screen in Figure 6.10.)

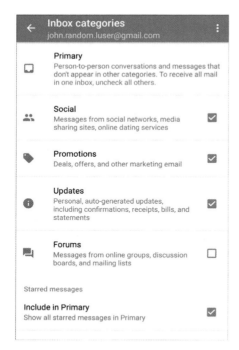

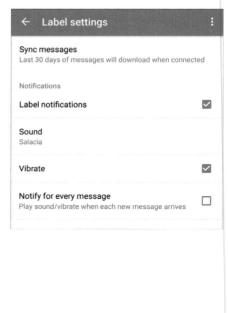

FIGURE 6.10

On the Inbox Categories screen (left), check the box for each category you want to use in your Default Inbox. On the Label Settings screen (right), choose which notifications to receive. You can also choose which messages to sync.

> **NOTE** By default, the Gmail app places any message you mark with a star in your Primary category. This behavior is normally helpful, but if you don't want it, uncheck the Include in Primary box on the Inbox Categories screen.

If you want to receive notifications when messages arrive in your Inbox, check the Notifications box. You can then tap the Inbox Sound & Vibrate button or the Priority Inbox Sound & Vibrate button and choose options on the Sync & Notify screen. (See the right screen in Figure 6.10.) These are the options:

■ **Sync Messages.** Tap this button to display the Priority Inbox dialog box (for a Priority Inbox) or the Primary dialog box (for a Default Inbox). You can then tap the Sync: None radio button, the Sync: Last *NN* Days radio button (which shows the number of days you choose in the Days of Mail to Sync dialog box, discussed later in this chapter), or the Sync: All radio button.

> **NOTE** If your device doesn't have a vibration motor, you'll see the Priority Inbox Sound button instead of the Priority Sound & Vibrate button. Similarly, you'll see the Inbox Sound button instead of the Inbox Sound & Vibrate button.

- **Label Notifications.** Check this box to receive notifications for messages with certain labels. This is the overall control for receiving label notifications. You then specify the labels for which to receive notifications, as discussed in the section "Managing Your Labels," later in this chapter.

- **Sound.** Tap this button, tap the ringtone you want to use for the notification, and then tap the OK button.

- **Vibrate.** Check this box if you want your device to vibrate to notify you of messages. This box appears only if your device has a vibration motor.

- **Notify for Every Message.** Check this box if you want Gmail to notify you for every incoming message, not just for the first message of a batch.

SAVING TIME WITH SIGNATURES

If you need to sign the messages you send from this account in a consistent way, you can create a signature for the account. A signature is text that the Gmail app automatically inserts in each outgoing message—each new message, each reply, and each forwarded message you create.

Tap the Signature button on the account settings screen to open the Signature dialog box. Type in the text—you can create multiple lines by tapping the Enter key—and then tap the OK button.

> **TIP** At this writing, the Gmail app enables you to have only one signature per account. It automatically inserts the signature in every outgoing message; you can't create a signature and turn it off temporarily. If you need more flexibility with signatures, create text shortcuts for the lines you want to have available, such as your position and company or your contact data, and use them to insert custom signatures as needed in your messages.

CREATING A VACATION RESPONDER

The Gmail app includes a built-in Vacation Responder feature that you can set up to respond automatically to incoming messages. Here's how to set up Vacation Responder:

1. Tap the Vacation Responder button on the account settings screen to display the Vacation Responder screen. (See the left screen in Figure 6.11.)

2. Set the Vacation Responder switch to the On position.

3. Tap the First Day button and choose the date.

4. Tap the Last Day button and choose the end date if necessary.

5. Tap the Subject field and type the message subject.

6. Tap the body text field and type the body text.

7. Check the Send Only to My Contacts box if you want to send the message only to your contacts. Checking this box is often a good idea because it prevents sending vacation messages to promotional messages (unless you've added such senders to your contacts).

8. Tap the Done button.

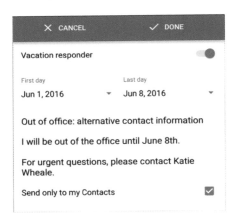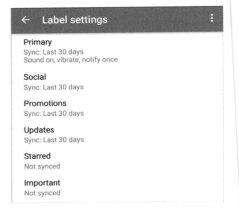

FIGURE 6.11

Set up the Vacation Responder (left) to reply automatically to incoming messages. On the Label Settings screen (right), tap the label for which you want to configure notifications.

CHOOSING WHICH MESSAGES TO SYNC

In the Data Usage section of the account settings screen, choose which messages to sync. Normally, you'll want to check the Sync Gmail box to sync your Gmail messages with the Gmail app on your device. Then tap the Days of Mail to Sync button and use the dial in the Days of Mail to Sync dialog box to set the number of days. Tap the OK button to apply your choice.

MANAGING YOUR LABELS

As you'll know if you've used the service for any length of time, Gmail uses labels instead of folders. So instead of moving a message to a folder for storage, you simply mark it with one or more labels. You can then browse or search by label to find the messages you need.

> **☑ TIP**　The advantage of labels over folders is that you can apply multiple labels to an individual message, enabling yourself to locate the message by browsing or searching any of those labels. By contrast, with folders, you can put a message in only a single folder; to get a message into multiple folders, you need to make an extra copy of the message for each folder beyond the first.

To use labels effectively, you need to make sure each account has the labels it needs. At this writing, you can't create labels by using the Gmail app on your Android device. Instead, open a browser, log in to your Gmail account, and then create the labels. You can do this on your Android device, but if you have a computer handy, you might want to use that instead.

Here's how to create a new label using your browser:

1. Click or tap the Create New Label link to open the New Label dialog box.
2. Type the name in the Please Enter a New Label Name box.
3. To nest the label under another label (like a subfolder), click or tap the pop-up menu, and then click or tap the existing label. The browser checks the Nest Label Under box automatically, so you don't need to check it manually.
4. Click or tap the Create button.

After you've customized your list of labels, you can choose notification settings for each label using the Gmail app on your Android device like this:

1. On the account settings screen, make sure you've checked the Notifications check box. If this check box is unchecked, notifications are off for the account as a whole, so you can't set notifications for individual labels.
2. Tap the Manage Labels button to display the Label Settings screen. (See the right screen in Figure 6.11.)
3. Tap the label you want to configure. The settings screen for the label appears, and you can choose settings as explained in the section "Configuring Your Inbox," earlier in this chapter.

CHOOSING DOWNLOAD ATTACHMENTS AND IMAGES SETTINGS

Check the Download Attachments box if you want the Gmail app to automatically download attachments when your device is connected to Wi-Fi.

Tap the Images button to display the Images dialog box, and then tap the Always Show radio button or the Ask Before Showing radio button to control whether the Gmail app always displays images in messages for this account.

WHY WOULD YOU TURN OFF IMAGES IN MESSAGES?

You may want to select the Ask Before Showing radio button for a couple of reasons.

First, images in messages can take time to load over a slow connection; and if the images are large, they can put a dent in your data allowance when your device is using a cellular connection.

Second, by including in a message a reference to an image stored on a server, someone can learn when you read the message (because the Gmail app requests the image from the server) and may be able to determine your approximate location. By selecting the Ask Before Showing radio button, you can display images only when you're confident you can do so without giving away this potentially sensitive information to anyone you don't trust.

CONFIGURING A PERSONAL ACCOUNT

To configure a personal account, tap the account's button on the Settings screen. The account's Settings screen appears, showing the account's name at the top. (See the left and right screens in Figure 6.12.)

These are the settings you can configure for a personal account:

- **Account Name.** Tap this button to change the descriptive name for the account.

- **Your Name.** Tap this button to change the name displayed on messages you send.

- **Signature.** Tap this button to display the Signature dialog box, in which you can type or paste the text you want the Gmail app to insert automatically at the end of outgoing messages. You can create multiple lines by tapping the Enter key.

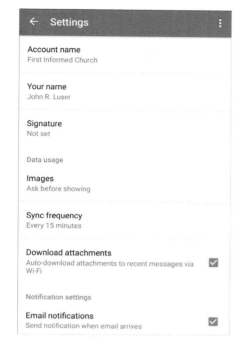
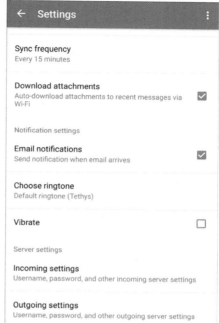

FIGURE 6.12

Use the controls on a personal account's Settings screen to make the account behave the way you prefer.

- **Images.** Tap this button to display the Images dialog box, and then tap the Always Show radio button or the Ask Before Showing radio button to control whether the Gmail app always displays images in messages for this account.

- **Sync Frequency.** Tap this button to display the Sync Frequency dialog box, in which you can choose how frequently the Gmail app checks for mail. If the Push setting is available, choose it if you want to get your messages as soon as possible.

- **Download Attachments.** Check this box to download attachments on recent messages automatically when your device has a Wi-Fi connection.

- **Email Notifications.** Check this box to make the Gmail app give you a notification when you receive messages.

- **Choose Ringtone.** Tap this button to choose the ringtone used for the email notification.

- **Vibrate.** Check this box to make your device vibrate when the Gmail app gives you a notification. This check box appears only if your device includes vibration.

- **Incoming Settings.** Tap this button to display a dialog box for configuring the account's incoming mail server.

- **Outgoing Settings.** Tap this button to display a dialog box for configuring the account's outgoing mail server.

> **NOTE** As with the general settings, the account-specific settings screen on your device may show different settings, or a different arrangement of settings, than the stock Android screen shown here. Explore the settings available to you so that you know all your options for configuring each account.

CONFIGURING AN EXCHANGE ACCOUNT

To configure an Exchange account, tap the account's button on the Settings screen. The account's settings screen appears, showing the account's name at the top. (See the left and right screens in Figure 6.13.)

These are the settings you can configure for an Exchange account:

- **Account Name.** Tap this button to change the descriptive name for the account, such as Work or Exchange Account.

- **Your Name.** Tap this button to set the name displayed on messages you send.

- **Signature.** Tap this button to display the Signature dialog box, in which you can type or paste the text you want the Gmail app to insert automatically at the end of outgoing messages. You can create multiple lines by tapping the Enter key.

- **Vacation Responder.** Tap this button to display the screen for setting up a vacation responder. See the section "Creating a Vacation Responder," earlier in this chapter, for more details.

- **Images.** Tap this button to display the Images dialog box, and then tap the Always Show radio button or the Ask Before Showing radio button to control whether the Gmail app always displays images in messages for this account.

- **Sync Frequency.** Tap this button to display the Sync Frequency dialog box, in which you can choose how frequently the Gmail app checks this account for mail. Choose the Automatic (Push) setting if you want to get your messages as soon as possible.

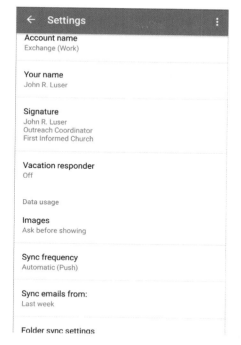 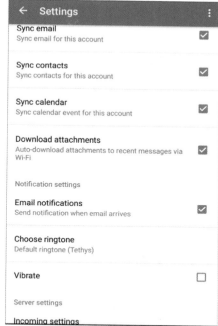

FIGURE 6.13

Use the controls on the Settings screen for an Exchange account to specify your name and signature, to control data usage and sync, and to choose notification and server settings.

- **Sync Emails From.** Tap this pop-up menu and choose what to sync: Last Day, Last Three Days, Last Week, Last Two Weeks, Last Month, or All.

- **Folder Sync Settings.** Tap this button to display the Sync Options screen (see the left screen in Figure 6.14), which shows a list of your folders. You can then tap the folder you want to configure, such as the Inbox, and then choose settings on the screen that appears. (See the right screen in Figure 6.14.) Check the Sync This Folder box if you want to sync the folder, tap the Days of Mail to Sync button to display the Days of Mail to Sync dialog box, and then tap the appropriate radio button: Use Account Default, Last Day, Last Three Days, Last Week, Last Two Weeks, Last Month, or All.

- **Sync Email.** Check this box to sync email for your Exchange account.

- **Sync Contacts.** Check this box to sync contacts for your Exchange account.

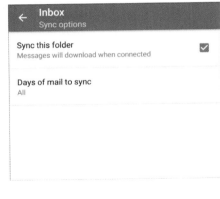

FIGURE 6.14

On the Sync Options screen (left), tap the Exchange folder you want to configure. On the screen that appears (right), choose whether to sync the folder and, if so, how many days of mail to sync.

- **Sync Calendar.** Check this box to sync calendar data for your Exchange account.
- **Download Attachments.** Check this box to download attachments on recent messages automatically when your device has a Wi-Fi connection.
- **Email Notifications.** Check this box if you want the Gmail app to notify you when you receive messages.
- **Choose Ringtone.** Tap this button to choose the ringtone used for the email notification.
- **Vibrate.** Check this box to make your device vibrate when the Gmail app gives you a notification. This check box appears only if your device includes vibration.
- **Incoming Settings.** Tap this button to display a dialog box for configuring the account's incoming mail server.

TRIAGING AND READING YOUR MESSAGES

Now that you've configured the Gmail app and your email accounts to your satisfaction, you're ready to deal with your messages quickly and smoothly.

In this section, you learn how to navigate among your accounts, labels, and folders; work in the conversation list; and read your messages.

NAVIGATING AMONG YOUR ACCOUNTS, LABELS, AND FOLDERS

The Gmail app enables you to navigate quickly among your email accounts, your folders, and your Gmail labels:

1. Tap the navigation button in the upper-left corner of the screen to display the navigation panel.

2. Tap the pop-up menu at the bottom of the colorful area at the top of the navigation panel, just above the All Inboxes button. The list of accounts appears. (See the left screen in Figure 6.15.)

3. Tap the button for the account you want to use. The folders or labels in that account appear. (See the right screen in Figure 6.15.)

> **TIP** You can also change accounts quickly by tapping the picture or letter circle for the account to which you want to switch.

4. Tap the folder or label you want to view.

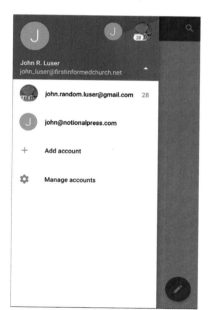
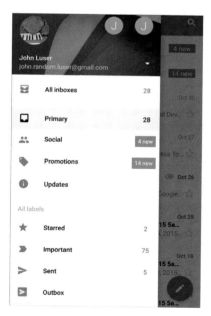

FIGURE 6.15

To navigate among your accounts, folders, and labels, display the navigation panel (left). Switch to the appropriate account by tapping its picture or letter or by tapping the pop-up menu and then tapping the account. You can then tap the folder or label you want to view (right).

WORKING IN THE CONVERSATION LIST

The conversation list (see Figure 6.16) presents a list of your messages with the newest at the top. You can refresh the conversation list by tapping the conversation list, pulling down the screen a little way, and then releasing the list.

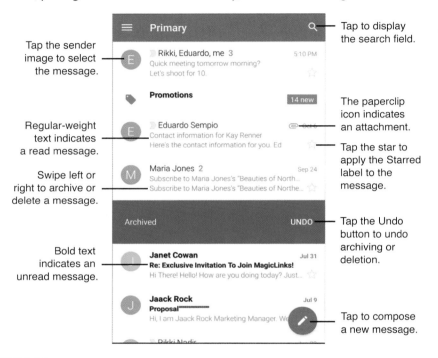

Tap the sender image to select the message.

Regular-weight text indicates a read message.

Swipe left or right to archive or delete a message.

Bold text indicates an unread message.

Tap to display the search field.

The paperclip icon indicates an attachment.

Tap the star to apply the Starred label to the message.

Tap the Undo button to undo archiving or deletion.

Tap to compose a new message.

FIGURE 6.16

The conversation list provides an easy-to-navigate compilation of your messages and conversations.

The sender's name and subject of each unread message appear in boldface, whereas the sender's name and subject of each read message appear in regular (nonbold) font.

> **TIP** The yellow arrow to the left of a message's sender indicates that Google considers the message important. The reason may be that you are the only recipient or that you have marked similar messages as important.

The sender image (or sender initial) circle to the left of the sender name gives you a quick way of seeing who the message is from.

> **TIP** If you turn off sender images, you can select a message by tapping and holding it. Doing so turns on Selection mode; you can then tap other messages to select them.

Tap the sender image square to select the message; the circle changes to display a white check mark on a gray circle. Selecting a message puts the conversation list into Selection mode, and three buttons for manipulating the selected messages appear at the top of the screen. (See Figure 6.17.)

- **Archive.** Tap this button to archive the selected messages.
- **Mark as Unread.** Tap this button to mark the selected messages as unread.
- **Delete.** Tap this button to delete the selected messages.

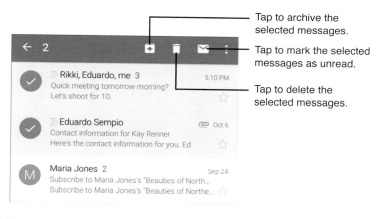

Tap to archive the selected messages.

Tap to mark the selected messages as unread.

Tap to delete the selected messages.

FIGURE 6.17

Use the three buttons at the top of the conversation list to archive the selected messages, mark them as unread, or delete them.

Also in the conversation list, you can swipe a conversation left or right off the list to archive or delete it, depending on the Default Gmail Action setting you chose on the General Settings screen. The Archived bar or Deleted bar appears, confirming the action you've taken with the conversation. You can tap the Undo button at the right end of the Archived bar or Deleted bar if you've gotten rid of the wrong message.

> **TIP** If Gmail identifies an unimportant message as important, select the message, tap the Menu button, and then tap Mark Not Important on the menu. If you do this consistently, Gmail gradually learns which messages are important to you and which are not.

READING YOUR MESSAGES

Tap a message in the conversation list to open it for reading. You can then use the controls shown in Figure 6.18 to take actions with the message:

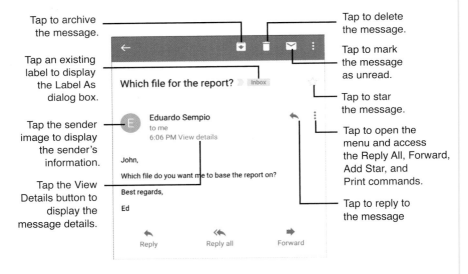

Tap to archive the message.

Tap an existing label to display the Label As dialog box.

Tap the sender image to display the sender's information.

Tap the View Details button to display the message details.

Tap to delete the message.

Tap to mark the message as unread.

Tap to star the message.

Tap to open the menu and access the Reply All, Forward, Add Star, and Print commands.

Tap to reply to the message

FIGURE 6.18

After opening a message for reading, you can reply to it, forward it, archive it, or move it.

- **Reply to the message.** Tap either the Reply button (the left-curling arrow) to the right of the sender's name or the Reply button at the bottom of the message.

- **Reply to all recipients of the message.** Tap the message's Menu button—the Menu button to the right of the sender's name—and then tap Reply All on the menu. Alternatively, tap the Reply All button at the bottom of the message.

- **Forward the message.** Tap the message's Menu button and then tap Forward on the menu. Alternatively, tap the Forward button at the bottom of the message.

- **Print the message.** Tap the message's Menu button and then tap Print on the menu.
- **Delete the message.** Tap the Delete icon at the top of the screen.
- **Star the message.** Tap the Star icon to the right of the subject line.
- **View the message details.** Tap the View Details button to display the From field, To field, and Date field.
- **Change the message's labels.** Tap the current label button above the message's Menu button to display the Label As dialog box, check the box for each label you want to apply, and then tap the OK button.
- **Display the sender's information.** Tap the sender image to display the sender's information. Here, you can tap the Star icon to star the contact, adding the contact to the Starred group.
- **Archive the message.** Tap the Archive button on the toolbar.
- **Mark the message as unread.** Tap the Mark as Unread button on the toolbar.
- **Move the message to a label.** Tap the Menu button in the orange bar at the top of the screen, and then tap the Move To button on the menu to display the Move To dialog box. Tap the destination label.

> **NOTE** If the message is part of a conversation, you can tap the Show Quoted Text button to display the quoted text and tap the resulting Hide Quoted Text button to hide it. Tap the Older Messages button to view older messages in the conversation.

WRITING AND SENDING MESSAGES

Gmail makes writing and sending messages easy: tap the Compose button (the orange circle with a pencil icon) in the lower-right corner of the screen; fill in the recipient, subject, and message body on the Compose screen; and then tap the Send button, the arrow button to the left of the menu button.

You can also change the account, add Cc or Bcc recipients, and attach files:

- **Choose the account.** If you have set up multiple Gmail accounts, tap the From pop-up menu and then tap the account to use.

> **NOTE** The Gmail app selects the account you were viewing as the sending account for the message.

- **Add Cc or Bcc recipients.** Tap the down-arrow button at the right end of the To field to display the Cc and Bcc fields. Tap the Cc field or the Bcc field as appropriate, start typing the contact's name or email address, and then tap the contact in the pop-up list of matches.
- **Attach a file to the message.** Tap the Attach button (the paperclip icon) at the right end of the Compose bar at the top of the screen, and then tap Attach File on the menu. Use the Open From panel to select the source of the file, such as Images or Videos, and then tap the file to select it. If you want to attach a file from Google Drive, tap Insert from Drive on the menu instead, and then select the file. Either way, the file appears as a large button showing the file's name. If you need to remove the file, tap the X button.

> **TIP** If you want to label a message you're composing, save it as a draft either by tapping the Menu button and then tapping Save Draft on the menu or by tapping the Back button twice. You can then open the Drafts folder, label the message, and then reopen it so that you can send it.

> **NOTE** If you decide not to send the message, you can discard it. To discard the message, tap the Menu button and then tap Discard on the menu.

LABELING, ARCHIVING, AND MOVING YOUR MESSAGES

To keep your messages in order, you will normally want to label them, archive them, and move them to folders.

- **Labeling.** In Google accounts, labeling assigns one or more labels, such as Personal or Work, to the message, enabling you to find it later by browsing through those labels or searching with them. When you label a message, it remains in the same folder, such as your Inbox.
- **Archiving.** In Google accounts, archiving moves a message out of your Inbox.
- **Moving.** In Google accounts or in other types of email accounts, you can move a message to a specific folder for storage.

> **NOTE** Between them, labeling and archiving in Google accounts have an effect similar to moving a message to a folder in other email systems. But because you can label and archive messages separately, Google accounts give you more flexibility. The Move To command and Move To dialog box enable you to label and move a message in a single move.

LABELING AND ARCHIVING MESSAGES IN A GOOGLE ACCOUNT

In a Google account, you can label either the message you have open for reading or selected messages in the conversation list by tapping the Menu button and then tapping Change Labels on the menu. The Label As dialog box opens (see the left screen in Figure 6.19), and you can check the boxes for the labels you want to apply. Then tap the OK button.

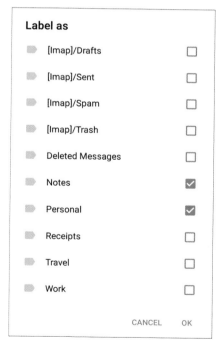

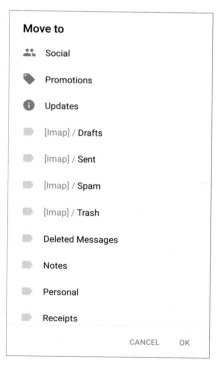

FIGURE 6.19

Use the Label As dialog box (left) to label a message and leave it in its current location. Use the Move To dialog box (right) to label a message and archive it at the same time.

> ☑ **TIP** You can also open the Label As dialog box by tapping a label's button on a message you've opened for reading.

> ✎ **NOTE** Google accounts use the Inbox label to determine which messages should appear in the Inbox. Removing the Inbox label from a message moves it out of the Inbox; applying the Inbox label to a message makes it appear in the Inbox.

To archive a message, tap the Archive button at the top of the screen for either a message you have opened for reading or selected messages in the conversation list.

To label a message and archive it at the same time, tap the main Menu button and then tap the Move To button on the menu. You can do this either for the message you have open for reading or the messages you have selected in the conversation list. The Move To dialog box opens (see the right screen in Figure 6.19), and you can tap the label to which you want to move the message.

MOVING MESSAGES IN PERSONAL AND EXCHANGE ACCOUNTS

In personal accounts and Exchange accounts, you simply move messages to the folders in which you want to keep them.

Select a message by tapping the sender image, tap the Menu button, and then tap the Move To button on the menu. In the Move To dialog box that opens, tap the folder to which you want to move the message.

DEALING WITH SPAM AND PROBLEM SENDERS

If you receive spam messages on your Google account, you can report them to Google. With the message either open for reading or selected in the conversation list, tap the main Menu button and then tap Report Spam on the menu.

> **TIP** Gmail doesn't give you a way to block specific senders, but you can create filters to put messages from them straight into the Trash. Using a web browser, log in to your Gmail account; if you're using your Android device, you need to open the menu and check the Request Desktop Site box. Click or tap the down-arrow button at the right end of the Search box, choose the details in the Filter pane, and then click the Create Filter with This Search button.
>
> For heavier-duty blocking, you can use an email proxy provider that filters your messages for you and permits only those messages that pass your specified criteria to reach you.

SEARCHING FOR MESSAGES

When you need to locate particular messages, you can search for them. You can do a straightforward search using one or more keywords in any type of account. In Google accounts, you can also use advanced search operators and Boolean operators for more power.

SEARCHING WITH KEYWORDS IN ANY TYPE OF ACCOUNT

To search for messages using keywords, tap the Search icon at the top of the conversation list and type the keywords. If the Gmail app displays a list of suggested matches, tap the appropriate one.

> **TIP** When you use multiple keywords, Gmail searches for messages containing them all. For example, if you search for *relocation project*, Gmail searches for messages containing both *relocation* and *project*. To search for an exact phrase, place the keywords in quotation marks—for example, *"relocation project"*.

The results list appears, and you can tap the message you want to view.

SEARCHING WITH ADVANCED SEARCH OPERATORS IN GOOGLE ACCOUNTS

For more advanced searching in Google accounts, use operators in your searches. Table 6.5 explains the search operators, with examples.

Table 6.5   Advanced Search Operators for Gmail

Search Operator	Meaning	Example
from:	The sender.	from:bill
to:	The recipient.	to:dan@surrealmacs.com
cc:	A Cc recipient.	cc:hr@surrealmacs.com
bcc:	A Bcc recipient on messages you have sent.	bcc:hr@surrealmacs.com
subject:	A subject word.	subject:relocation
after: older:	Messages sent or received after the date given.	after:2016/05/11 older:2016/05/11
before: newer:	Messages sent or received before the date given.	before:2016/08/04 from:bill newer:2016/05/20
older_than:	Messages older than the relative date given using days (d), months (m), or years (y).	older_than:6m older_than:1y
newer_than	Messages newer than the relative date given using days (d), months (m), or years (y).	newer_than:7d
label:	The label.	label:money
has:attachment	The message has an attachment.	from:bill has:attachment
filename:	The whole or partial filename of an attachment.	filename:sales.xlsx filename:docx
list:	The mailing list.	list:info@surrealmacs.com
in:	The location.	in:inbox in:trash
in:anywhere	Includes the Spam and Trash folders, which Gmail excludes by default.	from:bill in:anywhere
is:important	Messages that Priority Inbox has marked as important.	from:bill is:important
label:important	Messages that Priority Inbox has marked as important.	from:bill is:important
is:starred	The message has a star.	is:started subject:budget
is:unread	The message status is unread.	is:unread from:bill

Search Operator	Meaning	Example
is:read	The message status is read.	is:read subject:analysis
has:yellow-star has:red-star has:orange-star has:green-star has:blue-star has:purple-star	The message has a star of the given color.	has:blue-star from:bill
has:red-bang has:yellow-bang	The message has an exclamation point of the given color.	has:yellow-bang
has:orange-guillemet	The message has orange angle-quotes.	has:orange-guillemet
has:green-check	The message has a green check mark.	has:green-check
has:blue-info	The message has a blue info mark.	has:blue-info
has:purple-question	The message has a purple question mark.	has:purple-question
is:chat	The message is a chat message.	is:chat delivery
circle:	Your Google+ circle to which the message's sender belongs.	circle:family subject:Thanksgiving
has:circle	The sender is someone in your Google+ circles.	has:circle subject:park
category:	The category that contains the message.	category:social
size:	The minimum message size in bytes.	size:2000000
larger:	The minimum message size, using abbreviations for numbers (such as M for million bytes).	large:5M
smaller:	The maximum message size, using abbreviations for numbers.	smaller:1M
+	An exact match of the search term.	+result
has:userlabels	The message has user labels applied.	has:userlabels
has:nouserlabels	The message has no user labels applied.	has:nouserlabels
deliveredto:	The message's header contains the address in the Delivered-To line.	deliveredto:info@ surrealmacs.com
rfc822msgid:	The SMTP message ID (found in the message headers).	rfc822msgid: 0059ac168294@ surrealmacs.com

SEARCHING WITH BOOLEAN OPERATORS AND GROUPING

As you saw earlier, when you enter multiple search terms, Gmail searches for messages that contain them all. This is a Boolean AND operator: Searching for *budget spreadsheet 2015* is the equivalent of searching for *budget AND spreadsheet AND 2015*.

You don't need to specify the AND operator, but you can if you want. You can also use the OR operator and the NOT operator:

- **OR.** Use the OR operator to search for one item or another item. For example, *subject:relocation OR subject:planning*.

- **NOT (–).** Use the NOT operator, represented by the minus sign (–), to specify items you don't want to find. For example, *from:bill –meeting*.

You can use parentheses to group terms. For example, you can use *subject:(office project)* to messages whose subject lines contain both "office" and "project" (but not necessarily the phrase "office project").

SETTING UP 2-STEP VERIFICATION FOR YOUR GOOGLE ACCOUNT

To protect your Google account against attackers, you should set up 2-Step Verification for it. This process uses your phone as well as your password to help keep attackers out of your account.

Here's how 2-Step Verification works: Each time you sign in to your Google account using a computer or device on which you haven't signed in before, Google accepts your username and password but then prompts you for a code that it has just sent to your phone. Type in that code, and you can choose whether to authorize that computer or device so that you don't need to enter a code for it again in future.

You can set up 2-Step Verification using either a computer or just your Android device. The following sections explain what to do.

SETTING UP 2-STEP VERIFICATION USING A COMPUTER

If you use a computer as well as your Android device, use the computer to set up 2-Step Verification like this:

1. Open a web browser and go to the Gmail website.
2. Sign in to your Google account by providing your username and password.
3. Click your name or picture in the upper-right corner of the window, and then click My Account to display the settings screen for the account.

4. Click Sign-In & Security to display the Sign-In & Security screen.

5. In the Password & Sign-In Method box, click the 2-Step Verification button to display the Signing In with 2-Step Verification screen.

6. Click the Start Setup button.

7. Enter your password, and then click the OK button.

8. On the Set Up Your Phone screen, enter your phone number and select the Text Message (SMS) radio button or the Voice Call radio button, as appropriate.

> **✓ TIP** If you don't know your Android device's phone number by heart, open the Settings app, tap the About Phone button, tap the Status button, tap the SIM Status button, and then look at the My Phone Number readout.

9. Tap the Send Code button to send the verification code to your phone (or to receive a phone call).

10. On the Verify Your Phone screen, type in the verification code and click the Verify button.

11. On the Trust This Computer screen, check or uncheck the Trust This Computer box as needed, and then click the Next button.

> **! CAUTION** Check the Trust This computer box only if this is your own computer or you entirely trust all the other people who use it.

12. On the Confirm screen, click the Confirm button.

REINFORCING YOUR 2-STEP VERIFICATION SECURITY

After setting up 2-Step Verification, use the settings on the 2-Step Verification screen to add security mechanisms.

First, go to the Verification Codes tab and click the Add a Phone Number button to add a backup phone in case yours go missing. Then click the Print or Download button in the Backup Codes area to print or download backup codes you can use to get into your account if you have problems with your phone. Backup codes are also useful for travel, when you may have trouble connecting.

Next, click the App-Specific Passwords tab, click the Manage Application-Specific Passwords button, and follow through the process for setting passwords for specific apps, such as Mail apps, that access your Google account.

Last, click the Registered Computers tab and use its controls to configure your list of registered computers. These are computers you can use to manage your account when your phone isn't available, such as when it pits its delicate electronics against gravity or water.

You'll notice that the 2-Step Verification screen has a fourth tab: the Security Keys tab. This tab enables you to set up a physical security key for signing into your Google account. You might need this level of security for corporate use, but most likely not for a personal account.

SETTING UP 2-STEP VERIFICATION USING AN ANDROID DEVICE

If you use your Android device on its own, without a computer, you may be able to set up 2-Step Verification directly on the device by using the Google Authenticator app. Open the Play Store app on your device, search for **Google Authenticator**, tap the correct search result, and then install the app. When the installation completes, tap the Open button to open Google Authenticator, and then follow the prompts for choosing the appropriate Google account and setting up 2-Step verification on it.

> **NOTE** If Google Authenticator cannot sign you in, it may prompt you to sign in using the web interface instead. Follow the prompts to complete the verification. If Google Authenticator prompts you to continue on a computer instead, do so.

LOGGING IN TO YOUR ACCOUNT WITH 2-STEP VERIFICATION ENABLED

After you enable 2-Step Verification, you need to go through the extra step of verification the first time you log in to your Google account using a computer or device on which you haven't logged in to your account. Google apps such as Gmail will refuse your password and prompt you to log in using the web-based interface instead.

When you do, the 2-Step Verification screen shown in Figure 6.20 appears. The device on which you verified the account receives a text with a six-digit verification code. Type the code, tap the Next button, and then tap the Accept button on the Terms & Conditions screen.

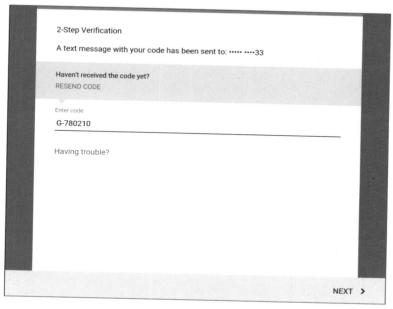

FIGURE 6.20

Type your verification code into the box on the 2-Step Verification screen, and then tap the Next button.

7

USING GOOGLE NOW AND MAPS

In this chapter, you'll first dig into getting Google Now to do your bidding, including setting time- and location-based reminders and using the Now on Tap information-gathering feature if your device runs Marshmallow rather than Lollipop. After that, you'll learn how to get around in the Maps app.

STREAMLINING YOUR LIFE WITH GOOGLE NOW

Google Now is a powerful tool for locating information that will be helpful to you in your current situation. It automatically displays a series of cards containing information about topics in which you have expressed an interest, such as weather for your current location, listings for the stocks you're tracking, and traffic details for your upcoming appointments. You can find further information by asking questions, either speaking them into your device's microphone or typing them into the Search box.

Google Now predicts your needs and offers information it judges may be helpful to you. You can adjust the information to make it suit your needs better.

DECIDING WHETHER TO USE GOOGLE NOW

To work effectively, Google Now needs to know a good deal of information about you. Before you start using Google Now, you should understand the nature and extent of this information to make sure you're comfortable sharing it with Google. As you probably know, Google makes something like nine-tenths of its money from delivering advertisements, and the more information Google knows about you, the better it can target you. This extensive data-gathering concerns some people, whereas others accept it as a fact of modern life.

First, Google Now needs to know about your web browsing. So it monitors any web page you visit in the Chrome app on any computer or device logged into the same Google account, including your full browsing history—plus web content you browse in other apps. Google Now also monitors your web searches to see what you're interested in to help it give you more relevant suggestions. This category of information is called Web & App Activity.

Second, enabling Google Now gives it access to a large amount of information stored on your Android device. This category of information is called Device Information and includes your apps, your music, your contacts, your calendars, the device's battery life and battery usage, and any sensor readings the device is capable of.

Third, Google Now records your voice input to help it recognize your specific voice and improve speech recognition. If you use the OK Google feature, Google Now listens for your voice in case you're trying to activate the feature. This category of information is called Voice & Audio Activity.

As you'll see later in this section, you can rein in some of Google Now's actions by configuring its settings. But broadly speaking, if you're going to use Google Now extensively, you should be prepared to give Google all the information detailed in this sidebar.

NAVIGATING AND CUSTOMIZING GOOGLE NOW

To use Google Now, open it in one of these ways:

- **Marshmallow.** Swipe right from your first Home screen.
- **Lollipop.** Tap and hold the Home button until the Google circle appears, and then slide your finger up to the circle.

> **NOTE** If the Google Now circle doesn't appear when you tap and hold the Home button in Lollipop, you may need to install Google Now. Most devices come with Google Now, but some don't. Tap the Play Store icon on the Home screen, search for *Google search*, and then install the app. For an older device, you may need to install the Google Now Launcher app.

SETTING UP GOOGLE NOW

If you haven't yet set up Google Now, Android prompts you to set it up the first time you try to access it. Read the information and tap the Yes, I'm In button to get started.

GETTING STARTED WITH NOW CARDS

Once you've opened Google Now, you see the current selection of cards containing information intended to be useful to you. Figure 7.1 shows an example of Google Now on a tablet.

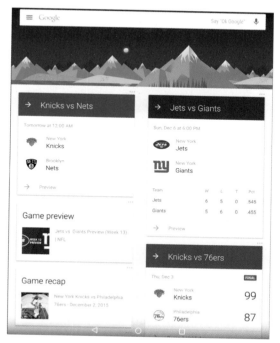

FIGURE 7.1

Google Now displays cards containing information intended to be useful to you.

If you don't want a card, swipe right to remove it from the screen. Google Now briefly displays a Done for Now button, with an Undo button that you can tap to recover the card if you swiped it by accident.

If the selection of cards extends off the bottom of the screen, swipe up to scroll down so that you can see them.

ENABLING AND USING THE NOW ON TAP FEATURE IN MARSHMALLOW

Marshmallow includes a new Google Now feature called Now on Tap that displays Now cards related to whatever is onscreen in the app you're using. For example, if you're reading an email message that mentions a song or a movie, Now on Tap can display cards related to that song or movie. Similarly, if you're writing a text and you mention a date and time, Now on Tap can display calendar information for that date and time.

> **NOTE** As of this writing, Now on Tap is an ingenious and experimental feature that is more successful with some input than with other input.

To enable the Now on Tap feature, tap and hold the Home button until the Want Help with Any Screen? Turn On Now on Tap dialog box opens. (See Figure 7.2.) Then tap the Get Started or the Turn On button, depending on which appears.

FIGURE 7.2
Tap the Get Started button in the Want Help with Any Screen? Turn On Now on Tap dialog box to start using Now on Tap in Marshmallow.

Once you've enabled Now on Tap, you can activate it by tapping and holding the Home button. When you do this, Now on Tap quickly analyzes the information on the screen, creates Now cards that may be relevant, and displays them. The left screen in Figure 7.3 shows an email message open in the Gmail app. The right screen in Figure 7.3 shows the cards that Now on Tap has derived from the message.

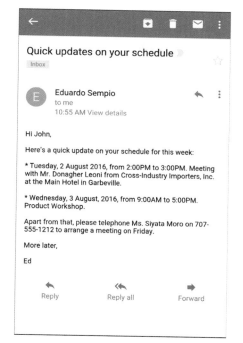
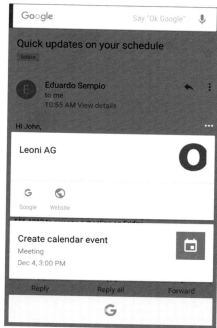

FIGURE 7.3

The Now on Tap feature attempts to analyze the current screen, such as an email message (left), and derive helpful Now Cards from it (right).

CUSTOMIZING GOOGLE NOW TO SUIT YOUR NEEDS

To customize Google Now to suit your needs, open the navigation panel by either tapping the Navigation Panel button or by swiping in from the right. The left screen in Figure 7.4 shows the navigation panel on a phone.

To start customizing Google now, open the navigation panel and tap the Customize button. The Customize Google Now screen appears. (See the right screen in Figure 7.4.)

When you're setting up Google Now, the How Do You Usually Get Around box appears at the top of the Customize Google Now screen. Tap the Biking button, the Driving button, the Public Transit button, or the Walking button, as needed. If the Get Updates for Commuting to Work dialog box opens, tap the Yes button or the No button, as appropriate.

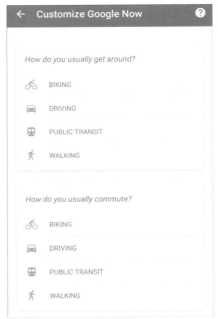

FIGURE 7.4

To start customizing Google Now to suit your needs, open the navigation panel (left) and tap the Customize button. On the Customize Google Now screen (right), specify how you normally get around and how you commute.

Once you've dealt with the How Do You Usually Get Around box, the box disappears. Next, deal with the How Do You Usually Commute box. Again, you can tap the Biking button, the Driving button, the Public Transit button, or the Walking button. This box also disappears when you've made your choice, leaving the items you can configure at any time. Here are brief details on these items:

- **Apps & Websites.** Tap this button to display the Apps & Websites screen. Here, you can choose whether to receive Now cards from apps and websites and whether to receive location-based Now cards from apps and websites.

- **Places.** Tap this button to display the Places screen. Here, you can tap the Home button (on the screen) to set or change your Home location, or you can tap the Work button to set or change your Work location. Google Now uses these locations to get accurate commuting information (if you choose to receive commuting updates).

- **Sports.** Tap this button to display the Sports screen. Here, you can build a list of the sports teams you're interested in by tapping the Add a Team button, starting to type the team's name in the Add a Team dialog box that opens, and then tapping the appropriate team from the list of matches that appears. The teams appear in the Interested In list on the Sports screen.

- **Stocks.** Tap this button to display the Stocks screen. Here, you can build a list of the stocks you're interested in by tapping the Add a Stock button, typing its tracker or the beginning of its name in the Add a Stock dialog box that opens, and then tapping the appropriate stock in the last of matches that Google Now shows. The stocks appear in the Interested In list on the Stocks screen.

> **TIP** To remove a team from the Sports screen or a stock from the Stocks screen, tap the team or stock in the Interested In list. A dialog box opens asking if you're interested in that team's games or in that stock and noting whether you added this team or stock or Google Now added it for you. Tap the No button to remove the team or stock.

- **Transportation.** Tap this button to display the Transportation screen. Here, you can tap the How Do You Usually Commute button or the How Do You Usually Get Around button and then tap the Biking button, the Driving button, the Public Transit button, or the Walking button.
- **TV & Video.** Tap this button to display the TV & Video screen. Here, you can tap the TV Provider button and specify your TV provider; tap the Video on Demand Providers button and select your providers in the Video on Demand Providers dialog box; and tap the Show Only Programs That I Can Cast While Chromecast Is Detected button to choose whether, when your Android device detects a Chromecast device within striking distance, Google Now should restrict the programs shown to those you can play via a Chromecast.
- **Everything Else.** Tap this button to display the Everything Else screen. Here, you can choose whether to receive updates for commuting to work, weather updates for work, and weather updates for home.

When you return to the Google Now screen, it displays information related to the interests you specified.

CHOOSING SETTINGS FOR GOOGLE NOW

Google Now gives you a range of settings that enable you to make it work your way. Many of these settings are important, so we'll go through all of them.

To access the settings, first open the navigation panel by either tapping the Navigation Panel button or swiping in from the right. The Settings screen appears. (See the left screen in Figure 7.5.)

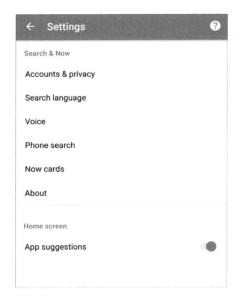
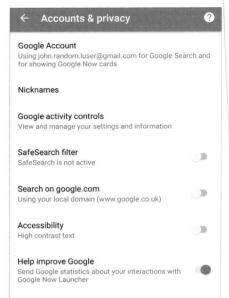

FIGURE 7.5

The Settings screen for Google Now (left) gives you access to the various Search & Now categories and enables you to turn off app suggestions for the Home screen. The Accounts & Privacy screen (right) enables you to switch accounts, create nicknames for contacts, and enable or disable SafeSearch.

In the Search & Now list, tap the category of settings you want to configure. The following subsections explain your main choices.

CONFIGURING ACCOUNTS & PRIVACY SETTINGS

Tap the Accounts & Privacy button to display the Accounts & Privacy screen. (See the right screen in Figure 7.5.) Here, you can configure the following settings:

- **Google Account.** To change the account you're using for Google Now, tap this account and then tap the appropriate account in the Google Account dialog box that opens. You can tap the Sign Out radio button to sign out of this account.

- **Nicknames.** Tap this button to display the Nicknames screen, which shows the nicknames you've created. You can remove a nickname by tapping it in the list and then tapping the Remove button in the Remove This Nickname dialog box that opens.

■ **Google Activity Controls.** Tap this button to display the Activity Controls screen. (See the left screen in Figure 7.6.) You can then tap the Web & App Activity button, the Device Information button, the Voice & Audio Activity button, the YouTube Search History button, the YouTube Watch History button, or the Google Location History button. On the screen that appears, such as the Web & App Activity screen (see the right screen in Figure 7.6), you can enable or disable the feature by setting the master switch at the top to On or Off, as needed. For some features, if you set the master switch to On, you can also configure other features, such as choosing whether to include history from Chrome and other apps in your Web & App Activity.

> **NOTE** The section "Managing Your Activity in Google Account History," later in this chapter, shows you how to work with your Google account history in more detail.

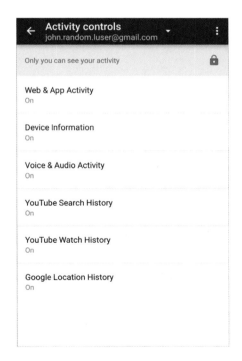
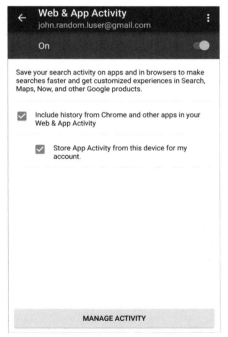

FIGURE 7.6

On the Activity Controls screen (left), tap the activity type you want to configure. On the resulting screen, such as the Web & App Activity screen (right), you can set the master switch to On or Off and configure any other options.

- **SafeSearch Filter.** Set this switch to On if you want to use the SafeSearch filter on your device. SafeSearch attempts to screen out websites that contain explicit content.

> **! CAUTION** Like most Internet safety tools, SafeSearch Filter isn't 100% effective, so you shouldn't rely on it alone to protect sensitive eyes and minds from offensive content. Even if you turn on SafeSearch Filter for a child, you should still supervise her web browsing.

- **Search on Google.com.** Check this box to search on the main Google.com website. If you uncheck this box, Google searches on the local domain for your geographical region, such as www.google.com/au for Australia. If the main Google.com website is your default, this button doesn't appear.
- **Accessibility.** Set this switch to On if you want Google Now to use high-contrast text to improve visibility.
- **Help Improve Google.** Set this switch to On if you want Google Now to share your usage statistics anonymously with Google in the hope of improving the service.

CREATING CONTACT NICKNAMES IN GOOGLE NOW

To help Google Now identify the contacts you want to get in touch with (or ignore), you can create nicknames for them. For example, instead of trying to specify the right Joan out of the dozen of Joans among your contacts, you can use the nickname "my wife." This feature isn't available on all devices, but it's well worth trying if your device has it.

To create a contact nickname, open Google Now, say "OK Google" or tap the microphone icon, and then announce the person and the nickname. For example, say "Joan Smith is my wife" or "Alan Jones is the head honcho."

The first time you try to create a contact nickname, Android may prompt you to enable the Contact Recognition feature. Do so, and you can then create the contact nickname and start using it.

CHOOSING YOUR SEARCH LANGUAGE AND VOICE SETTINGS

Next, tap the Search Language button to display the Search Language screen, and then tap the language you want to use for searches.

Back on the Settings screen, tap the Voice button to display the Voice screen. (See the left screen in Figure 7.7.) Here, you can choose the following settings:

- **Languages.** Tap this button to display the Languages dialog box. You can then check a language's box to add that language. To change your default language, tap and hold the language you want to use. When you finish selecting languages, tap the Save button.

- **"OK Google" Detection.** Tap this button to display the "OK Google" Detection screen. (See the right screen in Figure 7.7.) Here, you can set the From the Google App switch, the Always On switch or the From Any Screen switch (depending on your device and its Android version), and the Trusted Voice switch to On or Off, as needed. In the "OK Google" Voice Model area, you can tap the Retrain Voice Model button to run through the voice-model training again or tap the Delete Voice Model button to delete your existing voice model.

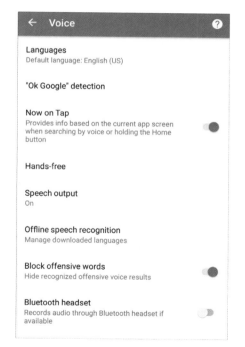
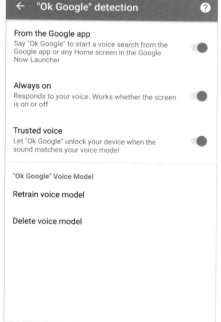

FIGURE 7.7

On the Voice screen (left), set your default language and choose the other voice features you want to use. On the "OK Google" Detection screen (right), choose when to use the "OK Google" feature, and retrain it if necessary.

> **☑ TIP**   If you want to be able to access Google Now quickly from the lock screen, go to the "OK Google" Detection screen and set the From the Google App switch, the Always On switch or the From Any Screen switch, and the Trusted Voice switch to On.

- **Now on Tap.** Set this switch to On to enable the Now on Tap feature, discussed in the section "Enabling and Using the Now on Tap Feature in Marshmallow," earlier in this chapter.

- **Hands-Free.** Tap this button to display the Hands-Free screen. Here, you can set the For Bluetooth Devices switch and the For Wired Headsets switch to On or Off to control which types of devices can make voice requests when your device is locked.

- **Speech Output.** Tap this button to display the Speech Output dialog box, in which you can select the On radio button or the Hands-Free Only radio button, as needed.

- **Offline Speech Recognition.** Tap this button to display the Download Languages screen. This screen has three tabs: Installed, All, and Auto-Update. On the Installed tab, you can see which languages you have installed. On the All tab, you can tap a language to download and install it. On the Auto-Update tab, you can select the Do Not Auto-Update Languages radio button, the Auto-Update Languages at Any Time radio button, or the Auto-Update Languages over Wi-Fi Only (usually the best choice).

- **Block Offensive Words.** Set this switch to On to make Google Now hide any offensive words it recognizes in voice results.

- **Bluetooth Headset.** Set this switch to On if you want your Android device to record audio through a Bluetooth headset when one is connected.

CHOOSING PHONE SEARCH OR TABLET SEARCH SETTINGS

To specify which items Google Now should use when searching your phone or tablet, tap the Phone Search button or the Tablet Search button. On the Phone Search screen (see the left screen in Figure 7.8) or the Tablet Search screen, you can configure the following settings:

- **Apps.** Check this box to allow Google Now to search the names of installed apps.

- **Books.** Check this box to allow Google Now to search your e-books.

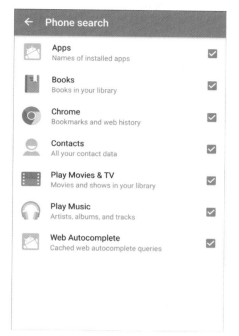
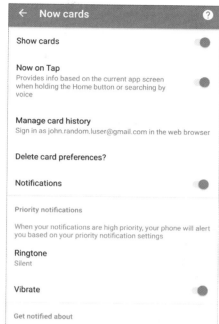

FIGURE 7.8

On the Phone Search screen (left) or Tablet Search screen, check or uncheck the boxes to specify what to search. On the Now Cards screen (right), choose which cards to show, configure priority notification preferences, and decide which types of notifications to receive.

- **Chrome.** Check this box to allow Google Now to search your bookmarks and your browsing history.
- **Contacts.** Check this box to allow Google Now to search through all your contact data.
- **Play Movies & TV.** Check this box to allow Google Now to search the movies and TV shows in your library.
- **Play Music.** Check this box to allow Google Now to search the artists, albums, and song names in your library.
- **Web Autocomplete.** Check this box to allow Google Now to search the data stored in your cached autocomplete queries.

CHOOSING NOW CARDS SETTINGS

The last category of settings to choose for Google Now is the Now Cards category. Tap the Now Cards button to display the Now Cards screen. (See the right screen in Figure 7.8.) Here, you can configure the following settings:

■ **Show Cards.** Leave this switch set to On unless you want to turn off Google Now. If you do want to turn off Google Now, set the switch to Off. In the Turn Off Google Now dialog box that opens, tap the Turn Off button.

> **!CAUTION** In the Turn Off Google Now dialog box, check the Also Delete Your Google Now Preferences box only if you want to disable Google Now on all your devices, not just on the device you're currently using.

■ **Now on Tap.** Set this switch to On to enable the Now on Tap feature, discussed in the section "Enabling and Using the Now on Tap Feature in Marshmallow," earlier in this chapter.

> **NOTE** The Now on Tap switch on the Now Cards screen has the same effect as the Now on Tap switch on the Voice Search screen.

■ **Manage Card History.** Tap this button to switch to the Chrome app and sign in to your Google account so that you can manage your card history. See the section "Managing Your Activity in Google Account History," later in this chapter, for more information on this.

■ **Delete Card Preferences.** Tap this button, and then tap the Delete button in the Delete Card Preferences dialog box that opens, only if you want to delete your Google Now customizations and turn off Now Cards on all your devices.

■ **Notifications.** Set this switch to On if you want to receive notifications from Google Now. If you set this switch to Off, all the controls in the Priority Notifications section and the Get Notified About section disappear because they depend on you receiving notifications.

■ **Priority Notifications.** In this section, first tap the Ringtone button and use the Ringtone dialog box to select the ringtone you want to use. Then, if your device has a vibration motor, set the Vibrate switch to On or Off, as needed.

■ **Get Notified About.** If this section appears on your device, set the Weather switch, the Commute and Time to Leave switch, the Sports switch, the Stories and Videos switch, and the Places switch to On or Off as needed.

ENABLING OR DISABLING APP SUGGESTIONS

In the Home Screen section at the bottom of the Settings screen, set the App Suggestions switch to On if you want to allow Google Now to suggest apps; otherwise, set this switch to Off.

After you finish choosing settings for Google Now on the Settings screen, tap the arrow button or the Back button below the screen to return to Google Now itself. The Google Now screen shows cards updated to reflect the settings you chose.

MANAGING YOUR ACTIVITY IN GOOGLE ACCOUNT HISTORY

The Google Account History feature gives you a window into the huge amount of information that Google can receive about you and what you do on your Android device—and other devices or computers—and on the Internet. But better than that, it enables you to manage your activities and delete those you want to remove from the record.

Follow these steps to access your Google account history:

1. Open Google Now. (For example, on Marshmallow, swipe right from your first Home screen.)

2. Open the navigation panel by tapping the Navigation Panel button or by swiping in from the left side of the screen.

3. Tap the Settings button to display the Settings screen.

4. Tap the Accounts & Privacy button to display the Accounts & Privacy screen.

5. Tap the Google Activity Controls button to display the Activity Controls screen.

> **NOTE** If you've set up multiple Google accounts on your device, make sure the pop-up menu at the top of the Activity Controls screen shows the right account. If not, tap the pop-up menu, and then tap the account you want to manage.

6. Tap the button for the activity category you want to review. (For example, tap the Web & App Activity button to display the Web & App Activity screen.)

7. Tap the Manage Activity button at the bottom of the screen to display the Manage Activity screen for that category. At this point, Android switches to your default browser, such as Chrome. The left screen in Figure 7.9 shows the Manage Activity screen for Web & Activity, which displays a list of your searches, the apps you've used, and the content you've browsed in Chrome and other apps.

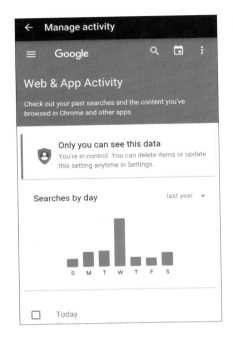 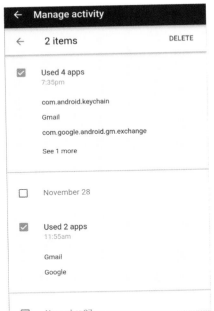

FIGURE 7.9
The top of the Manage Activity screen (left) enables you to restrict your search to specific dates. After selecting items you want to remove (right), tap the Delete button to remove them.

> **NOTE** The information on the Manage Activity screen may take a few seconds to load because your device is downloading it from Google's servers.

8. Look at the Searches by Day chart to see which days you've used Google Now the most. (In the example, Wednesday is the standout search day, for reasons unknown.) You can tap the Searches by Day pop-up menu and switch among Last Week, Last Month, Last Year, and All Time (for your Google account rather than eternity itself).

9. Swipe up to scroll down the list to examine its contents.

> **TIP** If you're looking for something particular, you can tap the Search icon (the magnifying glass) at the top of the screen and type in the term. And if you want to go to a particular date, tap the Date icon (between the Search icon and the three-dot menu button) and then tap the date on the pop-up panel that opens.

10. When you find an item you want to remove, check its box. The Delete button appears at the top of the screen. (See the right screen in Figure 7.9.)

11. Tap the Delete button. A message appears briefly at the bottom of the screen to confirm the deletion.

> **TIP** You can quickly delete information for today, yesterday, or a specific period by tapping the Menu button (the three vertical dots) and then tapping Delete Options on the menu. The Delete dialog box opens, showing the activity category—for example, when you're browsing the Device Information category, you'll see the Delete Device Information For dialog box. Specify the period by tapping the Today radio button, tapping the Yesterday radio button, or tapping the Advanced radio button and then specifying the period in the pop-up menu; and then tap the Delete button.

12. To switch to another category, tap the Navigation Panel button, and then tap the category on the navigation panel. The category's information appears, and you can browse it in the same way.

> **NOTE** Switching from one category to another may take a few seconds, again because your device is downloading the data from Google's servers. So if you tap a button on the navigation panel, and it seems to have no effect, wait for a few seconds for the data to download.

MANAGING YOUR NOW CARD HISTORY VIA A WEB BROWSER

Google Now also enables you to manage your Now Card history. You manage your Now Cards separately from your other Google Now information, but you use a similar technique and interface.

To manage your Now Cards, open Google Now, tap the Navigation Panel button (or swipe in from the left) to open the navigation panel, and then tap Settings to display the Settings screen. Tap the Now Cards button to display the Now Cards screen, and then tap the Manage Card History button to sign into your account using your default web browser (such as the Chrome app).

On the Now Card History screen, you can browse or search the Now Cards that Google has sent to your device. If you need to remove an item from the list, check its box, and then tap the Delete button that appears at the top of the screen.

ACCESSING GOOGLE NOW FROM THE LOCK SCREEN

If you've turned on "OK Google" detection, as explained in the section "Choosing Your Search Language and Voice Settings," earlier in this chapter, you can say "OK Google" to access Google Now from the lock screen.

WORKING WITH REMINDERS IN GOOGLE NOW

Google Now enables you to create reminders to track things you need to do.

To start working with reminders, first display the Google Now screen as usual:

- **Marshmallow.** Swipe right from your first Home screen.
- **Lollipop.** Tap and hold the Home button until the Google circle appears, and then slide your finger up to the circle.

Open the navigation panel by either tapping the Navigation Panel button or swiping in from the right, and tap the Reminders button to display the Reminders screen. (See the left screen in Figure 7.10.)

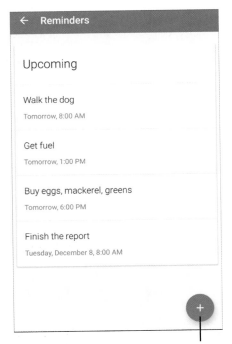
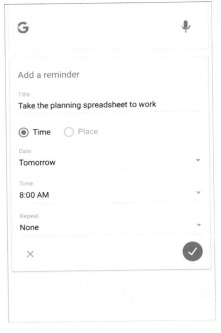

Add a Reminder button

FIGURE 7.10

On the Reminders screen (left), tap the Add a Reminder button to start creating a new reminder. You can set a reminder in Google Now (right) either by speaking the reminder or by typing its details.

From the Reminders screen, you can start creating a reminder either by tapping the Add a Reminder button and then typing in the details or by saying "Remind me" and the specifics. For example, you could say "Remind me to take the planning spreadsheet to work at 8 o'clock tomorrow morning" to produce the new reminder shown on the right screen in Figure 7.10.

> **TIP** For a time-based reminder, you can use general times such as "morning," "afternoon," or "evening" as well as specific times. You can also set a timer-based reminder by saying "in five minutes," "in one hour," or a similar phrase.

You can tie a reminder either to a time or to a place. To use a place, tap the Place radio button on the screen for setting a reminder, and then choose the place from the Location pop-up menu. You can choose a place you've already defined, such as Home or Work, or tap the Set Location button to set a different location.

> **TIP** You can create a location-based reminder by using a phrase such as "when I get to work" when speaking a reminder.

After you've put all the details in place, tap the blue circle with the check mark to add the reminder to your list. The Reminder Saved screen appears, and you can tap the View Reminders button to return to the Reminders screen.

> **TIP** If a Google search returns a card that includes a Remind Me on Google Now button, tap that button to quickly set a reminder about that item.

When a time or place triggers a reminder, your device displays a notification. You can tap the reminder to display it in Google Now or tap the Remind Me in 1 Hour button to snooze the reminder.

To delete a reminder, tap it on the Reminders screen, and then tap Delete in the Edit Reminder dialog box that opens.

NAVIGATING WITH MAPS

Google's Maps app enables you to find your location, explore a variety of places and optionally share them with others, and get directions from one place to another. You can save map sections for offline access, and you can choose settings to make the app work your way.

To get started, open the Maps app by tapping the Maps icon on the Apps screen.

MAKING SURE YOU KNOW ESSENTIAL MAPS MOVES

The Maps app is largely straightforward to use after you've grasped the essential moves:

■ **Navigate around the map.** Tap and drag to move the map. Flick to move a larger distance, and then tap to slow down the movement if necessary.

■ **Choose which map layers to display.** Tap the Navigation Panel button or swipe in from the left to open the navigation panel. Then tap the Traffic button, the Public Transit button, the Bicycling button, the Satellite button, or the Terrain button, as needed.

> ✅ **TIP** The Satellite and Terrain layers are mutually exclusive: You can view one or the other, but not both at once. Similarly, you can view only one of the Traffic, Public Transit, and Bicycling layers at a time.

■ **Go quickly to one of your places.** Tap the Navigation Panel button or swipe in from the left side to open the navigation panel, and then tap Your Places to display the list of your places. Tap the place you want to display in Maps.

■ **Explore your timeline.** Tap the Navigation Panel button or swipe in from the left side to open the navigation panel, and then tap Your Timeline. The first time you do this, the Explore Your Timeline screen appears, showing a brief explanation; tap the Let's Go button to proceed. You can then review the places you've been.

> 🗒 **NOTE** Tap the Google Earth shortcut on the navigation panel to switch to the Google Earth app and display the same place you're viewing in Maps.

■ **Show your location.** Tap the Location button in the lower-right corner of the screen.

■ **Turn the map to show the direction your device is facing.** Tap the Location button again. The Location button changes to a compass symbol. The Compass icon appears in the upper-right corner of the screen, with the red needle pointing north.

■ **Zoom in.** Place your finger and thumb together on the screen and pinch apart.

■ **Zoom out.** Place your finger and thumb apart on the screen and then pinch together. Alternatively, double-tap with two fingers.

TIP You can also zoom by double-tapping. Simply double-tap to zoom in by one zoom increment on the point where you double-tap; double-tap again to zoom further. Double-tap with two fingers to zoom out by increments. You can also double-tap and hold to activate the Zoom feature, and then scroll down to zoom in or scroll up to zoom out.

- **Rotate the map.** Place two fingers on the screen and turn them as needed. The Compass icon appears in the upper-right corner of the screen, with the red needle pointing north.
- **Return the map to north orientation.** Tap the Compass icon.
- **Search for a place.** Tap the Search box at the top of the screen, and then type or speak your search terms. Tap the icon for the type of result you want: food places, bars, gas stations, and so on. You can search using natural-language queries such as "Mexican restaurants in El Cerrito" or "museums in Albuquerque."

TIP If you want to see all the places Google Maps contains information about in the area you're viewing, type * in the Search box and tap the Search button. Maps displays a red dot for each place. For busy places, this move works best when you've zoomed in a long way.

- **Get directions.** Tap the Route arrow in the lower-right corner of the screen, and then specify the start location and the destination. Tap the button at the top of the screen to specify the transit type: driving, public transit, walking, or cycling.

TIP After getting directions, you can specify items to avoid by tapping the Options button and then checking the Avoid Highways box, the Avoid Tolls box, or the Avoid Ferries box in the Options dialog box.

- **Drop a pin on the map.** Tap and hold where you want to drop a pin. You can then tap the pin's label to display the place info sheet. From here, you can tap the Save button to save the place to your Places list, tap the Share button to share the place with others, or tap the Route button to get directions to the place.

> ⌐🗒 **NOTE**   When you want to remove a pin you've placed on the map, tap elsewhere on the map.

■ **Jump into Street View.** Drop a pin for the place (as described in the previous paragraph), tap the pin's label, and then tap the Street View button to go to the place in Street View. You can then look around by tapping and dragging, and move by tapping the white arrows that appear on the road. Tap the arrow button or the Back button below the screen when you're ready to leave Street View.

> ⌐🗒 **TIP**   In Street View, tap the screen to display the onscreen controls, and then tap the button with the two curling arrows to make Street View change direction as you turn your device. This feature is great for using Street View to explore the place you're actually in.

■ **Measure distance.** Drop a pin on the starting point, tap the pin's label to display the place info sheet, and then tap Measure Distance. A marker appears. Drag the map, stretching out a dotted green line from the marker to the starting point, and then tap Add Point when you need to add a turning point. The distance so far appears in the lower-left corner of the screen. Tap the arrow button or the Back button below the screen when you finish.

SAVING MAPS FOR OFFLINE USE

When you want to be able to access a map even if you have no Internet connection, you can save it for offline use. You can then view the map as needed, update it when your device is online, and delete it when you no longer require it.

SAVING A MAP FOR OFFLINE USE

Here's how to save a map for offline use:

1. Display a map of the area you want to save for offline use. You can do this either by browsing or by searching.

2. Tap the Navigation Panel button or swipe in from the left to display the navigation panel.

3. Tap the Offline Areas button to display the Offline Areas screen.

4. Tap the Download a New Offline Area button (the + icon). Maps display the Download This Area screen, showing the map you were viewing in step 1.

> **☑ TIP** Look at the "Download may take up to" readout at the bottom of the Download This Area screen, which shows how much space the download may take up and how much space is available on your device.

5. Tap the Download button. The Name Offline Area dialog box opens.
6. Type the name you want to give the saved map.
7. Tap the Save button. Maps downloads the area and briefly displays the Offline Area Download Complete readout to let you know it has done so.

DISPLAYING AND WORKING WITH YOUR SAVED MAPS

To display or work with saved maps, first display the Offline Areas screen by tapping the Navigation Panel button and then tapping the Offline Areas button on the navigation panel.

You can then open a map by tapping it in the list. From the map's screen, you can tap the Update button to update the map with the latest information available, or tap the Delete button to delete the map.

> **☑ TIP** You can set the Maps app to update offline areas automatically. To do so, tap the Settings button (the gear icon) on the Offline Areas screen, and then set the Automatically Update Offline Areas switch on the Offline Settings screen to On. Next, tap the Download Preferences button to open the Download Preferences dialog box and tap the Over Wi-Fi Only (Default) radio button or the Over Wi-Fi or Mobile Network radio button, as needed. Unless you have an unlimited data plan, the Over Wi-Fi Only setting is the better choice.

> **✎ NOTE** The Maps app automatically deletes your saved maps after 30 days. By updating your maps, you can keep them longer.

To rename a map, tap the Edit button (the pencil icon). In the Rename Area dialog box that opens, type the new name, and then tap the Save button.

CHOOSING KEY SETTINGS FOR MAPS

If you use the Maps app heavily, spend a few minutes configuring its settings. Tap the Navigation Panel button or swipe in from the left to display the navigation panel, and then tap the Settings button to display the Settings screen. (See the left screen in Figure 7.11.) You can then configure these settings:

■ **Edit Home or Work.** To set or change your home address or your work address, tap this button, and then tap the Enter Home Address button (or the Edit Home Address button) or the Enter Work Address button (or the Edit Work Address button).

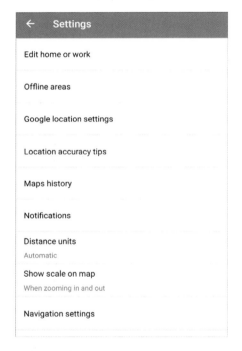
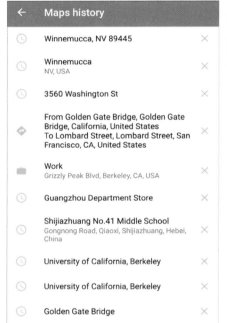

FIGURE 7.11

From the Settings screen (left) in the Maps app, you can edit your home and work addresses, delete indiscretions from your Maps History (right), and change the distance units.

■ **Google Location Settings.** Tap this button to jump to the Location screen in the Settings app, where you can choose the location mode and see which apps have requested your location recently.

■ **Offline Areas.** Tap this button to display the Offline Areas screen. You can then choose settings as explained in the nearby tip.

- **Google Location Settings.** Tap this button to display the Location screen in the Settings app, where you can change your location mode.

- **Location Accuracy Tips.** Tap this button to display the Location Accuracy Tips dialog box, which tells you the Google Location Settings you can choose to improve location accuracy. If you're already using the most accurate settings, Maps displays a message telling you that your location setting is already optimized.

- **Maps History.** Tap this button to display the Maps History screen (see the right screen in Figure 7.11), which shows a list of the places you've visited in Maps. You can tap the × icon on the right of a history item to display the Delete dialog box, and then tap the Delete button to delete that item from your Maps History.

- **Notifications.** Tap this button to display the Notifications screen. Here, you can check the Questions About Places box if you want to share information about places you've visited. You can also check the Traffic from Nearby Events box if you want to receive warnings about nearby events, such as road closures, that may affect traffic.

- **Distance Units.** Tap this button to display the Distance Units dialog box. You can then tap the Automatic radio button, the Kilometers radio button, or the Miles radio button, as needed.

- **Show Scale on Map.** Tap this button to display the Show Scale on Map dialog box, and then tap the When Zooming In and Out radio button or the Always radio button, as needed.

- **Navigation Settings.** Tap this button to display the Navigation Settings screen. Here, you can tap the Voice Level button to display the Voice Level dialog box, and then tap the Louder radio button, the Normal radio button, or the Softer radio button, as needed. You can check the Play Voice over Bluetooth box to have Maps play the voice through the Bluetooth device you have connected; tap the Play Test Sound button to make sure this is working. You can also check the Tilt Map box if you want to be able to change the perspective by tilting the map away from you.

- **Shake to Send Feedback.** Check this box if you want to be able to start giving feedback by shaking your device. Tap the Send Feedback button in the Shake to Send Feedback dialog box that opens.

EXPLORING THE HEAVENS WITH GOOGLE SKY MAP

If you enjoy exploring maps on your Android device, download and install the Google Sky Map app. This app is free from the Play Store and provides a fascinating view of the stars and planets.

The app follows the direction your device is pointing, so you can hold it up to the skies and see which heavenly bodies you're gazing at. The Time Travel feature enables you to whizz through time to view the positions of the stars and planets at a particular point, such as the next sunset, the next full moon, or the Apollo 11 moon landing.

8

BROWSING WITH CHROME

This chapter shows you how to get the most out of Chrome, the Google-built browser that comes with Android. You'll learn how to make the most of Chrome's integration with your Google account to share bookmarks and tabs among your Chrome-enabled devices and to send web pages from Chrome on your desktop computer to Chrome on your Android device for online or offline viewing.

This chapter will also show you where to find the many clever features hidden in and behind Chrome's apparently straightforward interface. You'll learn how to configure Chrome for best performance and to keep your private information secure because even the apparently harmless activity of browsing the Web exposes you to a variety of attacks.

NOTE Some Android devices come with other browsers as well as Chrome or instead of it. For example, most Samsung smart phones and tablets include Samsung's browser, which is usually called Internet but also sometimes called Browser, as well as Chrome. Chrome is free, so if your device doesn't have Chrome, open the Play Store app, search for *google chrome*, and install it.

CHOOSING ESSENTIAL CHROME SETTINGS

To get the most out of Chrome and to protect yourself online, spend a few minutes configuring the app with suitable settings before you use it on the Web.

Launch Chrome by tapping its icon on the Home screen or the Apps screen. Chrome displays the Most Visited tab, from which you can quickly open one of your frequently visited websites. For now, tap the Menu button to open the menu, and then tap the Settings button to display the Settings screen. (See Figure 8.1.)

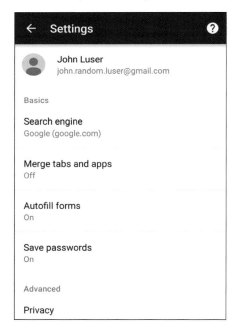 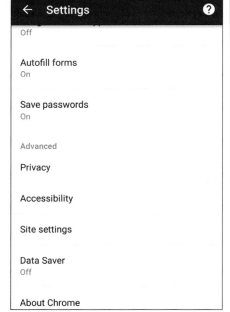

FIGURE 8.1

From the Settings screen, you can change your Google account and search engine; configure the Autofill Forms feature; and choose settings for privacy, accessibility, content settings, and bandwidth management.

✓ TIP Instead of tapping the Menu button, lifting your finger, and then tapping Settings on the menu, you can tap the Menu button, keep your finger on the screen, slide your finger down to Settings, and then lift it. See if you find this method of giving menu commands more comfortable than regular tapping.

CONFIGURING YOUR GOOGLE ACCOUNT

To get Chrome to sync the material you want, you must set it up with your Google account. At the top of the Settings screen is a button that shows the account that Chrome is set up to use. If this is the wrong account, you can change it easily enough; but even if it's the right account, you should make sure it's set to sync the right items. You should also encrypt some or all of the data you're syncing.

So tap the button with the Google account name to display the settings screen for the account. (See the left screen in Figure 8.2.)

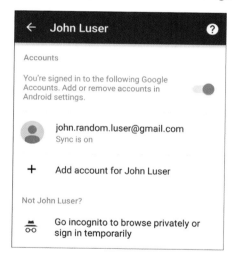
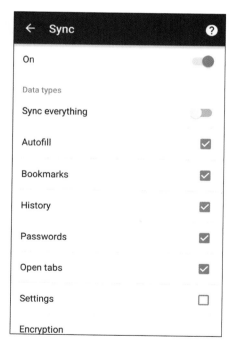

FIGURE 8.2

On the screen for your Google account (left), you can access that account's settings, add another account for the same person, or go incognito to browse privately. On the Sync screen (right), choose which data types to sync and whether to apply encryption.

> **NOTE** If Chrome is using the wrong Google account, you can tap the Add Account for [Your Name] button to display the Add Your Account screen, and then set up a different account. If you want to browse privately, tap the Go Incognito to Browse Privately or Sign In Temporarily button. We'll look at incognito browsing in the section "Browsing Incognito," later in this chapter.

Tap the button with your account name to display the Sync screen. (See the right screen in Figure 8.2.)

You can turn sync on or off by moving the switch at the top of the screen. Normally, you'll want to keep sync turned on so that you can enjoy its benefits.

Set the Sync Everything switch to On if you want to sync all the items. This is normally your best move unless you don't want to sync particular items, such as history or passwords. If you want to pick and choose, set the Sync Everything switch to Off, and then check the box for each item you want to sync:

- **Autofill.** Autofill, also called Autofill Forms, automatically fills in standard data, such as your address, in web forms. See the section "Setting Up Autofill Forms," later in this chapter, for details.

- **Bookmarks.** Your bookmarks enable you to quickly return to the web pages you mark. You can share bookmarks among the devices on which you use Chrome.

- **History.** Your history contains the list of web pages you've visited using Chrome on your devices.

- **Passwords.** Chrome can store your passwords and enter them automatically for you.

- **Open Tabs.** Chrome syncs the list of open tabs with your Android device, enabling you to pick up your browsing seamlessly on your phone or tablet viewing the same pages you left open on your computer.

- **Settings.** Chrome syncs applicable settings across your devices. Syncing settings is usually a good idea.

Your next move is to set up encryption on what you're syncing. You can encrypt only your passwords if you want, but normally it's best to encrypt all the data you sync.

Tap the Encryption button to display the Encryption dialog box, and then tap the radio button for the setting you want:

- **Encrypt Passwords with Google Credentials.** Tap this radio button to use your Google account credentials to encrypt your synced passwords.

■ **Encrypt All with Passphrase.** Tap this radio button to encrypt all your data using a passphrase of your choice that you enter in the Encrypt All with Passphrase dialog box. This is the more secure option. Choose a strong password and commit it to memory. Chrome stores the passphrase on your device and doesn't send it to Google.

TIP To create a strong password, use at least 8 characters and preferably 12 to 20. Combine uppercase and lowercase letters with numbers and symbols (such as $ or %). Avoid using any word or misspelling of a word in any language.

CAUTION After you encrypt all your synced data using a passphrase, you cannot change to encrypting only passwords unless you completely reset synchronization. To reset synchronization, tap the Manage Synced Data button at the bottom of the Sync screen to display the Chrome Sync page in your Google account, and then tap the Reset Sync button in the Having Trouble with Sync or Your Passphrase area.

After choosing your sync options, tap the arrow button in the upper-left corner of the screen or the Back button below the screen to return to the screen for your Google account. Tap the arrow button or the Back button again to return to the Settings screen.

CHOOSING YOUR SEARCH ENGINE

Chrome can use several different search engines. To choose the one you want, tap the Search Engine button on the Settings screen, and then tap the appropriate button in the Search Engine dialog box. (See the left screen in Figure 8.3.)

The available search engines vary depending on your device's manufacturer and your location. But you'll typically be able to choose from the major engines such as Google, Yahoo!, and Bing.

Your selected search engine shows *"Location is allowed"* or *"Location is blocked"* in blue under its name. To change whether the search engine may use your location, tap this blue Location message. On the Site Settings screen that appears (see the right screen in Figure 8.3), tap the Location Access button in the Permissions area, and then tap the Allow radio button or the Block radio button in the dialog box that opens.

 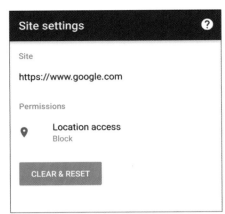

FIGURE 8.3

In the Search Engine dialog (left), tap the search engine. You can then tap the blue Location readout to display the Site Settings screen (right), and tap Location Access to enable or disable location access.

CHOOSING WHETHER TO MERGE TABS AND APPS ON A PHONE

On a phone, you can choose whether to merge Chrome's tabs with the apps and windows on the Overview screen or whether to use Chrome's built-in tab-switcher. On the Settings screen, tap the Merge Tabs and Apps button to display the Merge Tabs and Apps screen, and then set the Merge Tabs and Apps switch to On or Off, as needed.

> **TIP** Merge Tabs and Apps is a divisive feature. Some people love having their Chrome tabs appear on the Overview screen; others prefer to keep the tabs within Chrome. So try enabling Merge Tabs and Apps and see whether it suits you; if it doesn't, go back to the tab-switcher.

SETTING UP AUTOFILL FORMS

The Autofill Forms feature enables you to store data you need for filling in online forms, such as your name, address, and credit card details. You set up Autofill Forms by turning it on and adding your profile and any credit cards you want to be able to use easily.

On the Settings screen, tap the Autofill Forms button to display the Autofill Forms screen (shown in the left screen in Figure 8.4 with an address and a credit card added). Set the switch to On, and then tap the Add (+) button on the Addresses line to display the Add Address screen. Fill in the data you want to be able to use in the appropriate fields—Full Name, Address Line 1, and so on—and then tap the Save button. Lather, rinse, and repeat until you've set up all the profiles you need.

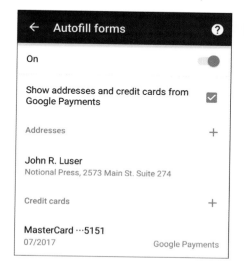
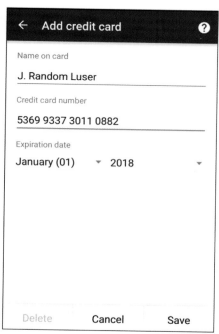

FIGURE 8.4

On the Autofill Forms screen (left), tap the Add (+) button on the Addresses line or the Credit Cards line. On the Add Credit Card screen (right), enter your card details.

If you want to save your credit card data, tap the Add (+) button on the Credit Cards line to display the Add Credit Card screen, type in the data, and then tap the Save button.

> **NOTE** At this writing, Autofill doesn't enable you to assign descriptive names (such as Capital One Visa or Work MasterCard) to your cards, so you need to be able to identify them by their last four digits.

WORKING WITH THE SAVE PASSWORDS FEATURE

Chrome can save your passwords for websites. This has two advantages: First, you don't have to laboriously type the passwords on your device's onscreen keyboard; and second, you can easily use passwords that are longer, more complex, and more secure.

To set Chrome to save your passwords, tap the Save Passwords button on the Settings screen to display the Save Passwords screen, and set the switch at the top to the On position. Now when you visit a website and enter your password, Chrome prompts you to allow it to save your password. Tap the Yes button or the Never button, as appropriate; if you want to postpone the decision until next time, tap the × button to close the prompt box.

The Passwords section at the top of the Save Passwords screen lists the sites for which you've saved passwords. To delete a password, tap the site's button, and then tap the Delete button on the Edit Saved Name/Password screen that appears.

The Never Saved section (further down the Save Passwords screen) lists sites for which you've entered a password but not saved it in Chrome. If you want to remove one of these sites, tap it to display the Edit Saved Name/Password screen, and then tap the Delete button.

CHOOSING PRIVACY SETTINGS AND CLEARING BROWSING DATA

Chrome includes a handful of privacy settings that you should configure to protect your privacy. From the Privacy screen, you can also clear your browsing data to remove potentially sensitive information.

Tap the Privacy button on the Settings screen to display the Privacy screen. (See the left screen in Figure 8.5.) You can then choose the following settings:

- **Navigation Error Suggestions.** This setting controls whether Chrome displays suggestions for web addresses it cannot resolve or reach. For example, if you type in **qupublishing.com** (missing the *e*) instead of **quepublishing.com**, Chrome cannot resolve the address. With Navigation Error Suggestions turned on, Chrome suggests the correct website. With Navigation Error Suggestions turned off, Chrome simply reports that the web page is not available.

- **Search and URL Suggestions.** This setting controls whether Chrome displays suggestions from a prediction service when you type in the omnibox. The suggestions may be helpful, but they could compromise your privacy.

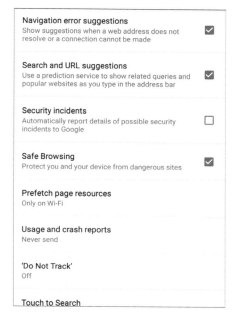

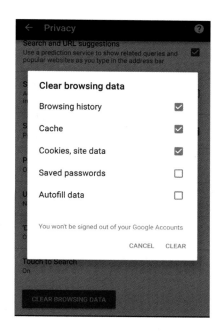

FIGURE 8.5

The Privacy screen (left) includes controls for choosing which suggestions to see and for clearing your browsing data. In the Clear Browsing Data dialog box (right), check the box for each item you want to clear, and then tap the Clear button.

- **Security Incidents.** Check this box to allow Chrome to automatically report to Google the details of any possible security incidents that occur while you're browsing.

> **NOTE** At this writing, the Security Incidents box and the Safe Browsing box do not appear on Chrome on tablets.

- **Safe Browsing.** Check this box to use the Safe Browsing feature, which attempts to warn you about any dangerous sites you try to access.
- **Prefetch Page Resources.** This setting controls whether Chrome looks up the IP addresses of all the links on the current web page so that it can more quickly load the page for whichever link you click. Tap the Prefetch Page Resources button to display the Prefetch Page Resources dialog box, and then tap the Always radio button (on a phone or cellular-capable tablet), the Only on Wi-Fi radio button, or the Never Radio button, as needed.

! CAUTION Prefetch Page Resources can speed up your browsing, so it's well worth trying. However, because it increases the amount of data that Chrome transfers, you normally don't want to choose the Always radio button unless you have an unlimited data plan or a generous plan within whose limits you normally stay without effort.

◻ NOTE The Prefetch Page Resources setting replaces the Network Action Predictions setting in earlier versions of Chrome. Prefetch Page Resources does pretty much the same thing as Network Action Predictions.

- **Usage and Crash Reports.** To control whether Chrome sends anonymized reports about your usage of the app and any crashes that occur, tap this button, and then tap the appropriate radio button in the Usage and Crash Reports dialog box: Always Send, Only Send on Wi-Fi, or Never Send. If you want to help Google develop Chrome, Only Send on Wi-Fi is the best choice.
- **'Do Not Track'.** If you want to request that websites not track you, tap this button to display the 'Do Not Track' screen, and then set the switch to the On position.

! CAUTION Some websites don't honor the Do Not Track request, so don't rely on Do Not Track to protect your privacy.

- **Touch to Search.** Tap this button to display the Touch to Search screen, on which you can set the switch at the top to On or Off, as needed. Touch to Search enables you to tap a word on a web page and have Google Search display results for it in its content. We'll look at how to use this feature later in this chapter. If the Touch to Search button doesn't appear on the Privacy screen on your device, see the next sidebar titled "Using chrome://flags to Enable Touch to Search" for instructions on enabling this feature.

If you want to clear your browsing data, tap the Clear Browsing Data button to display the Clear Browsing Data dialog box. (See the right screen in Figure 8.5.) You can then check the box for each item you want to delete:

- **Browsing History.** Your browsing history is the list of web pages you have visited.
- **Cache.** The cache contains data that Chrome has stored temporarily to enable itself to quickly load web pages when you return to them.

- **Cookies, Site Data.** Cookies are small text files that web servers store on your device to help them track what you do on their websites. For example, some websites use cookies to implement shopping carts or to give you a quick-access list of products you have browsed recently.

> **✓ TIP**   You can delete data for websites one by one instead of deleting all your cookies and site data. You can also refuse cookies. See the section "Choosing Site Settings," later in this chapter.

- **Saved Passwords.** This setting enables you to get rid of all your saved passwords at once instead of deleting them one by one, as discussed earlier in this chapter.
- **Autofill Data.** This setting deletes your Autofill data. See the section "Setting Up Autofill Forms," earlier in this chapter.

After making your choices, tap the Clear button.

USING CHROME://FLAGS TO ENABLE TOUCH TO SEARCH

If the Touch to Search button doesn't appear on the Privacy screen in Chrome's Settings on your device, you can enable it by going to the chrome://flags screen.

Tap the omnibox, type **chrome://flags**, and then tap the Go button (the green circle with a white arrow pointing to the right) on the keyboard. You'll see a page titled Careful, These Experiments May Bite, which contains an Experiments list full of cryptic settings such as Enable Slimming Paint and Enable Support for WebRTC Stun Origin Header.

Tap the Menu button to open the menu, and then tap Find in Page to display the Find in Page box at the top. Start typing **contextual** and then tap the Enable Contextual Search item. (Tapping hides the onscreen keyboard.) Tap the pop-up menu under the Enable Contextual Search heading, and then tap Enabled in the pop-up menu.

To make the change take effect, tap the Relaunch Now button that appears at the bottom of the screen. Chrome closes and then reopens to the Careful, These Experiments May Bite page.

If the change doesn't seem to have positive effects, or if you decide to play with any of the other experiments, you can tap the Reset All to Default button to the right of the Experiments heading on the Careful, These Experiments May Bite page to restore Chrome's normal settings.

CHOOSING ACCESSIBILITY SETTINGS

If you find the size of text on web pages hard to read, you can use Chrome's Text Scaling feature to enlarge it. Tap the Accessibility button on the Settings screen to display the Accessibility screen, and then drag the Text Scaling slider until the text in the Preview box is the size you want. You can then apply text scaling by double-tapping a paragraph on a web page.

Some websites request that web browsers not let you zoom in on the site. Usually, the reason is that the website designer wants to ensure you view the site at a standard size for artistic reasons. This may make the site unreadable on a small screen even if you have good eyesight.

To deal with this problem, check the Force Enable Zoom box on the Accessibility screen. Chrome then enables you to zoom in even if the website requests no zooming.

CHOOSING SITE SETTINGS

Next, tap the Site Settings button to display the Site Settings screen. (See Figure 8.6.) "Site Settings" sounds pretty harmless, but the settings here can make a huge difference to your browsing and your security, so take a minute to choose suitable settings.

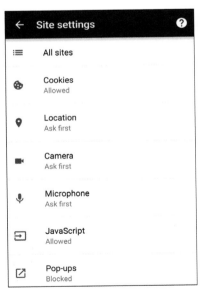
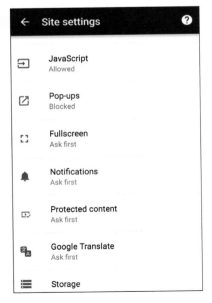

FIGURE 8.6
On the Site Settings screen (left and right), you can control cookies; access to location data, the camera, and the microphone; JavaScript; pop-ups; and more.

The following list explains the site settings. The settings appear in slightly different orders in different versions of Chrome, so if you're following along on your phone or tablet, you may need to skip backward and forward at times. Some settings, such as Images, don't appear in some versions.

■ **All Sites.** Tap this button to display the All Sites screen (shown on the left in Figure 8.7). You can then tap a site to display its Site Settings screen (shown on the right in Figure 8.7). Here, you can see how much data the site has stored. You can get rid of all the data the site has stored by tapping the Delete icon (the trash can) and then tapping the Clear All button in the Clear Stored Data dialog box that opens. If you want to clear all the data the site has stored *and* reset the permissions for the site, tap the Clear & Reset button on the Site Settings screen, and then tap the Clear & Reset button in the Clear & Reset dialog box that opens.

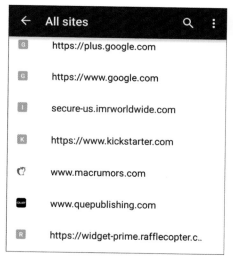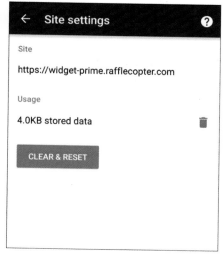

FIGURE 8.7

On the All Sites screen (left), browse the list of sites that have stored data on your device. Tap a site's button to display the Site Settings screen for the site (right), on which you can clear and reset the site's data.

■ **Cookies.** Tap this button to display the Cookies screen. (See the left screen in Figure 8.8.) You can then set the Cookies switch to On or Off to control whether sites may store cookies, the text files that web servers use to track your movements on their sites, on your device. If you set the Cookies switch to On, you can check or uncheck the Allow Third-Party Cookies box to control whether third-party sites can store cookies.

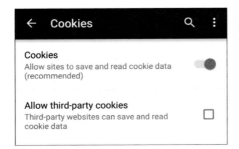 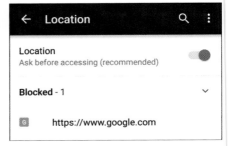

FIGURE 8.8

On the Cookies screen (left), set the Cookies switch to On, and then uncheck the Allow Third-Party Cookies box. On the Location screen (right), set the Location switch to On.

> **! CAUTION** Turning off cookies helps protect your privacy, but it prevents many websites from working properly. Normally, it is best to set the Cookies switch to On but to uncheck the Allow Third-Party Cookies box. Doing this allows the sites you visit to store cookies on your devices but prevents third-party parties, such as advertisers on those sites, from storing cookies on your device.

■ **Location.** Tap this button to display the Location screen. (See the right screen in Figure 8.8.) You can then set the Location switch to On or Off to enable or disable websites to request access to location data. If you have blocked any sites, they appear in the Blocked list, which you can expand or collapse by tapping its heading. If you set the Location switch to On, you get to approve or deny each request for location access.

> **! CAUTION** Setting the switch on the Location screen to the Off position disables Location Services for all apps, not just for Chrome. Normally, it's best to set the switch to the On position and confirm or deny the individual location requests when Chrome displays them. Judge the requests individually: Some websites require your location—for example, to provide information about novel dining experiences within strolling distance—but others are just plain nosy.

■ **Camera.** Tap this button to display the Camera screen. Here, you can tap the Android Settings link to display the App Info screen for the Chrome app. On this screen, tap the Permissions button to display the App Permissions screen for Chrome. You can then set the Camera switch to On to enable Chrome to use the cameras.

> **NOTE** In early versions of Marshmallow, the Camera screen shows a Camera switch that you can set to On or Off to control whether websites can request access to your device's cameras. If you set the Camera switch to On, you get to approve or deny each request for camera access. Similarly, the Microphone screen shows a Microphone switch that you can set to On or Off to control whether websites can request to use the microphone. If you see these switches on the Camera screen and Microphone screen, see if an update to a new version of Marshmallow is available for your device.

■ **Microphone.** Tap this button to display the Microphone screen. Here, you can tap the Android Settings link to display the App Info screen for the Chrome app. On this screen, tap the Permissions button to display the App Permissions screen for Chrome. You can then set the Microphone switch to On to enable Chrome to use the microphone.

■ **Notifications.** Tap this button to display the Notifications screen, on which you can set the Notifications switch to On or Off to control whether websites can request to send you notifications. Again, you get to approve or deny these requests.

> **NOTE** The settings for JavaScript work differently from those explained so far. If you set the JavaScript switch to On, there's no confirmation about running scripts—you've enabled the capability, and sites can use it. But if you set the JavaScript switch to Off, the Add Site button appears. You can tap this button and use the Add Site dialog box to enter a site for which you will permit scripts while blocking scripts for the rest of the Web. Sites you enter this way appear in the Exceptions list.

■ **JavaScript.** Tap this button to display the JavaScript screen, on which you can set the JavaScript switch to On or Off to control whether sites can run scripts (small programs) written in the JavaScript scripting language. Websites use JavaScript to display dynamic content, such as displaying a moving series of images or news headlines.

> **TIP** JavaScript is different from Java, which is a full-power programming language with capabilities that can threaten a computer's security. Many security experts recommend disabling Java on desktop computers to help avoid problems. Android devices don't normally run Java, so it's not a threat.

- **Pop-Ups.** Tap this button to display the Pop-Ups screen, on which you can set the Pop-Ups switch to On or Off to control whether websites can display pop-up windows. Blocking pop-ups is a good idea, but you may need to disable pop-up blocking for all the features on some websites to work.

- **Fullscreen.** Tap this button to display the Fullscreen screen, on which you can set the Fullscreen switch to On or Off to control whether websites can switch Chrome to full-screen mode without asking (On) or whether they must ask first (Off; usually a good idea).

- **Protected Content.** Some websites provide premium videos that require Chrome to authenticate your device, proving it is authorized to play the videos. To enable Chrome to authenticate your device, tap the Protected Content button and set the Protected Content switch on the Protected Content screen to On if you want to allow websites to request authentication (with your approval each time) or to Off if you want to block such requests.

- **Language.** If you want to enable Chrome to use Google Translate to translate pages written in other languages, tap this button to display the Language screen, and then check the Google Translate box. On the Language screen, you can also check the Auto Detect Encoding box to make Chrome automatically determine which character encoding to use for displaying text.

- **Storage.** Tap this button to display the Storage screen, which displays a list of the websites that have stored data on your device. This list is similar to that on the All Sites screen (shown in Figure 8.7, earlier in this chapter) except that each entry includes the amount of space the site is occupying. The sites are sorted in descending order, so the greediest sites appear at the top. You can tap a website to display its Site Settings screen, on which you can work as explained earlier in this chapter: You can tap the Delete icon (the trash can) and then tap the Clear All button in the Clear Stored Data dialog box that opens to delete all the site's data; or you can tap the Clear & Reset button on the Site Settings screen and then tap the Clear & Reset button in the Clear & Reset dialog box that opens to clear all the data the site has stored *and* reset the permissions for the site.

ENABLING THE DATA SAVER FEATURE

Chrome includes a Data Saver feature that reduces the amount of data your device must download to display a web page. Enabling this feature routes the pages you download through Google's servers, which compress them to reduce the file size. Using the Reduce Data Usage feature also turns on Chrome's Safe Browsing system, which helps protect you against malicious web pages and malware.

To use the Data Saver feature, tap the Data Saver button on the Settings screen. On the Data Saver screen that appears, set the switch at the top to On. While the switch is set to Off, the Data Saver screen displays an explanation of the feature; when the switch is set to On, the Data Saver screen displays a graph showing your data savings by using the feature.

> **TIP** The Reduce Data Usage feature is well worth trying. However, if you find that it prevents you from accessing premium data services that your carrier provides, turn it off.

GIVING CHROME MORE RAM

If you use Chrome extensively, opening many tabs and visiting chunky sites, the app may run low on RAM. If you find Chrome starts to run slowly but other apps appear to be running normally, you can try giving Chrome more RAM.

Before you do this, if your device is running Marshmallow, look to see how much RAM Chrome has been using recently. Open the Settings app, tap Apps to display the Apps screen, and then tap Chrome. At the bottom of the App Info screen, look at the Memory readout, which says something like "59 MB avg memory used in last 3 hours."

(You can't check RAM usage like this on Lollipop. You should be able to see how much RAM Chrome is using by choosing Settings > Apps > Running and looking at the readout on the Running tab of the Apps screen—but for some reason Chrome doesn't appear there.)

To give Chrome more RAM, tap the omnibox, type **chrome://flags**, and then tap the Go button (the green circle with a white arrow pointing to the right) on the keyboard. The Careful, These Experiments May Bite page appears.

Tap the Menu button to open the menu, and then tap Find in Page to display the Find in Page box at the top. Type **max** and then tap the Maximum Tiles for Interest Area item. (Tapping hides the keyboard.) Tap the pop-up menu under the Maximum Tiles for Interest Area heading to display a dialog for choosing the amount of RAM, and then tap the 128 radio button, the 256 radio button, or the 512 radio button. The Default setting gives 64 megabytes (MB), as does the 64 radio button, so you'll normally want to choose a higher number.

To make the change take effect, tap the Relaunch Now button that appears at the bottom of the screen. Chrome closes and then reopens to the Careful, These Experiments May Bite page.

BROWSING THE WEB WITH CHROME

Now that you've configured Chrome to suit your device, your eyes, and the way you browse, you're ready to use the app to browse the Web.

NAVIGATING AMONG WEB PAGES

With Chrome open, you can quickly navigate from one web page to another. Figure 8.9 shows Chrome open on a phone with the main controls labeled.

> **TIP** To zoom a page, place two fingers on the screen and pinch outward (to zoom in) or pinch inward (to zoom out). To zoom the page so that a column of content appears at its full width in Chrome, double-tap that column.

Omnibox   Menu

Bookmark
Forward | Information Reload

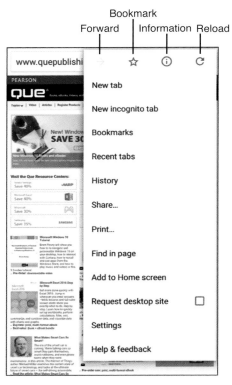

FIGURE 8.9

On a phone, Chrome hides its browsing power behind a straightforward interface (left). You access almost all the commands from the menu (right).

On a tablet, Chrome displays more controls because there's more space. Figure 8.10 shows Chrome open on a tablet with several tabs open (more on these later) and the same web page displayed as in Figure 8.9.

FIGURE 8.10

On a tablet, Chrome displays the tab bar for easy navigation, plus essential controls. The remaining controls are on the menu.

Here's how to navigate among web pages:

■ **Type in an address.** Tap the omnibox—the address box at the top of the screen—and type or paste in the address.

> ☑ **TIP** If the address appears as a link in another app, tap the link to open it in Chrome. For example, tap a link in an email message to open the linked page in Chrome. If the address appears but isn't a link, select it, copy it, and then paste it into the Chrome omnibox.

- **Open a linked page in the same tab.** Tap the link.
- **Open a linked page in a new tab.** Tap and hold the link, and then tap Open in New tab on the pop-up menu. (See Figure 8.11.) If you want to open the linked page in an incognito tab for private browsing, tap Open in Incognito Tab instead.

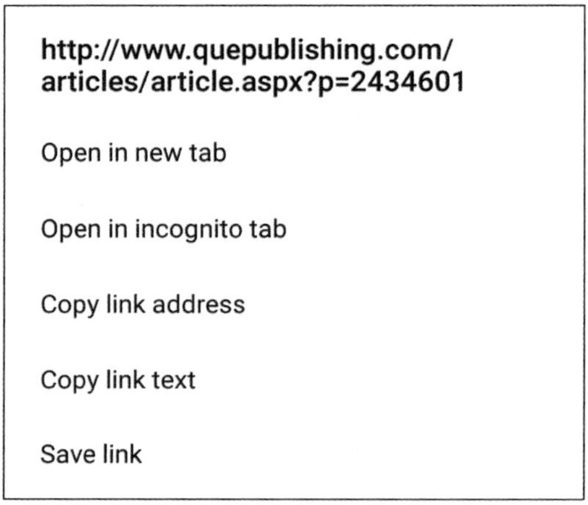

http://www.quepublishing.com/
articles/article.aspx?p=2434601

Open in new tab

Open in incognito tab

Copy link address

Copy link text

Save link

FIGURE 8.11

From the pop-up menu, you can open a link in a new tab or an incognito tab.

TIP To reload the current web page, tap the Reload button to the left of the omnibox on a tablet, or tap the Menu button and then tap Reload on a phone. You may want to reload the page to get updated information from it.

CHANGING YOUR DEFAULT BROWSER

If your device has multiple browsers installed, you can set one of them as the default browser. Your default browser is the one that opens when you tap a link in another app—for example, a link in an email message.

If you're not sure whether you have a default browser set, tap a link in another app and see what happens. (If you don't have a convenient link, send yourself an email message containing a link.) If a browser opens, that's the default. If the Open With dialog box opens, showing you a choice of browsers, tap the browser you want to make the default, and then tap the Always button.

If you want to change your default browser, open the Settings app and tap the Apps button to display the Apps screen.

On Lollipop, swipe left twice to display the All screen, and then locate the default browser in the alphabetical list. Tap the browser's button to display its App Info screen and then tap the Clear Defaults button.

On Marshmallow, tap the browser's entry on the Apps screen to display the App Info screen for the app. Tap the Open by Default button to display the Open by Default screen, and then tap the Clear Defaults button.

Now that you've cleared the default browser, you can set your default browser. On either Lollipop or Marshmallow, tap a link in another app, and the Open With dialog box opens. Tap the browser you want to use, and then tap the Always button.

MANAGING AND SWITCHING TABS

Chrome enables you to open multiple web pages at the same time by opening each page in a separate tab. You can open new tabs as needed, switch among your open tabs, and close any tabs you no longer need.

On a tablet, you switch among tabs by using the tab bar. As you'll see shortly, this is very straightforward.

On a phone, if you have enabled the Merge Tabs and Apps feature (as discussed in the section "Choosing Whether to Merge Tabs and Apps on a Phone," earlier in this chapter), you use the Overview screen to switch among tabs. If you have disabled Merge Tabs and Apps, you use Chrome's built-in tab-switcher instead.

OPENING A NEW TAB

You can open a new tab in a variety of ways:

- **From the menu.** Tap the Menu button and then tap the New Tab button.
- **From a link.** Tap and hold the link, and then tap Open in New Tab on the pop-up menu.
- **From the Tabs screen on a phone.** When Merge Tabs and Apps is disabled, tap the Tabs button in Chrome to display the Tabs screen (see the left screen in Figure 8.12), and then tap the New Tab (+) button. The Tabs button is the icon to the right of the omnibox, the icon showing a page outline and the current number of tabs.
- **From the tab bar on a tablet.** Tap the New Tab button, the short, blank tab button at the right end of the tab bar.

Tabs   New tab

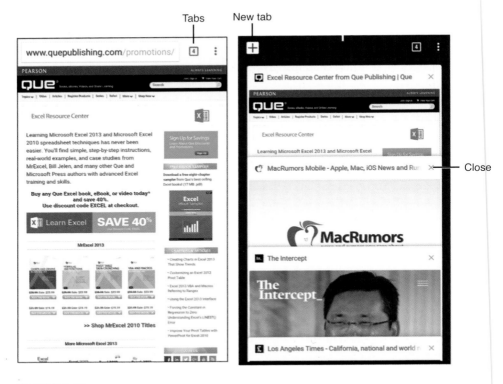

Close

FIGURE 8.12

On a phone with Merge Tabs and Apps disabled, tap the Tabs button (left) to display the Tabs screen (right) so you can open new tabs, close existing tabs, or display a different tab.

MANAGING AND SWITCHING TABS ON A PHONE

The way you manage your Chrome tabs on a phone depends on whether you've enabled or disabled the Merge Tabs and Apps feature.

When Merge Tabs and Apps is enabled, tap the Overview button below the screen to display the Overview screen. Your Chrome tabs appear mixed in with all your other app windows. Scroll down if necessary until you can see the thumbnail for the tab you want, and then tap that thumbnail to display the tab in Chrome. To close a tab, either tap its × button or swipe the thumbnail left or right off the Overview screen.

When Merge Tabs and Apps is disabled, tap the Tabs button in Chrome and work on the Tabs screen (shown on the right in Figure 8.12). Here you can do the following:

- **Examine a tab.** Tap a tab and drag your finger down to display more of the tab in the tab list.
- **Display a tab.** Tap the tab to display the web page full screen.
- **Close a tab.** Tap its × button or swipe it to the right off the list.
- **Close all tabs.** Tap the menu button and then tap Close All Tabs.

On a phone, you can switch tabs and display the Tabs screen by swiping at the top of the Chrome screen. If the Omnibox is displayed, swipe on that; if the Omnibox isn't displayed, swipe in the space where it would be. Swipe left or right to switch tabs, or swipe down to display the Tabs screen.

MANAGING AND SWITCHING TABS ON A TABLET

On a tablet, your open tabs appear on the tab bar (refer to Figure 8.10), which enables you to switch among them easily:

- **Display a tab.** Tap the tab you want to display.
- **Display a different section of the tab bar.** When you have many tabs open, tap and drag to display a different section of the tab bar.
- **Close a tab.** Tap its × button.

> **TIP** On a tablet, you can drag your tabs into a different order if you want. For example, you may want to group related tabs together for reference.

MAKING THE MOST OF BOOKMARKS

When you want to be able to easily return to a web page, create a bookmark for it. You can store bookmarks on your device, but to get more out of them, you can sync your bookmarks via your Google account, making bookmarks you create on your computer available on your Android devices, and vice versa.

CREATING A BOOKMARK

To create a bookmark for the current web page on a phone, tap the Menu button and then tap the empty star button at the top of the menu. The Add Bookmark screen appears, and you can name the bookmark and assign it to a folder.

> **NOTE** A bookmark stores only the address of a web page, so when you return to the bookmark, you see the latest version of the page. For example, if you bookmark the home page of a news site, the page will often have changed by the time you return.

To create a bookmark for the current web page on a tablet, tap the empty star button at the right end of the omnibox. The Add Bookmark dialog box opens, and you can name the bookmark and assign it to a folder.

The Add Bookmark screen and the Add Bookmark dialog box work in the same way:

- **Name.** Enter the name for the bookmark in this box. Chrome suggests the web page's title, but this is often awkwardly long, and you'll do better to type a short but descriptive name.
- **URL.** This box shows the web page's address. You can change the address, but if you started from the right page, you shouldn't need to change it.
- **Folder.** This box shows the folder into which Chrome will put the bookmark. To change the folder, tap the button, and then tap the right folder on the Choose a Folder screen or in the Choose a Folder dialog box. You can tap the New Folder button to create a new folder within the current folder.
- **Save.** After naming the bookmark and picking the folder, tap the Save button to save the bookmark.

> **TIP** Bookmarks are great, but if you need to go to a particular web page very frequently, put that page on your Home screen. Go to the page in Chrome, tap the Menu button, and then tap Add to Home Screen on the menu. The Add to Home Screen dialog box opens, and you can type the text for the shortcut in the text box and then tap the Add button.

GOING TO A BOOKMARK

After creating a bookmark, you can go back to the site in moments:

1. Tap the Menu button and then tap Bookmarks on the menu to display the Bookmarks screen.
2. Navigate to the folder that contains the bookmark.
3. Tap the bookmark to go to it.

> **TIP** To delete a bookmark, tap and hold it until the pop-up menu appears, and then tap Delete Bookmark. To edit the bookmark or move it to a different folder, tap and hold the bookmark, and then tap Edit Bookmark on the pop-up menu.

RETURNING TO A RECENT TAB OR A TAB OPEN ON ANOTHER DEVICE

To visit a tab you've recently closed, tap the Menu button, and then tap the Recent Tabs button on the menu to display the Recent Tabs screen. You can then tap the tab you want to reopen in the Recently Closed list.

The Recent Tabs screen shows a list of Chrome tabs open on the other devices that you sync using the same Google account. Tap the tab for the page you want to see, and you can pick up your browsing where you left off.

RETURNING TO A PAGE YOU VISITED EARLIER

When you want to return to a page that you visited earlier but that you didn't bookmark, you can use your history to find the page quickly. The history is a list of the web pages you have visited, with the most recent page first.

To view your history, tap the Menu button, and then tap History on the menu. The History screen appears. You can browse to find the page you want or tap the Search History box and type a search term. When you find the relevant history item, tap it to go straight to that page.

> **NOTE** If you've signed in to your Google account, the History screen displays the history from all your devices that are signed in to the same account. This enables you to browse more seamlessly no matter which device you're using.

> **TIP** If your history contains potentially embarrassing items, you can delete them by tapping the × button at the right end of their buttons. If there are too many sensitive items to delete individually, you can clear your history instead. See the section "Choosing Privacy Settings and Clearing Browsing Data," earlier in this chapter, for details.

SEARCHING FOR INFORMATION

Chrome allows you to search for information in three main ways:

- **Using your default search engine.** Tap the omnibox and type your search terms. In the list of suggestions that Chrome displays, tap the one you want.

> **☑ TIP** To search by voice, tap the omnibox (selecting its contents), and then tap the × button at the right end to delete the selection. Tap the microphone icon that appears in place of the × icon, and then say what you want.

- **Using another search engine.** You can use any web-based search engine by going to its web page and using the onscreen controls to search.
- **Using Touch to Search.** If you have enabled the Touch to Search feature, touch and hold a word onscreen to display a Google panel at the bottom containing brief information about that word. Tap this panel to expand it so that you can examine its contents, or drag it all the way to the top of the screen if you want to dig into the details.

BROWSING INCOGNITO

Normally, when you browse the Web, your browser adds the web pages you visit to your history list so that you can revisit them if you want. History can be a great way of returning to the past, but at times you may want to turn it off so that you can browse the Web without Chrome saving the details of where you went.

> **! CAUTION** Incognito browsing prevents pages from being added to your history list, but the websites you visit can still track your movements, as can your ISP. Government agencies may be able to get your browsing information from your ISP. Don't assume incognito browsing means anonymity.

When you want to turn off history, open an incognito tab by tapping the Menu button and then tapping the New Incognito Tab button. Chrome displays the tab, using different coloring and the incognito symbol (a head with hat, shades, and turned-up collar) to make clear that the tab is incognito. (See Figure 8.13.)

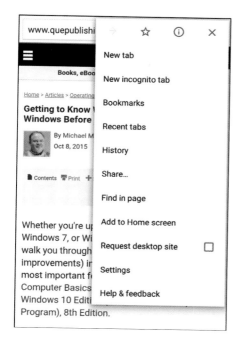

FIGURE 8.13

Open the menu and tap New Incognito Tab (left) to open an incognito tab (right) when you want to browse without adding the pages you visit to your history.

On a phone, if you've enabled the Merge Tabs and Apps feature, both the regular tabs and the incognito tabs appear on the Overview screen. Otherwise, if Merge Tabs and Apps is disabled on a phone, or if you're using a tablet, Chrome keeps incognito tabs separate from regular tabs so that you can easily distinguish the two. Here's how to switch between incognito tabs and regular tabs:

- **Phone.** Tap the Tabs button to display the Tabs screen. Swipe right to move from the list of incognito tabs to the list of regular tabs; swipe left to go from regular tabs to incognito tabs.

- **Tablet.** Tap the Switch Tabs button, the button that appears at the right end of the tab bar.

> **!CAUTION** When you finish using incognito mode, you must close all your incognito tabs to get rid of the details of your incognito browsing session.

REQUESTING A DESKTOP SITE

Many websites offer both a desktop version of web pages and a mobile version. The desktop version of a page is designed for a larger screen and a mouse or similar pointing device, whereas the mobile version of a page is designed for a smaller screen and touch-based controls. As a result, the desktop version and mobile version may differ hugely from one another.

> [✏️ **NOTE**] Some web servers don't honor the request for the desktop version.

Normally, when you access a web page using the Chrome browser on your Android device, the web server delivers the mobile version of the page. If that is not what you want, tap the Menu button and then tap Request Desktop Site, checking the box. Chrome reloads the web page, displaying the desktop version this time.

> [✏️ **NOTE**] The Request Desktop Site feature remains turned on for the tab on which you checked the box, but you need to turn it on separately for each new tab you open.

PLAY DINOSAUR-VERSUS-CACTUS WHILE OFFLINE

When you're offline, Chrome displays the message "You are offline" beneath a cartoon dinosaur icon. If you need entertainment on a phone, tap the dinosaur to start it running, and then tap the screen to jump each cactus the dinosaur approaches. The game ends when the dinosaur hits a cactus; tap the dinosaur again to start again.

IN THIS CHAPTER

- Managing your contacts and your schedule
- Transferring and syncing files with Google Drive
- Printing documents
- Using Chromecast devices

MAXIMIZING YOUR PRODUCTIVITY

In this chapter, you'll learn how to use your Android device to maximize your productivity. You'll go through managing your contacts with the Contacts app and managing your schedule with the Calendar app, and then you'll use Google Drive to transfer and sync files. Finally, you'll learn how to print documents from your device as well as other productivity-enhancing moves, such as cordoning off your work files from your personal files and controlling your computer using your Android device.

MANAGING YOUR CONTACTS

Android's Contacts app gives you an easy way to store the information about your contacts. After launching the Contacts app from the Apps screen, you can quickly browse your existing contacts by using the Favorites tab or the

All Contacts tab. (See the left screen in Figure 9.1.) To navigate between the Favorites tab and the All Contacts tab, either tap the tab buttons at the top of the screen or swipe left or right.

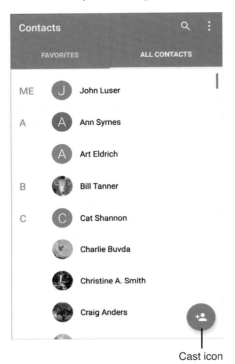
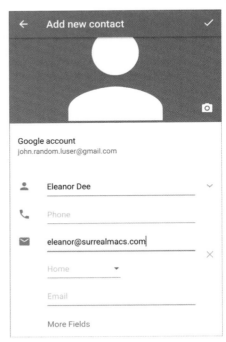

Cast icon

FIGURE 9.1

The Contacts app has a stripped-down interface featuring two tabs: Favorites and All Contacts (left). Tap the blue Add Contact button in the lower-right corner to display the Add New Contact screen (right). On a phone, you can access your contacts through the Phone app as well as through the Contacts app.

> ☑ **TIP** If you want to be able to tell from the ringing which of your contacts is phoning you, set a distinctive ringtone for each key contact. To set the ringtone, open the contact, tap the Edit button (the pencil icon) to display the Edit screen, tap the Menu button, and then tap Set Ringtone. In the Ringtones dialog box, tap the radio button for the ringtone you want, and then tap the OK button.

ADDING A NEW CONTACT

To add a new contact, tap the New Contact button in the lower-right corner of either the Favorites tab or the Contacts tab. If you have set up multiple accounts, the Contacts app may prompt you to choose the account in which to create the contact; alternatively, you can tap the Add New Account button to add another account, and then add the contact to that account.

After you've chosen the account, the Add New Contact screen appears, and you can fill in the information for the contact. In Marshmallow, the Add New Contact screen shows just a few fields—such as Name, Phone, and Email—at first; to see the remaining fields, tap the More Fields button. In Lollipop, the Add New Contact screen shows all the fields right from the start.

When you have entered all the available information, save the contact in one of these ways:

- **Marshmallow.** Tap the Done button (the check mark in the upper-right corner of the screen).

- **Lollipop.** Tap the arrow button or the Back button below the screen.

> **NOTE** You can add to a contact record at any point. Tap the contact to display the existing contact information, tap the Edit button (the pencil icon) to open the record for editing, and then enter the new information.

ORGANIZING YOUR CONTACTS INTO GROUPS

You can organize your contacts by allocating them to groups such as Friends, Family, Coworkers, or Inner Circle. The Contacts app comes with several built-in groups, but you can create as many other groups as you need. You can assign any contact to a single group or to multiple groups, and you can make the Contacts app display only the contacts in a particular group or in several groups.

> **NOTE** In KitKat and some earlier Android versions, the Contacts app included a Groups tab and group-editing functionality that enabled you to work with groups much more easily than the current Contacts app in Lollipop and Marshmallow does. Google seems to have removed the Groups tab and the group-editing functionality to streamline the interface, but the result is that groups are now much harder to work with.

To add a contact to a group, open that contact's record for editing. On Marshmallow, tap the More Fields button if necessary to display the remaining fields, including the Groups field. Tap the Group Name pop-up menu to display the list of groups (see the left screen in Figure 9.2), and then check the box for each group you want to add the contact to.

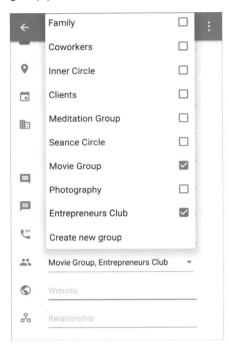
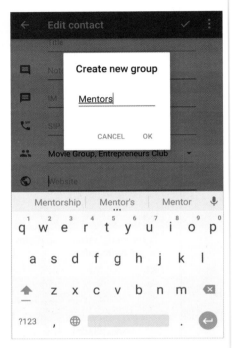

FIGURE 9.2

To add a contact to a group, tap the Group Name pop-up menu, and then check the box for the group (left). To create a new group, tap Create New Group at the bottom of the menu, type the name in the Create New Group dialog box, and then tap the OK button (right).

If you want to create a new group, tap the Group Name pop-up menu, and then tap the Create New Group button at the bottom of the list of groups. In the Create New Group dialog box that opens, type the group name, and then tap the OK button.

You can then start using the group, but you can only add contacts to the group or remove contacts from the group one at a time—by opening each contact's record, displaying the Group Name pop-up menu, and then checking or unchecking the group's name on the list.

DISPLAYING ONLY THE CONTACTS YOU WANT TO SEE

By default, the Contacts app displays all the contacts you've added to it. If you have many contacts, you may find it helpful to narrow down the display to only those groups you need to see at any particular time.

Here's how to control which contacts appear:

1. Tap the Menu button and then tap Contacts to Display to display the Contacts to Display screen. (See the left screen in Figure 9.3.)

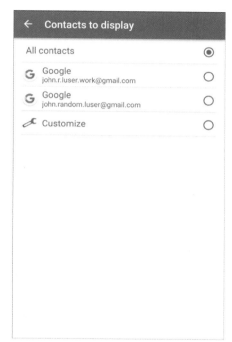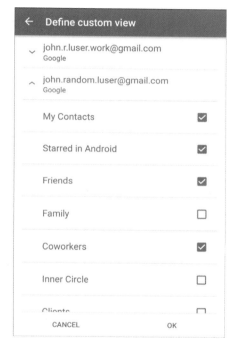

FIGURE 9.3

On the Contacts to Display screen (left), you can either tap an account's radio button or tap the Customize radio button to make a more complex selection on the Define Custom View screen (right).

2. If you want to display all the contacts in a particular account, tap the radio button for that account. If you want to display contacts from multiple accounts, tap the Customize radio button to display the Define Custom View screen. (See the right screen in Figure 9.3.)

3. Tap the downward caret to the left of an account's name to expand the account, showing the groups it contains.

4. Check the box for each contact group you want to display.

5. Tap the OK button.

> **NOTE** The Contacts app shows Contacts in Custom View or Contacts in *Account* at the top of the list to indicate that you've restricted the display to only some contacts. When you want to change the selection of contacts displayed, you can tap this bar to go straight to the Contacts to Display screen without having to open the menu.

MERGING AND SEPARATING CONTACTS

If you have two or more contact records for the same contact, you can combine the records to give a single record containing all the information. Marshmallow calls this *merging* contacts, whereas Lollipop and earlier versions of Android call it *joining* contacts.

Here's how to merge contacts:

1. Tap one of the contacts to open the contact record.

2. Tap the Edit button to open the contact for editing.

3. Tap the Menu button and then tap Merge (in Marshmallow) or Join (in Lollipop) to display the Join Contacts screen. (This screen is called Join Contacts in both Marshmallow and Lollipop.) The Suggested Contacts list at the top shows any contacts that Contacts thinks may be suitable.

4. Tap the appropriate contact. The Contacts Merged readout appears briefly in Marshmallow; in Lollipop, the Contacts Joined readout appears briefly.

5. Tap the Done button to stop editing the contact.

If you find you've merged two contacts by mistake, you can separate them. Open the contact for editing, tap the Menu button, and then tap Separate. The Separate Contact dialog box appears; tap the OK button to effect the separation.

> **NOTE** If you've merged more than two contacts, the Separate command separates them all; you can't separate one of the merged contacts without separating the others as well. So if you need to separate one contact but have two merged, you need to merge those two contacts again manually.

IMPORTING AND EXPORTING CONTACTS

The Contacts app makes it easy to import contacts from other sources and to export contacts you want to share. To get started, tap the Menu button and then tap Import/Export. In the Import/Export Contacts dialog box, tap the appropriate button:

- **Import from .vcf File.** Use this command to import contacts from either built-in storage or an SD card you've inserted. If you have set up multiple accounts on your device, tap the appropriate account in the Create Contact Under Account dialog box.

> **NOTE** Some devices and Android versions show Import from Storage rather than Import from .vcf File and Export to Storage rather than Export to .vcf File.

- **Import from SIM Card.** If you have contacts stored on your SIM card, you can use this command to import them into the Contacts app.

> **TIP** The Import from SIM Card command is most useful for transferring contacts from your old phone's SIM card to your new phone—providing that the phones take the same size SIM card or that you can get an adapter to make the old phone's SIM card fit in the new phone. If not, export the contacts from the SIM card using the old phone, and then use a different means (for example, your Google account) to put the contacts on the new phone.

- **Export to .vcf File.** Use this command to export your contact list to a file that you can then transfer to another device or save for backup. The Save To panel appears, enabling you to choose the location in which to save the file. After choosing the location, edit the default name for the file (contacts.vcf) and then tap the Save button.

> **NOTE** On some devices, the Import/Export Contacts dialog box also contains the Export to SIM Card command.

■ **Share Visible Contacts.** To share just some of your contacts, restrict the display to just that group using the technique explained in the previous section. Then give this command, select the app or service in the Share With panel, and tap the Just Once button. For example, you can tap the Gmail button to attach the vCard file containing the contacts to a new message in Gmail. You can then address and send the message.

MASTERING YOUR SCHEDULE WITH CALENDAR

The Calendar app gives you an easy way to track your events on your Android device. You can display only those calendars you want to see at a particular time, sync events with your other devices, and share a calendar with other people.

Best of all, you can configure the Calendar app so that it looks and works the way you prefer. Let's start there.

CONFIGURING THE CALENDAR APP

You can customize Calendar's behavior by configuring its settings. To get started, open the navigation panel by either tapping the Navigation button or swiping in from the left, and then tap the Settings button near the bottom of the panel. This brings you to the Settings screen (see the left screen in Figure 9.4), which gives you access to the general settings (which apply across all accounts) and the settings for each account (which affect only that account).

CHOOSING GENERAL SETTINGS

Tap the General button to display the General Settings screen. (See the right screen in Figure 9.4.) You can then choose these settings:

■ **Start of the Week.** Tap this button to display the Start of the Week dialog box, and then tap the Saturday box, the Sunday box, or the Monday box, to control which day appears at the start of the week. These check boxes act like radio buttons, in that only one of them can be selected at any time; selecting another check box deselects whichever check box was previously selected.

■ **Use Device Time Zone.** Set this switch to On to make the Calendar app use the time zone in which your device reports itself to be.

■ **Time Zone.** If this button shows the wrong time zone, tap it and use the resulting dialog box to select the right time zone. You must set the Use Device Time Zone switch to Off to be able to use the Time Zone button.

■ **Show Week Number.** Check this box to have Calendar show a readout such as "Week 35" above the month and year.

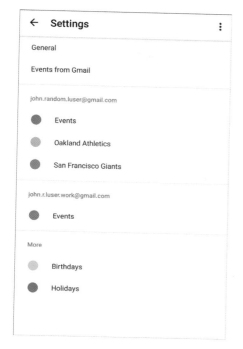
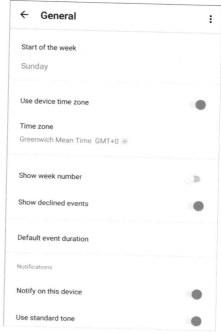

FIGURE 9.4

On the Settings screen (left), tap the General button to display the General screen (right). Here, you can configure the calendar view and your notifications and reminders.

■ **Show Declined Events.** Set this switch to On if you want to display events you've declined instead of displaying only those you've accepted (either definitely or tentatively).

■ **Default Event Duration.** Tap this button to display the Event Duration screen. Here, you can tap the current default time for an account to display the Default Event Duration dialog box, and then tap the button for the default duration: No End Time, 15 Minutes, 30 Minutes, 60 Minutes, 90 Minutes, or 120 Minutes.

■ **Notify on This Device.** Set this switch to On to receive Calendar notifications on this device.

■ **Use Standard Tone.** Set this switch to On if you want Calendar notifications to use the standard notification tone, which is called Calendar Notification. To use a different tone, set this switch to Off, tap the Tone button that appears, and select the tone you want in the Ringtones dialog box.

■ **Vibrate.** Set this switch to On if you want your device to vibrate when the Calendar app raises a notification. As usual, this setting appears only if your device has a vibration motor.

■ **Quick Responses.** Tap this button to display the Quick Responses screen, which contains four canned responses you can send in reply to invitations you receive—for example, "Be there in about 10 minutes" or "Go ahead and start without me." To change a quick response, tap it, edit it in the Quick Response dialog box, and then tap the OK button.

> **NOTE** You can't create new quick responses at this writing, so you need to make do by changing the existing four quick responses to suit your needs.

CHOOSING EVENTS FROM GMAIL SETTINGS

The Calendar app's Events from Gmail feature can automatically add events based on information in email messages you receive in your Gmail account. To configure Events from Gmail, tap the Events from Gmail button on the Settings screen, and then work on the Events from Gmail screen. (See the left screen in Figure 9.5.)

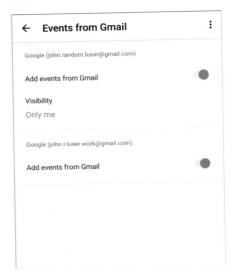
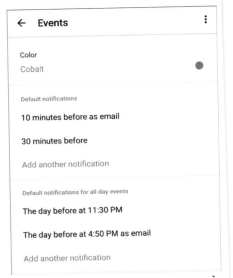

FIGURE 9.5

On the Events from Gmail screen (left), set the Add Events from Gmail switch for each account to On or Off, as needed, and specify the visibility for the events. On the settings screen for a calendar, such as the Events calendar (right), set the color and choose default notifications.

For each account, set the Add Events from Gmail switch to On if you want Calendar to pick up events from that app's messages. If the Visibility button appears for an account, tap it to display the pop-up panel of options, and then specify the visibility for the calendar events created from Gmail: Calendar Default, Private, or Only Me.

CHOOSING SETTINGS FOR INDIVIDUAL CALENDARS

To choose settings for an individual calendar, tap that calendar on the Settings screen in the Calendar app. For example, tap the Events calendar for your Gmail account to display an Events screen such as that shown on the right in Figure 9.5. Here, you can configure the following settings:

- **Color.** Tap the current color to display the Colors dialog box, and then tap the color you want.

- **Default Notifications.** Tap an existing default notification to display the dialog box for changing the notification, or tap the Add a Notification button to create a new notification.

> **NOTE** Whether you're editing a notification or adding one, you can tap the Custom button to display the Custom Notification dialog box, which enables you to set exactly the notification timing you want. To remove an existing notification, tap the No Notification button.

- **Default Notifications for All-Day Events.** Tap an existing default notification to display the dialog box for changing the notification, or tap the Add a Notification button to create a new notification.

CHOOSING WHICH CALENDARS TO DISPLAY

Sometimes it's useful to see all your commitments at once, but often you'll find it better to display only some of your calendars so that you can focus on their events. For example, you may want to view only your work calendar so that you can see your work commitments separate from all your other commitments.

To control which calendar the Calendar app displays, open the navigation panel by either tapping the Navigation button or swiping in from the left. You can then check the box for each calendar you want to display.

CONTROLLING HOW THE CALENDAR APPEARS

The Calendar app offers five views: Schedule, Day, 3 Day (on phones only), Week, and Month. The Schedule view displays a list of events for the upcoming days, enabling you to get an overview of your commitments. The Day, 3 Day, Week, and Month views show you the specified amount of time.

> **NOTE** To update your calendar with the latest information, tap the Menu button in the upper-right corner and then tap Refresh on the menu.

CREATING EVENTS

You can create a new event in any of these ways:

- **Manually in any view.** Tap the New button, the red circle containing a white + sign in the lower-right corner of the screen, and then tap Event on the pop-up menu. The New Event screen appears. Fill in the details of the event and then tap the Save button.

- **Manually in Day view.** Tap the appropriate time slot in the Calendar, placing a New Event box in it. You can then tap the New Event box to display a screen for adding the details to the event.

- **Manually in 3 Day view or Week view.** Tap the appropriate time slot in the Calendar, and then tap the + sign that appears in it. The New Event screen appears, and you can fill in the details of the event and then tap the Save button.

- **Manually in Month view on a tablet.** Tap a day that has no events. The Calendar app displays a pop-up panel saying "Nothing planned. Tap to create." Tap the Tap to Create prompt to display the New Event screen, enter the details, and then tap the Save button.

- **By voice.** Launch Google Now and tell it the event details. For example, say "Create a meeting Monday morning at 10 a.m. with Alice and Bill." Google Now is pretty good about getting the details straight, but if it doesn't, you can fix them on the event sheet that it displays.

- **Manually from an email message.** This approach works only with Gmail in a web browser, not in the Gmail app at this writing. If Gmail automatically underlines an event, move the pointer over it and click the Add to Calendar button that appears.

■ **Automatically from an email message.** If you've enabled the Events from Gmail feature (see the section "Choosing Events from Gmail Settings," earlier in this chapter), the Calendar app automatically picks up events that Gmail identifies in messages you receive.

> **TIP** If you've enabled Google Now, make sure you add the location to each calendar event so that Google Now can display the navigation information and driving time on your cards.

INVITING OTHERS TO AN EVENT

When creating an event to which you want to invite other people, tap the Invite People field and enter the invitees. Start typing the first name or email address, and then tap the appropriate result in the list of matches that pops up. The Calendar app adds a button showing the contact's name, and you can start typing the next name.

When you finish adding invitees, tap the Done button (the green circle with a white check mark) on the keyboard to return to the New Event screen.

DEALING WITH INVITATIONS

When you receive an invitation to an event, the Calendar app adds it to your calendar automatically. You can then tap the event to view its details, and then tap the Yes radio button, the Maybe radio button, or the No radio button in the Going area to give your response.

SHARING YOUR GOOGLE CALENDARS

Sending invitations works well for individual events, but if you need other people to be able to see every event in a particular calendar, you'll find that sending invitations for each new event grows old fast. Instead, you'll do better to share the calendar. As long as the calendar is a Google one, this is easy to do, but you need to use a web browser rather than the Calendar app at this writing.

Follow these steps to share a Google calendar:

1. Steer your web browser to calendar.google.com and log in if prompted.

> **NOTE** If you're already logged in to your Google account, click the Google Apps button (the grid of nine gray squares) to the right of your name in the upper-right corner of the screen, and then click Calendar on the pop-up panel to switch to Calendar.

2. In the My Calendars list, move the pointer over the calendar you want to share, click the pop-up menu button that appears, and then click Share This Calendar on the pop-up menu.

3. Click the Person box in the Share with Specific People section and type the email address of the first person with whom you want to share the calendar.

4. Click the Permission Settings drop-down menu and then click the appropriate level of permissions: Make Changes AND Manage Sharing, Make Changes to Events, See All Event Details, or See Only Free/Busy.

> **CAUTION** Give other people only the permissions they absolutely need for the calendar. If someone needs to be able to see your events, assign the See All Event Details permission; if someone will help you coordinate events, assign the Make Changes to Events permission (which includes seeing all the event details). Normally, you will want to keep the Make Changes AND Manage Sharing permission to yourself rather than assign it to others.

5. Click the Add Person button to add the person to the list.

6. Add other people as needed by repeating steps 3–5.

7. Click the Save button to make the changes.

> **CAUTION** Instead of sharing a calendar with specific people, you can check the Make This Calendar Public box to make the calendar appear in public Google search results. Do this only for information you're determined to share with the world at large. If what's important is letting people know when you're available and when you're not, check the Make This Calendar Public box, but then check the Share Only My Free/Busy Information box below it before clicking the Save button to effect the change. Using this setting, people can see when you're free and when you're busy, but they can't see the details of your events.

TRANSFERRING AND SYNCING FILES WITH GOOGLE DRIVE

As you saw in Chapter 2, "Loading and Syncing Your Device," you can use Google Drive as an easy way to put files on your Android device, but you'll likely also want to use it for day-to-day file operations. In this section, you'll look at how to set up Google Drive, navigate it, choose key settings, and add your documents to it and to your device.

SETTING UP GOOGLE DRIVE

To access Google Drive on your Android device, you use the Drive app. If you're not sure whether the Drive app is installed on your device, tap the Apps button on the Home screen and look for the Drive icon. If it's there, tap it to launch the Google Drive app; if not, tap the Play Store icon, search for *Drive* or *Google Drive,* and then install the app.

The first time you launch the Drive app, the app displays several introductory screens. Swipe left or tap the Next button (the > icon) to review the features, and then tap the Done button when you finish; or tap the Skip button if you'd prefer to explore on your own. The My Drive screen then appears. (See the left screen in Figure 9.6.)

NAVIGATING GOOGLE DRIVE

You can navigate your drive easily using these moves:

■ **Move among the different folders.** Tap the Navigation button or swipe in from the left to display the navigation panel (see the right screen in Figure 9.6), and then tap the button for the folder you want: My Drive, Shared with Me, Google Photos, Recent, Starred, Offline, or Uploads.

> **TIP** To refresh the view, tap on the My Drive screen and pull down a short way, and then lift your finger. Drive displays a curling arrow as it refreshes the information.

■ **Toggle between List view and Thumbnails view.** Tap the Thumbnails button (the six gray squares) or the List button (the three gray dots and horizontal lines) to switch views.

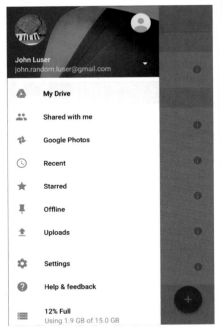

FIGURE 9.6

The My Drive screen (left) gives you quick access to the folders and documents you've stored on Google Drive. Use the navigation panel (right) to move quickly among the main areas of Google Drive.

- **Filter your files.** Tap the Menu button and then tap Filter By to display the Filter By dialog box. (See the left screen in Figure 9.7.) Tap the radio button—Folders, Presentations, Spreadsheets, Text Documents, Images, Videos, or PDF—for the type of item you want to view. Google Drive displays only items of the type you choose. A readout such as Filter: Folders or Filter: Images appears at the top of the screen.

> **NOTE** The Filter By button appears on the menu only in some versions of Android and Drive.

- **Sort your files.** Tap the Menu button and then tap Sort By to display the Sort By dialog box. (See the right screen in Figure 9.7.) Tap the radio button—Name, Last Modified, Last Modified by Me, Last Opened by Me, or Quota Used—by which you want to sort, and Google Drive displays the items in that order.

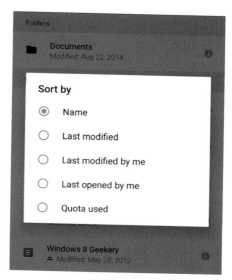

FIGURE 9.7

Use the Filter By dialog box (left) to filter your files to display only the types you want to see. Use the Sort By dialog box (right) to sort your files by name, by last modified date or last opened date, or by their usage of space. To remove a filter you've applied, tap the arrow button in the upper-left corner or the Back button below the screen. The My Drive screen appears again.

> ✅ **TIP**   Sort your files by Quota Used when you need to see which of them is taking up the most space—for example, when your Google Drive is getting full and you need to free up space.

- **Open a file or folder.** Tap the thumbnail or the name.
- **Download a file.** Tap and hold the file's button until the Drive app switches to Selection mode and a blue circle with a check mark appears on the file. (See the left screen in Figure 9.8.) On the selection bar that appears at the bottom of the screen, tap the Download button. You can also take other actions by tapping the Offline button or the Link button or by tapping the Menu button in the lower-right corner and then tapping the appropriate command on the menu.
- **View information for a document or folder.** Tap the Info (i) button on the thumbnail or the name button.
- **Search for a document or folder.** Tap the search icon at the top of the screen and type your search terms.

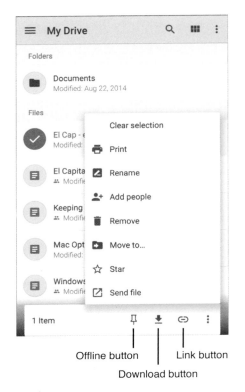
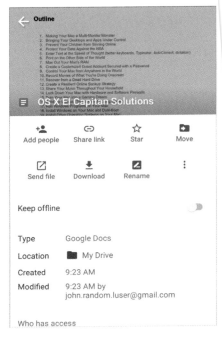

Offline button | Link button

Download button

FIGURE 9.8

To download a file, tap and hold its button, and then tap the Download button on the selection bar (left). To view information about a file or take other actions, tap its Info (i) button to display the Info panel (right).

CONFIGURING BACKUPS, CACHE, ENCRYPTION, AND DATA USAGE

To get the best out of Google Drive, you should configure the cache, turn on encryption, and make sure the app transfers files via the cellular connection only if you want it to. You can also enable the Auto Add feature for Google Photos; in Marshmallow, you can set the Drive app to back up your apps automatically as well.

Open the navigation panel by either tapping the Navigation button or swiping in from the left, and then tap Settings to display the Settings screen. (See the left and right screens in Figure 9.9.)

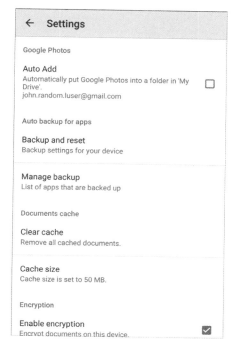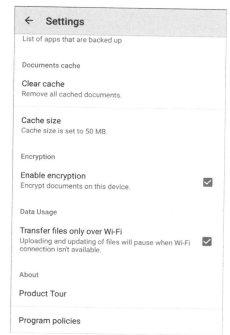

FIGURE 9.9

On the Settings screen for the Drive app, you can configure Google Photos, Auto Backup for Apps, the cache size, and encryption. On a phone, you may want to restrict the app to using Wi-Fi to transfer data.

CONFIGURING GOOGLE PHOTOS

In the Google Photos area, check the Auto Add box if you want your device to automatically upload your photos to Google Drive. Uploading the photos is great for keeping them safe, but it can mean uploading a lot of data and consuming space against your quota.

CONFIGURING AUTO BACKUP FOR APPS SETTINGS IN MARSHMALLOW

In the Auto Backup for Apps area, first tap the Backup and Reset button to display the Backup & Reset screen. If the Back Up My Data button's readout says Off, tap Back Up My Data to display the Back Up My Data screen in the Settings app, and then set the switch to On. If the Backup Account button's readout says "Need to set the backup account," tap the button to display the Set Backup Account dialog box, and then tap the appropriate account in the list. (If the account doesn't appear, tap the Add Account button, and then follow the prompts to add the account.) Tap the Back button below the screen to return to the Settings screen in the Drive app.

> **NOTE** Marshmallow enables you to back up your apps to Google Drive. Lollipop doesn't have this feature.

> **TIP** To see which apps have been backed up and how much space they're taking, tap the Manage Backup button to display the Manage Backups screen. As of this writing, this screen shows a straightforward list of the apps, the backup size, and the backup date; there is no management functionality as such, but it seems likely that Google will add some in future versions.

CONFIGURING THE DOCUMENTS CACHE

In the Documents Cache area, you can tap the Clear Cache button to clear all your currently cached documents. Normally, you'd do this only if some documents have become corrupt and won't open or sync.

Tap the Cache Size button to display the Cache Size dialog box, and then tap the radio button—25 MB, 50 MB, 100 MB, or 250 MB—for the cache size to use. If you use Google Drive extensively, set the Documents Cache to 250 MB (the maximum amount) to allow the app to cache plenty of data. The Drive app caches data so that it can provide it quickly on demand, without needing to download it from the Internet.

CONFIGURING ENCRYPTION AND DATA USAGE

In the Encryption area, check the Enable encryption box to encrypt your Google Drive documents on your device. If you have encrypted your Android device as a whole, you don't need to enable encryption in the Google Drive app, but you can if you want.

In the Data Usage area, check Transfer Files Only over Wi-Fi box if you want to prevent the Drive app using cellular data on your phone or cellular tablet.

> **! CAUTION** If you need your Google Drive files to be up to date all the time, uncheck the Transfer Files Only over Wi-Fi box, but keep a close eye on your data plan to make sure you don't go over your limits.

CREATING A FOLDER

Here's how to create a folder on Google Drive using the Drive app:

1. From the My Drive screen, navigate to the folder in which you want to create the new folder.
2. Tap the New (+) button to display the New panel.
3. Tap the Folder button to display the New Folder dialog box.
4. Type the name for the folder.
5. Tap the OK button.

Google Drive creates the folder and displays its contents—nothing so far. You can then upload files to the folder, create new files in it, or scan files to it.

ADDING FILES TO GOOGLE DRIVE

You can quickly add files to Google Drive in three ways using the Drive app. First, navigate to the folder in which you want to place the files. Then take the appropriate action:

- **Upload the file.** Tap the New (+) button to display the New panel. Tap the Upload button, navigate to the file, and then tap it. Google Drive starts the upload automatically.

- **Create a new file.** Tap the New (+) button to display the New panel. Tap the Google Docs button, the Google Sheets button, or the Google Slides button, as needed; then create the file in the Docs app, the Sheets app, or the Slides app, which opens automatically. Tap the check mark when you finish editing the file. Then tap the Close × button to close the file.

- **Scan a hard-copy document.** If your device has a rear camera, tap the New (+) button to display the New panel, and then tap the Scan button. Line up the document and tap the blue button to photograph it, and then use the cropping tools to crop the document as needed. You can tap the Type button (the color palette in the upper-right corner) and then check the box for the document type—None, Black & White, Color, or Color Drawing—on the Type pop-up menu. If you want to rename the file, tap the default name, type the new name in the dialog box that opens, and then tap the OK button. Tap the check mark when the file is ready for upload to Google Drive.

KEEPING FILES ON YOUR DEVICE

To keep a specific file on your device, tap the Info (i) button on the file to display the Information screen, and then set the Keep Offline switch to On.

> ☑ **TIP** From the Information screen, you can also share a file, send it to others, rename it, move it to a folder, or print it.

PRINTING DOCUMENTS

Even if you take your Android device with you everywhere, you may still need to print documents from it sometimes—for instance, so that you can show them to other people without having to hand over your device.

You have four main choices for printing from Android:

- Print to a Wi-Fi printer or Bluetooth printer that supports Android.
- Print to an HP printer using the HP Print Service Plugin.
- Print to a cloud printer. A *cloud printer* is one that connects directly to the Web, receives your print jobs from the Google Cloud Print server, and prints them.
- Print through your existing printer courtesy of your computer, Chrome, and your Google account.

PRINTING TO LOCAL PRINTERS

To print to a local printer, you need a printer that directly supports Android.

As you'd imagine, for a Wi-Fi printer, you need to connect your device to the same Wi-Fi network. Similarly, for a Bluetooth printer, make sure Bluetooth is enabled on your device, and pair the device with the printer.

If the app from which you want to print has a Print command, give that command, and work through the resulting dialog boxes or screens. For example, in Gmail, open a message for reading. To print the message, tap the Menu button and then tap Print on the menu. (See the left screen in Figure 9.10.) On the Print screen that appears (see the right screen in Figure 9.10), select the printer in the pop-up menu, choose other options such as the copies and paper size, and then tap the Print button.

Print button

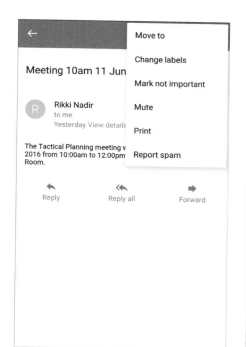

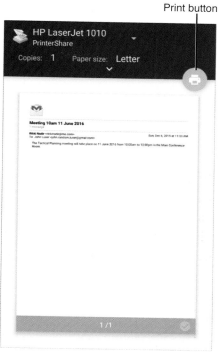

FIGURE 9.10

To print from an app such as Gmail, open the menu and tap the Print command (left). On the Print screen that appears (right), choose the printer and print options, and then tap the Print button.

If the app from which you want to print doesn't have a Print command, you need to use a third-party printing app. One example is PrinterShare, which you can download for free from the App Store. To print with such an app, you launch the app and use its controls to select the document you want to print. You can then choose which printer to use, select other options for printing, and send the document to the printer.

PRINT TO AN HP PRINTER USING THE HP PRINT SERVICE PLUGIN

The HP Print Service Plugin is a software component that comes preinstalled on some Nexus, Samsung, and HP Android devices. This plug-in enables those Android devices to print to a range of HP inkjet and laser printers.

To see whether your device has the HP Print Service Plugin installed, open the Settings app, go to the System section, and then tap the Printing button. On the Printing screen (see the left screen in Figure 9.11), see if the HP Print Service Plugin button appears. If it does, but the readout says Off, tap the HP Print Service Plugin button to display the HP Print Service Plugin screen (see the right screen in Figure 9.11) and set the switch to On.

> **NOTE** If the HP Print Service Plugin button doesn't appear, open the Play Store app, search for the plugin, and install it. You can then return to the Printing screen to enable the plugin.

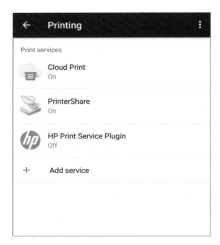
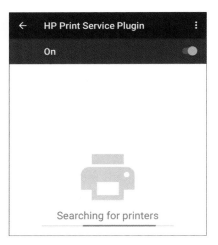

FIGURE 9.11

Look at the Printing screen in the Settings app (left) to see if the HP Print Service Plugin is installed; if it's not, install it. To enable the HP Print Service Plugin, tap its button on the Printing screen and then set the switch on the HP Print Service Plugin screen to On.

If your device has the HP Print Service Plugin installed, you can connect to a supported HP printer either via a wireless network or directly (if the printer supports direct wireless connections). Once connected, you can print to the printer.

PRINTING TO CLOUD PRINTERS

Google's overarching printing solution for its apps and devices is Cloud Print, an Internet-based service with which you can register a printer. To print using Cloud Print, you install the Google Cloud Print app or an equivalent app on your device, which enables your device to connect to printers registered on Cloud Print.

> **! CAUTION** Printing via Cloud Print raises moderate security concerns because each document you print has to be sent across the Internet to Google's servers so that it can then be transmitted to the printer. The documents you print are not private. Google keeps a copy of each document temporarily but deletes it when the print job is complete.

To print to a cloud printer, you open the document in the usual app you use for it and then give the Print command. Apps use different locations for the Print command, but you can usually find it easily. For example, in Google Docs, tap the Menu button, tap Share & Export, and then tap Print.

> **TIP** If no cloud printer is available, you can "print" from your device by saving the document to Google Drive. You can then print the document from there afterward.

PRINTING ON YOUR EXISTING PRINTER

To print on your existing printer that doesn't directly support Android, you need to install third-party software on your device. You may also need to install software on your computer to make the printer visible on the network.

The specifics depend on the software, but here's an example using the PrinterShare app, which is pretty straightforward. To set up printing with PrinterShare:

- Install the PrinterShare Print Service app on your Android device and use it to open the document you want to print.

- If the printer is connected to a Mac, you open System Preferences, go to the Sharing pane, and turn on Printer Sharing for the printer you want to use.

- If the printer is connected to a Windows PC, you install the PrinterShare app from the PrinterShare website (www.printershare.com).

> **NOTE** PrinterShare offers a free version of its software that enables you to print a modest number of pages on local printers and remote printers—for example, to test that it works—plus unlimited printing via Google Cloud Print. For unlimited printing to local printers and remote printers, you can buy the Premium version of PrinterShare for Android, which costs $9.95.

You can then print to the printer from your Android device. The left screen in Figure 9.12 shows the PrinterShare interface for selecting the printer to use and opening the item you want to print. The right screen in Figure 9.12 shows the Print Options dialog box for specifying print options such as the number of copies and the range of pages.

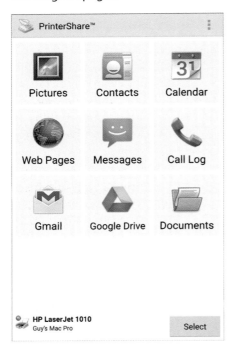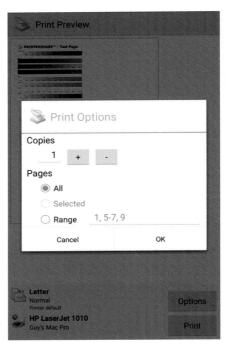

FIGURE 9.12

The main PrinterShare screen (left) enables you to select a printer and open a file to print. In the Print Options dialog box (right), you can set options such as the number of copies and the range of pages to print.

CONTROLLING YOUR COMPUTER FROM YOUR ANDROID DEVICE

If you want to do even more with your Android device, set it up to control your computer. This move is great both for when you're at home and don't want to go to the next room and for when you're at home and you need to access your computer at work without the commute.

To control your computer from your Android device, you typically need to install and run a server app on your computer and a client app on your device. The server app receives an incoming connection from the client and transfers data back and forth. The client app receives the data from the server, displays it for you (so that you can see what's happening on your computer's screen), and transmits your finger movements and your keystrokes to the server.

Various combinations of software are available, but these are the three most promising at this writing:

- **Splashtop.** Splashtop (www.splashtop.com) consists of a client app called Splashtop, which you install on the remote device (in this case, your Android device), and a server called Streamer, which you install on your PC, Mac, or Linux box. Splashtop comes in various different editions, such as Personal, Business, and Classroom.

- **LogMeIn.** LogMeIn (www.logmein.com) is a service that enables you to connect remotely to your PC or Mac across either a local network or the Internet. Using one of the LogMeIn client apps, such as the LogMeIn for Android app, you can use your Android device to control your PC or Mac after you have connected to it.

- **Remote Desktop Connection.** If your computer has one of the "business" versions of Windows, such as Windows 10 Pro or Windows 10 Enterprise, you can turn on the Remote Desktop feature and connect to your computer using a Remote Desktop client app. Start with the Microsoft Remote Desktop app for Android, which is free, and move on to other apps if you find it doesn't meet your needs.

- **VNC client.** Virtual Network Computing (VNC) is a feature for remotely viewing and controlling other computers. VNC consists of a server app and a client app. OS X includes a built-in VNC server that you can enable by checking the Screen Sharing box in the Sharing pane in System Preferences. You can then connect your Android device using a VNC client such as VNC Viewer from RealVNC Limited, which is available for free from the App Store.

USING A CHROMECAST DEVICE

Google's Chromecast devices enable you to display the content from your Android device on a large screen, such as an HDTV or a monitor, or to play audio through speakers.

The Chromecast device plays both audio and video, but Google also makes an audio-only version called Chromecast Audio. The first-generation Chromecast, released in 2013, is the size of a large thumb; the second-generation Chromecast, released in 2015, is a flattish circle. Both Chromecast versions connect to the HDTV or monitor via an HDMI port. The Chromecast Audio connects to speakers via a standard headphone jack. Your Android device connects to the Chromecast device or Chromecast Audio device via Wi-Fi and plays content on it.

> **NOTE** The device is simply called "Chromecast"—but the app you use to configure the device and to start casting your screen to it is also called "Chromecast." So, this section uses the terms *Chromecast device* and *Chromecast app* for clarity.

Android plays content on the Chromecast device in two ways, depending on what the content is:

- **Remote control.** If the media file is online, Android causes the Chromecast device to connect to the file. If the media file is on your device, Android transfers the media file to the Chromecast device. Android then uses remote control to play back the file on the Chromecast device.

- **Streaming.** The Android app you're using plays the media file but streams the playback to the Chromecast device, which displays the video content and outputs the audio content.

SETTING UP A CHROMECAST WITH YOUR ANDROID DEVICE

You can set up your Chromecast device using your Android device or another device or computer by following these steps:

> **NOTE** On a computer, take your web browser to www.chromecast.com/setup and follow the instructions.

1. On your Android device, go to the Play Store and install the free Chromecast app.

2. After installation, open the Chromecast app. The Chromecast app automatically searches for available Chromecast devices that need setting up. If the Chromecast app finds multiple Chromecast devices that need setting up, it displays the Devices screen, listing the devices. (See the left screen in Figure 9.13.) Tap the Set Up button for the device you want to configure,

and the Found screen appears. (See the right screen in Figure 9.13.) If the Chromecast app finds a single Chromecast device that needs setting up, it goes straight to the Found screen.

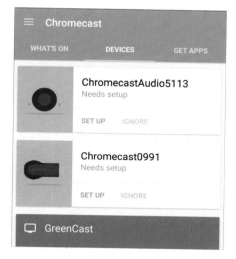

FIGURE 9.13

If the Devices screen (left) appears, tap the Set Up button for the Chromecast device you want to configure; the Found screen then appears. On the Found screen (right), tap the Set Up button to begin setup.

3. Tap the Set Up button and follow through the setup process until the Chromecast app displays the Name Your Chromecast screen. (See the left screen in Figure 9.14.)

> **NOTE** To enable you to verify you're configuring the right device, the setup process for a Chromecast device displays a code on the screen of the connected TV or monitor. For a Chromecast Audio, the setup process plays a sound through the connected speakers.

4. Type the name you want to give the Chromecast device.
5. Check the Enable Guest Mode box if you want to enable devices in the same room to access the Chromecast device without connecting to your Wi-Fi network.
6. Check the Send Chromecast Usage Data and Crash Reports to Google box if you want to provide usage data and crash reports to help Google improve the Chromecast devices and app.

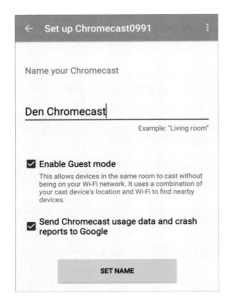

FIGURE 9.14

Type the name you want to assign your Chromecast device, choose whether to enable Guest mode and send usage data, and then tap the Set Name button (left). Use the controls on the Connect Chromecast to Your Wi-Fi screen (right) to connect your Chromecast device to your wireless network.

7. Tap the Set Name button. The Chromecast app displays the Connect Chromecast to Your Wi-Fi screen. (See the right screen in Figure 9.14.)

8. Tap the Network Name pop-up menu and then tap the network you want to use.

9. Tap the Wi-Fi Password field and then type the password. You can check the Show Password box if you need to verify the password.

10. Tap the Set Network button. The You're Ready to Cast screen appears.

11. Tap the Browse Your Cast Apps button to display the list of apps that can play content to Chromecast devices. You can then tap the app you want to use.

NOTE At this point, the Chromecast device connects to the Internet and checks automatically for updates. If it finds an update, it downloads and installs it. You'll see a message and progress readout on your TV screen while this is happening. During the update, the Chromecast device reboots. You don't need to do anything at this point—just wait until the Chromecast screen appears again on your TV.

CASTING YOUR SCREEN OR AUDIO TO THE CHROMECAST DEVICE

When a Chromecast device is available to your Android device, apps that support Chromecast display the Cast icon. For example, the YouTube app displays the Cast icon near the Menu button, as you can see in the left screen in Figure 9.15. Similarly, the Play Music app displays the Cast icon in the upper-right corner of the screen.

Cast icon

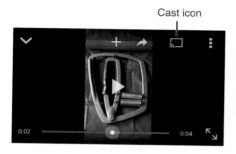 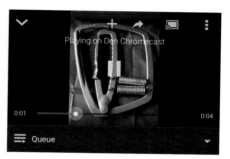

FIGURE 9.15

Tap the Cast icon in an app such as YouTube (left) to connect to a Chromecast device. Once connected (right), you can use your Android device to control playback on the Chromecast device.

Tap the Cast icon to display the Cast To dialog box, and then tap the Chromecast device you want to use.

Android connects to the Chromecast device, and the Chromecast device begins playing back the content. (See the right screen in Figure 9.15.)

When you're ready to stop casting, tap the Cast icon again, and then tap the Stop Casting button.

> **NOTE** When you're playing a music file that's stored online, Android causes the Chromecast device to stream it from the online site. If the music file is stored on your device, the device transfers the audio to the Chromecast device, and the Chromecast device then plays it back.

MAKING THE MOST OF PHONE AND HANGOUTS

In this chapter, you learn how to get the most out of the standard Phone app that comes with Android phones. You then dig into how to get the most out of Google's Hangouts app, which provides messaging, audio chat, and video chat.

BECOMING AN EXPERT WITH THE PHONE APP

Open the Phone app by tapping the Phone icon on the Home screen or on the Apps screen. You can then quickly start making calls, review recent activity, or choose settings to configure the Phone app.

> **NOTE** Many manufacturers customize the Phone app heavily, so your phone may have a substantially different look and layout than the Phone app shown here. Your phone may also have extra features added, but the essential features should be the same.

MAKING CALLS THE EASY WAY

When you first open the Phone app, it displays the Speed Dial tab. The left screen in Figure 10.1 shows the Speed Dial tab in Marshmallow; the right screen in Figure 10.1 shows the Speed Dial tab in Lollipop. As you can see, the Speed Dial tabs are similar but different. In Lollipop, a button for the most recent call appears below the Search Contacts & Places box; in Marshmallow, this button doesn't appear. In Lollipop, the three tab buttons have text names: the Speed Dial tab, the Recents tab, and the Contacts tab. In Marshmallow, the tab buttons have symbols instead of names.

Speed Dial   Recents   Contacts

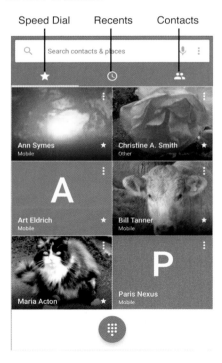
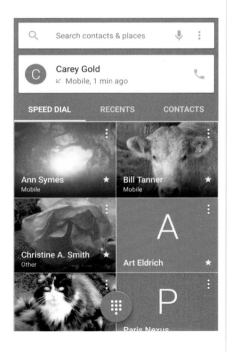

FIGURE 10.1

At first, the Phone app displays the Speed Dial tab. There are several differences between the Speed Dial tab in Marshmallow (left) and the Speed Dial tab in Lollipop (right).

From the Speed Dial tab, you can take the following actions:

- Tap the Search box at the top and search for a contact or a number.
- Tap the Last Call button to call that number. (Lollipop only)
- Tap a tile in the Speed Dial list to call that contact. If the contact has multiple numbers, the Choose Number dialog box opens. (See the left screen in Figure 10.2.) Check the Remember This Choice box if you want to use this particular number automatically in the future, and then tap the number to call.

> **TIP** The Speed Dial list shows those of your Favorites in the Contacts app that have one or more phone numbers. To add a contact to the Speed Dial list, open the contact in the Contacts app and tap the Favorite star. To remove a contact from the Speed Dial list in the Contacts app, open the contact and tap the Favorite star to remove it. To remove a contact from the Speed Dial list in the Phone app, tap and hold the contact, and then drag it to the Remove button that appears at the top of the screen. Doing this also removes the contact from the Favorites list.

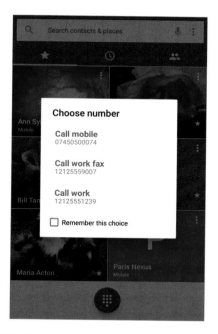
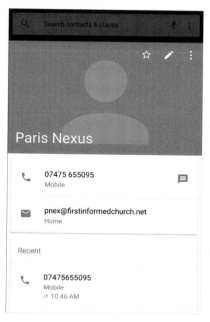

FIGURE 10.2

If the contact has multiple numbers, tap the appropriate one in the Choose Number dialog box (left). Tap the Menu button on a contact's tile to display a pop-up panel showing the contact's record, including recent communications (right).

■ Tap the Menu button on a tile to open a pop-up panel showing the contact's record. (See the right screen in Figure 10.2.) From here, you can choose a different way to communicate with the contact; for example, you can tap an email address to start an email message to the contact. You can also view the Recent section, which shows any recent communications with the contact.

> **TIP**   In addition, you can place phone calls from the Contacts app or from other apps that display contact information that includes phone numbers. If in doubt, try tapping the phone number and see what happens.

■ Tap the Recents tab button to display The Recents tab. The left screen in Figure 10.3 shows the Recents tab in Marshmallow; the Recents tab in Lollipop is similar but, like the Speed Dial tab, shows the Last Call button near the top. You can tap a button to call the contact or number shown on the button.

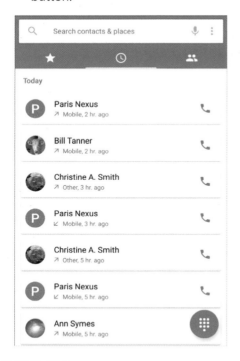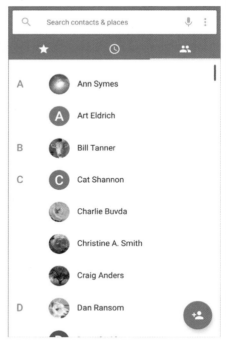

FIGURE 10.3

The Recents tab (left) shows the calls you've made and received recently. The Contacts tab (right) shows your full list of contacts in alphabetical order.

■ Tap the Contacts tab button to display the Contacts tab so that you can browse all your contacts. The right screen in Figure 10.3 shows the Contacts tab in Marshmallow; the Contacts tab in Lollipop is similar but (again) shows the Last Call button near the top.

> **NOTE** In either the Phone app or the Contacts app, you can tap the Menu button and then tap Clear Frequents to clear the Frequently Contacted list. This is the list that appears below the Favorites list in the Contacts app. It is separate from the Speed Dial list in the Phone app. On some phones, you can clear the list only from the Favorites tab of the Phone app.

SAVING TIME WITH YOUR CALL HISTORY

You can often save time and effort by using your call history, which tracks your incoming and outgoing calls. As you've seen already, the Recents tab displays the calls you've made and recently received. To go back further than that, tap the Menu button and then tap Call History on the menu. The Call History screen then appears in Marshmallow; in Lollipop, the History screen appears.

> **TIP** Place your vital contacts on the Home screen so that you can get in touch with them quickly. Open the contact in the Phone app or in the Contacts app, tap the Menu button, and then tap Place on Home Screen.

The Call History screen or History screen contains two tabs: the All tab and the Missed tab. The All tab appears at first. (See the left screen in Figure 10.4., which shows Marshmallow.) Here, a green arrow shows an outgoing call, a red arrow shows an incoming call you missed or ducked, and a blue arrow shows an incoming call you took; multiple arrows of the same color indicate multiple calls of the same type. You can tap the Missed tab button to restrict the list to calls you missed. (The right screen in Figure 10.4 shows the Missed tab of the History screen on a phone running Lollipop.)

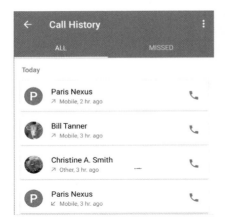
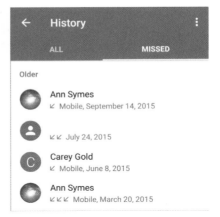

FIGURE 10.4

Use the Call History screen (in Marshmallow) or the History screen (in Lollipop) to view your past calls. You can view the All tab (left) or the Missed tab (right).

Tap a button on either the All tab or the Missed tab to display extra information. (See the left screen in Figure 10.5 for an example.) You can then take several actions depending on the call and the information available for the contact:

- Tap the Redial button to redial a call you placed.
- Tap the Call back button to return a call you missed.
- Tap the Send a Message button to send a text message to the contact.

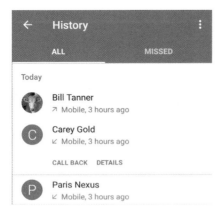
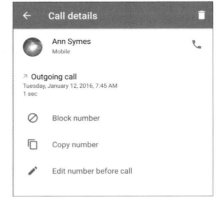

FIGURE 10.5

Tap a call button on the Call History screen or History screen to display buttons with actions you can take (left). Tap the Call Details button or the Details button to display the Call Details screen (right), where you can take further actions.

- Tap the Call Details button (in Marshmallow) or the Details button (in Lollipop) to display the Call Details screen (in both Marshmallow and Lollipop), on which you can block the number, copy the number, or edit the number before calling it.

> **TIP** When you've worked your way through the call history, you can clear it by tapping the Menu button and then tapping Clear Call History.

DIALING WITH THE SMART DIALER

To dial with the Smart Dialer, tap the Dialer button at the bottom of the screen and then tap the buttons to dial. You can also take the following actions:

- **Dial a contact.** As you dial, the Phone app displays contacts with matching numbers at the top of the screen. Tap the contact you want to dial.
- **Add a two-second pause.** Tap the Menu button to the left of the phone number and then tap Add 2-Sec Pause.

> **NOTE** The Menu button to the left of the phone number is available only after you've entered one or more digits. You can't start the number with a two-second pause or a wait.

- **Add a wait.** Tap the Menu button to the left of the phone number and then tap Add Wait.

MAKING MULTIPERSON CALLS WITH THE PHONE APP

The Phone app enables you to easily make multiperson calls: You simply place the initial call as usual and then add other calls one by one as needed.

> **NOTE** The maximum number of participants in a call depends on your carrier rather than on your phone. If you need to find out the limit, ask your carrier's support department.

To add a call, tap the Add Call button on the right of the control bar at the bottom of the call screen. (See the left screen in Figure 10.6.). The three tabs of the Phone app appear again, and you can dial the call by using the Speed Dial tab, the Recents tab, or the Contacts tab—or by tapping the Dialer button and then dialing the call.

Add Call   Merge

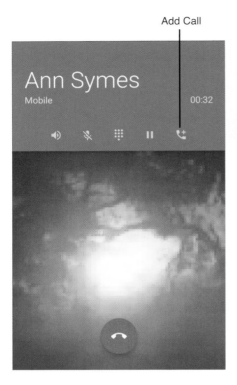

FIGURE 10.6

Tap the Add Call button (left) to start turning a single-person call into a multiperson call. Tap the Merge button (right) to merge the new call into the existing call.

> **✓ TIP** Tapping the Add Call button puts the first caller on hold, so it's a good idea to tell that person you're about to disappear temporarily.

After the new person you've called answers, exchange pleasantries, tell the person you're about to drop him in a multiperson call, and then tap the Merge button to merge the calls. (See the right screen in Figure 10.6.)

After you merge the calls, the Phone app displays the Conference Call screen. (See the left screen in Figure 10.7.) You can now add other calls if necessary (tap the Add Call button as before) or just talk, but you can also chat privately to individuals or drop people from the call.

End Call

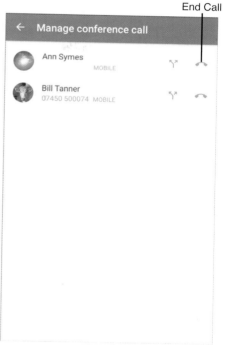

FIGURE 10.7

Tap the Manage Conference Call button on the Conference Call screen (left) when you need to speak individually to participants or to drop people from the call. From the Manage Conference Call screen (right), you can speak to a participant individually or hang up on a participant.

To manage the call like this, tap the Manage Conference Call button and work on the Manage Conference Call screen. (See the right screen in Figure 10.7.) Here you can tap the arrow button to speak to a participant privately or tap the End Call button to drop that participant from the call.

TAKING CALLS—OR AVOIDING THEM

When you receive a phone call, you can take it, decline it, or send a text response.

TAKING OR DECLINING A CALL

When you receive a call, your phone displays the calling number if it's available and any associated contact name and picture. The circle containing a phone receiver and the expanding concentric circles around it give a visual cue that the phone is ringing in case you've suppressed the sound. (See the left screen in Figure 10.8.)

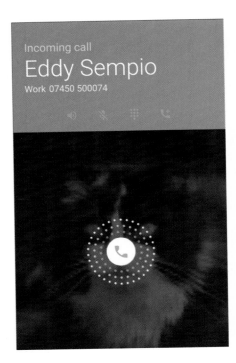

FIGURE 10.8

When a call comes in, your phone displays the number (if available) and any associated contact name and picture (left). Drag right to the green icon to take the call, drag left to the red icon to decline the call, or drag up to the text icon to send a text response (right).

Tap the receiver icon to display the available actions. (See the right screen in Figure 10.8.) You can then drag the receiver to the green icon on the right to accept the call or to the red icon on the left to decline it.

SENDING A TEXT RESPONSE TO A CALL

When you receive a call you can't take or don't want to take, you can send a text response. This can be either one of your predefined Quick Responses or a custom text you write. Drag the call circle straight up to the text icon. In the pop-up panel that appears, either tap the button for the appropriate Quick Response or tap the Write Your Own... button, type the response in the dialog box that opens, and then tap the Send button.

CONFIGURING THE PHONE APP TO WORK YOUR WAY

To get the most out of the Phone app with minimum effort and frustration, spend a few minutes configuring it to work your way. Open the Phone app, tap the Menu button, and then tap Settings to display the Settings screen.

The Phone app in Marshmallow and the phone app in Lollipop have similar settings, but the Settings screens are arranged differently. The left screen in Figure 10.9 shows the Settings screen in Marshmallow, which contains nine categories: Display Options, Sounds and Vibration, Quick Responses, Calls, Call Blocking, Accessibility, Caller ID by Google, Nearby Places, and About Phone. The right screen in Figure 10.9 shows the Settings screen in Lollipop, which has only three categories: General, Calls, and Advanced.

> **NOTE** Some manufacturers and carriers arrange the Settings screen for the Phone app in different ways, so you may need to do some exploring to find the settings discussed here. Some carriers do not offer all the settings.

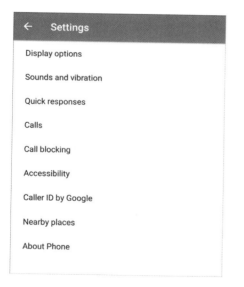
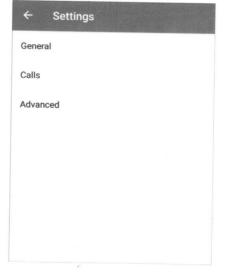

FIGURE 10.9

The Settings screen for the Phone app uses a different arrangement in Marshmallow (left) than in Lollipop (right).

CONFIGURING DISPLAY OPTIONS

The Phone app lets you choose the sort order for names and the format in which they appear. To make your choices, tap the Display Options button on the Settings screen in Marshmallow, and then use the buttons on the Display Options screen.

> **NOTE** In Lollipop, tap the General button on the Settings screen to display the General screen. The Contact Display section at the top of the General screen contains the Sort By button and the Name Format button.

- **Sort By.** Tap this button to display the Sort By dialog box, and then tap the First Name radio button or the Last Name radio button, as needed.
- **Name Format.** Tap this button to display the Name Format dialog box, and then tap the First Name First radio button or the Last Name First radio button, as needed.

CONFIGURING SOUNDS AND VIBRATION SETTINGS

To control sound and vibration, tap the Sounds and Vibration button on the Settings screen in Marshmallow and work on the Sounds and Vibration screen.

> **NOTE** In Lollipop, tap the General button on the Settings screen to display the General screen. The Sounds and Vibrate section on the General screen contains the Phone Ringtone button, the Dialpad Tones check box, and the Also Vibrate for Calls check box.

- **Phone Ringtone.** Tap this Phone Ringtone button to set the default ringtone—the ringtone that plays when the calling number isn't a contact to whom you've assigned a default ringtone or the calling number isn't available.
- **Also Vibrate for Calls.** Check this box if you want your phone to vibrate when it's ringing.
- **Dialpad Tones.** Check this box to have Android play touch tones as you dial numbers.

TAILORING YOUR QUICK RESPONSES TO YOUR NEEDS

The Phone app provides four preset Quick Responses, such as "I'll call you right back" and "Can't talk now. Call me later?" You can't create new Quick Responses, but you can edit the four preset ones by tapping the Quick Responses button on the Call Settings screen in Marshmallow and then working on the Edit Quick Responses screen.

> **NOTE** In Lollipop, tap the General button on the Settings screen to display the General screen. The Other section at the bottom of the General screen contains the Quick Responses button.

Tap a Quick Response to open it for editing, type the text you want in the Quick Response dialog box, and then tap the OK button.

> **TIP** You can tap the Enter button on the keyboard to create a new line or a new paragraph. Splitting up a longer Quick Response into multiple paragraphs can make it more readable for the recipient.

DISPLAYING THE CALL SETTINGS SCREEN

To move along with configuring settings, tap the Calls button on the Settings screen (in either Marshmallow or Lollipop) to display the Call Settings screen. The left screen in Figure 10.10 shows the Call Settings screen in Marshmallow for a Nexus 5X phone.

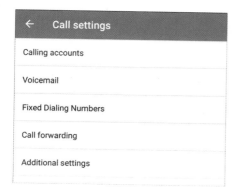
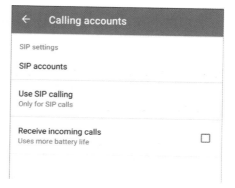

FIGURE 10.10

From the Call Settings screen (left), you can set up calling accounts, voicemail, Fixed Dialing Numbers (FDN), call forwarding, and more. On the Calling Accounts screen (right), set up any Internet calling accounts you want to use with your phone.

NOTE The Call Settings screen on your phone may contain different settings than those shown on the left screen in Figure 10.10. For example, you may see a TTY Mode button, a Hearing Aids check box, and a DMTF Tones button. See the sidebar "Choosing a TTY Mode to Help with Hearing Problems," a little later in this chapter, for coverage of TTY Mode. DMTF is the abbreviation for Dual Tone Multi Frequency, another name for Touchtone; you can tap the DMTF Tones button to choose between playing normal-length tones and long tones.

CONFIGURING INTERNET CALLING

If you want to use Internet calling as well as cellular calling, tap the Calling Accounts button on the Call Settings screen to display the Calling Accounts screen. (See the right screen in Figure 10.10.)

 NOTE Some phones and carriers don't offer Internet calling.

Tap the SIP Accounts button to display the SIP Accounts screen. You can then add an Internet calling account by tapping the Add (+) button, filling in the account's details on the SIP Account Details screen, and then tapping the Save button.

 NOTE SIP is the acronym for Session Initiation Protocol, the Internet protocol used for Internet calls.

On the Calling Accounts screen, tap the Use SIP Calling button to display the Use SIP Calling dialog box, and then tap the For All Calls radio button or the Only for SIP Calls radio button, as needed.

Check the Receive Incoming Calls box if you want your device to listen for incoming calls. Be aware that turning on this feature reduces your device's battery life.

CONFIGURING VOICEMAIL SETTINGS

To configure your voicemail, tap the Voicemail button on the Call Settings screen to display the Voicemail screen. (See the left screen in Figure 10.11.) Here, you can configure the following settings:

■ **Service.** Tap this button to display the Service dialog box, which shows available voicemail services. You may see only the Your Carrier radio button; you may see the Your Carrier radio button and the Google Voice radio button; or you may see other options.

NOTE The options on the Voicemail screen can vary depending on your carrier.

- **Setup.** Tap this button to display the Setup screen. This screen normally contains only the Voicemail Number button, which displays the phone number for the voicemail. You can tap this button and use the resulting Voicemail Number dialog box to change the number.

- **Sound.** Tap this button to display the Sound dialog box, tap the sound or ringtone you want to hear when you've got voicemail, and then tap the OK button.

- **Vibrate.** Check this box if you want your phone to vibrate to notify you that you have voicemail.

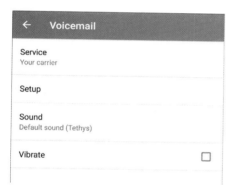
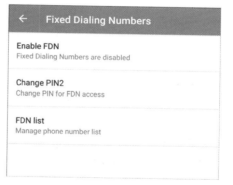

FIGURE 10.11

Use the controls on the Voicemail screen (left) to configure your voicemail. To limit outgoing calls to specific numbers, set up the FDN list and then enable the FDN feature on the Fixed Dialing Numbers screen (right).

LIMITING OUTGOING CALLS WITH FDN

The FDN feature enables you to limit the phone to call only specific numbers you save to the SIM card. You might want to set up FDN on a phone you give to a child.

NOTE The FDN feature is available only on phones that use the Global System for Mobile Communications (GSM) standard. If your phone uses the Code Division Multiple Access (CDMA) standard, FDN isn't available.

> **! CAUTION** To set up the FDN feature, you need to use a secondary PIN called PIN2. PIN2 is used to secure the FDN list against unauthorized access. PIN2 is separate from your unlocking PIN or your encryption passcode (or PIN).
>
> Some carriers put the PIN2 number on the SIM card, so it's worth looking there; failing that, you need to contact your carrier. Android phones typically allow you three attempts to enter PIN2 correctly and lock the FDN feature after three failures, so don't try to guess PIN2 more than twice.

Here's how to set up FDN:

1. Tap the Fixed Dialing Numbers button on the Call Settings screen to display the Fixed Dialing Numbers screen. (See the right screen in Figure 10.11.)

2. Tap the FDN List button to display the FDN List screen. You can then tap the Menu button and tap Add Contact to add a contact to the list. You'll need to type the contact name and phone number manually or copy and paste them from the Contacts app; you can't add this information directly from the Contacts app.

3. After you've set up the FDN list, tap the Enable FDN button on the Fixed Dialing Numbers screen. In the Enable FDN dialog box, type the PIN2, and then tap the OK button.

CHOOSING A TTY MODE TO HELP WITH HEARING PROBLEMS

If you have hearing problems, you can use the TTY Mode setting on the Call Settings screen to turn on a particular teletypewriter mode on your Android device. Tap the TTY Mode button to display the TTY Mode dialog box, and then tap the appropriate radio button: TTY Off (the default setting), TTY Full (for full teletypewriter features), TTY HCO (for Hearing Carry-Over functionality), or TTY VCO (for Voice Carry-Over functionality).

SETTING UP CALL FORWARDING

To set up Call Forwarding, tap the Call Forwarding button on the Call Settings screen to display the Call Forwarding Settings screen. Here you can configure these four settings:

- **Always Forward.** When you need to forward all calls, tap this button, enter the number in the Always Forward dialog box, and then tap the Turn On button.

> **NOTE** Some phones and carriers don't provide call forwarding. Others provide only some forwarding features, such as an All Incoming Calls button and an Unanswered button.

- **When Busy.** Tap this button to display the Forward When Busy dialog box, change the number if necessary, and then tap the Update button.

> **NOTE** The Forward When Busy, Forward When Unanswered, and Forward When Unreachable features are normally enabled and go to your voicemail service by default. You can redirect them as needed—for example, to a work colleague or a family member. You can also tap the Turn Off button in the feature's dialog box if you need to disable the feature.

- **When Unanswered.** Tap this button to display the Forward When Unanswered dialog box, change the number if necessary, and then tap the Update button.
- **When Unreachable.** Tap this button to display the Forward When Unreachable dialog box, change the number if necessary, and then tap the Update button.

CONFIGURING CALLER ID AND CALL WAITING

To configure Caller ID and Call Waiting, tap the Additional Settings button on the Call Settings screen. The Additional Settings screen appears. (See the left screen in Figure 10.12.) Tap the Caller ID button, and then tap the Network Default radio button, the Hide Number radio button, or the Show Number radio button in the Caller ID dialog box. (See the right screen in Figure 10.12.)

> **NOTE** Some phones name the Caller ID controls differently, such as Caller ID Readout. Other phones and carriers provide neither Caller ID nor Call Waiting.

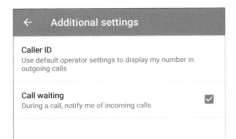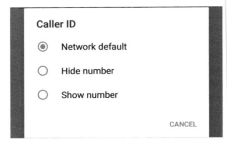

FIGURE 10.12

On the Additional Settings screen in the Phone app (left), you can configure Caller ID and Call Waiting. In the Caller ID dialog box (right), choose whether to show your number when calling, hide it, or go with the network default setting.

> **! CAUTION** Don't use the Network Default setting for Caller ID unless you know what it does. If you're not sure, ask your carrier or place a call to another mobile phone you can see to find out what the default setting for standard calls is.

Also on the Additional Settings screen, check the Call Waiting box if you want Call Waiting to notify you of incoming calls when you're already in a call.

Now that you've finished choosing call settings, tap the arrow button or the Back button below the screen to return from the Call Settings screen to the Settings screen.

> **TIP** In the United States, you can override your Caller ID blocking for a call by dialing *82 before the number. If you've turned on Caller ID, you can block it for a call by dialing *67 before the number. Other countries use different numbers for blocking and releasing; you can look them up easily on the Internet, but it's always a good idea to verify that they're working before relying on them.

TURNING ON CALLER ID BY GOOGLE

As you've seen earlier in this chapter, your phone can display the caller's name for any phone number in your contacts unless the caller has blocked Caller ID or there's another problem (for example, the call may be routed internationally or through a calling service). To see caller information for more numbers, you can enable the Caller ID by Google feature.

In Marshmallow, tap the Caller ID by Google button on the Settings screen to display the Caller ID by Google screen. In Lollipop, tap the Advanced button on the Settings screen to display the Advanced screen, and then tap the Caller ID by Google button. Then set the Caller ID by Google switch to On.

 NOTE Some phones don't offer the Caller ID by Google feature.

CHOOSING WHETHER TO USE THE NEARBY PLACES FEATURE

Apart from the About Phone button (which displays an informational screen), the last of the buttons on the Settings screen in Marshmallow is the Nearby Places button. Tap this button to display the Nearby Places screen.

NOTE Nearby Places uses your location (as determined by your device's GPS, by its cellular connection, or by known wireless networks nearby) to add nearby places from Google's database to your search results. Only some phones have the Nearby Places feature.

The left screen in Figure 10.13 shows the Nearby Places screen in Marshmallow. The right screen in Figure 10.13 shows the Nearby Places screen in Lollipop, which is a little different.

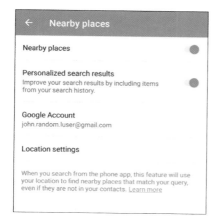
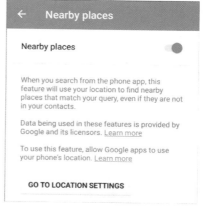

FIGURE 10.13

On the Nearby Places screen, set the Nearby Places screen to On if you want the results of your searches in the phone app to include nearby places that are not in your contacts. The Nearby Places screen in Marshmallow (left) includes the Personalized Search Results switch, which the Nearby Places screen in Lollipop (right) does not.

> **NOTE** In Lollipop, tap the Advanced button on the Settings screen to display the Advanced screen, and then tap the Nearby Places button to display the Nearby Places screen.

Set the Nearby Places switch to On if you want to use the Nearby Places feature. In Marshmallow, you can then set the Personalized Search Results switch to On if you want to allow Google to improve your search results by including items from your search history for the account specified on the Google Account button.

From the Nearby Places screen, you can tap the Location Settings button (in Marshmallow) or the Go to Location Settings button (in Lollipop) to display the Location screen. Here you can set the Location switch to Off if you want to turn off location reporting. You can also tap the Mode button and choose High Accuracy, Battery Saving, or Device Only on the Location Mode screen.

SETTING CUSTOM RINGTONES FOR IMPORTANT CALLERS

If you want to be able to distinguish your important callers easily, set a custom ringtone for each of them like this:

1. Open the contact in either the Phone app or the Contacts app.
2. Tap the Edit button (the pencil icon) to display the Edit Contact screen with the contact record open for editing.
3. Tap the Menu button and then tap Set Ringtone to display the Ringtones dialog box.
4. Tap a ringtone to listen to it.
5. After you've made your choice, tap the OK button.

> **TIP** If you tire of your device's built-in ringtones, you can download plenty more from the Internet. Alternatively, use an app such as Ringtone Maker from Big Bang Inc. (available free from the Play Store) to create custom ringtones from key sections of your favorite songs.

BLOCKING AND SCREENING CALLS

The great thing about having an Android phone is that anyone can call you at any time.

The bad thing about having an Android phone is that anyone can call you at any time.

To keep peace of mind and your privacy, you'll probably want to send some contacts' calls directly to voicemail, either sometimes or always. You may want to block some calls completely to prevent specific people (or specific phone numbers) from calling you. You may also want to screen your calls so that you can choose which to take and which to leave.

SENDING A CONTACT'S CALLS DIRECTLY TO VOICEMAIL

To send all of a contact's calls to voicemail, open the contact in the Contacts app or the Phone app, tap the Edit button, and then tap the Menu button and check the All Calls to Voicemail box.

BLOCKING CALLS

Sending a contact's calls to voicemail is straightforward. Blocking calls isn't. But here are four things you can do:

- **Have your carrier block specific numbers.** If you're being plagued by calls from a particular phone number, you can ask your carrier to block it. Setting up the blocking is a hassle, but it's effective.

> **TIP** If you are being troubled by telemarketing calls in the United States, you can register your phone number on the National Do Not Call Registry (www.donotcall.gov). The listing takes up to 31 days to become effective; not all telemarketers respect the Registry, but many do. If you're in another country, see if it has a similar registry or body.

- **Use a call-blocker app.** When you need to block calls from specific numbers, look at apps such as Call Control or Extreme Call Blocker. These apps let you choose which calls to take and which to avoid.

- **Use the Do Not Disturb feature in Marshmallow or the Interruptions feature in Lollipop.** See the section "Configuring and Using Do Not Disturb and Interruptions" in Chapter 1, "Getting Up to Speed with Android," for details.

- **Turn on Airplane mode.** When you need total peace and quiet, open the Quick Settings panel and tap the Airplane Mode button to silence all communications.

> **NOTE** Some phones have other blocking features. For example, if you have a Samsung phone, choose More, Settings, Call Blocking to display the Call Blocking screen. Tap the Block List button to display the Block List screen, where you can add phone numbers manually, from the call log, or from your contacts.

SETTING A SIM CARD LOCK

As you know, Android enables you to secure your phone or tablet against intrusion by setting a screen lock, such as a PIN or a password, and to secure your data by encrypting it. But a phone also has another point of vulnerability: Anyone who can get one-on-one time with the phone can remove the SIM card, insert it into another phone, and run up charges on your tab.

> **! CAUTION** To set a SIM card lock, you need to know the PIN Unlock Key, or PUK, for your SIM. Normally, you get the PUK from your carrier. For example, if your phone is on AT&T, log in to myAT&T, click Wireless, click Phone/Device, and then click Unblock SIM Card to get the PUK. On Verizon, log in to My Verizon, click About My Device, and then use the My PIN and Unblocking Key (PUK) controls.

To minimize the damage from someone filching your SIM card, you can lock it. Follow these steps:

1. Open the Settings app.
2. Tap the Security button to display the Security screen.

> **NOTE** Depending on your phone, you may need to take different steps here. For example, you may need to display the Security & Screen Lock screen or tap the button to assign a SIM PIN. On a Samsung phone, choose Lock Screen and Security, Other Security Settings, Set Up SIM Card Lock.

3. Tap the Set Up SIM Card Lock button to display the SIM Card Lock Settings screen.
4. Set the Lock SIM Card switch to On. The Lock SIM Card dialog box opens.
5. Type the SIM PIN.
6. Tap the OK button.

> **TIP** After enabling the SIM card lock, tap Change SIM PIN on the SIM Card Lock Settings screen and set a new SIM for security.

ADDING PHONE CALLING TO A TABLET WITH GOOGLE VOICE

If you have a tablet rather than a phone, and you're in the United States, consider adding the Google Voice app to it so that you can use the Google Voice telecommunications service. The app is free and the cost is minimal: Domestic and outbound calls from the United States and Canada are free, and calls from elsewhere cost $0.01 per minute. The main limitation is that the service is available only to Google account holders in the United States.

To get the Google Voice app, fire up the Play Store app, tap the Apps button, and then search for *Google voice*. Tap the right result, tap the Install button, and then review the extensive list of permissions that the app requires.

You first need to sign up for Google Voice. Open a web browser, either on your Android device or (easier) on a computer, and go to www.google.com/voice. Sign in with your Google account, and then go through the signup process for Google Voice. You need to verify your application using an existing U.S. phone number to prove that you're in the United States rather than maintaining a virtual presence through a virtual private network (VPN).

CHATTING, TALKING, AND CONFERENCING VIA HANGOUTS

Google's Hangouts app and Hangout service enable you to chat via text, via audio, or via audio and video across either a Wi-Fi connection or a cellular connection. Hangouts is the default app for text messaging in Marshmallow, Lollipop, Jelly Bean, and KitKat.

> **NOTE** Your Android device may let you choose between Messaging and Hangouts as your default messaging app.

Hangouts makes all three kinds of chat as simple as possible, but the underlying technologies are far from simple. Because of this, it's vital to configure your Hangouts account or accounts correctly so that you can get the most out of this app. You should also be aware of the wide range of configurable options that Hangouts offers, even if you choose to leave many of them set to their default settings.

> **NOTE** Google syncs your hangouts automatically across your devices that are logged in to the same Google+ account on Hangouts. This means that you can start a hangout on your phone, pick it up on your tablet, and then finish it on your computer.

GETTING AN ACCOUNT

To start using Hangouts, you need a Google account. Chances are that you'll have set up your Google account on your device already because you can't get far on Android without a Google account. But if you use multiple Google accounts on your device, you may need to set up another account at this point.

> **TIP** To get the most out of Hangouts, sign up for the Google+ service. With Google+, you can get up to nine people in a video chat in Hangouts; without Google+, you can have only yourself and one other person.

GETTING STARTED WITH HANGOUTS

To get started with Hangouts, tap the Hangouts icon on the Apps screen. If it's not there, open the Google folder and tap the Hangouts icon there.

> **NOTE** Hangouts may display the Find Your Friends screen, which prompts you to allow Hangouts to access your contacts. If you don't want to allow this, tap the Skip button. Otherwise, tap the Next button, and then tap the Allow button in the Allow Hangouts to Access Your Contacts dialog box that opens.
>
> The first time you launch Hangouts on a phone, the app prompts you to add your phone number to help people find you. Tap the I'm In button if you want to do this; otherwise, tap the Skip button. If you tap the I'm In button, the app prompts you to verify your phone number. Normally, you will want to do this.

Once you've gone through the preliminaries, the Hangouts screen appears. (See the left screen in Figure 10.14.) To get started with establishing yourself and configuring Hangouts to work your way, tap the Navigation Panel button or swipe right from the left edge of the screen to display the navigation panel. (See the right screen in Figure 10.14.)

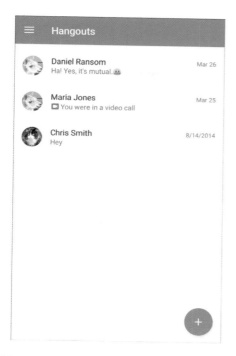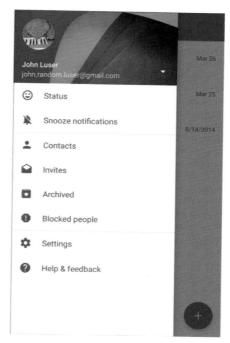

FIGURE 10.14

On the Hangouts screen (left), you can tap the + button to start a new hangout. Tap the Navigation Panel button or swipe right to open the navigation panel (right).

MAKING HANGOUTS COMFORTABLE FOR YOU

To make Hangouts comfortable for you, spend a few minutes setting your status and choosing settings.

SETTING YOUR STATUS IN HANGOUTS

Setting your status takes only a moment. Follow these steps:

1. Tap the Status button on the navigation panel to display the Share Your Status screen. (See the left screen in Figure 10.15.)

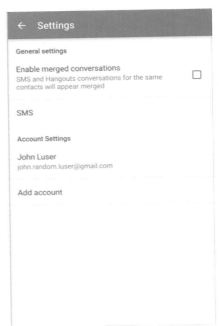

FIGURE 10.15

On the Share Your Status screen (left), type your current status and then tap the Update button. On the Settings screen (right), you can enable merged conversations, choose SMS settings, and choose account settings.

2. Type whatever you want your contacts to see—for example, how you're feeling or what you're doing. You can use up to 140 characters; the readout at the right end of the status line shows how many you've used.

3. Tap the Update button. Hangouts posts your status.

Tap the Navigation Panel button or swipe right from the left edge of the screen to display the navigation panel again. You'll see the status you just entered on the Status button for your reference.

CHOOSING GENERAL SETTINGS FOR HANGOUTS

Now tap the Settings button to display the Settings screen. (See the right screen in Figure 10.15.)

In the General Settings area, check the Enable Merged Conversations box if you want Hangouts to merge SMS conversations you have with a particular contact with Hangouts conversations with that same contact. Merging conversations is usually helpful.

CONFIGURING SMS FOR HANGOUTS

If you're going to use SMS in Hangouts, spend a few minutes choosing suitable settings. Tap the SMS button on the Settings screen to display the SMS screen. (See the left and right screens in Figure 10.16.) This screen has three sections: General, Notifications, and Advanced.

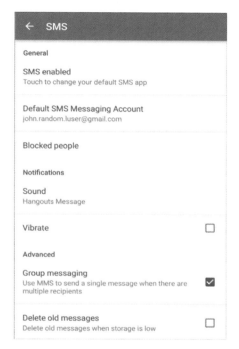
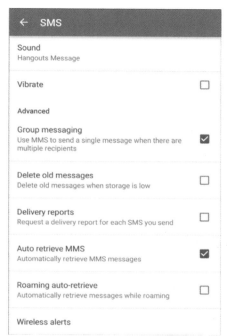

FIGURE 10.16

On the SMS screen (left and right), enable SMS for Hangouts and then choose how you want SMS to work.

In the General section of the SMS screen, you can configure the following settings:

■ **SMS Disabled/SMS Enabled.** If the SMS Disabled button appears, tap this button to make Hangouts your default SMS app. If the Change SMS App dialog box opens, tap the Yes button. If the Wireless & Networks screen in the Settings app appears, tap the Default SMS App button and choose a different SMS app (if you have installed one) in the Default SMS App dialog box.

> **⌨ NOTE**   On some devices, such as the Nexus 5, Hangouts is the default
> text-messaging app. You can't uninstall Hangouts, but you can install Google's
> Messenger app or a third-party messaging app and make it the default app instead
> of Hangouts. See the section "Sending Messages in the Hangout," later in this
> chapter, for information about other messaging apps.

- **Default SMS Messaging Account.** This button shows the Google account in Hangouts in which SMS messages sent to your Android phone will appear (if you have multiple accounts set up on it). To change the account, tap this button and then tap the appropriate Google account in the Select SMS Account dialog box that opens.

- **Blocked People.** Tap this button to display the Blocked People screen, which shows a list of people whose phone numbers you've blocked in Hangouts. Tap the Unblock button to unblock a number.

In the Notifications section of the SMS screen, you can configure the following two settings:

- **Sound.** Tap this button to choose the sound to play when an SMS message arrives in Hangouts.

- **Vibrate.** Check this box to have your phone vibrate when an SMS message arrives in Hangouts.

In the Advanced section of the SMS screen, you can configure the following settings:

- **Group Messaging.** Check this box to have Hangouts use Multimedia Messaging Service (MMS) instead of SMS to send a single message to multiple recipients.

- **Delete Old Messages.** Check this box to have Hangouts automatically delete old messages when your phone runs out of space. This feature is helpful unless you must keep your old Hangouts messages.

- **Delivery Reports.** Check this box to request a delivery report for each SMS message. You receive the delivery reports only if the recipient has allowed Hangouts to send them.

- **Auto Retrieve MMS.** Check this box to have Hangouts automatically retrieve MMS messages sent to your phone. This feature is usually helpful.

- **Roaming Auto-Retrieve.** You can check this box to have Hangouts retrieve MMS messages automatically when you are roaming. You may want to turn this feature off unless you have a generous data plan.

■ **Wireless Alerts.** Tap this button to display the Cell Broadcasts screen in the Settings app, which shows a list of emergency alerts broadcast on the cellular network.

CHOOSING ACCOUNT SETTINGS FOR HANGOUTS

On the Settings screen in Hangouts, tap your account name to display the settings screen for the account. (See the left and right screens in Figure 10.17.) This screen has five sections: General Settings, Notifications, How Others Get in Touch with You, Account, and Improve Hangouts.

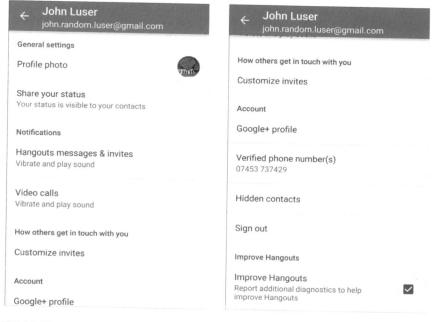

FIGURE 10.17

Use your account's settings screen in Hangouts to set your profile photo, choose notifications, and manage your profile and contacts.

In the General Settings section of the settings screen for your account, you can configure the following two settings:

■ **Profile Photo.** Tap this button to set your profile photo for Hangouts.

■ **Share Your Status.** Tap this button to display the Share Your Status screen. You can then check the Last Seen box if you want Hangouts to show the last time you were using Hangouts, and check the Device box if you want Hangouts to show which device you're currently using.

In the Notifications section of the settings screen for your account, you can configure the following two settings:

■ **Hangouts Messages & Invites.** Tap this button to display the Hangouts Messages & Invites screen. You can then check the Notifications box to receive notifications, tap the Sound button to choose the sound for incoming Hangouts messages and invitations, and check the Vibrate box to have your device vibrate (if it has a vibration motor).

■ **Video Calls.** Tap this button to display the Video Calls screen. This screen has the same options as the Hangouts Messages & Invites screen (discussed in the preceding bullet).

> **✓ TIP** On the Video Calls screen, choose a different sound than you're using for Hangouts Messages & Invites. This way, you'll be able to distinguish a video call by its ring.

In the How Others Get in Touch with You section of the settings screen for your account, tap the Customize Invites button to display the Settings screen for invitations. (See the left screen in Figure 10.18.)

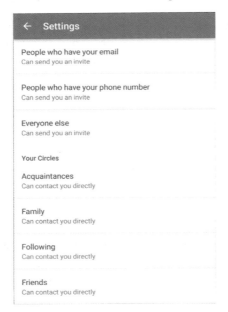
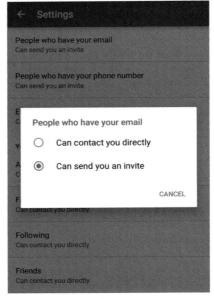

FIGURE 10.18

On the Settings screen for customizing invites (left), tap the group or circle you want to configure, and then tap the appropriate radio button in the dialog box that opens (right).

In the upper part of the screen, tap the People Who Have Your Email button, the People Who Have Your Phone Number button, and the Everyone Else button, in turn. In the dialog box that opens, tap the Can Contact You Directly radio button, the Can Send You an Invite radio button, or the Can't Send Invite radio button (if it's available).

In the Your Circles list, tap the button for each circle to open its dialog box, and then tap the Can Contact You Directly radio button, the Can Send You an Invite radio button, or the Can't Send Invite radio button.

When you finish working on the Settings screen for customizing invites, tap the arrow button or the Back button below the screen to return to the settings screen for your account. Then go to the Account section of the screen, where you can configure the following settings:

- **Google+ Profile.** Tap this button to open your Google+ profile in either the Google+ app or a browser.

> ## NOTE
> In some Android skins, the Google+ Profile button may not be available. If the Blocked Contacts button doesn't appear on your account's settings screen, look for it on the main Settings screen.

- **Verify Phone Number/Verified Phone Number.** If the Verify Phone Number button appears, tap this button to confirm the phone number to use for calls and SMS messages. If the Verified Phone Number button appears, you've already verified your phone number, and you don't need to do so again.

- **Blocked Contacts.** Tap this button to display the Blocked Contacts screen, which shows a list of the contacts you have blocked. Tap the Unblock button for anybody you want to reprieve.

- **Hidden Contacts.** Tap this button to display the Hidden Contacts screen, which shows a list of the contacts you have hidden. Tap the Unhide button to hide a contact.

- **Sign Out.** Tap this button to sign out of Hangouts. Normally, you can simply stay signed in to Hangouts.

In the Improve Hangouts section of the settings screen for your account, you can check the Improve Hangouts box to allow your device to send data to Google about how you use Hangouts so that Google can improve the app and the service.

COMMUNICATING VIA HANGOUTS

After you've set up Hangouts, communicating is largely straightforward—as soon as you know your way around the interface.

OPENING A NEW HANGOUT OR AN EXISTING HANGOUT

When you open Hangouts, the app displays the list of current hangouts (see Figure 10.20). A *hangout* is a chat session whose list of participants is saved, so you can easily return to chatting with the same person or group of people. Hangouts saves text chat history as well, so you can go back to previous chats.

> **✓ TIP** If you've set up Hangouts for multiple Google accounts, you can switch from one account to another by opening the navigation panel and then tapping the picture or account name for the account you want to use.

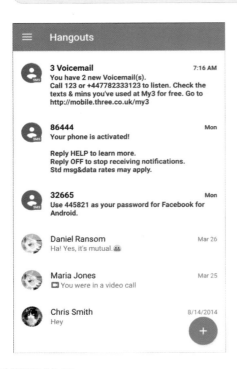

FIGURE 10.19

Hangouts displays your current hangouts so that you can easily return to them (left). To start a new hangout, tap the + button, and then tap New Video Call, New SMS, New Group, or New Conversation, as needed (right).

To start a new hangout, tap the + button to display the New Message icons. (See the right screen in Figure 10.19.) You can then tap the New Video Call button, the New SMS button (if your device has SMS and it is enabled), the New Group button, or the New Conversation button, depending on the type of hangout you want to create. This example uses New Conversation.

On the screen that appears, tap the first contact you want to add to the hangout. (See the left screen in Figure 10.20.) You can tap the contact either in the Frequent list at the top of the screen, which also shows an On Hangouts readout if the contact is currently on Hangouts, or in the Contacts list below it. The hangout then opens. (See the right screen in Figure 10.20.)

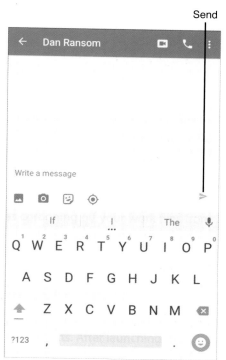

FIGURE 10.20

Tap the first contact you want to add to the hangout (left). Once in the hangout, you can send a message, a photo, an emoticon, or your location (right).

SENDING MESSAGES IN THE HANGOUT

After you've opened a hangout, you can chat with the other people in it. For a conversation hangout, simply type the message in the message box at the bottom of the screen and then tap the Send button to send it.

To switch to another type of chat, tap the appropriate icon at the top of the screen. The choices available depend on the device and the communications technology you're using. For example, on the right screen in Figure 10.20, you can tap the Phone icon to the left of the Menu button to place a phone call, or you can tap the Video icon to the left of the Phone icon to make a video call.

> **TIP** Hangouts enables you to record the history of a hangout. To do so, tap the Menu button in the hangout and then tap Turn History On.

CONFIGURING THE HANGOUT

To configure the hangout, tap the Menu button, and then tap People & Options to display the People & Options screen. (See the left screen in Figure 10.21.) Here you can take the following actions:

- **Add people to the hangout.** Tap the Add People button to display the screen for adding people. You can then add participants from the Frequent list or the Contacts list or by typing in the contact name, email address, phone number, or circle.

- **Block a participant.** You can block someone who is participating in a hangout via SMS by tapping the Block *Name* button on the People & Options screen for the hangout. Tap the Block button in the Block dialog box that opens. (See the right screen in Figure 10.21.) Blocking prevents the person from contacting you directly, and you no longer receive notifications about the person's messages. The person still appears in any group hangouts of which you're both members.

> **TIP** To unblock a contact, open the navigation panel, tap the Blocked People button to display the Blocked People screen, and then tap the Unblock button to the right of the contact's name.

- **Enable or disable notifications for the hangout.** Check or uncheck the Notifications box.

- **Set a distinctive chat message sound.** Tap the Chat Message Sound button and browse for a suitable sound.
- **Set a distinctive call ringtone.** Tap the Call Ringtone button and select a ringtone you will be able to identify easily.

Add People

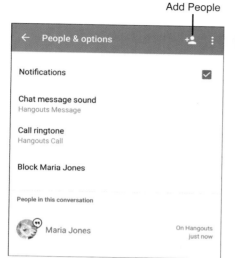
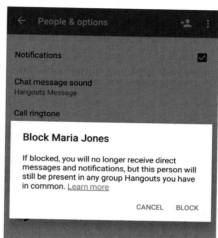

FIGURE 10.21

On the People & Options screen for the hangout (left), you can add other participants, block an existing participant (right), rename the hangout, or choose options to make the hangout easy to identify.

> **TIP** You can hide a contact from the Frequent list by tapping and holding until the Contact Options dialog box opens and then tapping Hide Contact. To get a hidden contact back, go to the main Hangouts screen, open the navigation panel, and then tap Settings. On the Settings screen, tap the account for which you hid the contact. Tap the Hidden Contacts button to display the Hidden Contacts screen, and then tap the Unhide button for the appropriate contact. The contact then reappears in the Frequent list.

MERGING HANGOUTS

If you've checked the Enable Merged Conversations box on the SMS screen in Hangouts Settings, Hangouts automatically merges your SMS messages from a particular contact with your other Hangouts messages from that contact.

> **✓ TIP** If you need to separate the SMS messages from the rest of the hang-
> out, tap the Menu button in the hangout and then tap Un-Merge SMS.

TROUBLESHOOTING THE MERGING OF HANGOUTS

If you've checked the Enable Merged Conversations box on the Settings screen, but SMS messages from a contact appear in a separate hangout from other messages from that contact, you may need to edit the contact's record to get the conversations to merge. In either the Contacts app or the Phone app, open the contact's record, and then tap Edit. Make sure that the contact record has both the right phone number (for SMS messages) and the right email address; if not, add the missing information. Save the changes.

Often, the problem is that you have two separate contact records: one with the phone number and the other with the email address. When this happens, open one of the contacts for editing, tap the Menu button, and then tap Link. Select the second contact record to link it, and then save the changes.

ARCHIVING A HANGOUT

When you've finished using a hangout for now, you can archive it. Archiving the hangout removes it from your Hangouts list and places it in the Archived Hangouts list, where you can access it again if you need to.

To archive a hangout, tap and hold the hangout in the Hangouts list until Hangouts switches to Selection mode. Then tap the Archive button (the folder icon bearing an arrow) at the top of the screen. The Hangout Archived pop-up message appears briefly at the bottom of the screen, with an Undo button that you can tap to undo the archiving if it was a mistake.

To return to a hangout you've archived, open the navigation panel and then tap Archived. On the Archived Conversations screen, tap the hangout.

DELETING A HANGOUT

When you no longer need a hangout, you can delete it:

1. Tap and hold the hangout in the Hangouts list until Hangouts switches to Selection mode.

2. Tap the Delete icon (the trash icon) at the top of the screen. The Delete Hangout dialog box opens.

3. Tap the Delete button.

11

EXPLOITING CAMERA, PHOTOS, AND VIDEOS

Always in your hand if not in your pocket or your bag, your Android device is perfectly positioned to take photos and videos of anything interesting you encounter.

Most Android phones and many tablets have both a front (screen-side) camera for taking shots and footage of yourself and your surroundings and a rear camera for shooting the rest of the world.

In this chapter, you'll explore how to get the most out of your device's cameras. That means configuring the Camera app to take the types of photos and videos you want, using the app's features to actually capture those shots and footage, examining your photos and videos, and editing your photos as needed. You'll also examine how to capture screenshots showing what's on your device's screen.

GETTING GREAT PHOTOS WITH THE CAMERA APP

In this section, you'll explore the Camera app, configure it to suit your needs, and then give its various modes a good workout.

> **NOTE** This section shows screens from the Nexus 5x running the Google Camera app in Marshmallow and screens from the Nexus 5 running the Google Camera app in Lollipop. Many phone and tablet manufacturers provide a custom camera app instead of Android's default. If your device has a different camera app or a different version of the Google Camera app, use the suggestions in this section for exploring the features that your device's app offers. If you have a Samsung device, see Chapter 14, "Using Samsung TouchWiz," for coverage of the Camera app on Samsung devices.

> **TIP** You can install the Google Camera app on any device that is running Lollipop or Marshmallow. The app is free from the App Store and is well worth trying. If your device is running Lollipop but has an older version of the stock Camera app, update to Google Camera to get the features described here.

OPENING THE CAMERA APP AND NAVIGATING ITS INTERFACE

Tap the Camera icon on the Home screen (it's usually there) or on the Apps screen to open the Camera app. The app has a stripped-down, uncluttered user interface, but there are some differences between the versions for Marshmallow and Lollipop and the versions for different devices. The left screen in Figure 11.1 shows the Camera mode, the mode you use to take regular photos, on the Nexus 5X running Marshmallow. The right screen in Figure 11.1 shows the navigation panel, which you display by tapping the Navigation Panel button and which gives you access to the various camera modes and the settings. This chapter refers to versions of the Camera app that looks like this as versions with the newer interface.

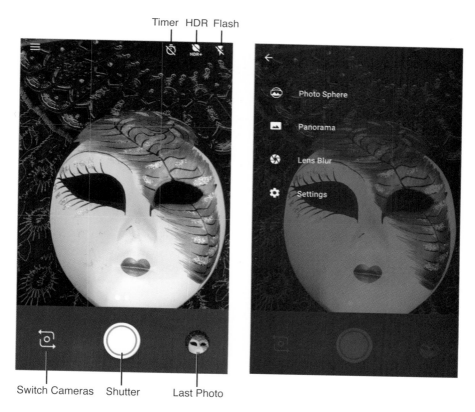

FIGURE 11.1

The Camera app in Camera mode on the Nexus 5X in Marshmallow (left). Tap the Navigation Panel button to display the navigation panel (right), which enables you to switch among modes and choose settings.

The left screen in Figure 11.2 shows the Camera app on the Nexus 5 in Lollipop. As you can see, the only visible control is the Options button (the ... button), to the left of which a small icon for any option currently in effect appears (in this case, the Flash Off icon). Tapping the Options button displays the Options bar (see the right screen in Figure 11.2), which enables you to quickly set options such as flash and HDR. This book refers to versions of the Camera app that looks like this as versions with the older interface.

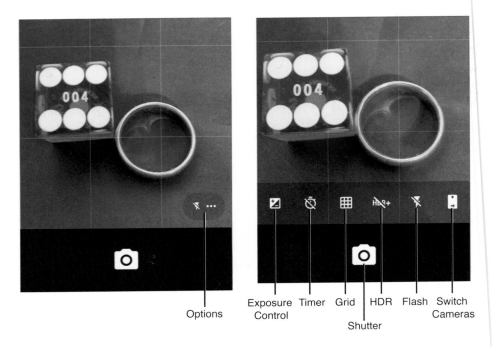

Exposure Timer Grid   HDR Flash Switch
Options   Control   Cameras
                              Shutter

FIGURE 11.2

The Camera app on the Nexus 5 in Lollipop (left). Tap the Options (...) button to display the Options bar (right) so you can choose options.

In this older version of the Camera app, there's no Navigation Panel button, so you swipe right to display the navigation panel.

The other main difference between the two interfaces of the Camera app is how you switch between Camera mode and Video mode. In the newer interface, you swipe left to switch to Video mode and swipe right to switch to Camera mode. In the older interface, you swipe right to display the navigation panel, and then you tap the Camera button for Camera mode or the Video button for Video mode— easy enough, but not quite as fast.

> **TIP** Some phones, such as the Nexus 5X, enable you to launch the Camera app quickly by double-clicking the Power button. To find out whether your device has this feature, open the Settings app, tap the Display button, and then look for the Press Power Button Twice for Camera switch. If the switch is there, set it to On to enable this feature.

ACCESSING THE CAMERA FROM THE LOCK SCREEN

To enable you to take photos quickly without messing about authenticating yourself, recent versions of Android let you access the Camera app directly from the lock screen. If the Camera icon appears in the lower-right corner of the lock screen, swipe left to display the Camera app.

You can then take photos as usual by tapping the Shutter button, or you can navigate the app as explained in the previous section. As usual, tap the Last Photo icon to display the last photo you took.

For security, the Camera app restricts you to taking photos and videos and viewing what you've just taken since the device was locked, so you can determine whether you've shot what you need or whether you need to keep shooting. After you swipe past the first photo or video you took, a lock screen icon appears. You can then unlock your device to view other photos.

Similarly, after displaying a photo or video in Lollipop, you can tap the Photos icon in the upper-right corner to jump to the Photos app—but to get there, you must unlock your device.

CONFIGURING THE CAMERA APP TO SUIT YOUR NEEDS

To get the most out of the Camera app, spend a few minutes configuring it to suit your needs. Open the navigation panel by tapping the Navigation Panel button or by swiping right (depending on which version of the Camera app you have), and then tap the Settings button to display the Settings screen. (See the left screen in Figure 11.3.)

> **NOTE** In older versions of the Camera app, the Settings button is the gear icon that appears on the right side of the screen when the navigation panel is open.

CHOOSING RESOLUTION AND QUALITY SETTINGS

Tap the Resolution & Quality button on the Settings screen to display the Resolution & Quality screen. (See the right screen in Figure 11.3.) You can then choose the following settings:

- **Back Camera Photo.** Tap this button to open the Back Camera Photo dialog box, and then tap the radio button for the resolution you want.

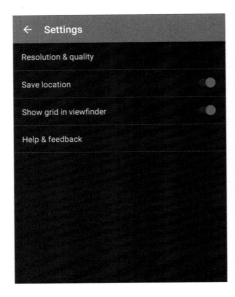

FIGURE 11.3

From the Settings screen for the Camera app (left), you can choose resolution and quality settings (right), turn on or off saving the location in photos, and toggle the display of the grid.

> **☑ TIP** When setting the Back Camera Photo resolution and the Front Camera Photo resolution, you'll normally want to use the highest resolution available. For some cameras, this means deciding whether to use the 4:3 aspect ratio or the 16:9 (widescreen) aspect ratio. Typically, the 4:3 aspect ratio uses all the camera's resolution, whereas the 16:9 resolution lops off the outer parts of the long sides. So unless you specifically need the widescreen format, you're usually better off shooting in the 4:3 format and then cropping the photos as required.

■ **Front Camera Photo.** Tap this button to open the Front Camera Photo dialog box, and then tap the radio button for the resolution you want.

> **✎ NOTE** The resolutions available for Back Camera Photo, Front Camera Photo, Back Camera Video, and Front Camera Video vary depending on your device's cameras.

■ **Back Camera Video.** Tap this button to open the Back Camera Video dialog box, and then tap the radio button for the video resolution to use.

> **TIP** You can down-resolve video as needed after shooting it, but doing so takes much more effort than down-resolving a photo. So it's a good idea to set the video resolution you'll normally want. If your device is short of space, shooting video at a lower resolution can help you avoid running out altogether.

> **! CAUTION** Some camera apps offer the CIF format for shooting video. CIF is the acronym for Common Intermediate Format, a standard video format that uses 352×288-pixel resolution. This resolution is low by today's standards, so avoid using it unless you're certain that it's what you need.

- **Front Camera Video.** Tap this button to open the Front Camera Video dialog box, and then tap the radio button for the video resolution to use.
- **Panorama Resolution.** Tap this button to open the Panorama Resolution dialog box, and then tap the High radio button, the Normal radio button, or the Low (Fastest) radio button, as needed.

> **TIP** To get the best Photo Sphere and panorama photos, tap the High radio button in the Panorama Resolution dialog box and use a tripod to keep your device steady while taking the photos.

CHOOSING WHETHER TO SAVE THE LOCATION IN YOUR PHOTOS

Back on the main Settings screen for the Camera app, set the Save Location switch to On or Off to control whether the Camera app saves the location in photos you take.

Saving the location enables you to sort your photos by locations, which is great for browsing and organizing your photos. The disadvantage of saving the location is that it enables anyone with whom you share the photo to see exactly where you took it. If you post photos online, this may be a privacy concern.

> **TIP** You can remove location information from a photo by using an app such as PhotoInfo Eraser or Pixelgarde Free, both of which you can download for free from the Play Store.

CHOOSING ADVANCED SETTINGS IN CAMERA VERSIONS WITH THE OLDER INTERFACE

In versions of Google Camera with the older interface, tap the Advanced button on the Settings screen to display the Advanced screen, and then choose from the available settings. At this writing, there's only one: You can set the Manual Exposure switch to On if you want to be able to control the exposure manually from the Settings bar. This switch controls whether the Exposure Control icon appears on the Options bar.

TAKING REGULAR PHOTOS

By this point, whether you've carefully chosen settings to suit your needs or you've decided to stick with the defaults, you should be ready to take photos. This section covers regular photos, the kind you'll likely want to take most of the time. The following sections cover the specialized photo types: Photo Sphere photos, panorama photos, and photos using the Lens Blur feature.

SWITCHING TO THE REGULAR CAMERA

If the Camera app doesn't display the regular Camera feature when you open the app, switch to it in one of these ways, depending on the version you're using:

- **Newer interface.** Swipe right from the Video screen.
- **Older interface.** Swipe right to display the navigation panel, and then tap Camera.

ZOOMING, FOCUSING, AND SHOOTING

To take a quick photo, aim the camera lens at your subject, and then tap the Shutter button.

> **TIP** You can press either the Volume Up button or the Volume Down button to take a photo.

To zoom in, place your finger and thumb (or two fingers) together on the screen and then pinch apart. To zoom back out, place your finger and thumb apart onscreen and then pinch together.

To focus, tap the point on which you want to place the focus. The Camera app displays a focus icon briefly (see the left screen in Figure 11.4) to indicate that it is adjusting the focus.

Tap where you want to focus.

FIGURE 11.4

Tap where you want to place the focus (left). In older versions of the Camera app, use the Manual Exposure bar (right) to adjust the exposure for the photos you take.

ELIMINATING CAMERA SHAKE

Camera shake—the camera moving while the shutter is open—can ruin a photo by making it blurred. The smaller and lighter the camera you're using, the easier it is to get camera shake when taking photos. With one of today's featherweight phones, getting camera shake is easier than falling off a log.

Some devices have automatic image stabilization for photos. But even so, you may need to use other means to steady your device when taking photos, especially when the light is low or when you have zoomed far in.

If you're taking photos of still subjects, a tripod remains the most effective means of stabilization. Where a tripod is impractical, try a monopod or a chest brace. You can also use a foot strap, which you slip around your foot and then hold the device under tension by pulling upward. To use any of these options, you need a tripod mount for your device.

When you have no hardware beyond your device, stabilize your position by using an available solid object, such as a tree, a building, or a vehicle. You may also be able to reduce camera shake by, instead of tapping the Shutter button to take a photo, tapping and holding the Shutter button while you line up the shot, and then releasing it when you're ready to take the photo. This trick doesn't work if your device has a Burst mode and you've enabled it because tapping and holding the Shutter button takes a burst of photos instead.

USING THE TIMER, GRID, HDR, AND FLASH

In versions of the Camera app with the newer interface, you can tap the icons at the top of the screen to control the timer, HDR, and flash. In earlier versions, tap the Options (…) button to display the Options bar, which contains these controls, the Grid button, and the Switch Cameras button.

- **Manual Exposure.** In versions of the Camera app with the older interface, tap this icon to display the Manual Exposure bar (see the right screen in Figure 11.4), and then tap the exposure you want: −2, −1, 0 (the default), +1, or +2.

> ☑ TIP Use the −1 exposure setting for backgrounds that are too bright for the automatic exposure control; use the −2 setting for extremely bright backgrounds, such as snow in sunshine. Use the +1 setting for a background that is too dark, and the +2 setting for photographing black cats in a coalmine at night.

- **Timer.** Tap this icon to cycle through the three settings: No Delay, 3 Seconds, and 10 Seconds.

- **Grid.** In versions of the Camera app with the older interface, tap this icon to toggle the grid on or off. Many people find the grid useful for composing their photos. You can use the grid simply to make sure that vertical objects are upright and horizontal objects are level on the screen, or you can use it to compose your photos according to the Rule of Thirds, a compositional guideline for placing your subjects in photos.

> ☑ TIP If you search online for *rule of thirds*, make sure you get the rule about photography rather than the rule about driving. (One-third of your gas supply is for the outward journey, one-third is for the return journey, and the last third is for safety).

■ **HDR+.** Tap this icon to toggle the HDR feature. HDR stands for High Dynamic Range. It improves the color and lighting balance of your photos, and sometimes it adds more detail by taking a series of shots in rapid succession and merging them into a single photo.

> **NOTE** Some cameras don't support HDR mode. Many support it on the rear camera but not on the front camera.

WHEN TO USE HDR AND WHEN NOT TO

HDR is a great feature in the Camera app and a great addition to your photography arsenal, so you'll probably want to use it often—but don't use it all the time.

Use HDR when you're taking photos of still subjects, such as landscapes, buildings, or still lifes (peaches, grapes, optional dead pheasant). Keep your device as steady as possible to make sure that each of the shots has the same alignment and contents, enabling Camera to merge them successfully. Use a tripod or other steadying device when you can, especially when shooting in low light.

Don't use HDR for anything involving movement, such as sports, children, or candid photos. You can't use HDR for any photos that need the flash because the Camera app disables the flash when you turn on HDR.

> **NOTE** Turning on HDR disables the flash and timer. It also disables Manual Exposure control in versions of the Camera app with the older interface (if you have set the Manual Exposure switch on the Advanced screen to On).

■ **Flash.** Tap this icon to cycle among the three flash settings: On (the lightning-bolt symbol), Automatic (the lightning-bolt symbol with an A to its right), and Off (the lightning-bolt symbol with a diagonal line through it).

> **TIP** Set the Flash feature to On when you need to force Camera to use the flash when it normally would not, such as when you need the flash to light up the shadowed face of a subject positioned in front of a bright background. Set Flash to Off when you need to be discreet or when you'll get a better effect with the ambient light.

- **Switch Cameras.** Tap this icon to switch from the rear camera to the front camera or vice versa.

> **NOTE** The capabilities of the front camera depend on the device, but a typical front camera has no flash and cannot use the HDR feature.

After selecting the settings you want, compose your photo and tap the Shutter button to take it.

REVIEWING YOUR PHOTOS QUICKLY

To see the photo or photos you've just taken, tap the Last Photo thumbnail in versions of the Camera app with the newer interface; in versions with the older interface, swipe left from the main Camera screen. The photo appears (see the left screen in Figure 11.5), and you can share it, edit it, or delete it by tapping the three icons at the bottom of the screen.

Share   Edit   Delete

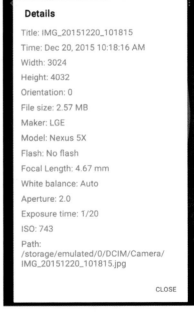

Details

Title: IMG_20151220_101815

Time: Dec 20, 2015 10:18:16 AM

Width: 3024

Height: 4032

Orientation: 0

File size: 2.57 MB

Maker: LGE

Model: Nexus 5X

Flash: No flash

Focal Length: 4.67 mm

White balance: Auto

Aperture: 2.0

Exposure time: 1/20

ISO: 743

Path:
/storage/emulated/0/DCIM/Camera/
IMG_20151220_101815.jpg

CLOSE

FIGURE 11.5

After displaying a photo for viewing (left), you can share it, edit it, or delete it. Open the Details dialog box (right) to see a photo's location, resolution, aperture, exposure time, and other details.

You can view the information for a photo by tapping the Menu button and then tapping Details. The Details dialog box opens (see the right screen in Figure 11.5), showing you a range of information from the date, time, and location; through the photo's resolution and orientation; whether the flash was used; and the focal length, aperture, exposure time, and ISO rating. Tap the Close button when you've seen enough.

Tap the arrow button or the Back button below the screen when you want to go back to the Camera screen so that you can take more photos.

IMPROVING YOUR PHOTOS USING TRIPODS AND LENSES

If you need to be able to keep your phone or tablet steady while taking photos, attach it to a tripod. All you need is a tripod mount for the device. Many of these are spring-loaded clips with a hole at the bottom threaded to receive a standard tripod screw—simple, but effective as long as they're strong enough. You can use any standard tripod, from a table-top toy to a professional monster.

Search online using terms such as *smart phone tripod mount, tablet tripod mount,* or *flexible tripod mount,* and you'll find plenty of options, usually starting from the price of a disappointing cup of coffee. Alternatively, see what your local electronics store can offer.

You can expand your photo-taking repertoire greatly by adding lenses to your phone or tablet. Many clip-on or stick-on lens sets are available that enable you to add macro, wide-angle, or fish-eye capabilities to your phone or tablet. These are straightforward to use, although you need to position them carefully to get the best effect. Both clip-on and stick-on lenses usually require you to remove any case from your device.

You can also get telephoto lenses and zoom lenses. Because these are typically bigger than macro, wide-angle, and fish-eye lenses, they need firmer fixing, such as a case with a lens mount built into it. This arrangement enables you to swap lenses easily and make sure the lenses are positioned correctly for the camera, so it's helpful if you use lenses a lot. But you have to remove any case from your device for these lenses as well.

TAKING PHOTO SPHERE PHOTOS

The Photo Sphere feature enables you to create panoramic photos that pan up and down as well as from side to side. These can be a lot of fun to view. The Camera app does a fine job of stitching together the component photos into a whole, but it helps to use a tripod with a smooth panning mechanism so you can keep the central point of the sphere the same.

In the Camera app, open the navigation panel, tap Photo Sphere, and then follow the prompts for aiming the lens. The Camera app displays white dots to indicate the areas you can go to next; when you track to a dot, it turns blue; and when you hold steady on a dot, Camera captures that section of the picture.

When you finish capturing the area for the Photo Sphere, tap the check mark.

TAKING PANORAMA PHOTOS

The Panorama feature enables you to take regular panorama photos—long, flat panoramas—but also vertical, square, and rounded panorama photos.

In the Camera app, open the navigation panel, and then tap Panorama. If you want to change the type of panorama, tap the icons at the top of the screen in versions of the Camera app with the newer interface; in versions with the older interface, tap the Options (…) button, and then tap the panorama type on the Options bar that appears. Tap the Shutter button, and then follow the dots.

When you finish capturing the panorama, tap the check mark.

TAKING PHOTOS WITH THE LENS BLUR FEATURE

The Lens Blur feature enables you to make a subject stand out more from the background. Lens Blur works with both the rear camera and the front camera on many devices, so you can use it for taking self-portraits as well as taking photos of other subjects.

> **TIP**   Lens Blur is mostly useful for close-up photos, such as portraits of people or pictures of objects, in which your subject is positioned in front of a background whose main features are some distance between them. For example, if you're taking a photo of your significant other in the park, you can use Lens Blur to make sure that the background is blurred to draw attention to the subject.

To use Lens Blur, take the photo and then move the device up to enable the Camera app to record information about the depth of objects in the picture. After taking the photo, you can adjust the amount of blur as needed. Follow these steps:

1. Open the navigation panel in the Camera app.

2. Tap Lens Blur to switch to Lens Blur mode.

3. Line up your shot and tap the Shutter button. Camera takes the initial photo and prompts you to move the device upward, keeping the subject centered.

> 📝 **NOTE**   If the light is low, Camera warns you of this and instructs you to move the device slowly.

4. Slowly raise your device, following the tracking arrow and keeping the subject centered in the frame until Camera displays a check mark.

5. Tap the Last Photo thumbnail (in versions of the Camera app with the newer interface) or swipe left (in versions with the older interface) to display the photo. You may have to wait while Camera processes the Lens Blur effect.

6. Tap the Lens Blur button (the shutter symbol, second from the left) to display the controls for editing the blurring.

7. If necessary, tap the point to which you want to move the focus.

8. Drag the slider to the left or right as needed. The left screen in Figure 11.6 shows a photo with a small amount of lens blur. The right screen in Figure 11.6 shows the same photo with blurring turned up all the way.

9. Tap the Done button when you are satisfied with the result.

FIGURE 11.6

Drag the slider on the Lens Blur screen to adjust the amount of blurring.

EDITING YOUR PHOTOS

It's great if you can get your photos perfect when shooting them, but chances are you'll need to edit many of your shots to get them just the way you want. Your Android device provides easy-to-use editing tools that enable you to make anything from subtle tweaks to wholesale changes.

To edit a photo from the Camera app, tap the Last Photo thumbnail (in the newer interface) or swipe left (in the older interface) to display the last photo you took. From here, swipe left as needed until you reach the right photo, and then tap the Edit button to open the photo for editing in the Photos app.

> **! CAUTION**   Many Android devices include multiple apps that can edit photos. So the first time you tap the Edit button for a photo in the Camera app, Android displays the Complete Action Using dialog box to let you decide which app to use. To follow these examples, tap Photos. If you want to use Photos for all your editing, tap the Always button; if you want to keep your options open, tap the Just Once button.

In Lollipop, you can also tap the Photos button in the upper-right corner of the screen to go to the Photos app. You can then browse the photos and start any editing directly in the Photos app.

The Photos app contains a variety of editing tools that range from basic moves (such as cropping and rotating photos) to more advanced moves (such as Tilt-Shift). These tools work in largely the same way, but some have extra features that you can switch to.

Here are the basic moves for using the editing tools:

1. Open the photo you want to change.

2. Tap the Edit button to turn on Editing mode.

3. At the bottom of the screen, tap the Tune Image button, the Effects button, or the Crop and Rotate button, depending on which type of edit you want to make. The left screen in Figure 11.7 shows these three buttons. The right screen in Figure 11.7 shows the Tune Image controls. The left screen in Figure 11.8 shows the Effects controls, and the right screen in Figure 11.8 shows the Crop and Rotate controls.

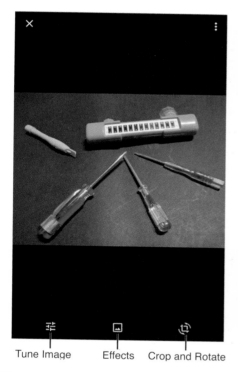
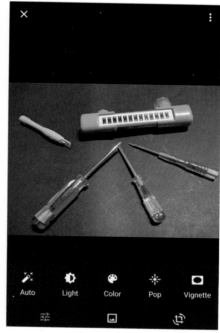

Tune Image   Effects   Crop and Rotate

FIGURE 11.7

In Editing mode (left), tap the Tune Image button, the Effects button, or the Crop and Rotate button. The editing controls appear, such as the Tune Image controls (right).

4. You use the tool's controls to manipulate the photo. For example, on the Crop and Rotate screen, drag the blue triangle on the rotation slider left or right as needed to straighten the photo.

> **TIP**   Tap and hold the screen to display the original photo temporarily so that you can see the effect of the changes you've made.

5. Tap the check mark to keep the changes you've made or tap the cross to discard them.

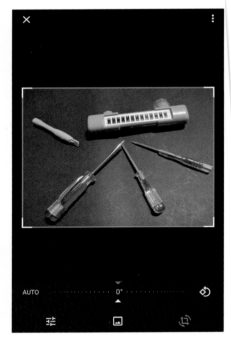

FIGURE 11.8

On the Effects screen (left), tap the effect you want to apply, drag the slider as needed, and then tap the check mark. On the Crop and Rotate screen (right), use the crop handles, rotation slider, and rotation button as needed.

SHOOTING VIDEOS

The Camera app makes it easy to shoot videos. Open the Camera app as usual by tapping its icon on the Home screen, and then switch to video mode:

- **Versions with the newer interface.** Swipe left from the Camera screen.

- **Versions with the older interface.** Swipe right to display the navigation panel, and then tap Video.

Any options available for video appear in the upper-right corner of the screen in the newer interface; in the older interface, you tap the Options (…) button to display the Options bar, and then tap the option you want to use. The options available depend on your device's camera and on the version of the camera app, but here are examples:

- **Switching cameras.** Tap the Switch Cameras button to switch between the rear camera and the front camera.

- **High-speed video.** Tap the Speed icon to switch between shooting at regular speed and shooting at high speed.
- **Grid.** Tap the Grid icon to toggle the grid on or off.
- **Flash.** Tap the Flash icon to enable or disable the flash.

After you've made those choices, tap the Shutter button to start shooting video. You can zoom in or out as needed by pinching outward or pinching together. Tap the Shutter button again when you're ready to stop filming.

 TIP While shooting a video, you can capture a still photo by tapping the screen.

CAPTURING SCREENSHOTS

Sometimes it's useful to capture what's on the screen of your Android device so that you can use it to amaze your friends or confound your carrier's tech support— or simply refer to it yourself later.

You can capture the screen on any stock Android device by pressing the Power button and the Volume Down button at the same time and holding them for a moment. This maneuver may be awkward until you get the hang of it, so it's worth practicing a few times before you need it. When you get it right, the screen gives a flash and displays a smaller version of what's onscreen, framed with a white border like an old-style photo, so you'll know you've captured the screen.

Android stores the screenshots in a folder called Screenshots inside the Pictures folder, so you can access them easily using any file browser.

TIP If you need to shoot a lot of screens on Android, install the Android SDK from the Android Developer website (http://developer.android.com), run the Monitor app, and use the Screenshot feature to capture screens. This method has the advantage of saving the screens directly to your computer. It's also useful for those (relatively few) screens you can't capture using the Power-and-Volume Down keypress.

IN THIS CHAPTER

- Getting your music onto your device or making it available online
- Enjoying music with the Play Music app
- Going further with other music apps

12

ENJOYING YOUR MUSIC EVERYWHERE

One of the great things about your Android device is that you can use it to enjoy high-quality music through headphones or speakers everywhere you go.

But should you put the music files on your device, or should you stream them across the Internet? Should you do both? And how do you get your existing music files, such as those on your CDs, onto your device? What format and compression should you use to get as much music as possible on your device at the quality you need, and how can you make it sound as good as possible?

In this chapter, you'll learn about the Play Music app. Stock Android devices come with this app, which provides plenty of features for playing back music either stored on your device or streamed across the Internet. Along the way, you'll discover options for dealing with the space problems that music addiction tends to bring to Android devices. Finally, you'll learn about some of the other music apps you may want to try on your device.

UNDERSTANDING YOUR OPTIONS FOR LISTENING TO MUSIC ON YOUR DEVICE

You have three main options for listening to music on your device:

- **Put your own music on your device and play it back from the device.** This is what you might call the old-school approach, but it remains simple and effective, and many people prefer it. The two disadvantages are that you need to get the music files, and your device must have enough space to hold them—plus all the other files you need to carry with you, not to mention preferably leaving several gigabytes free for you to shoot the next viral video.

- **Stream music from an online service.** Various online services (Spotify, Pandora, and so on) enable you to stream music from their servers across your Internet connection and play the music on your device. On the plus side, you can access a wide variety of music that you don't own, and you don't need to store the music files on your device. The disadvantage is that you may need to pay for the online service (typically via a subscription), and you always need an Internet connection to be able to play the music.

- **Put your music online, stream it, or store it on your device.** You can combine the two preceding approaches by putting your music collection online using a service such as Google's Play Music or Apple's iTunes Match. You can then either stream the music when you have a suitable Internet connection or put specific songs on your device so that you can play them anywhere, even when you don't have an Internet connection. The advantage of this approach is that you can play your music on a variety of devices (usually up to a set number of devices). The disadvantage is that you may need to pay for the service, and you need an Internet connection when streaming music.

GETTING YOUR MUSIC ONTO YOUR DEVICE

You can transfer your music files onto your device by using the techniques discussed in Chapter 2, "Loading and Syncing Your Device":

- **Windows 10 or Windows 8.** Use File Explorer to copy files.
- **Windows 7 and earlier versions.** Use Windows Explorer to copy files.
- **OS X.** Use Android File Transfer or another app to copy files.

> **NOTE** If you're going to use Google's Play Music service, you don't necessarily have to put music on your device because you can simply stream it all instead. Skip ahead to the section "Getting the Most Out of the Play Music App" to read about streaming with the Play Music app. The same goes for other streaming services: You don't need to put the music on your device.

Alternatively, if your device takes an SD card, you can copy the music files to the SD card using your computer and then insert the SD card in your device.

> **TIP** If your device doesn't take an SD card, you can copy the files to a USB On-the-Go drive and connect it to your device's micro-USB port. You can then either play the files from the drive or use a file-management app to copy them to the Music folder or another convenient folder.

> **NOTE** Android's default file system includes a folder called Music, which is the central repository for music files. To keep your device's file system neatly organized, you may want to put your music files here. But you can also store them in other folders because Android automatically makes all music files available to music-player apps, no matter which folder the files are in. If your device has limited built-in storage but enables you to add an SD card, putting your music on the SD card is usually the best approach.

UNDERSTANDING WHICH MUSIC FORMATS YOUR DEVICE CAN PLAY

Android can play music in the following formats:

- **MP3.** Technically, MP3 stands for "MPEG-1 Audio Layer III" or "MPEG-2 Audio Layer III," where MPEG stands for Moving Picture Experts Group, so it's no surprise that people simply use the abbreviation. MP3 is a lossy audio format (see the next tip) that sounds okay for music at bit rates of 128Kbps and pretty good at higher bit rates, such as 256Kbps or 320Kbps.

TIP Audio formats use either lossless compression or lossy compression to reduce the amount of space needed for an audio file. *Lossless compression* retains the full audio quality, whereas *lossy compression* loses some of the details—ideally the details that the human ear would normally miss anyway because they're masked by other sounds. Lossy compression is adjustable, so you can choose the quality, but typically it can compress audio far more than lossless compression.

NOTE Audio encoders use several settings to determine the quality and—indirectly—the file size. The key setting is the *bit rate*, which is the number of bits (individual pieces) of data per second. The bit rate can be either constant or variable. Variable bit rate (VBR) gives better quality than constant bit rate (CBR) at the same bit rate because it can use the bits more intelligently to store the data.

- **AAC.** Advanced Audio Coding (AAC) is a lossy audio format that provides slightly better quality than MP3. AAC is technically superior to MP3 and is Apple's preferred format for lossily compressed audio; it's widely used on Macs and on the various iPhone, iPad, and iPod models. Still, overall, MP3 is more widely used than AAC.

- **OGG.** Ogg Vorbis (variously referred to as "Ogg," "Vorbis," and "Ogg Vorbis") is a lossy audio format that delivers similar quality to MP3 and AAC at similar file sizes. At this writing, Ogg Vorbis is not widely used.

NOTE Ogg Vorbis and FLAC are open-source formats, which means that anyone can use them without paying licensing fees. By contrast, MP3 and AAC are both proprietary formats that require the payment of licensing fees. Usually, the manufacturers of the devices pay these fees, so you, as the user of a device, don't need to pay.

- **FLAC.** Free Lossless Audio Codec (FLAC) is a lossless compression format. FLAC delivers full-quality sound, but its files are large. As a result, FLAC is not a good choice for an Android device unless either the device has plenty of storage or you are happy to carry only a small amount of music with you.

- **PCM/WAV.** Pulse Code Modulation (PCM) and Waveform Audio File Format (WAVE or WAV, after the three-letter file extension) are uncompressed audio formats. This means they deliver full-quality audio, but the file sizes are huge, so you wouldn't normally want to use them on an Android device. These formats also don't have containers for the tag information in which the other formats store the artist, album, song name, and so on, so the only way to identify PCM and WAV files is by their filenames.

> ### 🗒 NOTE
> The preceding formats are built into Android. Some apps may support other music formats, but you're generally better off sticking with the main ones.

> ### ☑ TIP
> Opinions vary, but normally, you're best off using MP3 or AAC for audio files on your Android device. If possible, spend some time listening to MP3 files and AAC files encoded at 128Kbps and higher bit rates to decide the minimum level of quality you need. Listen to the songs on both your Android device and your computer (if you use one), and listen through both headphones and speakers.

GETTING YOUR CDS ONTO YOUR ANDROID DEVICE

If you have CDs containing songs you want to play on your device, you'll need to create digital files from the CDs. This process is called *ripping*, and you can perform it with many different apps on computers.

At this writing, iTunes is arguably the best free app for ripping audio files from CDs. iTunes comes built into OS X, so if you have a Mac, you already have iTunes installed. If you have Windows, you can download iTunes for free from Apple's website, www.apple.com/itunes/download/.

Here's how to configure iTunes with suitable settings for ripping your CDs:

1. Open the Preferences dialog box by pressing Ctrl+, (Ctrl+comma) in Windows or Cmd+, (Cmd+comma) on the Mac.
2. Click the General button on the tab bar to display the General pane.
3. In the When Insert a CD Is Inserted pop-up menu, choose Show CD.
4. Check the Automatically Retrieve CD Track Names from Internet box.
5. Click the Import Settings button to display the Import Settings dialog box. The left screen in Figure 12.1 shows the Import Settings dialog box in Windows.

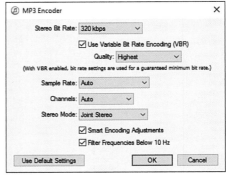

FIGURE 12.1

In the Import Settings dialog box for iTunes (left), choose the encoder and setting for the file format you want. To create high-quality files, choose custom settings in the MP3 Encoder dialog box (right) or the AAC Encoder dialog box.

6. Open the Import Using pop-up menu and click the encoder to use. Normally, you'll want to choose either AAC Encoder or MP3 Encoder.

7. Open the Setting pop-up menu and click the setting to use. The settings available depend on the encoder. For example, for AAC, you can choose High Quality (128Kbps), iTunes Plus, or Spoken Podcast. For MP3 Encoder, you can choose Good Quality (128Kbps), High Quality (160Kbps), or Higher Quality (192Kbps). To get other—or higher—quality on either MP3 Encoder or AAC, click Custom and work in the AAC Encoder dialog box or the MP3 Encoder dialog box. The right screen in Figure 12.1 shows the MP3 Encoder dialog box in Windows.

TIP For highest quality of AAC and MP3 files, choose the 320Kbps setting in the Stereo Bit Rate pop-up menu, leave the Sample Rate pop-up menu and Channels pop-up menu set to Auto, and check the Use Variable Bit Rate Encoding (VBR) box.

For MP3 Encoder, choose Highest in the Quality pop-up menu, choose Normal in the Stereo Mode pop-up menu, and check both the Smart Encoding Adjustments box and the Filter Frequencies Below 10 Hz box.

For AAC Encoder, check the Use High Efficiency box, but uncheck the Optimize for Voice box.

! CAUTION Use the Spoken Podcast setting only for spoken-word audio. It uses high compression that makes music sound horrible.

8. Check the Use Error Correction When Reading Audio CDs box. Using error correction slows down the ripping process a little but helps avoid getting skips and crackles in your audio files.

9. Click the OK button to close the Import Settings dialog box.

! CAUTION Don't choose the Apple Lossless Encoding option in the Import Settings dialog box in iTunes. This format is great for Apple devices (such as iPhones, iPads, and Macs), but most Android devices don't play it.

10. Click the OK button to close the Preferences dialog box.

NOTE In Windows, you can use Windows Media Player to rip CDs to MP3 files. Windows Media Player uses Microsoft's Windows Media Audio file format by default, so you need to change the settings. Click the Organize menu and then click Options to open the Options dialog box, click the Rip Music tab, and then open the Format drop-down list and choose MP3. Drag the Audio Quality slider to set the bit rate you want, and then click the OK button.

TIP If you want to create Ogg Vorbis files or FLAC files in Windows, use an app such as Total Audio Converter, which you can download from many software sites online. There's a 30-day trial, after which the app costs $19.90. The Audacity audio editor app (free from http://audacity.sourceforge.net) can also export audio in both Ogg Vorbis and FLAC formats. The easiest way to create Ogg Vorbis files or FLAC files on the Mac is by using XLD, which is available for free from various software sites.

After you've chosen your import settings, you can insert a CD in your computer's optical drive and rip it. Assuming you checked the Automatically Retrieve CD Track Names from Internet box, iTunes downloads the CD's details from the Gracenote database on the Internet and displays the results.

At this point, you can simply click the Import CD button to start importing the songs. But before you do, it's usually a good idea to look through the details that iTunes has retrieved and correct any errors. The Gracenote database contains an impressive amount of information, but it has many typos and other errors.

If any item of the CD info as a whole is wrong, click the CD Info button and use the CD Info dialog box to change it. This dialog box contains fields for the artist, composer, album title, disk number (for example, disk 1 of 2), genre, and year. You can also check the Compilation CD box if this CD is a compilation by different artists.

! CAUTION Check the Compilation CD box in the CD Info dialog box only if the CD is a compilation by different artists, not a compilation from the works of a single artist. Checking this box makes iTunes store the file in the folder called Compilations instead of in the artist's folder. When the CD is by a single artist, store the files in the artist's folder, where you can find them easily.

To change the information for an individual track, you can click a field twice to open it for editing. Pause between the clicks so that iTunes doesn't receive a double-click, which starts the track playing. For more extensive changes, right-click or Ctrl+click the track name and then click Get Info to display the Information dialog box, which gives you access to a wide range of fields for the track.

TIP When importing CDs, you'll often need to change the genre allocated to the music. Music fans can argue all day long about exactly which genre any given track belongs to, and iTunes and other apps enable you to assign a genre to each track rather than having to assign the genre at the album level (so that each track must have the same genre). To keep your music library straight and enable you to find the types of music you want easily, assign the genre that you will find most useful, no matter what genre other people suggest.

TRANSCODING EXISTING FILES

If you have music files in formats that your device can't play, you have two options: Either install an app that can play back the files, or transcode the files to a supported format so that you can play them with your existing app.

Usually, transcoding the files is the better option because it enables you to use your preferred music player for all your music. If the files in question are lossless, you can transcode them to another lossless format without losing quality or transcode them to your preferred lossy format with the normal loss in quality. Transcoding lossy files to another lossy format sacrifices more audio quality—you get any defects the first lossless format produced plus any defects the transcoding adds—but usually produces acceptable results. (If the results aren't acceptable, you can delete the transcoded files and figure out a plan B.)

In Windows, iTunes can transcode WMA files to a format such as MP3 or AAC. Otherwise, you'll need an app such as Total Audio Converter for Windows or XLD for the Mac.

GETTING THE MOST OUT OF THE PLAY MUSIC APP

The Play Music app is the app Google provides for enjoying music on mobile devices. Play Music can play music stored on your phone or device, but its most compelling feature is its ability to stream songs stored online. You can store 50,000 songs in your Google account. And if you subscribe to Google Music or to YouTube Red, you can also listen to any of the millions of songs in the Google Music catalog.

> **TIP** If your device doesn't have the Play Music app installed, open the Play Store app, search for **play music**, and then install the app. It's free.

GETTING STARTED WITH PLAY MUSIC

To get started with Play Music, tap the Play Music icon on the Home screen or on the Apps screen and then click Listen Now. The first time you launch the Play Music app, you need to decide between standard use (tap the No Thanks button) or sign-ing up for a trial subscription (tap the Get Started button). You may want to start with standard use, which enables you to upload 50,000 of your songs to Google Play and listen to them on your devices.

After you've made that decision, the Listen Now screen appears. (See the left screen in Figure 12.2.) This screen gives you access to your recent activity, such as songs you've played or purchased, and to instant mixes of songs. To navigate to the My Library screen, which enables you to access your music, tap the Navigation Panel button to display the navigation panel (see the right screen in Figure 12.2) and then tap My Library.

If your device contains songs, you can start playing them by navigating to one of them and tapping it. For example, on the Listen Now screen, tap an album to open it, and then tap the song you want to play.

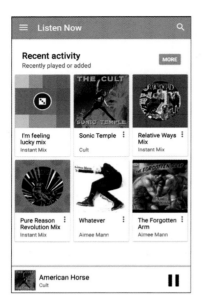
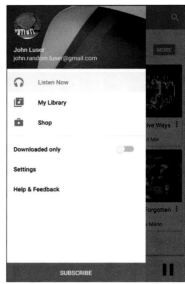

FIGURE 12.2

The Listen Now screen (left) gives you access to your recent music and to instant mixes. To navigate to your library, tap the Navigation Panel button and then tap My Library on the navigation panel (right).

SETTING UP AN ACCOUNT

If you've set up a Google account on your Android device, the Play Music app automatically uses that account. If necessary, you can switch to another account by following these steps:

1. Tap the Navigation Panel button to display the navigation panel.
2. Tap Settings to display the Music Settings screen.
3. In the Account section, tap the Google Account button to display the Select an Account screen.
4. Tap the existing account to use, or tap the Add Account button and follow through the resulting screens to set up a new account.

SYNCING YOUR 50,000 SONGS TO PLAY MUSIC

If you plan to sync songs to Google Play so that you can play them back with the Play Music app on your device, download and install the Google Music Manager app from https://music.google.com/music/listen#manager_pl. Click the Download

Music Manager button to download the app's distribution file, and then install it by double-clicking the file in Windows or by dragging the app's file from the disk image to the Applications folder on OS X.

After installing Music Manager, open it from the Start screen or Start menu (in Windows) or from Launchpad on the Mac. The Music Manager setup routine runs, and you can configure the app by doing the following:

1. On the Sign In with Your Google Account screen, sign in using the Google account you will use for music on your computer and your device.

2. On the What Would You Like to Do screen, select the Upload Songs to Google Play radio button and click the Continue button.

3. On the Where Do You Keep Your Music Collection screen (see Figure 12.3), select the iTunes radio button, the Music Folder radio button, or the Other Folders radio button, as appropriate. If you select the Other Folders radio button, click the Add Folder button and add the folders to the list box. Click the Continue button when you're done.

FIGURE 12.3

On the Where Do You Keep Your Music Collection screen, specify the folders you want Music Manager to search for music to upload to your Google Play account.

4. On the screen that asks whether you want to automatically upload songs you add to your selected folders in the future, click the Yes button or the No button, as appropriate. Uploading the songs automatically can be helpful, but you may want to perform quality control on your computer first to avoid loading songs you don't like into your Google Play account.

5. Follow through the remaining screens until the Your Music Is Being Added screen appears. You can then click the Go to Music Player button to open the online music player in your default web browser or click the Close button to close the Music Manager setup routine without opening the online music player.

> **NOTE** Uploading your songs will likely take hours or maybe days, depending on how many songs you're uploading and how fast your Internet connection is. Instead of simply uploading each song from your computer, Music Manager identifies as many matching songs as possible in Google's online library and makes those songs available to you; it then uploads those songs of yours for which Google has no matches.
>
> You can pause the upload at any time by giving the Pause command from the Music Manager icon in the notification area in Windows or toward the right end of the menu bar in OS X. From the pop-up menu, you can also click Go to Music Player to display the music player in your browser.

BUYING SONGS FROM THE PLAY STORE

The Play Music app makes it easy for you to buy music from the Play Store. From within the Play Music app, you can get to the Music section of the Play Store in a couple of ways:

- **Go to the Home screen of the Music section.** In the Play Music app, open the menu panel and then tap Shop. The Shop button is dimmed if you have set the Downloaded Only switch (which you'll learn about shortly) to On.

- **Go to a particular artist.** Tap the menu button for an artist, album, or song, and then tap Shop This Artist on the menu.

In each case, the Play Music app switches you over to the Play Store app. If you prefer, you can simply start with the Play Store app by tapping its icon on the Home screen or on the Apps screen. On the Home screen of the Play Store, either tap the Music button to start browsing music, or simply search by the name of the artist, album, or song you're looking for.

You can preview a song by tapping the Play button to its left. When you find a song you want to buy, tap its price button and then follow through the payment process.

> ☑️ **TIP** If you'd like some free music, look at the Free & Discounted Music area on the Home page of the Music section of the Play Store. You can tap the More button to display the Free Music screen, which shows all the free songs. These songs are genuinely free, but you still have to specify your means of payment and tap the Buy button to approve the payment of $0.00.

NAVIGATING THE PLAY MUSIC APP

The Play Music app has two main areas:

- **Listen Now.** The Listen Now screen provides quick access to the music you've added recently, music you've played recently, and music that Google Play recommends for you.

- **My Library.** The My Library screen has multiple tabs that enable you to browse by playlists (see the left screen in Figure 12.4), by instant mixes, by genres, by artists, by albums, or by songs (see the right screen in Figure 12.4). Tap the tab by which you browse; alternatively, swipe left or right to move from tab to tab. Tap the menu button for an item (such as a song) to display the menu of actions you can take with it, such as Play Next or Go to Artist.

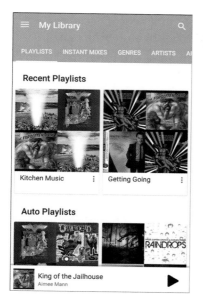
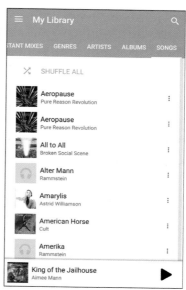

FIGURE 12.4

On the My Library screen, tap Playlists, Instant Mixes, Genres, Artists, Albums, or Songs. You can then browse your music or start it playing.

The songs in your music library are those you've loaded onto your device and those you've uploaded to the Play Music service. You can download songs from the Play Music service and store them on your device so that you can play them directly from the device without streaming. We'll look at how to do this a little later in this chapter.

> **NOTE** The Playlists screen contains three categories of playlists. The Recent Playlists category contains playlists you've created or edited recently. The Auto Playlists category contains playlists that the Play Music app maintains for you, such as the Last Added playlist and the Free and Purchased playlist, to give you easy access to particular categories of music. The All Playlists category shows all the playlists you've created.

Apart from the Listen Now button and the My Library button, the menu panel also contains one control and two other commands (plus the Help command and the Send Feedback command):

- **Shop.** Tap this command to go to the Music section of Google Play in the Play Store app.

- **Downloaded Only.** Tap this switch, turning it from gray (off) to orange (on), to set the Play Music app to display only the music on your device. You'd do this when your device doesn't have an Internet connection or when you don't want to use up your cellular allowance by streaming music.

- **Settings.** Tap this command to display the Music Settings screen. You'll look at this in the section "Configuring the Play Music App," later in this chapter.

PLAYING SONGS

To play a song, navigate to it and then tap it. Here's an example:

1. Tap the Navigation Panel button to display the navigation panel.
2. Tap My Library to display the My Library screen.
3. Tap the Artists tab button to display the Artists screen. (See the left screen in Figure 12.5.)
4. Tap the artist to display the list of albums.
5. Tap the album to display the list of songs from the album.
6. Tap the song you want to play. A playback indicator showing three moving vertical bars appears. (See the right screen in Figure 12.5.)

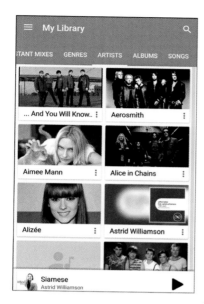

FIGURE 12.5

You can navigate easily to a song via the Artists screen (left). When you start a song playing, the playback indicator appears.

From here, you can tap another song to play it or tap the Now Playing button at the bottom of the screen to display the Now Playing screen. (See Figure 12.6.) You can easily control the music:

- Use the playback controls to pause or resume playback, fast-forward or rewind, skip to the next song, or go back to the previous song.
- Drag the Playhead to scrub quickly through the song.
- Tap the Repeat button to cycle through Repeat Off, Repeat All, and Repeat One.
- Tap the Shuffle button to toggle shuffling on or off.
- Tap the thumbs-up icon to like the song or the thumbs-down icon to dislike it.
- Tap the Queue button to display the queue of songs due to play next. You can then tap another song to start it playing.
- Tap the Menu button to display the menu, which contains commands such as Start Instant Mix, Add to Playlist, Go to Artist, Go to Album, Clear Queue, and Shop This Artist.

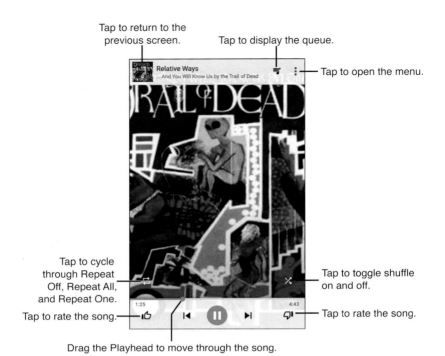

Tap to return to the previous screen.

Tap to display the queue.

Tap to open the menu.

Relative Ways
...And You Will Know Us by the Trail of Dead

Tap to cycle through Repeat Off, Repeat All, and Repeat One.

Tap to toggle shuffle on and off.

Tap to rate the song.

1:25   4:43

Tap to rate the song.

Drag the Playhead to move through the song.

FIGURE 12.6

From the Now Playing screen, you can drag the Playhead to move quickly through the song, turn on repeat or shuffle, rate the song, and display the track list.

TIP The queue contains the list of songs that will play next. You can add a song to the queue by opening the menu and then tapping Add to Queue. (If the song is already in the queue, the Remove from Queue command appears on the menu instead of the Add to Queue command.) To clear the current songs from the queue, tap the Menu button on the Now Playing screen and then tap Clear Queue. To save the contents of the queue as a playlist, tap the Menu button, and then tap Save Queue. In the Add to Playlist dialog box, you can either tap an existing playlist to add the queue's contents to it or tap New Playlist to create a new playlist.

NOTE If you lock your device while music is playing or Android locks it after the Sleep interval you have set, the music continues to play. Android displays playback controls on the lock screen enabling you to pause and resume the music without unlocking your device. You can also skip to the next song, return to the beginning of the current song, or go back to the previous song.

DOWNLOADING SONGS

The Play Music app shows both the songs that are actually on your device and those that are stored online in your Google Play library. When you start to play a song that isn't on your device, the Play Music app streams it across your device's Internet connection.

When you don't have a Wi-Fi connection, you may want to turn off streaming music so as not to use your cellular data plan. Tap the Navigation Panel button to display the navigation panel and then set the Downloaded Only switch to On to make the Play Music app show only the songs that are on your device and that you can play without streaming. The app displays a readout saying Downloaded Only near the top of the screen to remind you that you've restricted the library.

You can download songs from your Google Play library to your device as needed—preferably over a Wi-Fi connection. Tap the Albums button to display the albums screen, navigate to the album you want to download, tap the Menu button, and then tap Download.

DELETING SONGS FROM YOUR DEVICE AND YOUR LIBRARY

If you don't like a song, you can delete it. You may also want to delete songs if your device becomes too full and you need to clear some space on it.

> **!CAUTION** Because the Play Music app shows you both the songs actually on your device and those in your Google Play library, you need to be careful when deleting songs.

If the song is part of an album you've downloaded from your Google Play library, you'll usually do best to remove the album from your device. This keeps the album in your Google Play library so that you can play it again via streaming any time.

To remove an album, go to the album's screen, tap the album's Menu button, and then tap Remove Download. In the confirmation dialog box that opens, tap the Remove button; you can check the Don't Ask Me Again box first if you want to suppress this confirmation in the future.

You can also simply delete a song by going to the song, tapping its Menu button, and then tapping Delete. What happens then depends on whether you've copied the song to your device directly or it is in your Google Play library:

- **Song copied to your device.** A delete confirmation dialog box opens showing the song's name. (See the left screen in Figure 12.7.) Tap the OK button to delete the song.

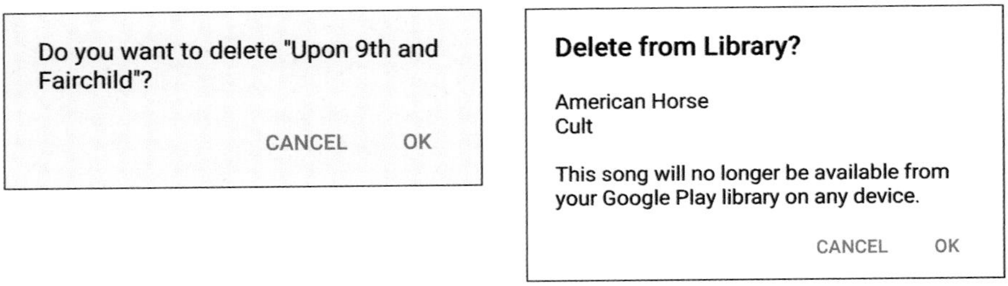

Do you want to delete "Upon 9th and Fairchild"?

CANCEL   OK

Delete from Library?

American Horse
Cult

This song will no longer be available from your Google Play library on any device.

CANCEL   OK

FIGURE 12.7

A delete confirmation dialog box (left) indicates the song is one that you've copied to your device. The Delete from Library dialog box (right) checks that you want to remove the song from your Google Play library, not just from your device.

■ **Song in your Google Play library.** The Delete from Library dialog box opens. (See the right screen in Figure 12.7.) You can tap the OK button to delete the song, but normally it's best to tap the Cancel button and then use the Remove Download command to remove the downloaded album, leaving the songs in your Google Play library.

CONFIGURING THE PLAY MUSIC APP

Like most apps, the Play Music app offers a variety of settings that you can customize to make the app work your way. To configure it, tap the Navigation Panel button to open the navigation panel, tap Settings, and then work on the Music Settings screen (see Figure 12.8).

TIP If you play streaming music with the Play Music app, it's important to configure your streaming and caching settings to make sure you don't run through your data allowance unintentionally.

The Music Settings screen has five sections: Account, General, Playback, Downloading, and About Play Music.

NOTE If you have an Android Wear device connected to your Android device, an extra section called Android Wear appears after the Downloading section on the Music Settings screen.

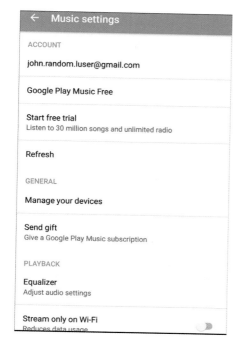
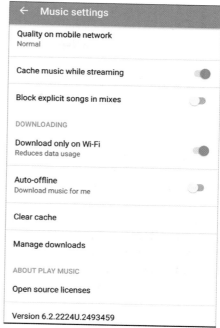

FIGURE 12.8

The Music Settings screen enables you to manage your devices, control downloading and caching, and access the Equalizer.

Here's what you can do with the Account settings:

- **Google Account.** Tap this button to display the Select an Account screen. You can then select the account you want to use for Google Play Music.
- **Google Play Music Free.** This button shows the status of your account.
- **Start Free Trial.** Tap this button to start setting up a free trial of access to all the music on Google Play. When the trial ends, continuing all access costs $9.99 per month.
- **Refresh.** Tap this button to refresh the list of music from Google Play. You'd want to do this after uploading songs from your computer to Google Play.

Here's what you can do with the General settings:

- **Manage Your Devices.** Tap this button to display the Your Devices screen, which lists the devices you're using for Google Play Music. You can use up to 10 devices at a time. To stop using a device, tap its button, and then tap the Deauthorize button in the Deauthorize Device dialog box that appears.

- **Send Gift.** Tap this button to access a screen for sending someone a sub-scription to Google Play Music.

Here's what you can do with the Playback settings:

- **Equalizer.** Tap this button to choose Equalizer settings. You'll look at how to do this a little later in this chapter.

- **Stream Only on Wi-Fi.** (Cellular-capable devices only.) Set this switch to On to prevent your device from streaming music across the cellular network. As with downloads, if your data plan is less than generous, you'll probably want to check this box.

- **Quality on Mobile Network** *or* **Mobile Networks Stream Quality.** (Cellular-capable devices only.) Tap this button, whose name varies between phones and tablets at this writing, to display the Quality on Mobile Network dialog box or the Mobile Network Stream Quality dialog box. Here, you can choose the Low radio button, the Normal radio button, or the High radio button to control how fast you burn through your data allowance while streaming audio across the cellular connection.

- **Cache Music While Streaming.** Set this switch to On to enable the Play Music app to *cache* (store) data temporarily while streaming music. Caching helps prevent interruptions, so it's usually helpful. Turn caching off only when your device is crammed full of data.

- **Block Explicit Songs in Mixes.** Check this box to prevent Play Music from including in mixes any songs that are marked as Explicit. This setting doesn't ensure complete sanitization of the music, but it's pretty solid—although it seems to block the occasional "explicit" instrumental that features too much sax and violins.

These are the Downloading settings you can choose:

- **Download Only on Wi-Fi.** (Cellular-capable devices only.) Set this switch to On to prevent your device from downloading music across the cellular net-work. If you've got a meager data plan, it's a good idea to set this switch to On.

- **Auto-Offline.** Set this switch to On to have Play Music automatically down-load music for you so that you can play it offline. This feature, introduced in November 2015, appears to try to download a moderate amount of the music you're most likely to want on your device. If you set the Auto-Offline switch to on, be sure to set the Download Only on Wi-Fi switch to On as well.

- **Clear Cache.** Tap this button to delete all the cached music. Normally, you'd want to do this only to reclaim the space the cached music is occupying. If your device is okay for space, leave the cached music in place to minimize streaming on songs you've played recently.

■ **Manage Downloads.** Tap this button to display the Manage Downloads screen so that you can see which songs the Play Music app is currently downloading.

> **NOTE** The About Play Music section of the Music Settings screen contains the Open Source Licenses button, which you can tap to see the details of the open-source licenses that the app uses, and the Version button, which displays the app's version number. You might need the version number when reporting or troubleshooting a problem with the app.

CREATING PLAYLISTS

The Play Music app makes it easy to create playlists containing only the songs you want to hear and in your preferred order. You can start creating a playlist from any song in your library. You can also quickly add songs to an existing playlist.

Here's how to create a playlist:

1. Navigate to the song or other item you want to put in the playlist.
2. Tap the item's Menu button and then tap Add to Playlist on the menu. The Add to Playlist dialog box opens. (See the left screen in Figure 12.9.)

FIGURE 12.9

From the Add to Playlist dialog box (left), tap New Playlist to start a new playlist, or tap the existing playlist. In the New Playlist dialog box (right), type the name and description for the playlist and decide whether to make it public.

3. Tap New Playlist. The New Playlist dialog box opens. (See the right screen in Figure 12.9, which has some settings already chosen.)

4. Type the name and description for the playlist.

> **☑ TIP**   The description is to help you identify the playlist from others with similar names, so it's a good idea to type something clear, no matter how redundant it seems now.

5. Set the Public switch to On if you want to make the playlist visible to other people on Google Play.

6. Tap the Create Playlist button.

Now that you've created the playlist, you can add other songs—or other items, such as an album or artist—to it by tapping each item's Menu button, tapping Add to Playlist, and then tapping the playlist's name in the Add to Playlist dialog box.

To play back a playlist, tap the Playlists tab on the My Library screen to display the Playlists screen. You can then tap the playlist to open it and tap a song to start it playing.

> **☑ TIP**   To change a playlist you've created, display the playlist. You can then drag a song up or down the playlist using the handle on the left side; alternatively, tap and hold the song until it becomes mobile, and then drag it up or down the list. To remove a song from the playlist, swipe it off to the left or to the right.

IMPROVING YOUR MUSIC WITH THE EQUALIZER

To make the music to which you listen sound as good as possible through your headphones or speakers, it's a good idea to use the equalizer built into the Play Music app. You can either apply an existing equalization, such as Folk or Heavy Metal, or create a custom equalization that suits your ears and your headphones or speakers.

> **☑ TIP**   If you often listen to music using your Android device, consider getting a headphone amplifier to improve the sound. A headphone amplifier is a small device that enables you to adjust the sound balance or turn up the volume.

TURNING ON THE EQUALIZER

Connect your headphones or speakers and set some music playing so that you can hear the effects of the changes you make. Then open the menu panel, tap Settings to display the Settings screen, and then tap Equalizer. On the Equalizer screen (see the left screen Figure 12.10), set the switch to On, enabling the other controls.

> **NOTE** The equalizer may not be available on all devices.

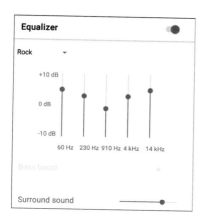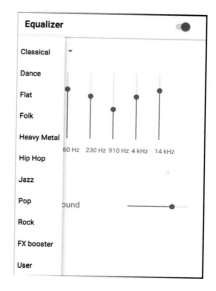

FIGURE 12.10

Set the Equalizer switch to On (left), pick an equalization from the pop-up menu (right), and then adjust the Bass Boost and Surround Sound as needed.

> **NOTE** The Bass Boost and Surround Sound features are available only if your device has the audio hardware needed for them.

You can then tap the pop-up menu and tap the preset equalization you want to apply: Normal, Classical, Dance, Flat, Folk, Heavy Metal, Hip Hop, Jazz, Pop, Rock, or FX Booster.

Now drag the Bass Boost and Surround Sound sliders (if they're available on your device) to tweak the sound to your preference.

> **NOTE** The Flat equalization has all the sliders at their midpoints, giving 0 decibel (dB) adjustment. This equalization has the same effect as turning the Equalizer off except that you can adjust the Bass Boost and Surround Sound settings (if your device supports them). The Normal equalization gives a slight boost to the lowest (60Hz) and highest (14kHz) frequencies to punch up the sound a little.

CREATING A CUSTOM EQUALIZATION

The Equalizer's presets offer a good range of equalizations, but if none meets your needs, you can create a custom equalization. Apply the existing equalization that sounds best to you, and then drag the frequency sliders to improve the sound. As soon as you adjust one of the sliders, Play Music selects the User item in the pop-up menu.

> **NOTE** You can also start creating your custom equalization by opening the pop-up menu and tapping User. This enables you to start with all the sliders at their midpoints.

When you've set up the equalization you want, tap the Back button twice to return to your music.

USING OTHER MUSIC APPS

Play Music can be great, but you can use a huge number of other Android apps to play music on your device. This section introduces you to three apps for identifying music you hear and three streaming services for exploring music and radio.

THREE APPS FOR IDENTIFYING MUSIC

These apps enable you to identify music easily:

- **Shazam.** Shazam is a free app that can automatically identify a song by listening to a snippet of it playing. Shazam enables you to share your music and TV discoveries via Facebook and Google+, but you can ignore these features if you don't need them.

- **SoundHound.** SoundHound is a free app that can automatically identify a song by listening to it being played nearby or by your humming the tune.

- **TrackID.** Also free, TrackID enables you to identify songs within range of your device's microphone. TrackID gives you access to artist biographies and links to music videos on YouTube.

> **☑ TIP** If you prefer to keep down the number of apps on your device, you can ask Google Now to identify a song for you. Say "OK Google" to activate the Google Now feature, then say something like "What song is this?" Google Now listens to the music and returns the information—including a link to the song on Google Play if it is available there.

THREE STREAMING SERVICES

If you like listening to a variety of music, try these three streaming services:

- **Spotify.** Spotify gives you access to a huge amount of music via streaming. You can browse through top lists or new releases, explore genres and moods, or simply search using keywords. The basic Spotify service is free and supported by ads. You can upgrade to the Premium service to get ad-free listening.

- **Pandora.** Pandora is a music-streaming service that plays selections based on the artists you choose. You can rate the songs that Pandora plays to tune the selections toward what you like. Pandora enables you to find information about the music played and to purchase it from various sources. Pandora also includes other features, such as enabling you to set alarm clocks and providing personalized radio recommendations.

> **☑ NOTE** At this writing, Pandora is available only in the United States, Australia, and New Zealand because of licensing constraints. To access Pandora from other countries, you need to use a VPN connection to one of these three countries.

- **TuneIn Radio.** TuneIn Radio is an online radio station that offers more than 100,000 real radio stations and millions of on-demand programs and podcasts. TuneIn Radio is a free service, but you can pay for the TuneIn Radio Pro upgrade if you want to be able to record radio to your device so that you can listen to it later.

> **! CAUTION** Streaming audio can take up a huge amount of bandwidth if you use it frequently. If you use streaming audio over the cellular network, keep a close eye on your data usage to make sure you don't rack up charges.

13

STAYING IN TOUCH VIA SOCIAL NETWORKING

Your Android device is great for keeping in touch with your contacts via social networking no matter where you go—or where they go. In this chapter, you'll learn how you can make the most of Facebook and Twitter on your device.

Both apps are largely straightforward to use, especially if you are familiar with how the two services work. But both have serious implications for your privacy, so it's essential that you configure them suitably. In particular, you should secure your Facebook account by setting up two-factor authentication and your Twitter account by applying login verification.

GETTING SERIOUS WITH FACEBOOK

If you're on Facebook, you'll probably want to use your Android device to keep up with your friends' latest news and to post your own.

Facebook makes it easy to share your information—too easy, many would say. You'll have no difficulty posting, liking, or commenting, so we'll concentrate on the other side of the equation: how to configure Facebook so that you're sharing only what you want to share, and no more.

Many Android devices include the Facebook app, but if yours doesn't, go to the Play Store and download it. You'll then need to log in using your account.

LOGGING IN TO FACEBOOK

The first time you launch the Facebook app on an Android device, you log into your Facebook account. Once you've done that, you normally stay logged into your account so that you can post items and receive updates. You can log out if you want—for example, so that you can log into a different Facebook account.

> **TIP** If you've already added your phone number to your Facebook account, you can use your phone number as your login identifier instead of your email address.

On a phone, the Facebook app may automatically pick up the phone number from the device and insert it in the Email or Phone field for you. On a tablet, you'll need to type (or paste) the number manually.

> **TIP** If you're having difficulty logging in using your phone number, make sure you've entered the full phone number, including the country code if your phone shows it. Omit any extra zero (0) characters or any + sign at the beginning of the number.

ADDING YOUR PHONE NUMBER TO YOUR FACEBOOK ACCOUNT

To add your phone number to your Facebook account, first log into your Facebook account via a web browser, either on a computer (usually easier) or on your Android device.

Open the menu in the upper-right corner of the screen and click Settings to display the Settings screen. In the left pane, click Mobile to display the Mobile Settings screen. Click the Add a Phone button to open the Activate Facebook Texts dialog box, and then click the Add Your Phone Number Here link. In the Confirm Your Number dialog box that opens, specify your country code in the Country Code pop-up menu, type your phone number in the Phone Number box, and select the Sending Me a Text radio button in the Confirm Number By area. Then click the Continue button.

Facebook then sends your phone a text message containing a confirmation code. Type this code in the Enter Your Confirmation Code dialog box that opens on your computer, and click the Confirm button. The Number Confirmed dialog box opens.

You've now added your phone number to your Facebook account—but you're not done quite yet because the Number Confirmed dialog box contains two other controls you should set. First, you can check the Turn On Text Notifications box if you want to receive texts about new messages, posts, and other Facebook happenings; be warned that you may get a barrage of notifications. Second, you should open the Share Your Phone Number With pop-up menu and choose who can see your phone number: Public (seldom a good idea), Friends (the default), or Only Me.

After making your choices, click the Save Settings button to close the Number Confirmed dialog box. Your phone number then appears on the Mobile Settings screen, marked Verified.

There's another way to add your phone number to your Facebook account: Use your phone to sign up for your Facebook account, and use the phone number as the identifier rather than using an email address. If you've already created your Facebook account using an email address, you don't have this option.

ADDING FRIENDS AND MANAGING INVITES AND IMPORTED CONTACTS

After you've logged in to Facebook, the app encourages you to use its Find Friends feature to connect to your friends. Find Friends can be a big help if you're looking to expand your social network on Facebook.

If you do choose to upload your contacts, you can use the Manage Invites and Imported Contacts screen to manage them.

UNDERSTANDING FIND FRIENDS AND CONTINUOUS CONTACTS UPLOAD

Find Friends works by uploading your contacts from your Android device to Facebook's servers so that it can find matching people who are signed up to Facebook. When you first run Find Friends, the feature uploads all your contacts; after that, it periodically uploads any new contacts it finds. Facebook calls this feature Continuous Contacts Upload, and you can turn it on and off as needed. Turning on Continuous Contacts Upload uploads all your contacts; turning off Continuous Contacts Upload deletes all your uploaded contact information from Facebook's servers.

Uploading your contacts is necessary for the Find Friends feature to work. But if it raises security concerns or you feel reluctant to provide Facebook with such a large amount of information, you should avoid using Find Friends. You can add contacts manually in Facebook instead.

ADDING FRIENDS BY USING THE FIND FRIENDS FEATURE

Tap the Find Friends button to display the Find Friends screen, and you'll see a short explanation of the feature. (See the left screen in Figure 13.1.) If you want to proceed, tap the Get Started button, and then tap the Allow button in the Allow Facebook to Access Your Contacts dialog box that opens.

The Facebook app then uploads your contacts to the Facebook servers. The Add Friends screen appears, showing a Contacts list and a People You May Know list. (See the right screen in Figure 13.1.) You can tap the Add Friend button next to a person's name on either list to send a friend request to that person.

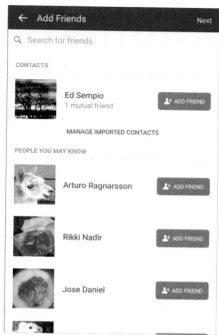

FIGURE 13.1

On the Find Friends screen (left), tap the Get Started button to start uploading your contacts to Facebook's servers. On the Add Friends screen (right), tap the Add Friend button for each person you want to add as a friend.

MANAGING INVITES AND IMPORTED CONTACTS

The Facebook app enables you to manage the contacts you have imported and the invitations you have sent. To get started, tap the Manage Imported Contacts button on the Add Friends screen to display the Manage Invites and Imported Contacts screen. (See the left and right screens in Figure 13.2.) This screen starts by displaying the first group of contacts; you can tap the See More button to move on to the next group.

To remove a contact, check the box to the left of the contact's name, and then tap the Delete Selected button.

Tap the Done button when you finish working on the Manage Invites and Imported Contacts screen.

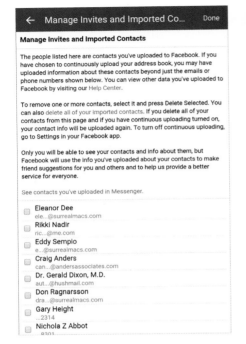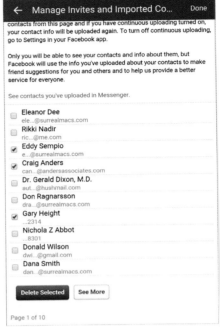

FIGURE 13.2

On the Manage Invites and Imported Contacts screen, check the box for any contact you want to remove from Facebook, and then tap the Delete Selected button.

> **TIP** You can tap the See Contacts You've Uploaded in Messenger link on the Manage Invites and Imported Contacts screen to display the list of contacts that you've uploaded using Facebook Messenger. These contacts are separate from those you've uploaded using the Facebook app itself.

TURNING THE CONTINUOUS CONTACTS UPLOAD FEATURE OFF OR BACK ON

You can change your Continuous Contacts Upload setting from within the Facebook app on your Android device. So if you decide that you want to stop uploading your contacts, take the following steps to stop the Facebook app from uploading your contacts anymore.

> **☐ NOTE** Turning off the Continuous Contacts Upload feature also deletes from Facebook's servers all the contact information the Facebook app has uploaded from your device.

1. Tap the More button to display the More screen.
2. Tap the App Settings button to display the Settings screen.
3. Set the Continuous Contacts Upload switch to Off. The Stop Continuously Uploading Your Contacts dialog box opens.
4. Tap the Turn Off button. The Contact Information Deleted message appears briefly to confirm that Facebook has deleted the contacts information you had uploaded.

> **☑ TIP** If you want to turn the Continuous Contacts Upload feature back on, select Menu, App Settings and then set the Continuous Contacts Upload switch on the Settings screen to On. The Find Friends screen then appears, and you can tap the Get Started button to start using the feature again.

GETTING AND CONFIGURING FACEBOOK MESSENGER

Until summer 2014, the Facebook apps for Android and other mobile platforms (such as Apple's iOS) enabled you to send messages from within the app. But in summer 2014, Facebook started requiring you to use its separate Facebook Messenger app for sending messages. At this writing, there's no way around using Messenger unless you're prepared to give up sending messages on Facebook.

> **☑ TIP** Facebook Messenger may already be installed on your device. To find out, tap the Home button, tap the Apps button, tap the Search Apps box at the top of the Apps screen, and then start typing **messenger**. Android displays matching results. The app normally appears under the name of Messenger rather than Facebook Messenger. If you see multiple Messenger apps, Facebook Messenger is the one with the icon of a blue speech bubble bearing a sideways white lightning flash.

GETTING FACEBOOK MESSENGER

If Facebook Messenger isn't already installed on your device, open the Play Store app, search for **Facebook messenger**, and then install the app.

> **NOTE** You may find the Facebook app prompts you to get the Facebook Messenger app. If this happens, you can click the Get App button to jump straight to the App Store.

Facebook Messenger requires a daunting set of permissions, including Identity, Contacts/Calendar, Location, Photos/Media/Files, Camera/Microphone, and Device ID & Call Information. These permissions are necessary for the many functions that Facebook Messenger provides, such as taking selfies and videos and sharing them with your contacts.

> **! CAUTION** Installing Facebook Messenger can cause Samsung devices to display the Potential Threat Alerts dialog box, which warns you that the app is authorized to access Messages. This looks like a problem, but it is not: If you want to be able to use Facebook Messenger, you need it to be able to send and receive messages.

After installing Facebook Messenger, tap the Open button on the Play Store screen to open the app. (If you've left the Play Store screen, go to the Apps screen and tap the Messenger icon there to open Facebook Messenger.)

On the Welcome to Messenger screen, verify that the Continue As button shows the user name you want to use for Messenger (for example, Continue As John Luser). If so, tap the Continue As button; if not, tap the Switch Account button, and then choose the account you want to use.

Next, the Text Anyone in Your Phone screen appears (on either a phone or a tablet). You can either tap the Turn On button to sync all your contacts continuously with Facebook, enabling you to see which of them are on Messenger (and, optionally, get in touch with them) or tap the Not Now button. If you tap the Turn On button, the Allow Messenger to Access Your Contacts dialog box opens; tap the Allow button to proceed.

> **NOTE** The Text Anyone in Your Phone screen offers pretty much the same choice as the Find Friends screen and the Continuous Contacts Upload feature in the Facebook app: It uploads all your contacts to Facebook's servers

to find matching people, and it periodically checks for new contacts. Facebook Messenger calls this feature Sync Contacts. But the two features are independent from each other, and you can configure them separately.

Whichever choice you make here, the What Number Can People Use to Reach You screen appears. Make sure that the correct phone number appears—type it in if the field is blank—and then tap the OK button. (If you don't want to provide your phone number at this point, tap the Not Now button and then tap the Skip button in the Skip Phone Number dialog box that opens to nag you for the phone number.)

NOTE Facebook doesn't make the phone number you specify on the What Number Can People Use to Reach You screen available to other people. Instead, it enables people who already have this phone number for you to contact you on this number.

Next, the Confirming Your Phone Number screen appears while Facebook sends you a confirmation code via instant message. Normally, Facebook Messenger receives this message automatically (because you gave it permission to access your messages) and dismisses the Confirming Your Phone Number screen. If not, type in the confirmation code manually and tap the OK button.

CAUTION Facebook also sends you an email confirming that it has added this phone number to your account. If you receive one of these emails without adding a phone number to your account, open your browser, go to www.facebook.com/hacked, and click the My Account Is Compromised button. Don't click the Secure Your Account link in the Facebook message about confirming your phone number because fraudsters can make convincing replicas of both the message and the Report Compromised Account page on Facebook's website.

NOTE If the Secure Your Account dialog box opens at this point, click the Continue button.

On the You're on Messenger screen, tap the Continue button to start using Facebook Messenger.

NAVIGATING THE FACEBOOK MESSENGER INTERFACE

Now that you have Facebook Messenger up and running, you'll find your way around easily. As you can see in Figure 13.3, Facebook Messenger has four tabs:

- **Recent.** Tap this tab to see recent activity. You can tap a chat to display it, or tap the New Message button to start a new message.

- **Groups.** Tap this tab to display your list of groups. You can create a new group by tapping one of the New Group placeholders or by tapping the New Group button in the lower-right corner.

- **Contacts.** Tap this tab to display the Contacts screen. This screen has two tabs: the Messenger tab and the Active tab. Tap the Messenger tab to display your list of contacts. Tap the Active tab to display your contacts who are active on Facebook or Facebook Messenger.

- **Settings.** Tap this tab to display the Settings screen. See the next section for details.

FIGURE 13.3

On the Recent screen, you can tap a chat to open it or tap New Message to start a new message.

CHOOSING SETTINGS FOR FACEBOOK MESSENGER

To make Facebook Messenger work the way you want, tap the Settings icon on the tab bar and work on the Settings screen. (See the left screen in Figure 13.4.) These are the settings you can choose on the main screen:

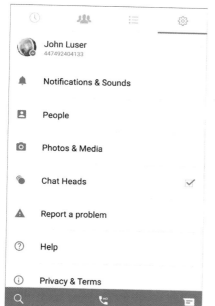 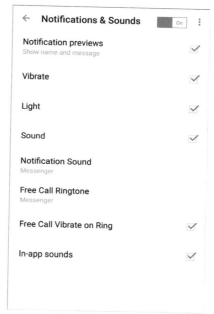

FIGURE 13.4

The Settings screen (left) gives you access to Facebook Messenger's categories of settings. On the Notifications & Sounds screen (right), choose whether to view notification previews and whether to use vibration, light, and sound for notifications.

- **Notifications & Sounds.** Tap this button to display the Notifications & Sounds screen. (See the right screen in Figure 13.4.) The next section explains the settings on this screen.
- **People.** Tap this button to display the People screen. Here, you can view your message requests, turn the Sync Contacts feature on and off, and block or unblock people. On some devices, you can also tap the Synced Call and Text History button or the Phone Call and SMS History button (the name varies) to view your call and SMS history.

NOTE Turning off Sync Contacts removes all your phone's contacts from Facebook Messenger.

- **Photos & Media.** Tap this button to display the Photos & Media screen. Here, you can check the Save Photos box to save incoming photos to your Gallery and check the Save on Capture box to save any new photos you capture in the Messenger app to your Gallery.
- **Payments.** Tap this button to display the Payments screen, on which you can configure your payment methods.
- **Chat Heads.** Check this box to use the Chat Heads feature.
- **Report a Problem.** Tap this button to start creating a problem report—for example, to report a bug in the Messenger app.

CHOOSING NOTIFICATIONS & SOUNDS SETTINGS FOR FACEBOOK MESSENGER

You can choose the following settings on the Notifications & Sounds screen for Facebook Messenger:

- **Notifications & Sounds.** Set this switch to Off if you want to suppress all notifications and sounds temporarily.
- **Notification Previews.** Check this box to display previews of the friend's name and the message. These previews are usually handy unless you get too many of them.
- **Vibrate.** Check this box to have your device vibrate when you receive a notification. This setting is available only on devices that have a vibration motor.
- **Light.** Check this box to have your device pulse its notification light when you have a notification.
- **Sound.** Check this box to have your device play a sound when you receive a notification.
- **Notification Sound.** Tap this button, select the ringtone in the Ringtone dialog box, and then tap the OK button.

> **TIP** The Free Call Ringtone setting enables you to use a different ringtone to identify free calls from paid calls.

- **Free Call Ringtone.** Tap this button, select your preferred free call ringtone in the Ringtone dialog box, and then tap the OK button.
- **Free Call Vibrate on Ring.** Check this box if you want your device to vibrate when you get a free call. This setting is available only on devices that have a vibration motor.
- **In-App Sounds.** Check this box to allow Facebook Messenger to play sounds.

MAKING FACEBOOK WORK YOUR WAY

Facebook has a large number of settings that you can configure to make the Facebook app and the Facebook platform work your way. The default settings tend to be configured in ways that suit Facebook, so you'd be wise to spend a few minutes understanding what the settings do and configuring them to suit your needs.

REACHING THE SETTINGS

To reach the settings, tap the More button on the right side of the main toolbar. This brings you to the More screen, which starts with your profile picture and your Favorites list. Scroll down past the Favorites list, the Apps list, the Feeds list, the Groups list, and the Pages list, and you'll find the Help & Settings section. (See the left screen in Figure 13.5.)

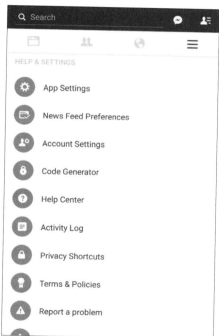 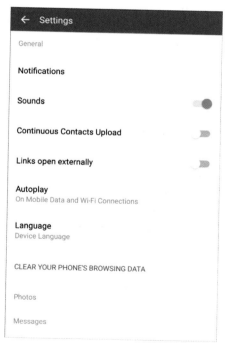

FIGURE 13.5

On the More screen (left), scroll down to the Help & Settings section, and then tap the App Settings button to display the main Settings screen (right), which enables you to configure notifications, sounds, Continuous Contacts Upload, and other features.

CHOOSING APP SETTINGS

To get started choosing settings, tap the App Settings button to display the Settings screen. (See the right screen in Figure 13.5.) Then tap the Notifications button to display the Notifications screen. (See the left screen in Figure 13.6.)

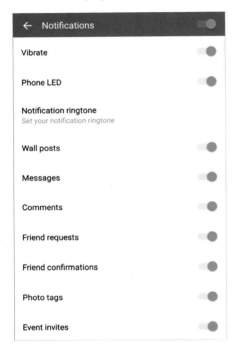
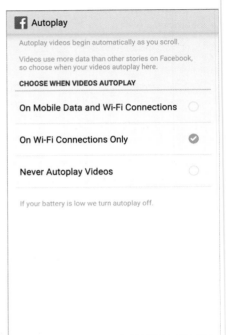

FIGURE 13.6

On the Notifications screen (left), specify which notifications you want and which items can raise the notifications. On the Autoplay screen (right), choose when videos are allowed to play automatically.

You can choose these settings on the Notifications screen:

- **Notifications.** Set this switch to On to make notifications active and to make all the other settings on the Notifications screen available.

- **Vibrate.** Set this switch to On to make your device vibrate to signal an incoming notification. This works only if your device has a vibration motor.

- **Phone LED.** Set this switch to On to have the phone LED flash to let you know there are incoming notifications.

- **Notification Ringtone.** Tap this button to display the Notification Ringtone dialog box, tap to select a distinctive ringtone, and then tap the OK button.

- **Wall Posts.** Set this switch to On to receive an alert when someone posts on your wall.
- **Messages.** Set this switch to On to receive alerts for messages.
- **Comments.** Check this box to receive alerts when people post comments.
- **Friend Requests.** Set this switch to On to receive alerts when you receive friend requests.
- **Friend Confirmations.** Set this switch to On to receive alerts when you receive friend confirmations.
- **Photo Tags.** Set this switch to On to receive alerts for tagged photos.
- **Event Invites.** Set this switch to On to receive alerts for event invites.
- **Application Requests.** Set this switch to On to receive alerts for application requests.
- **Groups.** Set this switch to On to receive alerts for changes to groups.
- **Place Tips.** Set this switch to On to see notifications on the lock screen about the location you're in.

When you finish choosing settings on the Notifications screen, tap the arrow button or the Back button below the screen to return to the Settings screen. Here, you can choose the following settings:

- **Sounds.** Set this switch to On to enable the Facebook app to play sounds.
- **Continuous Contacts Upload.** Set this switch to On to enable the Continuous Contacts Upload feature. See the sidebar "Understanding Find Friends and Continuous Contacts Upload," earlier in this chapter, for more information about Continuous Contacts Upload.
- **Links Open Externally.** Set this switch to On if you want links you follow in the Facebook app to open in your default apps for those types of links. For example, if you set the Links Open Externally switch to On, tapping a web page link may open the Chrome browser app.
- **Autoplay.** Tap this button to display the Autoplay screen. (See the right screen in Figure 13.6.) In the Choose When Videos Autoplay area, tap the appropriate radio button to specify when the Facebook app should automatically play videos when you scroll them into view. Your choices are On Mobile Data and Wi-Fi Connections, On Wi-Fi Connections Only, or Never Autoplay Videos. Tap the arrow button or the Back button below the screen to return to the Settings screen.

> **TIP** If you enjoy watching videos on Facebook, choose the On Wi-Fi Connections Only radio button on the Autoplay screen unless you have an unlimited data plan and can afford to select the On Mobile Data and Wi-Fi Connections radio button instead. If you prefer to start videos manually, choose the Never Autoplay Videos radio button.

- **Language.** If you need to change the language the Facebook app is using, tap this button to open the Language dialog box, and then tap the radio button for the language you want to use. Tap the Device Language radio button to make the Facebook app use the same language as your Android device is using.

- **Clear Your Phone's Browsing Data.** If you want to delete the cookies and cached data from websites you've visited while using the Facebook app, tap this button, and then tap the OK button in the Clear Your Phone's Browsing Data dialog box.

- **Photos** or **Photo Syncing.** Tap this button and use the Photo Syncing screen to choose which photos and albums to sync.

- **Messages.** Tap this button to configure messaging.

- **Facebook Chat.** Set this switch to On or Off to toggle Facebook Chat on or off.

MANAGING YOUR NEWS FEED

To manage your news feed, tap the News Feed Preferences button on the More screen, and then work on the Preferences screen. This screen has three main controls:

- **Prioritize Who to See First.** Tap this button to display the See First screen, and then tap the friends you want to prioritize, placing a star on their profile picture and a See First tag under their name. Tap the arrow button or the Back button below the screen to return to the Preferences screen.

- **Unfollow People to Hide Their Posts.** Tap this button to display the Following screen, and then tap each person you want to unfollow. Tap the arrow button or the Back button below the screen to return to the Preferences screen.

▪ **Reconnect with People You Unfollowed.** Tap this button to display the Unfollowed screen, and then tap each unfollowed person you want to follow again. Tap the arrow button or the Back button below the screen to return to the Preferences screen.

CHOOSING ESSENTIAL PRIVACY SETTINGS

To maintain as much privacy as you want while sharing your information on Facebook, you must make sure that you choose suitable privacy settings. This section concentrates on the most important settings—those that will make the greatest difference.

OPENING THE PRIVACY SHORTCUTS SCREEN

You can configure the absolute minimum of privacy settings from the Privacy Shortcuts screen. Here's how to display the Privacy Shortcuts screen:

1. In the Facebook app, tap the More button to display the More screen.
2. Scroll down to the Help & Settings section.
3. Tap the Privacy Shortcuts button to display the Privacy Shortcuts screen.

> **NOTE** Depending on your device and your region, you may see a different screen (such as the Privacy screen) from the Privacy Shortcuts screen.

CONTROLLING WHO CAN SEE YOUR POSTS

On the Privacy Shortcuts screen, tap the Who Can See My Stuff heading to display its contents. (See the left screen in Figure 13.7.)

Tap the Who Can See My Future Posts button to display the Select Audience screen. (See the right screen in Figure 13.7.) You can then tap the appropriate button: Public, Friends, Friends Except Acquaintances, Only Me, or a specific group. The final item shown in the right screen in Figure 13.7 is a custom option.

> **CAUTION** Share your posts with the Public audience only if you are certain that you want to share everything you post on Facebook with anybody in the world, both now and forever onward. Sharing your posts with the Friends audience is usually a much better choice.

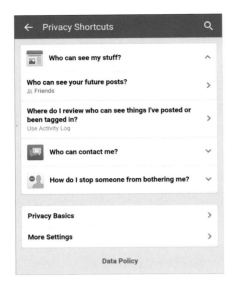
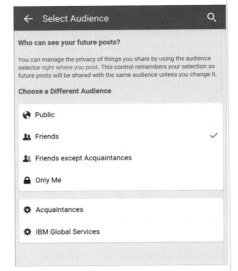

FIGURE 13.7
The Privacy Shortcuts screen (left) gives you access to the three most important privacy settings.
To control who can see your posts, tap the Who Can See My Stuff heading, tap the Who Can See
Your Future Posts button, and choose the audience on the Select Audience screen (right).

REVIEWING AND SANITIZING YOUR ACTIVITY LOG

Tap the arrow button or the Back button below the screen to return to the Privacy
Shortcuts screen, and then tap the Where Do I Review Who Can See Things I've
Posted or Been Tagged In button. The Facebook app displays the Activity Log
screen. (See the left screen in Figure 13.8.)

Tap the Filter button to display the Activity Log Options screen, and then tap the
button for the item type you want to view. (See the right screen in Figure 13.8.)
The Activity Log screen appears again, this time showing the items of the type
you chose.

> **NOTE**   You can filter by a long list of item types, from Your Posts, Posts
> You're Tagged In, and Photos all the way through Likes, Comments, and Friends to
> Questions, Saved, and All Apps.

Tap a downward-caret button to display a menu of actions you can take with it. For
example, on an action you've taken, you can tap the Hide from Timeline button to
prevent that action from appearing in your timeline.

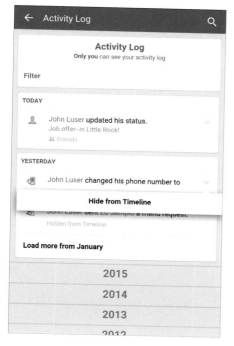 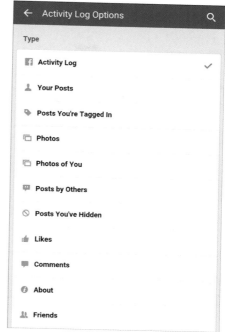

FIGURE 13.8

On the Activity Log screen (left), you can tap a downward-caret button to display a menu of actions, such as Hide from Timeline. Tap the Filter button to display the Activity Log Options screen (right), and then tap the button for the items you want to view on the Activity Log screen.

CONTROLLING WHO CAN CONTACT YOU

To control who can contact you, tap the Who Can Contact Me button on the Privacy Shortcuts screen to display its contents. You can then tap the Who Can Send Me Friend Requests button to display the Select Audience screen, on which you can check either the Everyone group or the Friends of Friends group.

> **NOTE** Friends of Friends is the sensible choice for friend requests except for a Facebook account that you use to maintain a public presence. For example, if you have a Facebook account for your band, you'd probably want to allow friend requests from everyone.

BLOCKING A PERSON WHO IS BOTHERING YOU

If someone is harassing you on Facebook, you can block that person. Follow these steps:

1. Tap the How Do I Stop Someone from Bothering Me button on the Privacy Shortcuts screen to display the section's controls. (See the left screen in Figure 13.9.)

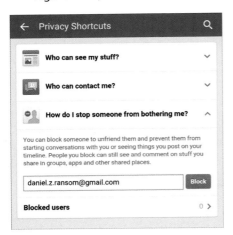 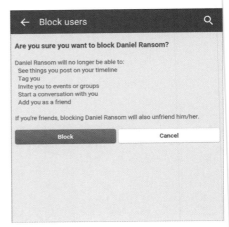

FIGURE 13.9

You can block someone from contacting you by typing his name or email address on the Privacy Shortcuts screen and then tapping the Block button (left). After choosing the person to block in the list of matches, tap the Block button on the Block Users screen (right) to implement the blocking.

2. Type the offender's name or email address in the Add Name or Email box.

> ☑ **TIP** If you know the email address of the person you want to block, type it into the Add Name or Email box. Searching by the email address should return only a single result, whereas searching by the name may return scores of results, out of which you'll need to pick the right result.

3. Tap the Block button. The Privacy Shortcuts displays a list of matches.

4. Tap the Block button for the person you want to block. The Block Users screen appears, making clear that the person will not be able to see items you post on your timeline, tag you, invite you to events or groups, start conversations with you, or add you as a friend. (See the right screen in Figure 13.9.)

> **TIP** If you're not certain which of the list of matches on the Privacy Shortcuts screen is the person you want to block, tap the person's name to display her profile.

5. Tap the Block button to block the person.

> **NOTE** Blocking someone with whom you're a currently a friend also unfriends that person.

> **TIP** To manage your blocked list, tap the Blocked Users button at the bottom of the How Do I Stop Someone from Bothering Me section on the Privacy Shortcuts screen. On the Block Users screen, you can review the Blocked Users list and tap the Unblock button to unblock someone if necessary.

> **NOTE** If you run into abusive content, spam, or policy violations, tap the Report a Problem button on the More screen and follow through the procedure for reporting the problem to Facebook.

SECURING YOUR FACEBOOK ACCOUNT WITH TWO-FACTOR AUTHENTICATION

As you know, the default means of authentication (proving your identity) to Facebook is entering your user ID and password. This is one-factor authentication and gives you only a modest amount of security. To help prevent someone from hacking into your account, you can set up two-factor authentication so that you have to enter a code each time you log in to Facebook from an unknown device.

> **TIP** Please do set up two-factor authentication to secure your account. It takes minimal time and effort and provides pretty good protection against hacking.

SETTING UP TWO-FACTOR AUTHENTICATION

Here's how to set up two-factor authentication:

1. In the Facebook app, tap the More button to display the More screen.

2. In the Help & Settings section, tap the Account Settings button to display the Settings screen.

3. Tap the Security button to display the Security Settings screen. (See the left screen in Figure 13.10.)

4. Check the Login Approvals On box. The Facebook app prompts you to re-enter your password.

5. Type your password.

6. Tap the Continue button. The first Login Approvals screen appears. (See the right screen in Figure 13.10.)

7. Tap the Start Setup button. The second Login Approvals screen appears, showing the phone number to which Facebook will text a code to confirm.

> **NOTE** If necessary, tap the Change Phone Number button and use the Set Up Security Code Delivery screen to add your mobile phone number to your account.

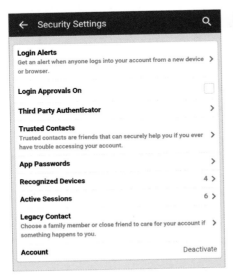

FIGURE 13.10

On the Security Settings screen (left), check the Login Approvals On box to start setting up two-factor authentication. On the first Login Approvals screen (right), tap the Start Setup button.

8. Tap the Continue button. The third Login Approvals screen appears, prompting you to enter the confirmation code that Facebook has texted to your phone. (See the left screen in Figure 13.11.)

9. Type in the code.

10. Tap the Continue button. The final Login Approvals screen appears. (See the right screen in Figure 13.11.)

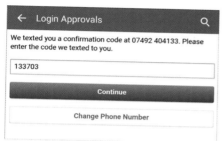
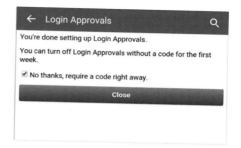

FIGURE 13.11

On the third Login Approvals screen (left), enter the confirmation code that Facebook has texted you, and then tap the Continue button. On the final Login Approvals screen (right), check the No Thanks, Require a Code Right Away box to tighten your security immediately.

11. Check the No Thanks, Require a Code Right Away box to decline Facebook's offer to let you turn off Login Approvals without a code for the first week.

12. Tap the Close button. The Security Settings screen appears again.

> **NOTE** Facebook sends you an email notifying you that Login Approvals is now activated.

LOGGING IN WITH A CODE

Now that you've turned on Login Approvals, you'll need to enter a code when you log in from a different device. The Facebook app displays the Login Approval Required dialog box (see Figure 13.12) to let you know.

Tap the OK button, enter the code when you receive it in a text, and then tap the Continue button to log in.

Login Approval Required

You will get an SMS shortly with a code to use for logging in.

OK

FIGURE 13.12
The Facebook app displays the Login Approval Required dialog box when you try to log in from a different device.

CREATING YOUR OWN LOGIN APPROVAL CODE

If you need to log in to Facebook using a different device but your phone isn't able to receive text messages, you can use the Code Generator to generate a code.

Tap the More button to display the More screen, and then tap the Code Generator button in the Help & Settings section. The Code Generator screen appears, showing a numeric code that changes every 30 seconds. Type in the code on the device that requires Login Approval, and then tap the Continue button.

USING MULTIPLE FACEBOOK ACCOUNTS ON THE SAME DEVICE

Android's Settings app includes a feature for setting up a Facebook account on your device. To get started, you open the Settings app, tap the Add Account button in the Accounts section, and then tap the Facebook button on the Add an Account screen. Android then walks you through the process of setting up the account.

This feature enables you to set up only one account on your device. If you go back to the Settings app and try to add another Facebook account, you get the message "Only one Facebook account is supported."

USING MULTIPLE ACCOUNTS BY LOGGING OUT AND LOGGING IN

The simplest way to use multiple Facebook accounts on your device is to log out of the account you've been using and then log in to the account you want to use next.

NOTE The Facebook app is set up to keep you logged in all the time so that you can share your news and views easily and receive updates from your friends and anyone else you have allowed to contact you. So normally you don't need to log out unless you want to unhook yourself from Facebook for a while or you need to change accounts.

Here's how to log out from Facebook:

1. Tap the More button to display the More screen.
2. Tap the Log Out button (at the bottom of the screen). The Log Out dialog box opens.
3. Tap the Log Out button. Facebook logs you out and displays the Log In screen.

Now that you've logged out of the account you were using, you can log in to the next account you want to use.

NOTE If you've implemented two-factor authentication on the account to which you're logging in, you'll also need to enter a Login Approval code. This is the code from a text that Facebook sends to your phone or a code that you generate using the Code Generator on your phone.

USING MULTIPLE ACCOUNTS BY USING A BROWSER

Another way of using multiple Facebook accounts is to open a browser, go to the Facebook website (www.facebook.com), and log in. You can log in using a different Facebook account than you're using in the Facebook app.

The advantage of this method is that you can be logged in to two or more accounts at once. The disadvantage is that some of the accounts are using the browser interface instead of the Facebook app, which is normally easier to use on a mobile device.

TIP If you need to use multiple Facebook accounts from within the same app, look at apps such as Fast (Client for Facebook) or Multi for Facebook. You'll find both of these apps, not to mention others, on the Play Store.

REMOVING YOUR FACEBOOK ACCOUNT FROM YOUR DEVICE

If you no longer need to use a particular Facebook account on your device, you can remove it.

> **! CAUTION** Removing a Facebook account from your device deletes all its messages and other data from your device. It also deletes all the contact information from Facebook.

First, log out of the Facebook app if it's running. Tap the More button, tap the Log Out button, and then tap Log Out in the Log Out dialog box.

Next, close the Facebook app. Tap the Overview button, and then swipe the Facebook app off the list to the left or right.

Last, remove your Facebook account. Open the Settings app and tap the Facebook button in the Accounts section to display the Facebook screen. Tap the Menu button, tap Remove Account, and then tap the Remove Account button in the Remove Account dialog box.

MAKING THE MOST OF TWITTER

If you enjoy using Twitter, you'll want to fully exploit it on your Android device. Twitter is pretty straightforward compared to Facebook, but you should still spend some time configuring the settings to suit your needs and avoid any unpleasant surprises. You'll probably want to implement the login verification feature to secure your account against unauthorized access.

SIGNING IN TO TWITTER

The first time you run the Twitter app, you sign in to your Twitter account. If you don't have an account, tap the Sign Up button on the Welcome to Twitter screen to create an account using your phone number or an email address.

When logging in, you need to pay attention to the check box called Upload My Address Book to Connect Me with My Friends or Upload My Address Book and Use My Phone Number to Connect Me with Friends and Send Me Text Updates. This box is checked by default, so you'll need to uncheck it if you don't want to upload all your contacts to Twitter.

> **TIP** If you do leave the Upload My Address Book (etc.) check box checked, go through the list on the Invite Friends screen and uncheck the boxes for any who won't appreciate an invitation to join you on Twitter. Alternatively, tap the Skip button to skip sending invitations altogether.

After you log in, the Twitter app prompts you to let it use your current location to "customize your experience"—in other words, to include location-specific information in what it shows you. If you're okay with this, tap the OK button in the dialog box, and then tap the Allow button in the Allow Twitter to Access This Device's Location dialog box that follows it. If you're not okay with sharing your location, or if you want to defer the decision, tap the Don't Allow button.

> **TIP** You can change Twitter's access to your location information afterward by tapping the Menu button, tapping Settings, tapping Location and Proxy in the General area of the Settings screen, and then checking or unchecking the Location box on the Location and Proxy screen.

> **NOTE** If you created a new Twitter account using an email address, Twitter sends you an email message for you to confirm the address. Click the Confirm Now button in the message to confirm the address.

NAVIGATING THE TWITTER APP

After you've finished setting up the app, you'll see your Home screen. (See Figure 13.13.)

These are the main screens of the Twitter app:

- **Home.** The Home screen displays a list of tweets for you to browse. At the top of the screen, the Who to Follow list suggests other people you may want to follow.

> **TIP** The Home screen is at the top level of the Twitter app, so you tap the Back button to go back to it after navigating to another screen.

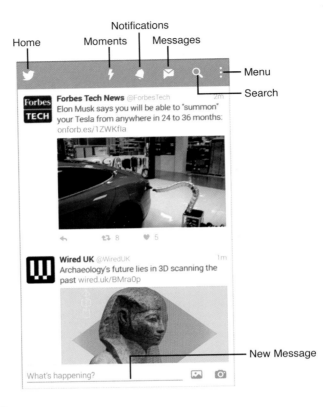

FIGURE 13.13

From the Home screen, you can quickly navigate to other areas of the Twitter app.

- **Moments.** This screen displays items for the biggest news happening on Twitter.
- **Notifications.** This screen displays updates when people follow you, retweet your tweets, make you a favorite, or mention you.
- **Messages.** This screen displays your private messages.

> **NOTE** When the Messages screen is empty, you can tap the Find Friends button on the screen to upload your contacts to Twitter so that it can help you find friends and suggest users you may want to follow.

- **Search Twitter.** Use this screen to search Twitter using keywords or to browse the top trends.

CONFIGURING THE TWITTER APP

Compared to Facebook, Twitter has refreshingly few settings, but there are enough to make a big difference to your Twitter experience.

Tap the Menu button, and then tap Settings to display the Settings screen. (See the left screen in Figure 13.14.)

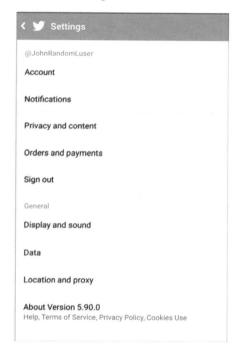
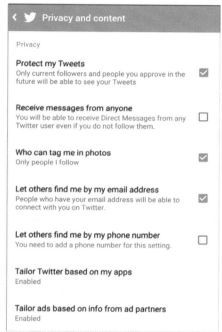

FIGURE 13.14

On the Settings screen (left), tap the category of settings you want to configure. For example, tap the Privacy and Content button to display the Privacy and Content screen (right).

CHOOSING ACCOUNT SETTINGS

To configure your Twitter account, tap the Account button. On the Account screen that appears, you can make the following changes:

- **Phone Number.** Tap this button to add your phone number to your account.
- **Email.** Tap this button to display the Update Email screen, which contains controls for changing the email address associated with your Twitter account.
- **Change Password.** Tap this button to display the Change Password screen, which allows you to change your Twitter password.

■ **Security.** Tap this button to display the Security screen, on which you can set up login verification. See the section "Securing Your Twitter Account with Login Verification," later in this chapter, for details.

CHOOSING NOTIFICATIONS SETTINGS

The Twitter app allows you to choose which types of notifications you receive and which items you receive them for. Tap the Notifications button on the Settings screen to display the Notifications screen. (See the left screen in Figure 13.15.) Then tap the Mobile Notifications button to display the Mobile Notifications screen. (See the right screen in Figure 13.15.)

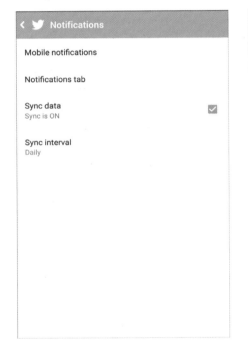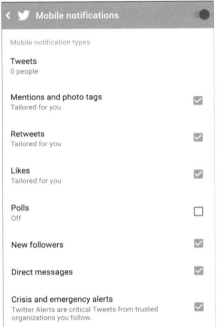

FIGURE 13.15

From the Notifications screen for an account (left), you can choose which types of notification to receive and which items to receive them for. The Mobile Notifications screen (right) allows you to specify the notification items and the notification styles.

NOTE At the top of the Mobile Notifications screen, you can set the Mobile Notifications switch to Off if you want to turn off all notifications temporarily.

These are the settings you can choose in the Mobile Notification Types section of the Mobile Notifications screen:

- **Tweets.** Tap this button to display the Tweets screen. You can then check the Tweets check box to enable receiving notifications for tweets, and choose which of the people you follow can send you notifications.

- **Mentions and Photo Tags.** Tap this button to open the Mentions and Photo Tags dialog box, and then tap the Tailored for You radio button, the From Anyone radio button, or the Off radio button, as needed.

- **Retweets.** Tap this button to display the Retweets dialog box, and then tap the Tailored for You radio button, the From Anyone radio button, or the Off radio button, as needed.

- **Likes.** Tap this button to display the Likes dialog box, and then tap the Tailored for You radio button, the From Anyone radio button, or the Off radio button, as needed.

- **Polls.** Tap this button to display the Polls dialog box, and then tap the Only Polls I Create radio button, the Polls I Create or Vote In radio button, or the Off radio button, as needed.

- **New Followers.** Check this box to receive notifications about new people following you.

- **Direct Messages.** Check this box to receive notifications about direct messages.

- **Crisis and Emergency Alerts.** Check this box to receive notifications about crisis and emergency alerts.

- **New Contacts.** Check this box to receive notifications about new contacts.

- **Highlights.** Check this box to receive notifications about Twitter highlights.

- **Moments.** Check this box to receive a notification when a moment you're following is about to start.

- **Recommendations.** Check this box to receive notifications about recommendations.

- **News.** Check this box to receive notifications about news.

- **First Look at New Features.** Check this box to receive notifications about new features on Twitter.

These are the settings you can choose in the Notification Styles section of the Mobile Notifications screen:

- **Vibrate.** Check this box to have your device vibrate when you receive a notification. As usual, this setting is available only if your device has a vibration motor.

- **Ringtone.** Tap this button to display the Ringtone dialog box; tap a distinctive tone that you like; and then tap the OK button.
- **Notification Light.** Check this box to make your device pulse its notification light when you have unread notifications.

Tap the arrow button or the Back button below the screen to return from the Mobile Notifications screen to the Notifications screen. You can then set these three settings:

- **Notifications Tab.** Tap this button to display the Notifications Tab screen. Here, you can check the Mentions Only box and the Only People You Follow box, as needed, to filter the notifications on your timeline.
- **Sync Data.** Check this box to enable data syncing.
- **Sync Interval.** If you check the Sync Data box, tap this button to display the Sync Interval dialog box, and then tap the sync interval to use, such as 15 Minutes.

CHOOSING PRIVACY AND CONTENT SETTINGS

To configure privacy and content settings, tap the Privacy and Content button on the Settings screen and then work on the Privacy and Content screen. (Look back to Figure 13.14, earlier in this chapter.) Here, you can choose the following settings in the Privacy section:

- **Protect My Tweets.** Check this box to protect your tweets, enabling you to control who is able to view them.
- **Receive Messages from Anyone.** Check this box if you want any Twitter user to be able to send direct messages to you. If you uncheck this box, only people you follow can send you direct messages.
- **Who Can Tag Me in Photos.** Tap this button to display the Who Can Tag Me in Photos dialog box, and then tap the Anyone radio button, the Only People I Follow radio button, or the Off radio button, as needed.
- **Let Others Find Me by My Email Address.** Check this box to enable people to find your Twitter name via your email address.
- **Let Others Find Me by My Phone Number.** Check this box to enable people to find your Twitter name via your phone number.
- **Tailor Twitter Based on My Apps.** Tap this button to display the Tailor Twitter Based on My Apps screen. You can then check or uncheck the Tailor Twitter Based on My Apps check box to enable this feature. Briefly, when this feature is on, Twitter periodically collects a list of the apps installed on your device and uses that list to deliver customized content to you.

■ **Tailor Ads Based on Info from Ad Partners.** Tap this button to display the Tailor Ads Based on Info from Ad Partners screen. You can then check or uncheck the Tailor Ads Based on Info from Ad Partners check box to enable or disable this feature. This feature causes Twitter to track which ads you seem to be interested in and to show you more ads for similar things.

In the Content section of the Privacy and Content screen, you can configure these three settings:

■ **Show Me Sensitive Media.** Check this box if you want to see photos or videos deemed sensitive (in other words, offensive to some people).

> **NOTE** If your device shows the Privacy screen instead of the Privacy and Content screen, look for the three content settings on the main Settings screen.

■ **Blocked Accounts.** Tap this button to display the Blocked Accounts screen, on which you can manage the list of accounts you've blocked.

> **TIP** The Imported tab of the Blocked Accounts screen enables you to import a preexisting block list. If you have such a block list, importing it can save you time over blocking the same accounts manually.

■ **Muted Accounts.** Tap this button to display the Muted Accounts, on which you can manage the list of accounts you've muted.

VIEWING YOUR ORDERS AND PAYMENTS

When you need to view your orders and payments, tap the Orders and Payments button on the Settings screen to display the Orders and Payments screen. You can then tap the Order History button to display the Order History screen, which shows your orders.

SIGNING OUT OF TWITTER

You can sign out of Twitter by tapping the Sign Out button on the Settings screen and then tapping the OK button in the Log Out dialog box that opens.

> **! CAUTION** Signing out of Twitter removes all your Twitter data from your Android device. So normally you won't want to sign out. Instead, just leave the Twitter app running so that you can access it quickly as needed, or close the app if you don't want to use it for a while.

CHOOSING DISPLAY AND SOUND SETTINGS

To configure display and sound settings, tap the Display and Sound button in the General section of the Settings screen and then work on the Display and Sound screen. (See the left screen in Figure 13.16.) Here, you can choose the following settings:

- **Sound Effects.** Check this box to enable sound effects.
- **Font Size.** Tap this button to display the Font Size dialog box and then tap the radio button for the font size you want.
- **Use In-App Browser.** Check this box if you want web page links to open in the Twitter browser. Uncheck this box if you want them to open in your default browser, such as the Chrome app.

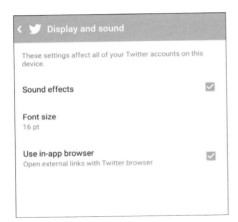
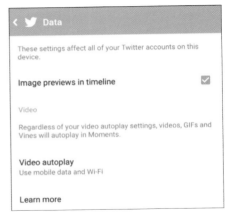

FIGURE 13.16

On the Display and Sound screen (left), choose whether to play sound effects, pick your font size, and decide whether to use the in-app browser. On the Data screen (right), specify whether to display image previews in the timeline and choose your preferred Video Autoplay setting.

CHOOSING DATA SETTINGS

To configure data settings, tap the Data button in the General section of the Settings screen and then work on the Data screen. (See the right screen in Figure 13.16.) Here, you can choose the following two settings; you can also tap the Learn More button to display information about playing videos in Twitter.

- **Image Previews in Timeline.** Check this box if you want to display image previews in the timeline. The previews are usually helpful for making tweets more comprehensible, but you may want to turn them off if you have a slow Internet connection.

■ **Video Autoplay.** Tap this button to display the Video Autoplay dialog box, and then tap the appropriate radio button: Use Mobile Data and Wi-Fi, Use Wi-Fi Only, or Do Not Automatically Play Video in Timelines.

> **!CAUTION** Select the Use Mobile Data and Wi-Fi radio button in the Video Autoplay dialog box only if you have an unlimited data plan. Otherwise, choose the Use Wi-Fi Only radio button if you like to have videos play automatically; choose the Do Not Automatically Play Video in Timelines radio button if you prefer to control video playback manually.

CHOOSING LOCATION AND PROXY SETTINGS

To configure location and proxy settings, tap the Location and Proxy button in the General section of the Settings screen. The Location and Proxy screen appears. (See the left screen in Figure 13.17.)

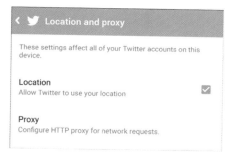
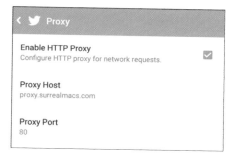

FIGURE 13.17

On the Location and Proxy screen (left), check the Location box if you want the Twitter app to be able to use your device's location. Tap the Proxy button to display the Proxy screen (right), on which you enable and configure the proxy server.

Check or uncheck the Location check box to control whether the Twitter app can use your device's location. Then tap the Proxy button to display the Proxy screen. (See the right screen in Figure 13.17.) Check the Enable HTTP Proxy box to turn on proxying, tap the Proxy Host button and specify the hostname or IP address of the proxy server, and tap the Proxy Port button and enter the port number for the proxy server in the Proxy Port dialog box.

A *proxy server* fulfills and redirects Internet requests. You may need to configure a proxy if your employer or organization blocks Twitter.

ADDING OTHER TWITTER ACCOUNTS

The Twitter app enables you to add multiple accounts to your device and use them alongside each other. To add an account, follow these steps:

1. Go to the Home screen.
2. Tap the Menu button to open the menu.
3. Tap the Accounts button to display the Accounts dialog box.
4. Tap the Add Existing Account button or the Create New Account button, as needed, and then follow the resulting prompts.

> **!CAUTION** On the Sign In screen on a phone, make sure you check or uncheck the box called Upload My Address Book and Use My Phone Number to Connect Me with Friends and Send Me Text Updates. This box is checked by default, so you'll need to uncheck it if you don't want to upload all your contacts to Twitter. If you do upload all your contacts, work through the list on the Invite Friends screen and uncheck the box for any contact who will not welcome an invitation to connect with you on Twitter.

SECURING YOUR TWITTER ACCOUNT WITH LOGIN VERIFICATION

To protect your Twitter account against being hacked, you should set up login verification on it. Here's how to do that:

1. Tap the Menu button, and then tap Settings to display the Settings screen.
2. Tap the Account button to display the Account screen.

> **NOTE** If you haven't added your phone number to your Twitter account, tap the Phone Number button on the Account screen to display the Add Phone screen, and then follow the prompts to add your number.

3. Tap the Security button to display the Security screen. (See the left screen in Figure 13.18.)
4. Check the Login Verification box. The Login Verification dialog box opens, making sure that you know that you will need this device to sign in to Twitter.
5. Tap the OK button. The Your Backup Code dialog box opens, offering to take a screenshot of your backup code and store it in your Android Gallery app.

FIGURE 13.18

On the Security screen (left), check the Login Verification box to start setting up login verification. Memorize or write down the code that appears on the Your Backup Code screen (right). You can also tap the Copy Backup Code to Clipboard button to copy the code and paste it elsewhere.

> **! CAUTION** Taking a screenshot is a good way to store your backup code—but only as long as nobody else can view the photos in the Gallery app. If you take the screenshot, be sure to use a secure means of locking your device. It is also a good idea to encrypt your device.

6. Tap the Yes button or the No button, as appropriate. The Your Backup Code screen appears. (See the right screen in Figure 13.18.)

7. Memorize the code or write it down.

8. Tap the Back button three times to leave the Settings screens and return to the Twitter screen you were using.

> **TIP** On the Security screen, you can tap the Login Requests button to review the login requests that have been made for your Twitter account.

> **NOTE** Now that you have applied login verification to your account, any login attempt displays the Verify Login screen prompting you for the login code. Type in the code that Twitter has just texted to you, and then tap the Send button. Once the login request is approved, you can start using the Twitter app.

USING MULTIPLE TWITTER ACCOUNTS

When you've set up multiple accounts in the Twitter app, you can easily switch from account to account by tapping the Menu button, tapping Accounts, and then tapping the appropriate account in the Accounts dialog box that opens.

IN THIS CHAPTER

- Using notifications, Quick Settings, and Multi Window
- Exploiting the Camera app and the Internet browser
- Improving performance by turning off TouchWiz features

14

USING SAMSUNG TOUCHWIZ

Most Samsung Android devices come with Samsung's TouchWiz skin. TouchWiz is a heavy skin that makes a huge difference to the way that devices look and work, all the way from the Home screen and the Quick Settings panel to the Internet browser app and the Camera app.

In this chapter, you'll take a whirlwind tour of the main features of TouchWiz, concentrating on what you need to know to use your device effectively.

! CAUTION Samsung has a vast number of different devices, ranging from miniature phones to colossal tablets, and these devices run many different versions of TouchWiz. This chapter covers Android 5.1.1 (Lollipop) running on typical Samsung hardware, but your device may well have some differences. If so, explore the commands available to see if Samsung has put the features described here in a different place—or removed them altogether.

GETTING UP TO SPEED WITH TOUCHWIZ ESSENTIALS

In this section, you get up to speed on the essentials of the TouchWiz interface, including its custom buttons, navigation of the Home screen and the Apps screen, and the gestures you can use to control your device.

SHOULD YOU CREATE A SAMSUNG ACCOUNT?

Samsung's software heavily encourages you to create a Samsung account both while setting up your Android device and afterward. A Samsung account is free, and you can set up one in moments, but it's worth evaluating whether you need an account rather than simply going ahead and creating one.

The main point of a Samsung account is to enable you to store certain data online and sync it among your devices. Inevitably, storing that data in a Samsung account gives Samsung information about you and the ways in which you use your Android device.

Some of Samsung's apps require you to have a Samsung account to use all the app's features. For example, the S Health app requires a Samsung account if you want to store your data online and back it up; the Internet app enables you to sync your browsing across your computers and devices by using your Samsung account. If you don't need to use apps such as S Health, and if you don't need to sync data in apps such as the Internet app, you may not need to get a Samsung account.

USING THE BUTTONS IN TOUCHWIZ

Instead of the default Android set of three soft buttons (the Back button, the Home button, and the Recent Apps button, looking from left to right), Samsung devices have a physical Home button located below the screen. On current devices, the

Recent Apps soft button appears to the left of the Home button, and the Back soft button appears to the right.

> **NOTE** A *soft button* or *virtual button* is an area of the touchscreen that acts as a button, as opposed to a physical button.

> **NOTE** Samsung devices designed for Android Jelly Bean (4.1 and 4.2) and older versions have a Menu soft button to the left of the physical Home button and the Back soft button to the right of the Home button.

The Home button works as usual—but with one added feature:

- **Press.** Displays the Home screen panel you were using last. Press again to display your main Home screen panel.
- **Press and hold.** Opens Google Now.

> **NOTE** Samsung devices that don't have a Recent Apps button require you to press and hold the Home button to display the Recent Apps screen, not to open Google Now.

- **Double-press.** Opens the Camera app. If this doesn't work, open the Camera app, tap the Settings icon (the gear icon), and then set the Quick Launch switch on the Camera Settings screen to On.

NAVIGATING THE HOME SCREEN

In TouchWiz, the Home screen consists of a horizontal series of panels among which you navigate by swiping left or right. The left screen in Figure 14.1 shows the Home screen with fairly typical contents. Some versions of TouchWiz include the Briefing screen, a customizable news feed, as the leftmost Home screen panel by default. The right screen in Figure 14.1 shows the Briefing screen.

> **NOTE** Briefing is a feature that provides a personalized set of current information based on the interests you exhibit. To customize Briefing, open it by swiping right from the Home screen, tap the Menu button, and then check the circles for the topics you want to see.

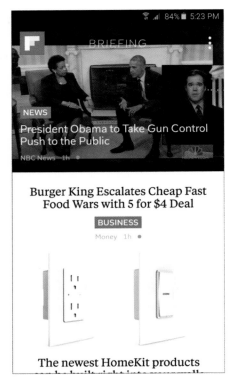

FIGURE 14.1

The TouchWiz Home screen (left) is a series of panels among which you can move by swiping left or right. The Briefing screen (right) shows a customizable news feed.

> **TIP** In some versions of TouchWiz, the Home screen panels work as a carousel. That is, you can swipe left or right to switch among the panels as usual, but when you reach the last panel or the first, you can swipe again to wrap around to the first panel or the last. This feature is helpful, but Samsung seems to be phasing it out as of this writing.

CUSTOMIZING YOUR HOME SCREEN

To start customizing your Home screen, either tap and hold an open space on it (as in stock Android) or pinch inward with two fingers on it. TouchWiz opens the

Home screen for customization. (See the left screen in Figure 14.2.) You can then make these changes:

- **Rearrange the Home screen panels.** Tap the thumbnail for a panel and then drag it to where you want it.
- **Remove a Home screen panel.** Tap the thumbnail for the panel and then drag it up to the Remove icon. When the Remove icon turns red, release the thumbnail.
- **Add a Home screen panel.** Scroll the thumbnails all the way to the left, and then tap the + button on the last panel.

 NOTE   You can have up to seven Home screen panels on TouchWiz.

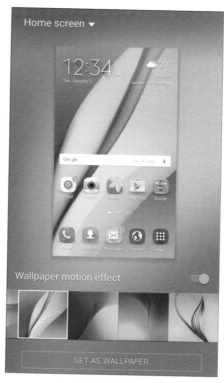

FIGURE 14.2

Pinch inward with two fingers to open the Home screen for customization (left). On the Set Wallpaper screen (right), use the pop-up menu in the upper-left corner to specify which screen to affect, choose the picture, and decide whether to use the motion effect.

- **Change the wallpaper.** Tap the Wallpapers button to display the Set Wallpaper screen. (See the right screen in Figure 14.2.) Tap the pop-up menu in the upper-left corner of the screen and then tap the Home Screen button, the Lock Screen button, or the Home and Lock Screens button, as appropriate. In the thumbnail strip at the bottom of the screen, tap the wallpaper so that it appears full screen. Set the Wallpaper Motion Effect switch to On or Off, as needed, and then tap the Set as Wallpaper button.

- **Add a widget.** Tap the Widgets button to display the Widgets screen. Navigate to the widget, tap and hold its icon until the Home screen panel thumbnails appear, and then drag the icon to the panel and position where you want it to appear.

- **Apply a theme.** Tap the Themes button to display the Themes screen. You can then tap a theme, such as Default, Pink, or Space. Tap the Theme Store button at the bottom of the screen if you want to visit the Theme Store for more themes. Some themes are free, but you must pay for others.

- **Adjust the screen grid.** Tap the Screen Grid button to display the screen for customizing the screen grid, the hidden framework that controls where you can put items on the screen. You can then tap the 4×4 button, the 4×5 button, or the 5×5 button to specify which grid to use. As you'd imagine, the more items on the grid, the more you get on the screen at once, but you may find that some of the arrangements feel cramped.

When you finish customizing the Home screen, tap the Back button to hide the customization options again.

USING GESTURES TO CONTROL YOUR SAMSUNG DEVICE

Over the years, Samsung has built various innovative gestures into TouchWiz to give you different ways of interacting with your device. Some gestures work for both phones and tablets, but others are specific to phones. Some gestures are available only on certain models of phones and tablets, such as the gestures that work only with the S Pen stylus on the Galaxy Note models.

NOTE Samsung keeps changing the set of gestures available, gradually removing those that users find confusing, awkward, or pointless, so your device may include different gestures from those explained here. But you should be able to figure them out easily from their descriptions or by searching their names on the Internet.

To find out which gestures your device offers, open the Settings app and tap the Motions and Gestures button in the Device section. The Motions and Gestures screen appears, showing a list of the gestures with a switch for enabling or disabling each of them. At the top of the Motions and Gestures screen is a panel that displays an explanation of a gesture; you can swipe this panel left or right to display the explanation for another gesture. (See the left and right screens in Figure 14.3.)

FIGURE 14.3

The Motions and Gestures screen in the Settings app enables you to enable or disable each gesture your device supports (left). Swipe the panel at the top to display an explanation of another gesture (right).

The following list explains the gestures:

- **Direct Call.** Pick up the phone to call the contact you have currently displayed in the Phone app or the Contacts app.

- **Smart Alert.** Pick up the device to view the calls and messages you have missed.

- **Mute.** You can mute the current music or an incoming phone call by turning the device over and laying it facedown. In theory, you can also pause music by putting your palm—or a convenient flat object—over the device's screen, but this gesture seldom works in my experience.

- **Palm Swipe to Capture.** This feature also appears as the Palm Motion check box on the Motion Control screen in some versions of TouchWiz. Swipe across the screen from right to left or from left to right using the side of your hand to capture what is onscreen. (The side of your hand is the fleshy part below the palm, between your little finger and your wrist.) This gesture may feel awkward at first, but it usually works. When it does, you'll hear a shutter sound and see a brief preview of the screenshot.

> ☑ **TIP** If you find the Palm Swipe to Capture gesture difficult to perform, use the standard method of capturing a screenshot: Press and hold the Power button and the Home button together for a moment.
>
> If your device is running too slowly, you may need to turn off some gestures and other features. See the section "Improving Performance by Turning Off TouchWiz Features," later in this chapter, for details.

CUSTOMIZING THE APPS SCREEN

To launch an app that's not on your Home screen, you touch the Apps button to display the Apps screen as usual, and then you touch the app's icon. The left screen in Figure 14.4 shows the Apps screen.

If you have many apps, you may want to customize the Apps screen so that you can find those you want more easily. The following subsections explain how to customize it.

CREATE A FOLDER

Here's how to create a folder:

1. Tap the Edit button to switch to Edit mode.
2. Tap and hold one of the apps you want to put in the new folder, drag the icon over another app you want to put in the folder, and drop it there. A new folder appears.
3. Tap the Enter Folder Name prompt and type the name.
4. Tap the color picker in the upper-right corner and tap the color for the folder.
5. Tap outside the folder to close it.
6. Tap and hold another app and drag it to the folder.
7. Tap the Done button if you've finished your customizations.

FIGURE 14.4

On the Apps screen (left), you can tap an app to launch it, tap A–Z to sort the apps alphabetically, or tap Edit to switch to Edit mode (right) so that you can create folders, rearrange the apps, or uninstall or delete apps.

DELETE A FOLDER

Here's how to delete a folder:

1. Tap the Edit button to switch to Edit mode.
2. Tap the white circle containing a red – sign on the upper-right corner of the folder you want to delete. A confirmation dialog box opens, telling you that the folder will be deleted but that apps within the folder will not be uninstalled.
3. Tap the Delete button.
4. Tap the Done button if you've finished your customizations.

- **Rearrange the apps.** Tap the Edit button to switch to Edit mode. Tap and hold the app you want to move, and then drag it to where you want it. Tap the Done button if you've finished your customizations.

> **TIP** When you want to put the apps back into alphabetical order, tap the A–Z button on the Apps screen, and then tap the Sort button in the confirmation dialog box that opens.

UNINSTALL OR DISABLE APPS

You can uninstall any app you've installed. You cannot uninstall any of the built-in apps, but you can disable them.

1. Tap the Edit button to switch to Edit mode. A white circle containing a red – sign appears on the upper-right corner of each app you can remove or disable.

2. Tap this circle to display the Uninstall Application dialog box (for an app you've installed) or the Disable Application dialog box (for a built-in app).

3. Tap the Uninstall button or the Disable button, depending on the dialog box.

4. Tap the Done button when you finish your customizations.

> **TIP** To get back the apps you've disabled, open the Settings app and tap the Applications button in the Device section. On the Applications screen that appears, tap the Application Manager button to display the Application Manager screen. Swipe left three times until the Disabled tab appears. Tap the button for a disabled app you want to get back, and then tap the Enable button on the Application Info screen that appears.

WORKING WITH THE NOTIFICATIONS PANEL, QUICK SETTINGS, AND SETTINGS

TouchWiz customizes the Quick Settings panel and the Settings app heavily, so if you're used to stock Android, you're in for some changes—and some welcome improvements.

USING THE NOTIFICATIONS PANEL AND THE QUICK SETTINGS BAR

When you want to see your notifications, pull down from the top of the screen with one finger. The Notifications panel opens, showing the list of notifications, which you can navigate as explained in the following list. (See the left screen in Figure 14.5.)

■ **Open the app that raised the notification.** Tap the notification.

■ **Expand the notification.** If the notification contains extra information, tap it and draw your finger down to expand it. For example, you can expand a Gmail notification about multiple messages to display details of the messages. (See the right screen in Figure 14.5.)

■ **Remove a notification.** Swipe left or right to remove the notification from the list.

■ **Clear all notifications.** Tap the Clear button.

■ **Open the Settings app.** Tap the Settings button.

Quick Settings bar   Settings

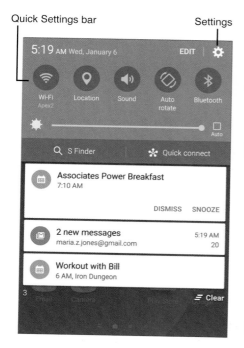

FIGURE 14.5

In TouchWiz, the Quick Settings bar appears at the top of the Notifications panel, giving you access to essential settings (left). You can expand a notification such as the Gmail notification here by tapping it and drawing your finger down a short way (right).

TouchWiz adds a Quick Settings bar across the top of the Notifications panel to give you even faster access to the settings you use most. Here's how to use the Quick Settings bar:

■ **Turn a feature on or off.** Tap the button for the feature. If the button doesn't appear on the first section of the Quick Settings bar, scroll left as needed.

■ **Display a feature's screen in the Settings app.** Tap and hold the button for the feature until the related screen appears. For example, you can tap and hold the Wi-Fi button to display the Wi-Fi screen.

■ **Customize the Quick Settings bar.** Open the Notifications panel and tap the Edit button to display the Customize Quick Settings screen. (See the left screen in Figure 14.6.) You can then choose which buttons to have on the Quick Settings bar by dragging them from the lower box to the upper box. You can also choose the order in which the buttons appear by dragging the buttons within the upper box. Check or uncheck the S Finder box and the Quick Connect box to control whether these features appear on the Notifications panel. Tap the Done button when you finish.

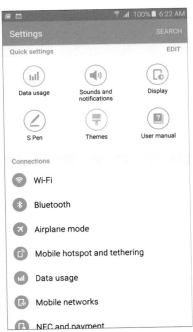

FIGURE 14.6

On the Customize Quick Settings screen (left), drag the Quick Settings buttons into your preferred order and choose whether to show the S Finder button and the Quick Connect button. The Quick Settings panel appears at the top of the Settings screen (right), giving you quick access to your preferred settings screens.

USING THE QUICK SETTINGS PANEL AND THE SETTINGS APP

Older versions of TouchWiz used to have a Quick Settings panel that worked in a roughly similar way to the Quick Settings panel in stock Android. But in Lollipop, Samsung has moved the Quick Settings panel to the Settings screen itself and greatly reduced its functionality, making it a group of shortcuts to the screens in the Settings app that you want to be able to access quickly.

USING AND CUSTOMIZING THE QUICK SETTINGS PANEL

To access the Quick Settings panel, open the Settings app and (if necessary) navigate to the top of the Settings screen. By default, the Quick Settings panel contains six icons for key features such as Data Usage, Sounds and Notifications, and Display. (See the right screen in Figure 14.6.) Tap one of these icons to go to the associated screen in Settings.

You can change the number of icons in the Quick Settings panel, adding icons up to a maximum of nine or removing icons until there are none left. You can also choose which icons appear. To choose, tap the Edit button in the upper-right corner of the Quick Settings panel, and then check and uncheck the boxes on the Edit Quick Settings screen as needed. Tap the arrow button or the Back button below the screen when you finish.

NAVIGATING THE SETTINGS APP

TouchWiz uses a heavily customized Settings screen with colorful icons. The Settings screen divides the settings into the following four categories:

- **Connections.** This category contains Wi-Fi, Bluetooth, Airplane Mode, Mobile Hotspot and Tethering, Data Usage, Mobile Networks, NFC and Payments, and More Connection Settings (which contains items such as Printing, MirrorLink, Download Booster, VPN, and Default Messaging App).

- **Device.** This category contains Sounds and Notifications, Display, S Pen, Motions and Gestures, and Applications.

- **Personal.** This category contains Wallpaper, Themes, Lock Screen and Security, Privacy and Safety, Easy Mode, Accessibility, Accounts, and Backup and Reset.

- **System.** This category contains Language and Input, Battery, Storage, Date and Time, User Manual, Developer Options (if you've enabled them), and About Device.

> **TIP** If you're having trouble finding the settings you need, tap the Search button in the upper-right corner of the Settings screen. Start typing a keyword, and you'll get a screen full of results. You can then tap the right result to display the screen that contains the setting.

USING MULTI WINDOW

TouchWiz includes a Multi Window feature that enables you to split the screen between two apps. They can be two different apps or two instances of the same app. Only some apps work in Multi Window—those that appear in the Multi Window panel.

Multi Window is great for tablets, where you have enough screen space to use the apps productively alongside each other, but some phones also offer Multi Window. You can turn Multi Window off if you don't need it.

Here's how to use Multi Window:

■ **Display the Multi Window panel.** From the Home screen, tap and hold the Recent Apps button until the panel appears in the lower half of the window. (See the left screen in Figure 14.7.) The upper half of the screen shows a message that the current screen (the Home screen) does not support split screen view.

> **NOTE** You can also open the Multi Window panel from the running app. If the app works in Multi Window, it appears in the upper half of the screen. If it doesn't, the Home screen appears with the message saying that the current screen doesn't support split screen view.

FIGURE 14.7

Tap and hold the Recent Apps button to display the Multi Window panel in the lower half of the screen (left). Tap an app to launch it in the upper half of the screen (right), and then tap the second app you want to launch.

- **Open the apps.** Scroll left or right as needed to locate the first app you want to launch, and then tap the app's icon to launch it in the upper half of the screen. (See the right screen in Figure 14.7.) Locate the second app and tap its icon to launch it in the lower half of the screen. (See the left screen in Figure 14.8.)

- **Work in the apps.** With the apps open, you can work in the apps much as usual—except that you have only half the amount of space for each. A blue line appears around the active app. (See the left screen in Figure 14.8.) Tap the other app when you need to make it active.

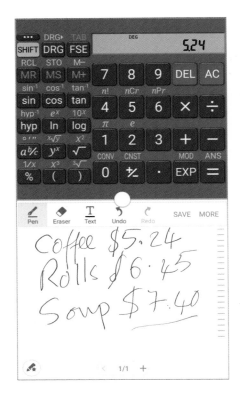
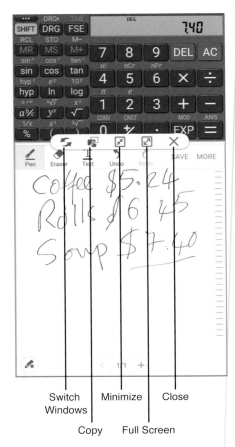

Switch Windows   Minimize   Close

Copy   Full Screen

FIGURE 14.8

After opening the apps in Multi Window, you can work in them as usual (left). Drag the white dot up or down to resize the panes, and tap the white dot to display the control buttons to take further actions (right).

- **Resize the window panes.** Tap the white dot on the line between the panes and drag it up or down, or left or right, as needed.

- **Switch the window panes.** Tap the white dot to display the control buttons, and then tap the Switch Windows button. (See the right screen in Figure 14.8.)

- **Copy text or an image from one window to another.** Tap the pane that contains the content so that a blue outline appears around it. Tap the white dot to display the control buttons, and then tap the Copy button. (Again, see the right screen in Figure 14.8.) Tap the paragraph or the image and drag it to the other window until it snaps into place.

- **Minimize the active window pane.** Tap the white dot to display the control buttons, and then tap the Minimize button.

- **Display the active window pane full screen.** Tap the white dot to display the control buttons, and then tap the Full Screen button.

- **Close a window pane.** Tap the pane you want to close so that the blue outline appears around it. Tap the white dot to display the control buttons, and then tap the Close button (the X button).

UNDERSTANDING THE GALAXY APPS AND S APPS

Samsung provides a range of apps for its Android devices. Some of the apps come preinstalled, whereas others are available for free download. As usual, the specifics depend on the device you're using and the version of TouchWiz it's running. This section summarizes the apps briefly so that you're clear what's what.

- **GALAXY Apps.** Formerly Samsung Apps, this app gives you access to Samsung's App Store for its mobile devices. You can browse using the Best Picks tab, the For GALAXY tab, or the Top tab, which offers "top" categories such as New, Most Downloaded, or Price: Low to High. Many of the apps are free, but others you must pay for.

> **!CAUTION** If the Samsung Apps app displays the Updates screen, you may need to tap the Update button to update it before you can use it. (Tapping the Update Later button often opens a Notice dialog box telling you that Samsung Apps will close if you don't update it now.) Updating Samsung Apps is a good move, but make sure your device is connected to a Wi-Fi network rather than using a cellular connection.
>
> On the Updates screen, don't check the box called I Want to Keep Samsung Apps Up to Date at All Times. This May Result in Additional Charges unless you have an unlimited data plan or a Wi-Fi–only device. Instead, use the Update button to update Samsung Apps manually as needed.

- **S Voice.** S Voice is a voice-driven assistant that you can ask for information in the same way that you can ask Google Now.

- **S Note.** S Note is a note-taking app designed for the Galaxy Note series. It includes handwriting and drawing features for the S Pen stylus.

- **Memo.** Memo is a straightforward note-taking app for devices that don't have the S Pen. You can enter text using the keyboard, and you can insert existing pictures or new photos you take.

- **S Planner.** S Planner is a calendar app that can sync data with various calendar accounts including Google Calendar and the calendar feature of Exchange Server.

- **S Health.** S Health is a health-management app that you can use to track your fitness goals and weight, calculate your nutritional needs and how you attempt to fulfill them, and measure activity using a pedometer and other features. If your device has a heart-rate sensor, you can use it to measure your heart rate. Note that you must remain "still and quiet," and the results are "not for medical or clinical use," which arguably reduces their worth.

> **TIP** Two things you need to know about S Health. First, using S Health fully requires a Samsung account. Second, when creating your profile in S Health, check the Hide My Profile Information from Other S Health Users box on the Create Profile screen unless you are certain that you want to share your information.

USING THE CAMERA APP'S EXTRA FEATURES

Samsung devices include a heavily customized Camera app. This section tells you what you need to know to get the most out of this app.

> **TIP** Because of the complexity of the Camera app, it's a good idea to spend some time working through the settings and modes to find out which are useful to you and which you can safely ignore.

MASTERING THE ESSENTIALS OF THE CAMERA APP

After launching the Camera app by tapping its icon on the Home screen or the Apps screen, you can take photos quickly. Figure 14.9 shows the Camera screen. Here are the essentials of the Camera app:

- **Zoom in or out.** Place your finger and thumb on the screen and pinch apart to zoom in or pinch together to zoom out.

> **TIP** You can open the Camera app from the lock screen by tapping the Camera icon in the lower-right corner and swiping upward. Alternatively, double-click the Home button.

FIGURE 14.9

From the main Camera screen, you can access the Settings screen; turn on HDR, the flash, or the timer; or simply shoot a photo or a video.

- **Display the Camera Settings screen.** Tap the Settings button. You'll learn about the settings on the Camera Settings screen in the section "Setting the Camera to Take the Photos and Videos You Want," later in this chapter.

- **Focus.** Tap the point on the screen where you want to focus.

- **Change the resolution.** Tap the Picture Size button to display the Picture Size pop-up panel, and then tap the resolution you want.

- **Use the flash.** Tap the Flash button to cycle among the three settings: Auto, On, and Off.

- **Use the timer.** Tap the Timer button to display the Timer pop-up panel, and then tap the Off radio button, the 2 Seconds radio button, the 5 Seconds radio button, or the 10 Seconds radio button, as needed.

- **Take High Dynamic Range (HDR) photos.** Tap the HDR icon at the top of the screen so that HDR ON appears instead of HDR OFF.

- **Apply an effect.** Tap the Effect button to display the Effect screen, and then tap the effect you want to use, such as Pastel or Vivid. (Tap the No Effect button when you want to remove the effect you've applied.)

- **Hide the settings.** Tap the Hide Settings button to hide the settings temporarily. Tap the Show Settings button (the < icon) when you want to display the settings again.

- **Change the camera mode.** Tap the Mode button and work on the Mode screen. See the next section for details.

- **Switch to the front camera.** Tap the Switch Cameras button to switch from the rear camera to the front camera; tap again to switch back.

- **Take a photo.** Tap the Take Photo button. Tap and hold the button to take a burst of photos (if your device has this capability).

- **Take a video.** Tap the Video button. The Camera app starts shooting video immediately.

- **View the last photo you took.** Tap the Last Photo thumbnail. From the last photo, you can navigate to other photos you've taken recently.

MAKING THE MOST OF THE CAMERA MODES

The Samsung Camera app includes a large number of different modes to help you take various kinds of shots. To switch modes, tap the Mode button, and then tap the appropriate mode on the Mode screen. (See the left screen in Figure 14.10.)

Different versions of the Camera app have different modes, but your device likely offers some of the following modes (and may even have more):

- **Auto.** Use this mode for general shooting—in other words, when you don't have a good reason to use any of the other modes.

- **Pro.** Use this mode when you need to take full control of the photos you shoot. As you can see in the right screen in Figure 14.10, Pro mode includes light metering, exposure adjustment, shutter speed control, ISO (film sensitivity) adjustment, white-balance adjustment, focus adjustment, and various color filters.

 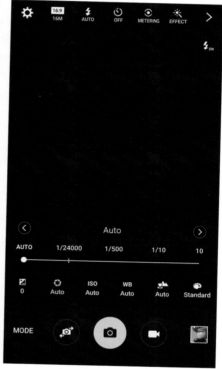

FIGURE 14.10

On the Mode screen (left), tap the Camera mode you want to use next. Pro mode (right) includes expert controls such as exposure value, shutter speed, and white balance.

■ **Selective Focus.** This mode enables you to adjust the focus on the photo after you take it. Selective Focus requires the subject of the photo to be positioned in the foreground with an appreciable distance between it and the background. Only some devices have Selective Focus.

■ **Panorama.** Turn on this mode when you want to take a panorama photo such as a landscape. The Camera app displays arrows to guide your movements of the camera.

■ **Video Collage.** Use this mode to make short collages of videos without having to put serious effort into editing. This mode is designed for creating videos suitable for sharing on social media.

■ **Live Broadcast.** Use this mode for broadcasting live on YouTube. The Camera app creates a link that you can share with your friends so that they can watch your broadcast in real time.

- **Slow Motion.** Switch to this mode when you want to shoot video clips at a high frame rate so that they play back in slow motion.
- **Fast Motion.** Use this mode when you need to shoot video clips for viewing in fast motion. Fast motion can create a dramatic effect if you use it the right way.
- **Virtual Shot.** Turn on this mode when you want to give a 360-degree tour of an object.

> ☑ **TIP** Tap the Download button on the Mode screen to see a list of other modes you can download for your device's camera. Most of these are free, but you may find some for which you have to pay.

SETTING THE CAMERA TO TAKE THE PHOTOS AND VIDEOS YOU WANT

The Camera app's modes are great for quickly taking substantially different types of photos, but you'll also want to dig into the settings that the Camera app offers to get exactly the photos you want. Tap the Settings button in the upper-left corner of the Camera screen to display the Camera Settings screen. (See the left screen in Figure 14.11.)

> ✐ **NOTE** Different versions of the Camera app have different settings, so you may need to do some exploring on your own. This section shows you the settings from the Camera app on the Galaxy Note 5, which is fairly typical of Samsung's higher-end devices.

Your device may offer the following settings:

- **Video Size (Rear).** Tap this button to display the Video Size (Rear) screen, and then tap the radio button for the resolution you want to use. (See the right screen in Figure 14.11.)

> ❗ **CAUTION** Shooting at a high resolution, such as UHD (3840×2160 pixels) or QHD (2560×1440 pixels), consumes storage space very fast. If your device is short of storage, you may do better to shoot at the FHD (1920×1080) resolution, which gives high enough quality for most purposes.

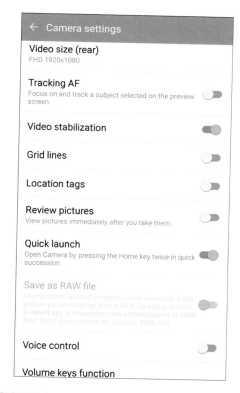
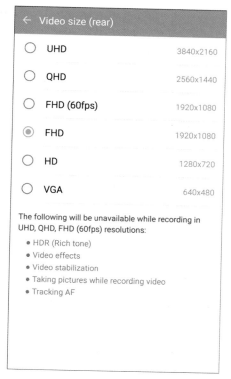

FIGURE 14.11

To make the most of your device's camera, explore the settings on the Camera Settings screen (left). When setting the video size on the Video Size screen, you may want to shoot at less than the camera's full resolution to save storage space (right).

■ **Tracking AF.** Set this switch to On if you want to use the Tracking Auto-Focus feature. This feature enables you to lock the focus onto an object in the view. The Camera app keeps the focus on this object even as you move your device so that the object moves to a different part of the screen.

■ **Video Stabilization.** Set this switch to On to enable video stabilization. It's a good idea to use video stabilization if you're not using a tripod or other support to keep your device steady.

> **NOTE** Video stabilization may not be available at the highest resolution your camera supports.

- **Grid Lines.** Set this switch to On to display the grid lines onscreen, which you can use to compose your photos and videos.

- **Location Tags.** Set this switch to On or Off to turn location tagging on or off.

> **TIP** Adding location data enables you to sort your photos by locations and see exactly where each photo was taken. But if you share your photos with others, the location data may be a threat to your privacy.

- **Review Pictures.** Tap this button to toggle the review feature, which automatically displays each photo or video you take so that you can see if it is good enough. Review is useful for leisurely shooting, but turn it off when you are shooting live action.

- **Quick Launch.** Set this switch to On if you want to be able to open the Camera app by double-clicking the Home button. This shortcut is great for getting to the Camera app quickly when you need it.

- **Save as RAW File.** Set this switch to On if you want to be able to shoot uncompressed photos in the RAW format when using Pro mode. RAW photos are great for serious work, but you may need to get a viewer app if you want to be able to view them on your device.

- **Voice Control.** Set this switch to On to enable the Voice Control feature. Voice Control enables you to take a shot by saying one of four control words: "Cheese," "Shoot," "Smile," or "Capture." Voice Control is good for group shots including yourself or for self-portraits using the rear camera.

- **Volume Keys Function.** Tap this button to display the pop-up menu, and then tap the Take Pictures button, the Record Video button, or the Zoom button, as needed.

- **Reset Settings.** Tap this button to reset the Camera's settings to their default values.

BROWSING WITH SAMSUNG'S INTERNET BROWSER

Most Samsung devices include Samsung's browser, which is usually called Internet but is also sometimes called Browser and is usually set as the default browser with a shortcut on the Home screen. We'll call it "the Internet app" here for clarity. The Internet app is pretty easy to use and offers standard features such as bookmarks, history, and private browsing (which it calls Secret mode).

GRASPING THE ESSENTIALS OF THE INTERNET APP

The Internet app has a straightforward interface. (See Figure 14.12.)

Refresh

FIGURE 14.12

The Internet app has a straightforward interface with an address box, Back and Forward buttons, a Home button, and a Bookmarks button (left). Tap the More button to display the menu with other commands (right).

> **NOTE** The Internet app hides its controls by default as soon as you leave the top of a page to which you've navigated, but you can display them at any time by tapping the screen and dragging your finger down a short way.

You can go to a web page by tapping the address box, typing the address, and then tapping the Go button on the keyboard. You can also get there by following a link on another page.

You can navigate back to the previous page by tapping the Back button. After you've gone back, you can tap the Forward button to go forward again.

You can tap a link to open its page in the same tab, or you can tap and hold to display a dialog box of actions. You can then tap the Open in New Tab command to open the linked page in a new tab.

> **TIP** Many web pages attempt to detect whether the browser you're using is on a mobile device or a full-bore computer and display mobile versions of pages for mobile devices. To request the desktop version of the current page, tap the Menu button and then check the Desktop View box. This setting persists for the current tab until you either uncheck the Desktop View box or close the tab.

SWITCHING FROM THE INTERNET APP TO CHROME

If the Internet app doesn't suit you, use Chrome instead. Many Samsung devices include Chrome, so look on the Apps screen or in the Google folder to see if it's there. If it's not, open the Play Store app and download Chrome.

You'll then want to stop the Internet app from being your default browser. Open the Settings app, tap the Applications button in the Device section, and then tap the Default Applications button on the Applications screen. Go to the Clear Defaults list, locate the Internet entry, and tap the Clear button to its right.

Now set Chrome as your default browser. Go to your Email app, find a link in a message, and tap it. In the Open With panel that appears, tap the Chrome button. After you've done this, Chrome always opens when you tap a link in another app.

SAVING WEB PAGES AND READING THEM LATER

When you don't have time to read an interesting web page you've found, tap the More button and then tap Save Web Page. You can then go to your Saved Pages list by tapping the Bookmarks button icon at the bottom of the screen, tapping the Saved Pages tab, and then tapping the page to open it.

> **TIP** Saving a page saves it in its current state, so when you return to it, you see the page as it was when you saved it. By contrast, when you return to a bookmark, you see the latest version of the page. Save a page instead of creating a bookmark when you need to be able to refer to the page as it was.

To delete a saved page, tap and hold its button on the Saved Pages tab until the Internet app goes into Selection mode and selects it. You can then check or uncheck the boxes for other saved pages as needed and tap the Delete button to delete them.

RETURNING TO WEB PAGES WITH BOOKMARKS

The Internet app makes it easy to bookmark web pages and then return to them. You can add a bookmark like this:

1. Go to the page you want to bookmark.
2. Tap the Bookmarks button to display the Bookmarks screen.
3. Edit the bookmark's name to something short and easily identifiable.
4. Choose the folder in which to save the bookmark.
5. Tap the Save button.

> **TIP** You can quickly add a bookmark for the current web page to the My Device folder by tapping the More button and then tapping Add to Bookmarks on the menu.

To go to a bookmark, tap the Bookmarks button to display the Bookmarks screen, navigate to a different folder if necessary, and then tap the bookmark for the page you want to view.

> **TIP** You can change the order of your bookmarks by tapping the More button on the Bookmarks screen, tapping Change Order, and then using the up-and-down-arrow handles to drag the bookmarks into the order you want. Tap the Back button when you finish.

OPENING MULTIPLE TABS AND NAVIGATING AMONG THEM

Like any decent browser, the Internet app enables you to open multiple tabs so that you can have multiple pages open at the same time. You can switch from tab to tab as needed and close any tab that you no longer require.

You can open a new tab in either of these ways:

- Tap and hold a link, and then tap Open in New Tab in the dialog box that opens.
- Tap the Tabs button to display the Tabs screen, and then tap the New Tab button.

Figure 14.13 shows the Tabs screen, which you also use to navigate among windows and close windows.

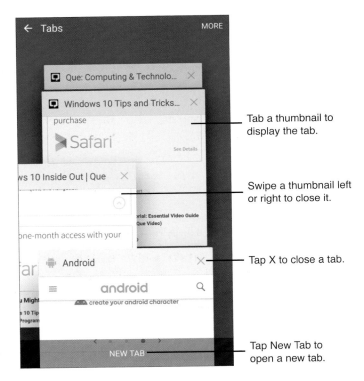

Tab a thumbnail to display the tab.

Swipe a thumbnail left or right to close it.

Tap X to close a tab.

Tap New Tab to open a new tab.

FIGURE 14.13
On the Tabs screen, tap the × button to close a tab, tap the New Tab button to open a new tab, or tap the thumbnail whose contents you want to display.

LOADING YOUR FAVORITE PAGES ONTO THE QUICK ACCESS SCREEN

Some versions of the Internet browser include a Quick Access feature that you can use to get to your favorite pages quickly. To add a page to the Quick Access screen, open the page, tap the More button, and then tap Add to Quick Access.

You can then tap the Home button to display the Quick Access screen. Following that, you can tap the icon for the page you want to display.

ADDING A WEB PAGE SHORTCUT TO YOUR HOME SCREEN

When you need to be able to access a particular web page quickly, add a shortcut for it to your Home screen. Go to the page, tap the More button, and then tap Add Shortcut on Home Screen (or Add Shortcut to Home in some versions of the Internet app).

BROWSING SECRETLY

When you want to browse without adding the trail of pages you visit to your history, tap the Tabs button to display the Tabs screen, tap the More button, and then tap New Secret Tab. The Internet app opens a Secret mode tab that stores the details of the pages you visit only during the Secret mode session (so that you can navigate back and forward as needed) and then disposes of them.

When you no longer need to use Secret mode, close the Secret mode tab.

SYNCING OPEN PAGES THROUGH A SAMSUNG ACCOUNT

The Internet app enables you to sync your open web pages across your computers and devices by signing in to your Samsung account on each computer or device.

To sign in to your Samsung account on your Samsung device, tap the Tabs button to display the Tabs screen, tap the More button to display the menu, and then tap Sync with Other Devices. In the Sign In to Account dialog box that opens, tap the Sign In button, and then follow through the sign-in process.

IMPROVING PERFORMANCE BY TURNING OFF TOUCHWIZ FEATURES

If your Samsung device is running slowly, you may be able to improve performance by turning off some of the TouchWiz features.

■ **Strip useless widgets off the Home screen.** Like most Android devices, Samsung's phones and tablets seem convinced that the more widgets on the Home screen, the fuller your life will be. But the widgets can slow down your device, so getting rid of any you don't need can improve performance.

> ☑ **TIP** If your Samsung device is running slower than usual, try restarting it: Press and hold the Power button until the Device Options dialog box appears, and then tap the Restart button. As with most computers and devices, restarting your Samsung device can clear up any number of slowdowns and niggling problems.

■ **Close any apps you're not using.** Tap the Recent Apps button, scroll up to the top, and swipe any apps you're not using off the list. This could hardly be easier to do, but it can give you an appreciable performance boost.

> ☑ **TIP** Another way to speed up your Samsung device is to replace the default TouchWiz launcher with another launcher. See Chapter 3, "Customizing Your Device," for a discussion of alternative launchers.

■ **Turn off gestures you don't need.** As you saw earlier in this chapter, Samsung's gestures for controlling your device are clever and can be helpful. But if you don't use some of the gestures, or if you don't use any, don't waste processor power trying to track your movements. Open the Settings app, tap the Motions and Gestures button in the Device section, and then set the individual switches on the Motions and Gestures screen to On or Off, as needed.

■ **Turn off Voice Wake-Up for S Voice.** If you don't need to have S Voice listening for you to wake it up, turn off the Voice Wakeup feature and run S Voice from the Apps screen when you need it. To make this change, tap the Apps button, tap S Voice to launch it, and then tap Settings (the gear icon) on the left of the S Voice bar. On the S Voice Settings screen, tap the Voice Wake-Up button, and then set the switch on the Voice Wake-Up screen to Off.

TURNING OFF DEVELOPER ANIMATIONS ON TOUCHWIZ

Samsung TouchWiz includes several animation settings that you can turn off on the Developer Options screen in the Settings app. You may want to try turning off these animations if you're trying to get the best performance out of your Samsung device.

First, you may need to make the Developer Options icon available because it's hidden by default. Open the Settings app and scroll down to the System section. If the Developer Options button doesn't appear between the User Manual button and the About Device button, tap the About Device button to display the About Device screen, tap the Software Info button to display the Software Info screen, and then tap the Build Number version three times.

A readout appears, saying you are four steps from becoming a developer; tap the button four more times, and you'll see a message that Developer Options have been turned on. Tap the Back button twice to return to the Settings screen.

Now tap the Developer Options button to display the Developer Options screen and scroll down to the Drawing section. You can now tap the Window Animation Scale button to display the Window Animation Scale dialog box, and then tap the Animation Is Off radio button to turn off the animation. Repeat the move with the Transition Animation Scale button and the Animator Duration Scale button to turn these animations off as well.

Index

D

E

G

H

O

S

X–Y

Z

Best-Selling My Books!

Learning to use your smartphone, tablet, camera, game, or software has never been easier with the full-color My Series. You'll find simple, step-bystep instructions from our team of experienced authors. The organized, task-based format allows you to quickly and easily find exactly what you want to achieve.

Visit quepublishing.com/mybooks **to learn more.**